P9-DCD-291

the sexual
person

Moral Traditions Series
James F. Keenan, SJ, Series Editor

The Global Face of Public Faith: Politics, Human Rights, and Christian Ethics
David Hollenbach, SJ

The Ground Beneath the Cross: The Theology of Ignacio Ellacuría
Kevin F. Burke, SJ

Heroes, Saints, and Ordinary Morality
Andrew Michael Flescher

Introduction to Jewish and Catholic Bioethics: A Comparative Analysis
Aaron L. Mackler

Jewish and Catholic Bioethics: An Ecumenical Dialogue
Edmund D. Pellegrino and Alan I. Faden, Editors

John Cuthbert Ford, SJ: Moral Theologian at the End of the Manualist Era
Eric Marcelo O. Genilo, SJ

John Paul II and the Legacy of Dignitatis Humanae
Hermínio Rico, SJ

Josef Fuchs on Natural Law
Mark Graham

Love, Human and Divine: The Heart of Christian Ethics
Edward Collins Vacek, SJ

Loyal Dissent: Memoir of a Catholic Theologian
Charles E. Curran

Medicine and the Ethics of Care
Diana Fritz Cates and Paul Lauritzen, Editors

The Moral Theology of Pope John Paul II
Charles E. Curran

The Origins of Moral Theology in the United States: Three Different Approaches
Charles E. Curran

Overcoming Our Evil: Human Nature and Spiritual Exercises in Xunzi and Augustine
Aaron Stalnaker

Prophetic and Public: The Social Witness of U.S. Catholicism
Kristin Heyer

The Sexual Person: Toward a Renewed Catholic Anthropology
Todd A. Salzman and Michael G. Lawler

Shaping the Moral Life: An Approach to Moral Theology
Klaus Demmer, MSC
James F. Keenan, SJ, Editor

Theological Bioethics: Participation, Justice, and Change
Lisa Sowle Cahill

Theology for a Liberating Church: The New Praxis of Freedom
Alfred T. Hennelly, SJ

United States Welfare Policy: A Catholic Response
Thomas J. Massaro, SJ

Who Count as Persons? Human Identity and the Ethics of Killing
John F. Kavanaugh, SJ

More praise for *The Sexual Person*

"This superb volume courageously explores Catholic teaching on sexual ethics. The authors' exploration of the biological, relational, and spiritual dimensions of human sexuality engages Catholic teaching respectfully, critically, and creatively. The book is a significant contribution to both sexual ethics and moral theology generally."

—Paul Lauritzen, director, Program in Applied Ethics,
John Carroll University

"This book is a much-needed contribution to the contemporary Catholic discussion of sexual ethics. The authors utilize the most recent sociological and psychological data to supplement their careful parsing of the Catholic theology of sex, gender, and embodiment. It is a work that manages to be highly theoretical while addressing everyday concerns about premarital sex, contraception, homosexuality, divorce, and reproductive technology.

Salzman and Lawler embrace the model of theology as dialogue, and as a result, their treatment of both traditionalist and revisionist views about human sexuality is constructive and helpful. They succeed in moving a seemingly stalled conversation forward."

—Aline Kalbian, associate professor, Department of Religion,
Florida State University

"A bold and brave book! Tightly argued and well documented, this book lays out an understanding of human sexuality that expresses the profound work that theologians do on behalf of the Church in order to find ever better understandings of what the Church teaches in light of the witness of scripture, the tradition, and our understanding of human experience."

—Richard M. Gula, SS, The Franciscan School of Theology,
Graduate Theological Union

the sexual

TOWARD A RENEWED CATHOLIC ANTHROPOLOGY

person

Todd A. Salzman

and

Michael G. Lawler

Georgetown University Press / Washington, D.C.

Georgetown University Press, Washington, D.C. www.press.georgetown.edu
© 2008 by Georgetown University Press. All rights reserved. No part of this book may be reproduced or utilized in any form or by any means, electronic or mechanical, including photocopying and recording, or by any information storage and retrieval system, without permission in writing from the publisher.

Library of Congress Cataloging-in-Publication Data

Salzman, Todd A.
    The sexual person : toward a renewed Catholic anthropology / Todd A. Salzman and Michael G. Lawler.
        p.   cm.— (Moral traditions series)
    Includes bibliographical references and index.
    ISBN-13: 978–1-58901–207–3 (cloth : alk. paper)
    ISBN-13: 978–1-58901–208–0 (pbk. : alk. paper)
    1. Sex—Religious aspects—Catholic Church.   2. Catholic Church—Doctrines.   I. Lawler, Michael G.   II. Title.
BX1795.S48S25   2008
241′.66088282—dc22

                                                                    2007046198

⊛ This book is printed on acid-free paper meeting the requirements of the American National Standard for Permanence in Paper for Printed Library Materials.

15 14 13 12 11 10 09 08   9 8 7 6 5 4 3 2
First printing

Printed in the United States of America

*To our wives, Katy Salzman and Sue Lawler, and to the people of
Old Parish, County Waterford, Ireland:*

*Ba mhaith linn ár mbuíochas a ghabháil do mhuintir an t-Sean
Phobal don féile chineálta agus don chairdeas a d'fhoghlaimear*

*We express our gratitude to the people of Old Parish for their
kind hospitality and friendship*

Contents

Foreword

THE AUTHORS OF THIS BOOK, Todd A. Salzman and Michael G. Lawler, write as Catholic theologians who both are married and are very familiar with the Catholic tradition. The book accepts the classical understanding of faith and reason, recognizing especially the importance of human reason in developing sexual marital morality. The authors ground their understanding of sexuality in a more personalistic and relational understanding of natural law theory. They enter into a dialogue almost exclusively with other Catholic authors who have been dealing with these issues. On the basis of their natural law theory, they propose a renewed Catholic anthropology that serves as the basis for their positions on marital morality dealing with contraception, cohabitation, and the process of marrying, homosexuality, and artificial reproductive technologies.

There is no doubt, especially in light of extensive media coverage, that the pedophile scandal has been a traumatic experience for the Catholic Church in the United States. But another crisis that has received much less media attention might in the end have more lasting effects on the life of the Church. I refer to the fact that the vast majority of Roman Catholics do not follow the teaching of the hierarchical Magisterium of the Church with regard to aspects of marital morality. In this book Todd Salzman and Michael Lawler cite sociological statistics to show that 75 to 85 percent of Catholics approve of contraception for married couples despite the official teaching. Many Catholics also disagree with other aspects of Catholic sexual teaching with regard to marriage.

This problem came to the fore with Pope Paul VI's 1968 encyclical *Humanae vitae*, which taught that each and every marriage act must remain open to the transmission of life. The pope grounded his teaching in the inseparable connection willed by God and unable to be broken by human beings of the two meanings of the conjugal act: the unitive and the procreative. Thus, every marital act must be open to procreation and be expressive of the loving union of husband and wife. As a result of this teaching, the hierarchical Magisterium has condemned artificial contraception for spouses, artificial reproductive technologies that do away with the conjugal act, and homosexual genital relationships.

Pope Paul VI referred to the "lively debate" set off by his encyclical, but it has truly been a crisis, with many Catholics leaving the Church because of it and others experiencing great tension with the Church because of their disagreement with this teaching. Some of the crisis and tension has been lessened by the recognition proposed by many Catholic theologians that a Catholic can dissent from such noninfallible Church teaching and still be a good Roman Catholic. One can solve this problem in the forum of conscience. But there are other disputed areas in the Church today that cannot be resolved in the forum of conscience. Think, for example, of the ordination of married men or the ordination of women, which require the leadership of the Church to make structural changes. Thus the forum of conscience does not offer any relief for these issues. Note here that I am not saying that conscience itself makes something right but rather, in the area of noninfallible teaching, that an informed conscience may dissent from such teaching. Although the forum of conscience provides a way to deal with some of the tensions in marital morality, the continued discrepancy between the hierarchical teaching and the actions and practices of many Catholics cannot be a good thing for the life of the Church.

Humanae vitae and the responses to it have also brought about serious theological tensions in the Catholic Church in the United States between revisionist theologians calling for a change in the hierarchical teaching and the hierarchical Magisterium itself. The day after the encyclical was published in 1968, theologians at Catholic University issued a statement ultimately signed by more than six hundred Catholic scholars in sacred sciences that maintained that the encyclical added nothing to the arguments that had already been presented. Because the teaching was noninfallible, the statement concluded that in theory and in practice one could disagree with the conclusion of the encyclical condemning artificial contraception for spouses and still be a loyal Roman Catholic. The trustees of Catholic University, half of whom were bishops and archbishops, mandated a faculty committee hearing to determine if by their declarations and actions the faculty members had violated their responsibilities as Catholic theologians. The faculty committee and the Academic Senate of the university strongly supported the declarations and actions of the subject professors. The Board of Trustees ultimately accepted the faculty committee report insofar as it pertains to the academic propriety of what the subject professors did, but this acceptance does not represent approval of the theological position expressed in the statement.

The publication of *Human Sexuality: New Directions in American Catholic Thought* in 1977 occasioned a deepening split within the Catholic moral theology community and triggered new tensions between revisionist Catholic moral theologians and the hierarchical Magisterium. This book originated as follows. In 1972 the Catholic Theological Society of America appointed a committee headed by Anthony Kosnik, a priest professor at Saints Cyril and Methodius Seminary in Michigan, to do a study of sexual ethics in the hope of providing useful guidelines for sexual activity. At the 1977 annual meeting, the society's board of directors received the report. The board's role was not to approve or disapprove of it. The report was ultimately published in book form and created quite a stir. The book rejected the act-centered approach of the hierarchical Magisterium's teaching and accepted the criterion proposed in *Gaudium et spes* of Vatican II with its norm of "the nature of the person and his acts." Rejecting the older physicalism, the book proposed seven values that should be present in sexual relations. On the basis of these values, the authors developed guidelines with respect to artificial contraception, masturbation, homosexual relations, and premarital sexuality that differ somewhat from the official hierarchical teaching. This publication and the role of the Catholic Theological Society in sponsoring the study played a major role in more conservative Roman Catholic theologians joining with other Catholic academicians in forming the Fellowship of Catholic Scholars, whose members commit themselves to supporting and safeguarding the teaching of the hierarchical Magisterium. The U.S. bishops and the Vatican's Congregation for the Doctrine of the Faith pointed out the errors in the book, and disciplinary action was taken against Father Kosnik, the chair of the committee.

In 1977, Philip S. Keane, a Sulpician priest, published *Sexual Morality: A Catholic Perspective*, which also employed a personalist criterion as opposed to the older physicalism with its emphasis on the physical structure of the sexual act. Keane employed a proportionalist methodology justifying some ontic evil for a proportionate reason. As a result, his conclusions disagreed with the hierarchical teaching in areas of contraception, masturbation, and homosexual genital relations. The Vatican pressured the archbishop of Seattle, Raymond Hunthausen, to withdraw his imprimatur from the book but took no disciplinary action against Father Keane.

In 1976, John McNeill, an American Jesuit priest, published the *Church and the Homosexual*, which argued that the homosexual condition is not determined by biology and is created good in accord with the will of God. Like many, he examined the teaching of scripture, the other sources of moral wisdom and knowledge for Catholic theology, and contemporary science and human experience. He found that homosexual acts in a loving and ethically responsible relationship based on mutuality, fidelity, and unselfishness are morally and spiritually good. In 1978, the Congregation for the Doctrine of the Faith condemned the book and prohibited McNeill from speaking about the book or the issue. McNeill publicly challenged the 1986 document from the Congregation on homosexuality and was dismissed from the Jesuits. In a more pastoral vein, Sister Jeannine Gramick and Father Robert Nugent were the founding codirectors of New Ways Ministries for Gays and Lesbians. They never publicly expressed their own position on the morality of homosexual relationships, but they explained the teaching of the hierarchical Magisterium as well as those of dissenting theologians. In 1999, the Congregation permanently prohibited them from any further pastoral work with homosexual persons.

The strongest Vatican action against a theologian came in 1986 when, after a seven-year investigation, the Congregation for the Doctrine of the Faith, with the pope's approval, concluded that I was neither suitable nor eligible to be a Catholic theologian because of my dissent. I had been the primary author and leader of the statement from Catholic University theologians over *Humanae vitae* in July 1968.

Since that time I have continued to write in areas of sexuality and other areas in moral theology. More than 750 Catholic theologians signed a statement supporting me. The Congregation condemned my position on dissent as well as my dissent on the specific issues of artificial contraception, the indissolubility of marriage, masturbation, premarital sexuality, homosexual acts, direct sterilization, direct abortion, and euthanasia.

Note that the theologians condemned by the Vatican have all been Catholic priests. The Vatican has much more control over priests and religious than it has over laywomen and laymen who are theologians. But a very significant development in Catholic theology in general since the 1980s has been the growing number of lay theologians, so that today laypeople are the predominant group of Catholic moral theologians in the United States. As Salzman and Lawler point out, Catholic women theologians coming from a feminist perspective have made a very significant contribution to Catholic marital and sexual ethics from a revisionist perspective. Margaret Farley, a Mercy sister, Lisa Sowle Cahill, Christine Gudorf, Barbara Andolsen, Patricia Jung, and others have written important volumes and articles on marital and sexual morality. At the same time, married male Catholic theologians such as William Roberts and Michael Lawler have written monographs and articles from a revisionist perspective.

Within the Catholic theological community, all recognize that the great majority of Catholic moral theologians writing today support revisionist positions in general, but a strong minority defends the positions of the hierarchical Magisterium. This school—often called New Natural Law Theory and headed by Germain Grisez, John Finnis, William E. May, and others—strongly endorses the positions of the hierarchical Magisterium. Some Catholic moral theologians disagree with New Natural Law Theory and follow the somewhat different neoscholastic understanding of natural law that was the basis for the traditional Catholic teaching on marital and sexual morality as found in the manuals of moral theology.

At the beginning of the twenty-first century, a new generation of voices began to address marital morality. These scholars—such as Florence Caffrey Bourg, David Matzo McCarthy, and Julie Hanlon Rubio—have no living memory of Vatican II and *Humanae vitae*. In general these married people emphasize that marital morality involves much more than just sexual issues. Theology must help Catholic spouses today to support and nurture the marital relationship of younger Catholic spouses who are committed to the equality of wife and husband and recognize that both have a public vocation in addition to their marital vocation. In many ways they are trying to move beyond the paralyzing debates of the last forty years of the twentieth century. Marital and family love must expand to include the neighborhood, the broader human community, and especially our community with poor people. However, the discussions about sexual marital morality are not going to disappear. The papal and hierarchical magisteria have continued to strongly uphold the existing Catholic teachings on these issues, grounded in the position that sexual relations are morally acceptable only in marriage and only if every sexual act is both open to procreation and expressive of a loving union.

In 1975, the Congregation for the Doctrine of the Faith reaffirmed the hierarchical teachings and the natural law basis for them in the Declaration on Certain Questions Concerning Sexual Ethics. In his long papacy, Pope John Paul II often and staunchly explained and defended the existing teachings. Early in his pontificate in his weekly audiences, he began a series of talks on sexuality and marriage. These were later published in book form in the *Theology of the Body: Human Love in the Divine Plan*. His 1981 apostolic exhortation *Familiaris consortio* dealt with marriage and the family. Above all, his 1993 encyclical *Veritatis splendor* is the first encyclical ever directed exclusively to moral theology. Here he staunchly defends and explains the Catholic natural law theory that serves as the basis for its sexual teachings.

Under John Paul II the Congregation for the Doctrine of the Faith issued three different documents on homosexuality defending the existing teaching. The Wojtyla papacy firmly emphasized the truth of the magisterial teaching in general and the need for Catholic theologians to accept and follow such teaching. The 1983 *Code of Canon Law*, the 1989 Profession of Faith and Oath of Fidelity, and the Congregation for the Doctrine of the Faith's 1990 *Instruction on the Ecclesial Vocation of the Theologian* all emphasized the decisive role of the hierarchical Magisterium and the submission required by theologians. The papal Magisterium has never explicitly recognized the validity of any dissent from its noninfallible teachings. In addition, all Catholic theologians teaching in Catholic institutions are required by Church law to receive a mandate from the local bishop.

Anyone familiar with the Catholic tradition and its history knows that arguments and even sharp differences between and among Catholic theologians are nothing new. In fact, in earlier times the differences were more severe than they are today. In the seventeenth and eighteenth centuries, Catholic moral theologians accused one another of laxism and rigorism. Some authors in the eighteenth century used pseudonyms in their sharp attacks on the moral theology of Alphonsus Liguori, who was later proclaimed a saint and the patron of moral theologians.

Conversely, John Paul explicitly wrote *Veritatis splendor* in light of the genuine crisis that seriously endangers the moral life of the faithful and the communion of the Church. Today it is no longer a matter of limited and occasional theological dissent but an overall and systematic calling into question of traditional moral teachings, which is occurring even in seminaries and in faculties of theology. This is a genuine crisis.

In this historical context, the present volume makes a significant contribution. Two long chapters analyze and criticize both the New Natural Law Theory approach and also the revisionist approach to morality and sexuality. Chapter 4 explains the authors' understanding of anthropology and the principle for making judgments about the morality of sexual acts. The subsequent chapters apply their carefully crafted anthropology and principle of judging sexual acts to the specific cases of cohabitation and premarital sexuality, homosexuality, and artificial reproductive technologies. Not all Catholic theologians will agree with what Salzman and Lawler propose here. But all must recognize that they have achieved their purpose of entering into a genuine and respectful dialogue in the search for the truth and meaning of human sexuality in the Catholic tradition today.

CHARLES E. CURRAN

Acknowledgments

No AUTHOR WRITES A BOOK in isolation; he is subject to multiple influences. We are happy to confess that we are no exception to that rule, and we freely express our gratitude to all those teachers, colleagues, students, and friends with whom we have had a dialogue over the years, and from whom we have learned what human sexuality means in the Catholic tradition. Because we cannot name all of them, it seems churlish to name any of them. We name only Katy, Sue, and the Old Parish community in County Waterford, Ireland, to whom this book is dedicated. We also thank Gail Risch for her painstaking editorial work on the manuscript.

Prologue

Two MAGISTERIAL PRINCIPLES capture the essence of the Catholic moral, sexual tradition. The first principle comes from the Congregation for the Doctrine of the Faith: "Any human genital act whatsoever may be placed only within the framework of marriage."[1] The second received its modern articulation in Pope Paul VI's *Humanae vitae:* "Each and every marriage act must remain open to the transmission of life."[2] In the Catholic tradition sexual activity is institutionalized within the confines of marriage and procreation, and sexual morality is marital morality.

These two principles that capture the essence of the Catholic tradition do not have the same theoretical underpinning. The first is founded in human *reason*: Attention to and understanding, evaluation, and rational judgment of the various aspects of an issue reveal to attentive, rational, and responsible human beings what right sexual conduct ought to be. The second is founded in what is called *nature* or *natural order.* The structure of sexual acts reveals to the attentive and rational person the form that each and every sexual act must take to be in accord with nature and the will of nature's Creator. These two different ways of arriving at moral principles have a long history in the Catholic moral tradition. Thomas Aquinas argues, for example, there are two ways in which a sexual act is rendered unbecoming: "First, through being contrary to right *reason.* . . . Secondly, because, in addition, it is contrary to the *natural order* of the sexual act as becoming to the human race."[3] In his influential 1951 speech to Italian midwives, Pius XII argued from both reason and "nature." On the one hand, he did not condemn the prevention of procreation in a *marriage*; on the other hand, he condemned the artificial prevention of procreation in *marital intercourse.*[4] In the first case, *right reason* dictates how a married life should be lived; in the second, the "nature" of the sexual act dictates how it should be performed within marriage. These two ways of arriving at moral principle and judgment on sexual ethical questions are evident throughout Catholic tradition and will recur regularly throughout this book. They reflect a deeper tension within this tradition between methodological and anthropological developments and the norms that are formulated and justified in light of those developments. This tension and its implications for a living and evolving Catholic tradition and theologians within the tradition are well illustrated in Bernard Lonergan's concept of conversion.

1

Lonergan introduced the important notion of the conversion of the knowing subject in his groundbreaking *Insight*, and he further developed it in his *Method in Theology*.[5] Conversion, a process that involves "a radical about-face in which one repudiates characteristic features of one's previous horizon,"[6] may be threefold. *Intellectual conversion* abandons "the myth that fully human knowing is to be conceived on an analogy with seeing, and replaces it with the affirmation of a self that knows because it understands correctly."[7] *Moral conversion* is "a shift in the criterion of one's decisions and choices from satisfaction to values."[8] *Religious conversion* is simply "falling in love with God."[9] Lonergan's initial analysis of conversion occurred within the analysis of the development of the human knower in general, and reoccurred within the analysis of the theologian-knower in particular. Conversion, it is important to note, is not a development in what the theologian *says* but "a fundamental and momentous change in the human reality that a theologian *is*."[10] Conversion changes what the theologian *is*; it is a radical development of personal foundations and horizons.[11] It is clear that from different foundations and horizons unconverted and converted theologians will interpret the Catholic tradition, and the methodological and anthropological developments of that tradition, in different ways and will draw radically different conclusions from it. But such different conclusions do not warrant the conclusion that one unconverted theologian is not a Catholic theologian and another converted theologian is one. This dialectic between theologians will occur throughout this book, with no implied judgment that one theologian is converted and the other is not.

The conversion that we explore in this book is primarily intellectual conversion that reflects, stimulates, and affects moral and religious conversion. In examining the tradition of Catholic sexual teaching, we note a conversion in this tradition that is reflected in a disconnect between many of the Magisterium's absolute proscriptive sexual norms and the methodological and anthropological developments explicitly recognized and endorsed throughout Catholic tradition, especially since the Second Vatican Council. This conversion is marked by methodological and anthropological developments that invite a reconsideration of norms and their justification. The methodological developments include a fundamental shift from a primarily classicist worldview to a primarily historically conscious worldview. The classicist worldview asserts that reality is static, necessary, fixed, and universal. The method utilized, anthropology formulated, and norms taught within this worldview are timeless, universal, and immutable, and the acts condemned by these norms are always so condemned. Historical consciousness, grounded in existentialism, fundamentally challenges this view of reality. According to the historically conscious worldview, reality is dynamic, evolving, changing, and particular. The method utilized, anthropology formulated, and norms taught within this worldview are contingent, particular, and changeable, and the acts condemned by these norms are morally evaluated in terms of evolving human knowledge and understanding.

The shift from the classicist to the historically conscious worldview is reflected, for example, in the Magisterium's endorsement of the historical-critical method for interpreting scripture articulated in *Divino afflante spiritu* and *Dei verbum*, which requires that scriptural texts be read in the "literary forms" of the writer's "time and culture."[12] Though this method is clearly established and marks an explicit shift in the Catholic tradition in how scripture is to be read, interpreted, and applied to ethical issues, magisterial teaching continues to proof-text scripture to justify absolute norms condemning certain sexual acts, which reflects the exegetical method of the moral manuals rather than the historical-critical method of recent tradition. The *Catechism of the Catholic Church*, for example, references Genesis 19:1–29, the story of Sodom and Gomorrah, as a scriptural foundation for the absolute prohibition of homosexual acts.[13] Most biblical scholars, however, relying upon the historical-critical method, assert that the central meaning of this passage is about hospitality or homosexual rape and has virtually no relevance to the discussion of people with a homosexual orientation in monogamous, committed, loving relationships. Though the Magisterium espouses the historical-critical method for interpreting scripture and advocates utilizing other methodological resources such as the sciences to formulate its teaching,[14] it fails to fully consider and integrate the normative implications of those methodological developments into its teaching, especially with regard to many absolute sexual norms. It continues to cite certain scriptural passages to condemn many sexual acts, whereas its own method indicates that these passages are peripheral, if not irrelevant, to the acts it is condemning. The historical-critical method does not support this classicist approach to justifying norms.

A similar disconnect exists between sexual anthropological developments in Catholic tradition and the formulation and justification of absolute sexual norms. *Gaudium et spes* marks a radical evolution in Catholic sexual teaching and, by implication, the sexual anthropology reflected in this teaching, by eliminating the language of the hierarchy of the ends of marriage. Before the Second Vatican Council, procreation was the primary end of marriage and union between spouses was the secondary end of marriage. In *Gaudium et spes*, hierarchical language for the two ends of marriage is rejected and "the nature of the human person and his acts" is posited as the foundational principle for harmonizing the ends of marriage.[15] This marked a fundamental shift and development in Catholic sexual teaching and anthropology, but there is little evidence that the Magisterium has fully incorporated this shift into its sexual anthropology or into its formulation and justification of norms. As we will demonstrate throughout this book, the emphasis in its teaching continues to be on the "nature" of the act rather than on the "nature" of the human person and his or her acts.

This book includes two objectives, one explicit and one implicit. The explicit objective is to explore the normative implications for sexual ethics of the methodological and anthropological developments in Catholic tradition. Given the importance of history in the process of conversion, we begin by providing a historical overview (chapter 1) of the Christian understanding of human sexuality, which spans from Genesis to Vatican II. This historical overview provides a context for the current theological discussions and debates on the nature and existence of absolute sexual norms, but more fundamentally, on ethical method and anthropology. We move from history to contemporary debates and explain traditionalist (chapter 2) and revisionist (chapter 3) ethical methods and sexual anthropologies. Building on revisionist sexual anthropology, we articulate our own anthropology, drawing insights from tradition and utilizing methodological resources in the tradition to formulate a foundational sexual ethical principle (chapter 4). The subsequent chapters apply this principle to marriage (chapter 5), cohabitation (chapter 6), homosexuality (chapter 7), and reproductive technologies (chapter 8).

The implicit objective of this book is to stimulate further dialogue among theologians, and between theologians and the Magisterium. John Paul II teaches that dialogue is rooted in the nature and dignity of the human person. It "is an indispensable step along the path towards *human self-realization*, the self-realization of *each individual* and of *every human community*. . . . It involves the human subject in his or her entirety."[16] We agree that every dialogue involves the subjectivity of each individual in the dialogue. Each individual must, therefore, attend carefully to the data emerging in the dialogue, and must inquire intelligently into the data, come to understand them, and formulate this understanding in mutually understandable concepts. Each individual must then rationally reflect, marshal the evidence, and eventually pass judgment on the truth or falsity, certainty or probability, of his or her understanding. It is only after this rational judgment is passed that any true knowledge is achieved in the dialogue. After the passing of judgment, there is the final step of considering possible courses of action, evaluating them, making a decision about which course of action to follow, and then translating this decision into action. In all this, the participants in the dialogue must be equal partners, with none being privileged over any other, for it is only on the basis of this equality that any individual in the dialogue may reach intellectual and, perhaps, also moral conversion.

We are wide open to dialogue in this book. We have to be, given the theological positions we embrace in it and in our theological lives. We are like two men at a third-story window getting only a restricted third-story perspective on the landscape outside the window, and we have to be open to the complementary perspectives provided by women and men at the sixth-, ninth-, and twenty-first-story windows. In theological parlance, therefore, we situate this book in the category of *quaestio disputata*, the disputed question, so beloved of the medieval Scholastics. The Scholastic master had three tasks: *lectio*, or commentary on the Bible; *disputatio*, or teaching by objection and response to a theme; and *praedicatio*, or proclamation of the theological word.[17] Peter Cantor speaks for all of them when he argues that "it is after the *lectio* of scripture and after the examination of the doubtful points thanks to the *disputatio, and not before*, that we must preach."[18] It is important for the reader to be aware that this book is *lectio* and *disputatio* before it is theological and pastoral *praedicatio*.

We freely confess that it is not for theologians alone to formulate the theological or moral doctrine and practice of their Church. That task is for the whole communion-Church. The task of the theologian in the Church is a different and critical one, that of "interpreting the documents of the past and present Magisterium, of putting them in the context of the whole of revealed truth, and of finding a better understanding of them by the use of hermeneutics."[19] The theologian "is charged with developing the tradition beyond its current state so that it can meet new questions, needs, and circumstances."[20] It is this difficult theologian's task of "maintaining the balance between 'immobilism' and 'eccentricity'" that we seek to fulfill, positively and not destructively, in this book.[21] Because we believe that genuine and respectful dialogue about sexual morality, and indeed about all that is involved in the life of Christian discipleship, is sorely needed to clarify Christian truth today, we intend this book to be part of a genuine dialogue. Our dialogue partners in the book, as the reader will discover, are Christians who argue from different starting points and reach different conclusions about sexual morality than we do. Our intent is neither to prove ourselves right or them wrong. Convinced of the central role that love, desire, and fertility play in a human life, and therefore also in a life of Christian discipleship, we seek only to suggest a sexual anthropology that might lead to the enhancement of human and Christian sexual relationships.[22] What we have written here is to be submitted to the experience, attention, intelligence, reasonableness, decisiveness, and response of our fellow believers in the communion-Church, particularly of our fellow theologians trained in the tools of scientific theology. Because we do not dare suggest, in a pilgrim Church,[23] that the Spirit of God has breathed the final word about either the communion-Church or the sexuality of its members, we invite our dialogue partners to be as critical in their reading as we have been in our writing. Both our critiques and theirs, however, should not be destructive of the communion instituted by Christ and constituted by the Spirit of Christ, who is at once the Spirit of God and the Spirit of "righteousness and peace and joy" (Rom 14:17).

Chapter One

Sexual Morality in the Catholic Tradition

A Brief History

Human sexual activity and the sexual ethics that seeks to order it are both sociohistorical realities and are, therefore, subject to historicity, the quality of the human animal that follows inevitably from his and her situation in real time and space and "provides him with a [human] world that he must accept in freedom."[1] Before we embark on a presentation of contemporary Catholic sexual anthropology and ethics, therefore, it behooves us to look at their past history. In this chapter we do that in two stages. First, and briefly because it is already well known and well documented, we consider the pre-Christian history that helped to shape Western understanding of human sexuality, sexual activity, and sexual ethics. Second, and more extendedly because it is central to our project, we consider their understanding in specifically Catholic history. This historical conspectus is offered here for readers who do not already understand it and may therefore be surprised by it. Readers who believe they already know this history may skip this chapter and proceed immediately to the meat of the book in chapter 2. Before embarking on the history, however, we must first say a word about historicity.

Historicity

Bernard Lonergan delineates what he calls "the theoretical premises from which there follows the historicity of human thought and action." They are as follows: "(1) that human concepts, theories, affirmations, courses of action are expressions of human understanding; . . . (2) that human understanding develops over time and, as it develops, human concepts, theories, affirmations, courses of action change; . . . (3) that such change is cumulative; and (4) that the cumulative changes in one place or time are not to be expected to coincide with those in another."[2] From these premises flows the conclusion that the articulations of the meanings, values, moral norms, and moral actions of one sociohistorical era are not necessarily the articulations of another era or, indeed, of different groups in the same era. The world—both the "already, out, there, now real"[3] world free of every human intervention and the human world fashioned by socially constructed and interpersonal meanings—is in a permanent state of change and evolution. It is essentially for this reason that Joseph Fuchs argues, correctly in our judgment, that anyone wishing to make a moral judgment about any human action in the present on the basis of its givenness in the past must keep at least two facts in mind.

The first fact is that those living in the past simply did not know either the entire reality of the human person, from its emergence to its full development in the future, nor its individual elements, from the mysterious powers of the physical universe to the long-hidden possibilities of human biology and human sexuality considered physiologically, psychologically, and sociohistorically. "If one wishes to make an objective moral judgment today," Fuchs points out, "then one cannot take what Augustine or the philosophers of the Middle Ages knew about sexuality as the exclusive basis of a moral reflection."[4] The second fact is that "we never simply 'have' nature or that which is given in nature." We know "nature," rather, "always as something that has already been interpreted in some way."[5] The careful attention, understanding, interpretation, judgment, and responsible decision of rational persons about "nature" and what it demands is what constitutes *natural law*, never simply the pure givenness of "nature" alone. In the Catholic moral tradition, argument is never from "nature" alone or reason alone, but always a question of "nature" *interpreted by* reason. For the human person subject to historicity, moral decision making and action are always the outcome of a process of hermeneutics controlled by reason. They are never the outcome of merely looking at the facticity of "*nature*." (As we discuss in chapter 2, because "nature" is not pure uninterpreted "nature"— because it is, as philosophers and sociologists say, socially constructed—throughout this book we speak of it always within quotation marks, that is, as "nature.")

Bernard Lonergan was convinced that something new was happening in history in the twentieth century and that, because a living theology ought to be part of what was taking place in history, Christians were living in a new theological age that required a new theological approach. This new approach, he prophesied correctly, would be necessarily historical and empirical. His distinction between a classicist and an empirical notion of culture has itself become classical: "The classicist notion of culture was normative: at least *de iure* there was but one culture that was both universal and permanent." The empirical notion of culture was "the set of meanings and values that informs a way of life. It may remain unchanged for ages. It may be in the process of slow development or rapid resolution."[6] Classicist culture is static; empirical culture is dynamic. Theology, which is necessarily part of culture, mirrors this distinction.

In its classicist mode, theology is a static, permanent achievement that anyone can learn; in its empirical mode, it is a dynamic, ongoing process requiring a free person who is committed and trained. This distinction is as valid for moral theology as for any other discipline. The classicist understanding, Fuchs writes, conceives of the human person as "a series of created, static, and thus definitively ordered temporal facts." The empirical understanding conceives of the person as a subject in process of "self-realization in accordance with a project that develops in God-given autonomy, that is, along a path of human reason and insight, carried out in the present with a view to the future."[7] Classicist theology sees moral norms coming from the Magisterium as once and for all definitive; sexual norms enunciated in the fifth or sixteenth centuries continue to apply absolutely in the twenty-first century. Empirical theology sees the moral norms of the past not as facts for uncritical and passive acceptance but as partial insights that are bases for critical attention, understanding, evaluation, judgment, and decisions in the present sociohistorical situation. What Augustine and his medieval successors knew about sexuality cannot be the exclusive basis for a moral judgment about sexuality today. The Second Vatican Council adopted a historical, empirical approach to theological (including moral theological) judgments as well as a focus on the *person* rather than on the person's *acts*, but the Roman Magisterium continues to support its teaching on sexual morality by quoting the past tradition as if it did not suffer from historicity.

In reality, of course, the Magisterium is more than a little schizophrenic when it speaks of making moral judgments. In sexual ethics, it follows the classical approach enshrined, for instance, in the writings of Pius XII; in social ethics it follows the historical approach validated by the Second Vatican Council. The *Catechism of the Catholic Church* teaches that "the Church's social teaching proposes *principles for reflection*; it provides *criteria for judgment*; it gives *guidelines* for action."[8] This trinity of principles for reflection, criteria for judgment, and guidelines for action came into Catholic social teaching via Paul VI's *Octogesima adveniens* in 1971.[9] It was repeated in the Congregation for the Doctrine of the Faith's (CDF's) important *Instruction on Christian Freedom and Liberation* in 1986,[10] and it was underscored again a year later in John Paul II's *Sollicitudo rei socialis*.[11] This sociomoral teaching, now an established part of the Catholic moral tradition, introduces a model of personal responsibility that increasingly underscores the responsibility of each person. John Paul accentuates this point of view by teaching that, in its social doctrine, the Church seeks "to *guide* people to *respond*, with the support of rational reflection and of the human sciences, to their vocation as *responsible* builders of earthly society."[12] The relationship of Magisterium and individual believer advanced in this teaching merits close attention. The Church guides;[13] responsible persons, drawing on the Church's guidance, their own intellectual abilities, and the findings of the human sciences, respond responsibly.

The notion of responsibility introduces the important personal dimension of human freedom and autonomy to the unnuanced notion of response.[14] In social reality, the Magisterium does not pretend to pronounce on every last detail or to impose final decisions; it understands itself as informing and guiding believers and as leaving the final judgment and application to their faithful and responsible con-science.[15] Sociomoral principles are guidelines for reflection, judgment, and action, not unchanging moral imperatives based on divine, "natural," or ecclesiastical law, and demanding uncritical obedience to God, "nature," or the Church. John Paul adds what the Catholic moral tradition has always taken for granted. On the one hand, the Church's social teaching is "constant." On the other hand, "it is ever new, because it is subject to the necessary and opportune adaptations suggested by the changes in historical conditions and by the unceasing flow of the events which are the setting of the life of people and society."[16] Principles remain constant. Judg-ments and actions might well change after reflection on changed sociohistorical conditions and the ongoing flow of human events illuminated by rational reflection and the data of the social sciences.

There is, however, a problem. This model of relationship–responsibility seems to apply in the contemporary Catholic moral situation only in *social morality*. A model antithetical to personal freedom and responsibility applies in *sexual morality*, where propositions from the past tradition are accepted not as principles and guidelines for reflection, judgment, and action but as laws to be universally and uncritically obeyed. How this can be is, at least, debatable. Because social and sexual morality pertain to the same person, this double and conflicting approach seems illogical. In fact, because the whole personality is more intimately involved in the sexual domain, should it not "be *more than any other* the place where all is referred to the informed conscience."[17] The choice between the two moral approaches is neither self-evident nor free from risk. But it is a choice that must be made to find the best theological and pastoral approach to the experience of contemporary women and men. Bressoud judges that the choice is clear, and that there is "a manifest link between the notions dear to social morality, namely, person, freedom, relationship, and responsibility, and the notions of individual sexual development and progression toward mar-riage."[18] We are not convinced that the choice is clear or that the link is manifest to everyone, but in this book the conflict between the two Catholic approaches to morality cannot be avoided and will recur regularly.

Sexuality and Sexual Ethics in Ancient Greece and Rome

Generalizations about ancient Greece and Rome are fraught with difficulties, both because their histories were in general written by elite males to the detriment of women's sexual histories and because we know today more about Athens and Rome than about other Greek city states and other parts of the earlier and later Roman Empire. Yet we can safely say that in both societies sexuality was generally accepted as a natural part of life and that attitudes toward sex were permissive, especially for men.[19] In both societies, marriage was monogamous and regarded as the foundation of social life, but sexual activity was not restricted to marriage. Hallett demonstrates that, at least among elite men and women, erotic intercourse could be sought with partners other than spouses,[20] and concubinage, male and female prostitution, and male intercourse with slaves were also permitted and common. The ancient aphorism attributed to Demosthenes is famous. "Mistresses we keep for the sake of pleasure, concubines for the daily care of our persons, but wives to bear us legitimate children and to be faithful guardians of our households."[21] Divorce was readily available in Greece and the later Roman Empire, with both societies legislating for the economic situation of divorced women. Abortion and infanticide were commonly accepted forms of birth control. Marriage was not about love, which is not to say that marital love was never present between spouses. Men were expected to marry to produce an heir, but for them the greatest love was to be had in relationship, sexual or otherwise, with other men, for between men there was an equality that a woman could never attain.

Both Greece and Rome were male-dominated societies in which women were regarded as inferior to men, indeed as belonging to men, either to their fathers or to their husbands. Male homosexual activity was accepted in both as a function of a patriarchal ethos, and female homosexual activity was regarded as adultery because wives were the property of their husbands.[22] The approved male homosexual activity was not because some men had an intrinsic homosexual orientation, which was unknown at the time, but because men were generally considered more beautiful than women and a man might reasonably be attracted to the more beautiful. It is misleading, however, to speak of sexual relations between men; relations were most often between adult men and boys. Those relations were to cease when the boy reached a certain age,[23] not because homosexual relations per se were problematic but because adult *male passivity* was problematic.[24] We will encounter this same problematic when we consider in chapter 7 the biblical texts proscribing male homosexuality.

Greek and Roman attitudes toward sexuality were fashioned in large part by their great philosophers. The Greek dualism between body and soul, with the body being the inferior component, led to a distrust of physical sex and the categorization of sexual pleasure. Both Plato and Aristotle judged sexual pleasure to be a lower pleasure shared with other animals.[25] Plato urged its transcendence for the sake of higher pleasures of good, beauty, and truth; Aristotle urged, in keeping with his general approach, not its transcendence, but its moderation. Though Plato offered in both the *Republic* and the *Laws* a design for the equality of men and women, Aristotle always opposed this. It was not, however, Plato or Aristotle who had the greatest influence on the Christian approach to sexuality. It was the Stoics. We will deal with these in some detail in the next section. Here we make only two summary statements. The Stoics Musonius Rufus, in his *Reliquiae*, and Seneca, in his *Fragments*, considered sexual desire and activity to be irrational and liable to excess. They sought, therefore, to rationally order it by situating it in a larger context of human meaning, and they did this by asking about its *telos*, its purpose or end. That end, they judged, was the procreation of children and, therefore, sexual activity was moral *only* when it was engaged in for the sake of procreation. The later Stoics went further. Not only was sexual activity for procreation but also it was to be limited to marriage; there could be no moral sex outside of marriage. Foucault's ultimate judgment summarizes the Stoic position well: "The conjugal family took custody of [sexuality] and absorbed it into the serious function of reproduction. On the subject of sex, silence became the rule. The legitimate and procreative couple laid down the law. The couple imposed itself as model, enforced the norm, safeguarded the truth, and reserved the right to speak while retaining the principle of secrecy."[26] Stoic philosophers both "conjugalized" and "procreationalized" sexual relations.

Sexuality and Sexual Ethics in the Catholic Tradition

In 1976, the CDF asserted that, to be moral, "any human genital act whatsoever may be placed only with the framework of marriage."[27] Earlier, in 1968, Pope Paul VI asserted that in marriage "each and every marriage act [*quilibet matrimonii actus*] must remain open to the transmission of life."[28] In traditional Catholic sexual morality, therefore, every sexually moral act takes place only within the institution of marriage, and within marriage each and every such act must be open to procreation. Traditional Catholic sexual morality is essentially *marital* morality; sexuality was carefully confined in the home. Foucault's comment cited above accurately describes the Catholic sexual tradition. "The conjugal family took custody of [sexuality] and absorbed it into the serious function of reproduction." Sexual intercourse is exclusively for marriage and procreation. In the Catholic moral tradition, every intentional genital act outside of marriage is seriously sinful.[29]

The consonance of that teaching with Stoic philosophy is clear. It would be wholly inaccurate, however, to assume that philosophy is the only root of Catholic sexual morality. Catholicism is "a textualized religion,"[30] and its first instinct is to consult not ancient Hellenistic philosophers but its equally ancient sacred text, the Bible, *Dei verbum*,[31] the very word of God. As Catholic theologians, it is also our first instinct, and so we begin our analysis of the development of traditional Catholic sexual morality with an exploration of, first, the Old Testament and, then, the New Testament. Following the lead of the Second Vatican Council, we then follow the biblical tradition through its subsequent history, in which, under the grace of the Spirit of God, "there is a growth in insight into the realities and words that are being passed on."[32]

Ultimately, as the Second Vatican Council taught, "sacred tradition and sacred scripture make up a single sacred deposit of the Word of God entrusted to the Church."[33] Abandoned is the Tridentine distinction between sacred scripture *and* tradition as two distinct sources;[34] abandoned also is the post-Tridentine debate about whether all truth is contained in the sacred writings alone or whether some truths not in the writings are found only in the ongoing tradition. There is only one source of the Word of God for humans, and that source is interpretive tradition,

sometime in the form of sacred writings, sometime in the form of oral interpretation.[35] It is necessary to study both the sacred writings and the historical interpretive
development to understand not only what is the Catholic moral tradition with
respect to sexuality, already enunciated at the opening of this chapter, but also how
and why that tradition came to be. Both need to be read and interpreted in light of
the sociohistorical background of the times when they were created. Given the
almost three-thousand-year time differential between the writing of the first Old
Testament document and the present day and the fact of historicity—that is, the
effect of sociohistorical circumstance on the conceptual and verbal formulation of
ideas—it is not surprising to find different interpretive traditions at different junc-
tures of the development.

Reading Sacred Scripture

Christianity is a religion of the book, and Christians automatically appeal to their
sacred scripture, believed to be *Dei verbum*, the very word of God, to substantiate
their theological claims, including their moral theological claims.[36] A special question arises here, namely, whether or not the canonical writings that constitute the
Christians scriptures are as subject to historicity as any other writings. The Catholic
answer to that question is an unqualified "yes they are," but this answer requires
careful explanation. The contemporary Catholic approach to biblical exegesis was
established by Pope Pius XII's 1943 encyclical letter on the promotion of biblical
studies, *Divino afflante spiritu*. The pope left no doubt about the historicity of the
biblical corpus. Having first stated that the biblical exegete's "foremost and greatest
endeavor should be to discern and define clearly that sense of the biblical words that
is called literal,"[37] Pius goes on to insist that that literal sense "is not to be determined by the rules of grammar and philology alone. The interpreter must go back
wholly in spirit to those remote centuries of the East and with the aid of history,
archaeology, ethnology, and other sciences, accurately determine what modes of
writing the authors of that ancient period would be likely to use, and did use."[38]
The Second Vatican Council picked up that instruction and put it forcefully: "The
exegete must look for that meaning that the sacred writer, *in a determined situation
and given the circumstances of his time and culture*, intended to express and did express
through the medium of a contemporary literary form."[39] Sociohistorical circumstance—that is, historicity—is a factor in the correct translation, interpretation, and
inculturation of the biblical Word of God.[40]

The Pontifical Biblical Commission's 1994 document *The Interpretation of the
Bible in the Church* insists that "holy scripture, in as much as it is 'the word of God
in human language,' has been composed by human authors in all its various parts
and in all the sources that lie behind them. Because of this, its proper understanding
not only admits the use of [the historical-critical] method but actually requires it."[41]
It further insists that "religious texts are bound in reciprocal relationship to the

societies in which they originate [in the way we have explained above]. . . . Consequently, the scientific study of the Bible requires as exact a knowledge as possible of the social conditions distinctive of the various milieus in which the traditions recorded in the Bible took shape."[42] The very "nature" of the biblical texts requires the use of a historical methodology for the their correct interpretation. "*Diachronic research*," the commission insists, "will always be indispensable for exegesis."[43]

Of particular relevance to this book is the Pontifical Biblical Commission's applications of its principles for biblical exegesis to moral theology. Though the Bible is God's word to the Church, "this does not mean that God has given the historical conditioning of the message a value which is absolute. It is open both to interpretation and being brought up to date." It follows, therefore, that it is not sufficient for moral judgment that the scripture "should indicate a certain moral position [e.g., the practice of polygamy, slavery, or divorce, or the "prohibition" of homosexual acts] for this position to continue to have validity. One has to undertake a process of discernment [as we have explained above]. This will review the issue in the light of the progress in moral understanding and sensitivity that has occurred over the years."[44] And so Fuchs writes that what Augustine, Jerome, Aquinas, and Trent said about sexuality cannot exclusively control what moral theologians say today.

A characteristic of sacred scripture, then, is the historicity it shares with every other document subject to sociohistorical conditions. If that is the case with scripture, the normative theology of the earliest churches, it will be the case also with the theology and doctrine of every later church. That this is so is demonstrated from magisterial documents. In 1965, in his encyclical letter on the Eucharist, *Mysterium fidei*, Pope Paul VI claimed that doctrinal formulas "are not tied to a certain specific form of culture, or to a certain level of scientific progress";[45] that is, they do not have the characteristic of historicity. Eight years later, in its 1973 document on the Church, *Mysterium ecclesiae*, which Paul VI approved, the Congregation for the Doctrine of the Faith (CDF) asserted with no demur that "difficulties arise from the historical condition that affects the expression of revelation. . . . It sometimes happens that some dogmatic truth is first expressed incompletely (but not falsely) and at a later date, when considered in a broader context of faith or human knowledge, is expressed more fully and perfectly."[46] Doctrinal and theological, including moral, formulations share the characteristic of historicity with scriptural formulations. They are subject, therefore, to the same historical-critical hermeneutic.

Scripture, then, and traditional theological, doctrinal formulations are the result of reflexive, critical, human construal and have to be, therefore, as sociohistorically conditioned as its construers themselves.[47] It cannot be otherwise. If God is to be really revealed to concrete, historical women and men, there is no alternative but for the revelation to be mediated in sociohistorical symbols. If the foundational revelation is to be expressed in human language, oral or written, as it is in scriptural, doctrinal, and theological formulations, there is no alternative but for the expression to be in a language that is sociohistorically mediated. There is no synchronic, transhistorical, transcultural language valid for all times and for all peoples. The condition of the possibility of real human encounter with God, as transcendentalists like

Heidegger, Rahner, and Lonergan will say, *pace* Milbank, is precisely that it be sociohistorically mediated in the symbols available to them. Because the scriptural rule of faith and the theological writings selectively derived from it are historically and culturally conditioned, they will require translation, interpretation, and inculturation to truly disclose God in every different historical and cultural situation. Because the translators, interpreters, and inculturators may stand in different sociohistorical contexts, their interpretations of the classic tradition will almost certainly be pluriform, which will lead to dialectic. That dialectic will be resolved only by intellectually, morally, religiously, and psychically converted theologians in respectful dialogue.

Discovering what scripture says about sexual morality, therefore, is never as straightforward as simply reading the text. The reader must get behind the text to understand how the Church and its theologians construe scripture and what authority they assign to it.[48] The standard answer is that scripture is construed as a normative authority for the Catholic Church and, therefore, for Catholic theology. Kelsey's detailed case study of seven Protestant theologians, however, demonstrates the diversity of ways in which that authority is construed.[49] It is construed with equal diversity by Catholic theologians. We begin our analysis with the Catholic teaching of how the sacred scriptures came to be and how they are to be interpreted. They came to be in a four-stage process: a first generation of followers construed their experience of the life, death, and resurrection of Jesus of Nazareth as religious and revelatory of God; the growth of interpretive traditions about that experience; the preservation of those traditions in written form in the third generation;[50] and the canonization of certain writings as authoritative Church scripture.[51] How theologians understand this four-stage process, we suggest, determines how they construe scripture and its authority in theology.

With the Second Vatican Council, the Catholic Church embraced this four-stage scheme with respect to the writing of the four gospels and issued instruction on how the scriptures of both the Old and New testaments are to be read. "Those who search out the intentions of the sacred writers," it teaches, "must, among other things have regard for 'literary forms.' For truth is proposed and expressed in a variety of ways, depending on whether a text is history of one kind or another, or whether its form is that of prophecy, poetry, or some other type of speech. The interpreter must investigate what meaning the sacred writer *intended to express and actually expressed* in particular circumstances as he used contemporary literary forms in accordance with the situation of his own time and culture."[52] It is never enough simply to read the text to find out what it says about sexual morality. Its original sociohistorical context must first be clarified and then the text can be translated, interpreted, and inculturated in a contemporary context. An example of how sexual morality and sociohistorical context are connected appears from an analysis of patriarchy.

The dominant characteristic of patriarchy is that it describes women in relation to men, and in ways that serve and further men's interests. Patriarchy is the "social order in which women are declared to be the possessions of, first, fathers and, later, husbands—the aim of which is to produce children who 'belong to' the father and take his name."[53] It is "the systematic social closure of women from the public sphere by legal, political, and economic arrangements which operate in favor of men."[54] There are minority strands in both testaments that are critical of patriarchy: the Hebrew midwives refusal of Pharaoh's order to murder the male children (Ex 1:15–22); Lot's two daughters who get their father drunk in order to become pregnant by him (Gen 19:30–38); Ruth making herself sexually available to Boaz by her own free choice (Ruth 3:1–15); Queen Vashti's refusal to obey her drunken husband's command to flaunt herself before him (Esther 1:1–12); Jesus' open attitude toward women; Paul's assertion of equality between men and women in Christ (Gal 3:28), and in sexual intercourse (1 Cor 7:3–4). Anne Carr calls these examples of nonpatriarchal behavior "liberating strands."[55]

In spite of these liberating strands, patriarchal assumptions abound in both testaments and the New Testament uses them to enforce women's subordination to men (1 Cor 11:7–12; Col 3:18), to silence them in church, and to suggest the way for women to atone for their collective guilt in causing men to sin is to bear men children (1 Tim 2:12–15). Genesis 2–3 is the aetiological and mythical justification for all patriarchy in the Bible. In this account, the earlier creation account, woman is created as an afterthought from man and for man. She is to be "a helper fit for him" (Gen 2:20). A quite different perspective is given in the later account in Genesis 1, where both male and female are created together "in [God's] own image" and together are declared to be *'adam*, humankind (Gen 1:27). This presumed equality between male and female as human vanishes in Genesis 3, where the woman is blamed for the man's sin (Gen 3:12) and condemned to be under the man's rule (Gen 3:16).

If we accept the Bible as a source for moral judgments about sexual morality, the Catholic tradition requires that we first examine the sociocultural assumptions that underpin what is said about sexual morality. If what is said is inseparably linked to the underpinning judgment that the proper relationship between a man and a woman is a patriarchal relationship with the man as superior, then a careful process of separating what is synchronically true but culturally limited and what is diachronically and transculturally true must be undertaken. The criterion for such a refining process is provided by the New Testament and Jesus' behavior toward women, the woman with the issue of blood (Mark 5:25–34), the sinful woman in the house of the Pharisee (Luke 7:36–50), and the Samaritan woman at Jacob's well (John 4:8–30). Jesus deals with and speaks to none of these women in a demeaning or patriarchal way. In the Israel of Jesus' time, women were surely among the oppressed promised liberation in Luke's Magnificat: "he has put down the mighty from their thrones and has exalted the lowly" (Luke 1:52). It was but a small further step to Paul's egalitarian judgment that, for Christians in the fictive family of Jesus ("whoever does the will of God is my brother, my sister, my mother," Mark 3:35), "there is neither male nor female, for you are all one person in Christ" (Gal 3:28).

Hayter is correct. There are "two views of womanhood in the Bible, the subordinationist and the egalitarian."[56] The two need to be discriminated in a dialogue that includes the Bible, Christian tradition, and contemporary human experience. Only such discrimination will yield a true sexual theology rather than a theology of sexuality,[57] which results from unidirectional instruction from the Bible and Christian tradition to human sexual experience. This book presents a sexual theology in which the contemporary human experience and understanding of sexuality and sexual activity are equal partners in the moral dialogue.

Old Testament Teaching

Old Testament teaching on sexuality and marriage must be situated in the context of the ancient Near Eastern cultures with which the biblical peoples had such intimate links. It is not our intention here, because it is not necessary to our purpose, to dwell at length on these cultures and their approach to sexuality and marriage. They were all syncretistic, and a brief overview will provide a sufficient sense of both the general context and its specific distinction from what we find in the Hebrew Bible. Underlying the themes of sexuality and marriage in the cultures surrounding Israel are the archetypal figures of the god-father and the goddess-mother, the sources of universal life in the divine, the human, and the natural realms. Myths celebrated the marriage, the sexual congress, and the fertility of this divine pair, simultaneously divinizing sexuality and legitimating the marriage, the intercourse, and the fertility of every earthly pair. Rituals acted out the myths, establishing a concrete link between the divine and the earthly worlds, enabling men and women to share in both the divine action and the efficacy of that action. This is especially true of sexual rituals, which bless sexual intercourse and ensure that the unfailing divine fertility is shared by a man's plants and animals and wives, all important elements in his struggle for survival in those primitive cultures.

The Hebrew view of sexuality and marriage makes a radical break with this polytheistic perspective.[58] Sexuality is not divinized. There is no god–goddess couple, only Yahweh who is unique (Deut 6:4). There is no goddess associated with God who creates. In the later Priestly account, God creates merely by uttering a creative word (Gen 1) and, in the earlier Yahwist account, by shaping creation as a potter (Gen 2–3). At the apex of Yahweh's creation stands 'adam, man and woman together: "Male and female he created them and he blessed them and named them 'adam" (Gen 5:2). The fact that Yahweh names male and female together 'adam, that is, earthlings or humankind, founds the equality of man and woman as human beings. They are "bone of my bones and flesh of my flesh" (Gen 2:23), and because they are equal they can marry and become "one body" (Gen 2:24). In marriage, equal man and woman take on the unequal gendered roles of husband ('ish) and wife ('ishsha),[59] which gives aetiology and foundation for biblical patriarchy. These ideas are taken from the Yahwist creation account in Genesis 2, written about 950 B.C.E., but the Priestly account in Genesis 1, written four hundred years later around

550 B.C.E., also records the creation of 'adam "in the image of God, . . . male and female" (1:27).

Equal man and woman, and their separate sexualities, do not derive from a divine pair whom they are to imitate. They are called into being by the creative action of the sovereign God. "It was not the sacred rites that surrounded marriage that made it a holy thing. The great rite which sanctified marriage was God's act of creation itself."[60] It was God alone, unaided by any partner, who not only created 'adam with sexuality and for marriage but also blessed him and her, making them fundamentally good. Man and woman, humankind, 'adam, their sexuality, and their marriage are all good, because they are the good gifts of the Creator God. Later Christian history, as we shall see, will have recurring doubts about the goodness of sexuality and its use in marriage, but the Hebrew tradition had none.

That a man and a woman become one body in marriage has often been restricted in the Western tradition to only one facet of marriage, namely, the act of uniting bodies in sexual intercourse. That facet is undoubtedly included in becoming one body, but it is far from all there is, for "body" in Hebrew implies the entire person: "One personality would translate it better, for 'flesh' in the Jewish idiom means 'real human life.' "[61] In the debate on sexuality and marriage at the Second Vatican Council, the biblical scholar Bernard Cardinal Alfrink pointed out that "the Hebrew verb dabaq, in Greek kollao, does suggest physical, bodily, sexual union, but it suggests above all spiritual union which exists in conjugal love."[62] In marriage a man and a woman unite in an interpersonal union, not just a sexual or genital one. In such a union they become one coupled social person and one life, so complementing one another that they become again, as in the beginning, 'adam. They enter into a union that establishes not just a juridical relationship but also a quasi-blood relationship that makes them one social person. Rabbis go so far as to teach that it is only after marriage and the union of man and woman into one person that the image of God may be discerned in them. An unmarried man, in their eyes, is not a whole man. The mythic stories, interested as always in etiology, the origin of things, proclaim that it was so "in the beginning," and that it was so by the express design of God. For both Jew and Christian, there could be no greater foundation for the human and religious goodness of sexuality and marriage. Nor could there be a secular reality better than marriage for pointing to God and his steadfastly loving relationship with Israel. That was the next step in the development of the religious character of marriage. Before we consider that, however, we should consider the different mythic meanings we find in Genesis 1 and 2.

The older Yahwist creation account in Genesis situates sexuality in a relational context. "It is not good that the male ['ish] should be alone," God judges, "I will make a helper ['ezer] fit for him" (2:18). The importance of the helper to the one helped may be gleaned from the fact that twice in the Psalms (30:10 and 54:4) God is presented as such a helper ('ezer) of humans. The equality of the partners in this helping relationship is underscored. Male and female are "bone of my bones and flesh of my flesh" (2:23), they have the same strengths and the same weaknesses, and the myth asserts that it is precisely because of their equality and, therefore, potential intimacy that male and female may marry. Significantly, they are presented as being totally comfortable with each other's sexuality, for they "were both naked and not ashamed" (1:25), a comfort that is celebrated frankly in that great Jewish love song, the Song of Songs.

About four hundred years later, the Priestly tradition has God bless 'adam, male and female, and enjoin them to "be fruitful and multiply, and fill the earth and subdue it" (1:28). Male and female, their sexuality, and their fertility are blessed by God; ever afterward there can be no doubt that sexuality is good. The Priestly myth situates sexuality in a procreative context, that is, a context of cooperation with the creator in both the creation of children and caring providence for them. Collins notes that "procreation was valued in Israel insofar as large Israelite families were considered to be the fulfillment of the promise made to Abraham."[63] From the beginning of the biblical tradition, therefore, sexuality as created by God is linked to two perspectives, to the relationship of mutual help between male and female and to their procreative activity together. These two perspectives are the ones we found also in the Greco-Roman, Stoic tradition. The Stoic Musonius Rufus argues that marriage is a natural institution[64] with two broad purposes, the one sexual intercourse (homilia) and procreation, the other community of life (koinonia) between the spouses,[65] and that it is the most important and venerable of all human communities.[66] These two broad purposes have convoluted histories in the postbiblical Catholic tradition.

Central to the Hebrew notion of their special relationship with God was the idea of the covenant. The Deuteronomist reminded the assembled people: "You have declared this day concerning you that you are a people for his own possession" (Deut 26:17–19). Yahweh is the God of Israel; Israel is the people of Yahweh. Together Yahweh and Israel form a union of salvation, a union of grace, a union, one could say, of one body. It was probably only a matter of time until the people began to image this covenant relationship in terms drawn from marriage, and the first to speak of marriage as image of the covenant was the prophet Hosea. He preached about the covenant relationship of Yahweh and Israel within the biographical context of his own marriage to a harlot wife, Gomer. To understand his preaching, about both marriage and the covenant, we must first understand the sociohistorical times in which Hosea lived.

Hosea preached in the middle of the eighth century B.C.E., at a time when Israel was well established in Canaan. Many Israelites thought, indeed, they had become too well adapted to their promised land, for among the new ways they learned was the cult of the fertility god Baal. This cult, which seriously challenged their worship of Yahweh, was situated in the classic mold presented earlier, that of the god–goddess pair, with Baal as the Lord of the Earth and Anat as his consort. The sexual intercourse and fertility of these two were believed to establish the pattern of the fertile intercourse of every human pair, and this belief was acted out in worship as ritual sexual intercourse in the temple of Baal. Such sexual rituals were prohibited in the cult of Yahweh (Deut 23:18), and any Jewish woman participating in them was regarded as a harlot. It was such a harlot, Gomer, whom Yahweh instructed Hosea to take for his wife (1:2–3).

It is irrelevant to our discussion whether the book of Hosea tells us what Hosea did in historical reality, namely, took a harlot-wife and remained faithful to her despite her infidelity to him, or whether it offers a parable about marriage as steadfast covenant. The only thing that is relevant is that Hosea found in marriage, either in his own marriage or in marriage in general, an image in which to represent the steadfastness of Yahweh's covenantal love for the people of Israel. On a superficial level, the marriage of Hosea and Gomer is like any other marriage. But on a more profound level, it serves as prophetic symbol, proclaiming, revealing, and celebrating in representation the covenant relationship between Yahweh and Israel. The names of Hosea's two younger children reflect the sad state of that relationship: A daughter is Not Pitied (1:6), and a son is Not My People (1:9). As Gomer left Hosea for another, so too did Israel abandon Yahweh in favor of Baal and become Not Pitied and Not My People. But Hosea's remarkable reaction to Gomer's infidelity proclaims and makes explicit in representation the remarkable reaction of Yahweh to Israel's infidelity. He redeems Gomer (3:2); that is, he buys her back. He loves her "even as Yahweh loves the people of Israel, though they turn to other gods" (3:1), and his unfailing love for Gomer reveals in representation Yahweh's unfailing love for Israel. As Hosea has pity on Gomer, so Yahweh "will have pity on Not Pitied," and will "say to Not My People 'you are my people,'" and they will say to him, "Thou art my God" (2:25). The covenant union, that between Hosea and Gomer as well as that between Yahweh and Israel, is unshakeable. A sundering of the marital relationship is not possible for Hosea because he recognized that his God is not a God who can abide the dissolution of covenant, no matter what the provocation.

There is a serious possibility of anachronism to be avoided here, connected to that overworked word *love*. In contemporary usage, love always means a strong affection for another person, frequently a passionate affection for a person of the opposite sex. When we find the word in our Bible, it is easy to assume that it means exactly these same things; but it does not, at least not exclusively. The covenant love of which Hosea speaks is more than the love of interpersonal desire and commitment; it is a love that is ultimately a decision for "loyalty [or fidelity], service and obedience."[67] When we read, therefore, of Hosea's steadfast love for Gomer and of Yahweh's faithful love for Israel, we ought to understand intentional fidelity, service, and obedience, not only felt interpersonal affection.

What ought we to make of the story of marriage that Hosea leaves to us? There is a first, and clear, meaning about Yahweh: God is faithful. There is also a second, and somewhat more mysterious, meaning about marriage. Not only is it, on one level, the intimate communion of a man and a woman, but it is, on another level, also a prophetic symbol, proclaiming and revealing in representation the steadfast love of Yahweh for Israel. First articulated by the prophet Hosea, such a view of marriage recurs again in the prophets Jeremiah and Ezekiel (Jer 3:6–14; Ezek 23:4).

Israel and Judah are as much the harlots as Gomer, but Yahweh's faithfulness is as undying as Hosea's. Yahweh offers a declaration of undying love: "I have loved you with an everlasting love; therefore, I have continued my faithfulness to you" (Jer 31:3; cf. Ezek 16:63; Isa 54:7–8). The belief in and experience of covenant fidelity creates and sustains the belief in and the possibility of fidelity in marriage, which then and only then becomes a prophetic symbol of the covenant. Yahweh's covenant fidelity becomes a characteristic to be imitated, a challenge to be accepted, first, in every Jewish marriage and, later, in every Christian one.

Another Old Testament book, the Song of Songs, is intimately related to a biblical analysis of sexuality. The Song has always been an embarrassment for interpreters, posing the difficulty of deciding whether it is a paean to divine or human love. For centuries, under the shadow of the negative presuppositions about sexuality that developed in the postbiblical Church and, therefore, unwilling to assign erotic love a place in the sacred writings, Christian commentators opted for a spiritualized meaning. The Song, they prudishly and allegorically explained, was about the love of Yahweh for Israel, even the love of God for the individual soul. This argument ignores the historical fact that the Song was included in the Hebrew canon before there was any suggestion of an allegorical interpretation, which in itself provides "a powerful argument for believing that Israel's faith did not see its profane nature as an impediment to its acceptance as 'biblical literature.'"[68] Embodied men and women need no elaborate literary or philosophical argument; they need only listen to the extraordinarily explicit words and imagery of sexual love to know what the poetry means.

"I am sick with love," the woman exclaims (Song 2:5; 5:8). "Come to me," she cries out in desire for her lover, "like a gazelle, like a young stag upon the mountains where spices grow (2:17; 8:14). When he comes and gazes upon her nakedness, he is moved to poetry. "Your rounded thighs are like jewels. . . . Your vulva[69] is a rounded bowl that never lacks wine. Your belly is a heap of wheat encircled with lilies. Your two breasts are like fawns, twins of a gazelle. . . . You are stately as a palm tree and your breasts are like its clusters. I say I will climb the palm tree and lay hold of its branches" (7:1–8). Her response is direct and far from coy. "I am my beloved's and his desire is for me. Come, my beloved, let us go forth into the fields. . . . There I will give you my love" (7:10–13). No woman or man who has ever been sick with love and desire can doubt the origin of the language or its intent. Karl Barth, who argued that the Song was a "second *Magna Carta*" that develops the relationship view hinted at in Genesis 2,[70] notes the equality between the man and the woman in the Song: "It is to be noted that in this second text we hear a voice which is lacking in the first. This is the voice of the woman, to whom the man looks and moves with no less pain and joy than she to him, and who finds him with no less freedom . . . than she is found. Implicitly, of course, this voice is heard in Genesis as well. But now it finds expression in words. And what words!"[71]

Such explicitly erotic language has always raised doubt about the claim that the Song of Songs is about divine love, and today a consensus has emerged among scholars that its clear and literal meaning is the one enshrined in any human love song.[72] The Song may be an allegory about divine love but only secondarily; it may be about spiritual love, but only derivatively. The primary analogate is human, erotic love, love that makes every lover "sick with love" (2:5). This love is celebrated as image of the love of the creator God who loves women and men as the two lovers love one another. It is celebrated as good, to honor both the Giver and the gift, and also the lovers who use the gift to make both human and, in representation, divine love. It is as intentional and explicit analogy that human love and sexual intercourse become outward sign or sacrament of the God who is Love (1 John 4:8) and loving. Sexuality is no more divinized in the Song than anywhere else in the Old Testament; it may provide the basis for spiritual analogy, but the basis remains a secular, profane, and good reality. What this love poetry celebrates, and what we can learn from it, is "not eroticism for its own sake, and certainly not ribaldry or promiscuous sex, but rather the desires of an individual woman and man to enjoy the bond of mutual possession" (Song 2:16; 6:3; 7:10).[73] Barth notes an item of importance, namely, the woman speaks as openly as the man, and just as often. "There is no male dominance, no female subordination, and no stereotyping of either sex."[74] Nor is there any mention of marriage or procreation to justify sexuality. The Song is a far cry from Plato's and Aristotle's downgrading of sexual desire and pleasure; it is a celebration of human love and of the sexual desire of the lovers. Christian history will seriously patriarchalize the equal sexual relationship between male and female, will institutionalize it within the confines of marriage and procreation, and will follow Plato and Aristotle in their suspicion of sexual pleasure.

In summary, sexuality plays a relatively small role in the Old Testament. At the apex of Yahweh's creation stands 'adam, created "in the image of God, . . . male and female" (Gen 1:27), that is, sexual. Male and female are "bone of my bones and flesh of my flesh" (Gen 2:23); that is, they are equal as human, and because they are equal they can marry and become "one body" (Gen 2:24). The common Western interpretation of this text refers it to the sexual union of man and woman in marriage. In its sociohistorical context, however, it refers to their becoming one coupled life together, one social person. The early Yahwist creation account sets this couple in a *relational* context; "it is not good that the male should be alone" (Gen 2:18). The later Priestly account sets it in a *procreational* context; male and female are to "be fruitful and multiply" (Gen 1:28). This twofold relational and procreational purpose of both sexuality and marriage will continue in the Catholic tradition to the present day, and will be widely controverted. Marriage, however, and sexuality within marriage, are simply "good," because they were created good in the beginning by the good God. They will be so good that, in the prophet Hosea, the marital union of man and woman will become the prophetic symbol of the covenant union between God and God's people and, in the Song of Songs, sexual union will be celebrated in itself and as the image of the love of God who loves women and men as two human lovers love one another. This Old Testament judgment of both sexuality and marriage pass naturally into the New Testament.

New Testament Teaching

"It is striking," Lisa Cahill judges, "that sexuality plays a relatively small role in the New Testament at all. Only twice does Jesus direct his concern toward it [Jn 8:1–11 and Matt 5:31–32], and in both cases he protects women from the customs of his day and culture."[75] The New Testament provides no more of a systematic code of sexual ethics or even an approach to a sexual ethics than does the Old Testament. It records interpretations of the meaning of the deeds and words of Jesus "in view of the situation of the churches"[76] and their application in the sociohistorical situations in which Christians lived in the first century. The foundational presupposition for its every statement, including every statement about sexual ethics, is the belief that the followers of Jesus, the *ekklesia*-church, are the people of God of the last times. Jesus himself preached that the Kingdom of God was at hand (Mk 1:15), and Paul was convinced that "the form of this world is passing away" (1 Cor 7:31). Any interpretation of any statement about sexuality in the New Testament must be interpreted with this presupposition in mind.

The most extensive New Testament teaching about sexuality is in Paul's first letter to the Corinthians, apparently in response to a question the Corinthians had asked: "Is it better for a man not to touch a woman?" (1 Cor 7:1). Paul's answer, under the mistaken apprehension that the last days have arrived (7:31), is a mixed message. He prefers celibacy over marriage in the situation of the last days, but "because of the temptation to sexual immorality, each man should have his own wife and each woman her own husband" (7:2). It is "better to marry than to be aflame with passion" (7:9). Marriage is good, even for Christians, he seems to say, against the ascetical Encratites and Gnostics who urged celibacy on all Christians, even if only as a safeguard against sexual sins (7:5–9). Much more telling, however, than his lukewarm affirmation of marriage and sex in the circumstances is his countercultural assertion of the equality between husband and wife in marriage: "The husband should give to the wife her conjugal rights, and likewise the wife to her husband. For the wife does not rule over her own body, but the husband does; likewise the husband does not rule over his own body, but the wife does" (7:3–4).

A modern Christian might seize, as did medieval canonists seeking a precise juridical definition of marriage, on Paul's dealing with marital intercourse as an obligation owed mutually by the spouses one to the other. His contemporaries would have seized on something else, totally astounding to them, namely, his assertion of strict equality between husband and wife in this matter: "A modern Christian may wince at finding the apostle writing of sexual intercourse as an obligation, or even a debt, owed by spouses to one another, and writing of husbands' and wives' marital relationship as containing authority over one another's bodies. But Paul's contemporaries—at least those bred in the tradition of Torah and of its rabbinic interpreters—would have winced for another reason. This was Paul's assertion of equality between husbands and wives, and equality exactly on the juridical ground of authority and obligations owed."[77]

When a Christian man and a Christian woman marry, first-century Paul suggests, the covenant they make with one another is a covenant of equal and intimate partnership, and it embraces their human sexual activity within it. It is a suggestion that the Second Vatican Council would pursue twenty centuries later.[78]

Hosea's conception of marriage as a prophetic symbol of the mutually faithful covenant relationship is continued in the New Testament, with a change of dramatis personae, from Yahweh-Israel to Christ-Church. Rather than presenting marriage in the then-classical Jewish way as a symbol of the covenant union between Yahweh and Israel, the writer of the letter to the Ephesians presents it as an image of the relationship between the Christ and the new Israel, his church.[79] This presentation is of central importance to the development of a Christian view of marriage and sexuality and, unfortunately, has been used to sustain a diminished Christian view. We shall have to consider it here in some detail.

The passage in which the writer offers his view of marriage (Eph 5:21–33) is situated within a larger context (5:21–6:9), which sets forth a list of household duties that exist within a family in his time and place. This list is addressed to wives (5:22), husbands (5:25), children (6:1), fathers (6:4), slaves (6:5) and masters (6:9). All that concerns us here is what is said to wives and husbands. There are two similar lists in the New Testament, one in the letter to the Colossians (3:18–4:1), the other in the First Letter of Peter (2:13–3:7), but the list in Ephesians opens with a singular injunction: "Because you fear [or stand in awe of] Christ give way to one another" or, in the weaker translation of the Revised Standard Version, "be subject to one another out of reverence for Christ" (5:21). This injunction, commentators agree, is an essential element of what follows. Mutual giving way is required of all Christians, even of husbands and wives as they seek holiness together in marriage, and even in spite of traditional patriarchal relationships, which permitted husbands to lord it over their wives.

Because Christians have all been admonished to give way to one another, there is no surprise in the instruction that a Christian wife is to give way to her husband, "as to the Lord" (Eph 5:22). There is a surprise, however, at least for the ingrained male attitude that sees the husband as supreme lord and master of his wife and appeals to Ephesians 5:22–23 to ground and sustain that un-Christian attitude, that a husband is to give way to his wife. This follows from the general instruction that Christians are to give way to one another. It follows also from the specific instruction given to husbands. This instruction is not that "the husband is the head of the wife," the way in which the text is frequently cited, but rather that "*in the same way* that the Messiah is the head of the church the husband is the head of the wife." A Christian husband's headship over his wife is to be modeled upon and model of Christ's headship over the Church, and the way Christ exercises authority is never in doubt: "The Son of Man came not to be served but to serve, and to give his life as a ransom (redemption) for many" (Mark 10:45).

Diakonia, service, is the Christ way of exercising authority; it was as a servant that "Christ loved the church and gave himself up for her" (5:25). A Christian husband, therefore, is instructed to be head over his wife by serving, giving way to, and giving himself up for her. Marital authority modeled on that of Christ does not mean control, giving orders, making unreasonable demands, reducing another person to the status of servant or, worse, of slave to one's every whim. It means loving service. The Christian husband-head, as Markus Barth puts it so beautifully, becomes "the first servant of his wife."[80] It is such a husband, and only such a one, that a wife is to hold in awe (v. 33b) as all Christians fear or hold in awe Christ (v. 2lb). There is no reversal of Paul's judgment of equality between spouses in marriage, but rather a confirmation of it from another perspective, that of mutual and equal service, in every part of their life including the sexual.

A husband is further instructed to love his wife, for "he who loves his wife loves himself" (v. 28b; cp. v. 33a). Viewed within the perspective we have just elaborated, such reasoning makes sound sense. It makes even more Christian sense when we realize that it is a paraphrase of Jesus' great commandment: "You shall love your neighbor as yourself" (Lev 19:18; Mark 12:21). The great Torah and Gospel injunction applies also in marriage: "You shall love your neighbor as yourself." As all Christians are to give way to one another, so also each is to love the other as himself or herself, including a husband and a wife in marriage. This love is essential to marriage, and the marriage it founds reveals a profound mystery about Christ and his Church.

The mystery, most scholars agree, is embedded in the text of Genesis 2:24, cited in 5:31. As the Anchor Bible translation seeks to show, "this [passage] has an eminent secret meaning," which is that it refers to Christ and Christ's Church. The writer is well aware that this meaning is not the meaning traditionally given to the text in Judaism, and he states this forthrightly. Just as in the great antithesis of the Sermon on the Mount Jesus puts forward his interpretations of biblical texts in opposition to traditional interpretations ("You have heard that it was said to the men of old, . . . but *I* say to you"), so also here the writer asserts clearly that it is his own reading of the text ("*I* mean in reference to Christ and the Church," v. 32b). He acknowledges the meaning that husband and wife become one body in marriage; indeed, in verse 33, he returns to and demands that husband and wife live up to this very meaning. He chooses, however, to go beyond this meaning to insinuate another. Not only does the text refer to the union of husband and wife in marriage, but it refers also to that union of Christ and his church which he has underscored throughout Ephesians 5:1–33.

On one level, Genesis 2:24 refers to the covenant union between a man and a woman in marriage; on another level, it refers to the covenant union between Christ and his Church. It is a small step from there to interpret human marriage as prophetic symbol of the covenant between Christ and his Church, and to interpret the communion between Christ and his Church as providing a model for human marriage and for the mutual conduct of the spouses within it. It will take a thousand years for Catholic theologians to become comfortable with this notion of marriage as prophetic symbol, or sacrament,[81] of the Christ–Church covenant, and the constant stumbling block was the negative view of sexuality and, therefore, of marriage that came into the Christian tradition in the post–New Testament period.

In summary, then, we can say that the New Testament teaching does not mythicize sexuality and marriage as an imitation of the sexuality and marriage of some divine pair, nor does it idealize it beyond the capacity of any embodied man and woman. Rather, it leaves sexuality and marriage what they are, human realities in which a man and a woman seek to become one person in a communion of intimate and equal life, love, and service. What is added is only this, simple and yet mysteriously complex. As they become one body-person in covenant love, they provide through their marital and sexual union a prophetic symbol of a similar union that exists between their Christ and their Church. Marriage is not so secular a reality that Christ and his Church cannot be represented by it; not so base a sexual union that it cannot become image and symbol of another, more mysterious union; and not so mythical a reality that women and men cannot live it together as one. It is, as the Second Vatican Council will later teach, "an intimate partnership of conjugal life and love."[82]

The Fathers of the Church

The doctrine about sexuality and marriage in both Old and New testaments was a Jewish doctrine, developed in the originating Jewish culture of the Christian movement. The developing Church soon moved out of that Jewish culture into a Greco-Roman one in which Greek and Latin Fathers of the Church shaped the biblical doctrine about marriage and sexuality within their own cultural contexts and established the Catholic approach to sexuality we noted at the outset, namely, sexual morality as marital morality. To understand fully the Christian tradition about sexuality and marriage that came down to our day, we must seek to understand not only their teaching but also the sociohistorical situation in which it developed. As we have already discovered for the Bible, there was no systematic and full treatment of either sexuality or marriage as a social and Christian institution. The Fathers' teaching was almost exclusively a defense of marriage and marital sexuality against certain errors that threatened both its Christian value and its future. The majority of these errors had Gnostic sources, and it will be to our benefit to consider, however briefly, the Gnosticism from which they came.

Gnosticism, a Hellenistic religious philosophy characterized by the doctrine that salvation is achieved through a special knowledge (*gnosis*), antedated Christianity and exercised a great influence on many Christian communities in the Mediterranean basin. Christian Gnostics looked upon themselves as the only faithful interpreters of the Jesus movement. They disagreed with orthodox Christian teaching on two major points. First, they preached predestination, denying free will to humans in either salvation or damnation. Second, they preached a dualistic and pessimistic view of the world, a view in which good and evil are equally real. Both these views affected their attitude toward sexuality and marriage and, therefore, the Fathers' expositions on them in response. Because matter, and therefore sexuality and marriage with their very material bodily intercourse and bodily outcome, was essentially evil, the Gnostics believed, it could not have been created by a good God. That meant they had to revise the classic Jewish approach to creation, a task that was accomplished by Marcion. He taught there had to be two gods, one who created evil, the other who created good. The god who created evil is Yahweh, the god of the Old Testament; the god who created good is the Father of Jesus, who alone reveals him. The Old Testament, therefore, should be rejected along with all its doctrines and its laws. Among these doctrines is the one that men, women, sexuality, and marriage were created good by God; among such laws are those that legislate the relationships of men and women and their mutual sexual activity. Such attitudes generated, on the one hand, a negative, ascetic approach to sexuality and marriage and, on the other hand, a licentious, permissive approach, known as antinomianism. The second- and third-century Fathers had to defend marriage against attacks on both these fronts.

By the middle of the second century of the Christian era, Alexandria had become established as the intellectual capital of the Hellenistic world. We would expect to find powerful Gnostics there, and our expectation is verified via the writings of Clement, the bishop of Alexandria. He tells us of the two kinds of Gnostics we have noted, namely, the ascetics who abstained from marriage and sexual intercourse because they believed them to be evil, and the antinomians who believed they are saved by their special *gnosis* no matter what and are, therefore, above any law regarding sexuality and marriage.[83] He tells us of the ascetic Julius Cassianus, whose work *On Continence* he cites: "Let no one say that because we have these members, that because the female is structured this way and the male that way, the one to give the seed and the other to receive it, that the custom of sexual intercourse is allowed by God. For if this structure were from God, toward whom we tend, he would not have pronounced blessed those who are eunuchs."[84] We might note in passing the false biology in Cassianus' statement, a biology shared by the majority of thinkers of the time; the man is the one who gives "seed," the woman is but the "ground" or the "field" in which the seed is sown.[85] The woman has no active part in procreation.

Clement declares the opinion of Cassianus "impious" and responds with a simple argument. There is only one God, and that God is good; sexuality and marriage were created by the one God and, therefore, are good from their origin. "If marriage according to the law is sinful," he argues, "I do not see how anyone can say he knows God, and say that sin was commanded by God. But if the law is holy, marriage is holy. The apostle, therefore, refers this mystery to Christ and the church."[86] Irenaeus of Lyons employs this same argument in his extensive refutation of the Gnostics. He mentions Marcion and Saturnius, "who are called the continent," and accuses them of frustrating the ancient plan of God and of finding fault with him "who made both male and female for the begetting of men."[87] Marriage is primarily for procreation,[88] and for two other things secondarily. It is for a wife to bring help to her husband in the funding of his household, particularly in his sickness and old age,[89] and it is a union for a pious wife to seek "to persuade her husband, if she can, to be a companion to her in those things that lead to salvation."[90]

The early Greek Christian understanding of the nature of sexuality resembles that of the Stoic philosophers, represented in a statement from the Christian African Lactantius: "Just as God gave us eyes, not that we might look upon and desire pleasure, but that we might see those actions that pertain to the necessity of life, so also we have received the genital part of the body for no other purpose than the begetting of offspring, as the very name itself teaches. This divine law is to be obeyed with the greatest of devotion."[91] This was a commonly accepted teaching, which carried with it several conclusions. First, by its very nature sexual intercourse is for the procreation of children; second, any such intercourse for purposes other than procreation is a violation of nature and, therefore, immoral; and third, any sexual intercourse when conception is impossible is similarly immoral. From this established position, the Church Fathers would argue that the Gnostics, or anyone else, engaging in sexual intercourse for any purpose other than procreation, lovemaking, for instance, or pleasure were in violation of nature. It is an argument that the Latin Church Fathers continued to make into the twenty-first century.

Already in the second century, in his apology for Christians, Justin had replied to Roman accusations about the sexual immorality of Christians by insisting that "either we marry only to have children or, if we do not marry, we are continent always."[92] But Clement goes much further, arguing that the only purpose for sexual intercourse is to beget a child and that any other purpose must be excluded. "A man who marries for the procreation of children," he argues, "must exercise continence, lest he desire his wife whom he ought to love, and so that he may beget children with chaste and moderated will. For we are not children of desire but of will."[93] Origen, his fellow Alexandrian, is just as clear, arguing that the man who has sexual intercourse only with his wife, "and with her only at certain legitimate times and only for the sake of children," is truly circumcised.[94] He underscores what he means by legitimate times, insisting that once a wife has conceived, intercourse is no longer good. Those who indulge in sexual intercourse with their own wives after they are already pregnant are worse than beasts, "for even beasts know that, once they have conceived, they do not indulge their mates with their largesse."[95] So ruthlessly consistent was Origen in his belief that sexual activity was only for procreation in marriage that, having decided not to marry, he castrated himself.[96]

Tertullian also argued that abstinence from sexual activity is the surest way to the grace of God. Commenting on Paul's "It is better to marry than to burn with passion" (1 Cor 7:9), Tertullian adds that "it is better neither to marry nor to burn with passion."[97] Virgins, he goes on, have "full holiness" because "continence is more glorious" than marriage.[98] Tertullian seems to have been the first to make this evaluation of virginity as holier than marriage but, in the fourth century, that theological judgment was concretized in a new ascetic practice, the rejection of marriage and the embracing of virginity as a way to live a Christlike, holy life. It was not that the Fathers of the time were opposed to marriage; they were not. It was rather the way they expressed their preference for virginity in their Greek rhetorical styles that made marriage look less than good.[99] Tertullian can argue that Paul permits marriage as a concession and that something good needs no concession.[100] Athanasius can say both "blessed is the man who in his youth is joined in marriage for the procreation of children" and "there are two ways in life, one inferior and vulgar, namely marriage, the other angelic and supreme above all, namely, virginity."[101] John Chrysostom can say "I believe that virginity is a long way better than marriage, not because marriage is evil, for to those who would use it correctly [for procreation] it is the doorway to continence."[102] The same Chrysostom can also argue that "whoever denigrates marriage also diminishes the glory of virginity. . . . What appears good only in comparison with evil would not be particularly good. It is something better than what is admitted to be good that is the most excellent good."[103] Basil also affirms the goodness of sexual intercourse in marriage which is "entered into according to the sacred scriptures and legitimately," that is, for procreation, but he also excoriates marital intercourse sought for pleasure.[104]

Marriage is good, especially when sought for procreation; it has to be good because God created it. But virginity is better. This ambiguity about the goodness of sexuality and marriage, introduced early into the Catholic tradition, perdures to the present time. Writing an Apostolic Exhortation *On the Family*, John Paul II, citing Chrysostom as above, removes any ambiguity about the Church's position: "The Church throughout her history has always defended the superiority of this charism [virginity] to that of marriage, by reason of the wholly singular link which it has with the Kingdom of God."[105] When it comes to a comparison of sexual intercourse and marriage with virginity, one could say that John Paul has removed the Greek ambiguity.

Two Latin Fathers advanced the church's thinking on sexuality and marriage and left both with a theology that became a given in Christian thinking ever afterward. The lesser one is Tertullian, who wrote about marriage in both the orthodox Catholic and heretical Montanist periods of his life. In his first book, *To a Wife*, he exhibits the same ambivalence to sexuality and marriage that we have seen already in Origen. He grants that in the beginning marriage was necessary to populate the Earth but argues that, when the end of the world is near (note his sociohistorical assumption), there is no need for such activity. Paul may have allowed marriage as an antidote to desire, but Tertullian is in no doubt: "How much better it is neither to marry nor to burn [with concupiscence]." He will not even allow that marriage can be called good, for "what is *allowed* is not good, . . . nor is anything good just because it is not evil."[106] One would be excused for thinking that Tertullian has no time for marriage and the sexual intercourse it legitimates. This same man, however, who is so pessimistic about marriage in his first book, in a second book under the same title writes the most beautiful lines on Christian marriage that one could ever hope to find: "What a bond is that of two faithful who are of one hope, one discipline, one service; both are siblings, both are servants. . . . They are truly two in one flesh, and where there is one flesh there is also one spirit. They pray together, they sleep together, they fast together, teaching one another, exhorting one another, sustaining one another."[107] It would seem that between the first and second books, Tertullian had found a wonderful wife. When he became a Montanist, however, he regressed to his earlier judgment that Paul had simply allowed marriage and the sexual activity it encompasses, which is, though not a sin, none the less a blot on a perfect Christian life.[108]

When we reach Augustine, the great bishop of Hippo, we reach the systematic insight into sexual morality and marriage that was to mold and control the doctrine of the Latin Church down to our own day, so much so that Augustine is frequently called the doctor of Christian marriage. His influence is always present in Catholic talk about marriage. Pius XI, for instance, in the opening of his influential encyclical on Christian marriage, *Casti connubii*, turned to him as to the wellspring of the truths about Christian marriage to which the Catholic Church adheres. The Second Vatican Council also turned to him, developing its teaching about marriage within the schema of the threefold good of marriage as he described it.[109] Because Augustine's influence on the doctrine of marriage is beyond doubt, we must look closely at it. His teaching too must be viewed in its sociohistorical context, a context which is again largely a defense against attack. As the Alexandrians defended sexuality and marriage against the attacks of the Gnostics, so did Augustine defend them against the attacks of the Manichees, who at root were Gnostics, and of the Pelagians. We need to say a word, therefore, about these two groups.

The Manichees took their name from their founder, Mani, who was born in Babylonia about the year 216 C.E. Mani claimed to have received from an angel, at the ages of twelve and twenty-four years, the definitive revelation about the nature of the world and of history. Here we need to consider only those aspects of Manichaeism that impinge on its teaching on sexuality and marriage. First, it is a dualistic system, the dual opposites being, as always, good and evil, light and darkness, spirit and matter. Sexuality is listed among the dark and evil realities, along with wine and meat. Second, because Mani was looked upon as the ultimate prophet in the line of Jesus, he was said to have completed the latter's teachings and to have organized the ultimate church. That church had two kinds of members, a group of the perfect and a group of auditors, those we would call today catechumens. The perfect always abstained from wine, meat, and sexual activity; the auditors abstained only on Sundays. It is not difficult to imagine the Manichean approach to sexuality and marriage. Both were evil in themselves and, therefore, to be avoided. Against this approach Augustine repeated the argument of Clement and Irenaeus: Sexuality and marriage, created by God, must be essentially good.

Pelagianism derived its name from a Briton, Pelagius, who lived in Rome around the year 380, though the Pelagian debate with Augustine was led more by Pelagius' disciple, Julian, the bishop of Eclanum. The debate centered around the extent of *'adam*'s original fall from grace. Augustine taught that the original sin seriously impaired human nature, so that after the Fall men and women could not do without grace what they had been able to do without it before the Fall. Pelagius, on the contrary, taught that the Fall left human nature unimpaired, so that men and women could do after the Fall what they had been capable of doing prior to the Fall without any help from grace. Against the Pelagians Augustine taught that the results of the Fall make it very difficult to avoid sin in sexual intercourse, even in marriage. The Pelagians, therefore, accused him of being a Manichee and of teaching that marriage and sexual intercourse are necessarily sinful.[110] They will be followed in this by many a modern writer who adverts only to Augustine's anti-Pelagian writings. For such a complex writer, caught in the crossfire of two opposing heresies, that is too simple a procedure to be correct.

Augustine's basic statement about sexuality and marriage is ubiquitous, firm, and clear. Contrary to those Manichee heretics who hold that sexuality is evil and who condemn and prohibit marriage and sexual intercourse, he states that sexuality and marriage were created good by a good God and cannot lose that intrinsic goodness.[111] He specifies the good of marriage as threefold and insists that even after the Fall the marriages of Christians still contain this threefold good: fidelity, offspring, sacrament. "It is expected that in fidelity neither partner will indulge in sexual activity outside of marriage; that offspring will be lovingly accepted, kindly nurtured, and religiously educated; that in sacrament the marriage will not be dissolved and that neither partner will be dismissed to marry another, not even for the sake of offspring."[112] In this triple good, Augustine intends the mutual fidelity of the spouses, the procreation of children, and indissolubility. Procreation has priority because "from this derives the propagation of the human race in which a living community is a great good."[113] And yet, to some extent, the good of the sacrament is valued above the good of procreation, for he insists, as we have just seen, that a marriage cannot be dissolved, "not even for the sake of offspring." There may be here the seed of a Christian attitude toward marriage that moves away from the priority of procreation to the priority of communion between the spouses, in the image of the communion between Yahweh and Israel and between Christ and the Church. We shall see throughout this book that these two priorities have been given quite different weights at different times in Roman Catholic history, and that in the contemporary Roman Catholic approach they are given equal weights.

Alongside the tradition of the threefold good of marriage, Augustine advances yet another good, that of friendship between the sexes. In *The Good of Marriage*, after asserting that marriage is good, he gives an interesting explication of why it is good: "It does not seem to me to be good only because of the procreation of children, but also because of the natural companionship between the sexes. Otherwise, we could not speak of marriage in the case of old people, especially if they had either lost their children or had begotten none at all."[114] Later in the same work, he returns to that idea: "God gives us some goods which are to be sought for their own sake, such as wisdom, health, friendship, [and] . . . others for the sake of friendship, such as marriage or intercourse, for from this comes the propagation of the human race in which friendly association is a great good."[115] "In these passages," Mackin judges, "Augustine has enriched the source whence Catholic canonists and theologians will later draw one of their 'secondary ends' of marriage, . . . the *mutuum adiutorium* of the spouses, their mutual help, or support."[116] We believe Augustine has done more. He has falsified in advance the claim of those modern commentators who say that only in modern times have sexual intercourse and marriage been seen in the context of the relationship of spouses. But the source of what appears problematic in Augustine's teaching about marriage seems always to derive from what he says against the Pelagians. To this, therefore, we now turn.

The basic position can be stated unequivocally, and there can be no doubt about it: Sexual intercourse between a husband and a wife is created good by God. It can, as can any good, be used sinfully but, when it is used sinfully, it is not the good itself that is sinful but its disordered use. It is a balanced principle to which Augustine will return at the end of his life in his *Retractiones*. Evil and sin are never substantial; they are only in the will. Nevertheless, he believes there is in men and women a concupiscence that causes sin, a disordered pursuit by any appetite of its proper good, a pursuit that since the Fall is difficult to keep within proper limits. With this belief in mind, it is not difficult to understand all that Augustine says about sexuality and marriage. Against the Pelagian, Julian, he explains carefully: "Evil does not follow because marriages are good, but because in the good things of marriage there is also a use that is evil. Sexual intercourse was not created because of the concupiscence of the flesh, but because of good. That good would have remained without that evil if no one had sinned."[117] His judgment appears beyond doubt: There is one thing that is good, namely, sexual intercourse in marriage, and another thing that is evil, namely, concupiscence, that can mutate the good into evil. His position is much more nuanced than many notice or admit: Sexual intercourse is good in itself, but there are uses which can render it evil.

The condition under which intercourse is good is the classic Stoic condition we have already seen in the Alexandrians, namely, when it is for the begetting of a child. After the Fall, any other use, even between the spouses in marriage, is at least venially sinful. "Conjugal sexual intercourse for the sake of offspring is not sinful. But sexual intercourse, even with one's spouse, to satisfy concupiscence [disordered desire] is a venial sin."[118] It is not sexual intercourse per se between spouses that is sinful, but intercourse vitiated by concupiscence. Sexual intercourse for the stoically natural reason, the procreation of children, is good; intercourse that results from concupiscence is sinful. In effect, since the Fall of humankind and the rise of concupiscence, the sexual appetite is always threatened by disorder and, therefore, by sinfulness. It is not, however, the sexual appetite that is sinful; it is good. The Fathers of the Old Testament, Augustine argues, took a "natural delight" in sexual intercourse and it was not sinful because it "was in no way given rein up to the point of unreasoning and wicked desire."[119] It is clear that it is disordered and unreasonable sexual intercourse fired by concupiscence that is sinful, not sexual intercourse per se. "Whatever, therefore, spouses do together that is immodest, shameful, filthy, is the vice of men, not the fault of marriage."[120] And what is "immodest, shameful, and filthy" is the concupiscent desire for sexual pleasure.

Pope Gregory the Great shared Augustine's judgment that, because of the presence of concupiscence, even genital pleasure between spouses in the act of procreation is sinful. He went further and banned from access to the Church those who had just had pleasurable intercourse. "The custom of the Romans from antiquity," he explained, "has always been, after sexual intercourse with one's spouse, both to cleanse oneself by washing and to abstain reverently from entering the church for a time. In saying this we do not intend to say that sexual intercourse is sinful. But because every lawful sexual intercourse between spouses cannot take place without bodily pleasure, they are to refrain from entering the holy place. For such pleasure cannot be without sin."[121] Again, it is clear that it is sexual pleasure that is sinful, and it is not difficult to see how such a doctrine could produce a strong ambivalence toward sexuality and marriage. That ambivalence weighed heavily in subsequent history on the theory and practice of Christian marriage.

In summary of this section on the Fathers of the Church, we can say that, though the relational and procreational meanings of sexual activity we found in Genesis remain, they have been seriously prioritized. Though the judgment remains that sexuality and sexual activity are good because they were created good by the good God, their goodness is threatened by the pleasure associated with sexual intercourse and by the concupiscence engendered by sin. This position is much in evidence in Augustine, who taught that sexual activity in marriage is good when it is for the purpose of procreation and venially sinful when, "even with one's spouse, [it is] to satisfy concupiscence."[122] The Catholic aversion to sexual pleasure reached its high point when Pope Gregory the Great banned from access to church anyone who had just had *pleasurable* intercourse. We accept as accurate Brundage's judgment of the effect of that patristic history: "The Christian horror of sex has for centuries placed enormous strain on individual consciences and self-esteem in the Western world."[123] This might be the place, however, to introduce a linguistic caveat. Medieval Latin had no words for the modern concepts of "sex" and "sexuality." Payer, therefore, correctly points out that "in the strictest sense there are no discussions of sex in the Middle Ages." He goes on to point out that Foucault's claim that "the relatively late date for the invention of sex and sexuality is, I believe, of paramount significance. The concept of sex and sexuality as an integral dimension of human persons, as an object of concern, discourse, truth, and knowledge, did not emerge until well after the Middle Ages."[124] This caveat has significance for all that has gone before and all that comes after in this book.

The Penitentials

Many of the attitudes and teachings of the Fathers with respect to sexuality and marriage can be found in the manuals known as Penitentials, which flourished in ecclesiastical use from about the sixth to the twelfth century C.E. The Penitentials were designed to help confessors in their pastoral dealings with penitents in confession, providing lists of sins and corresponding penances. They were, however, more than just lists of sins and penances. They were also manuals of moral education for the confessor, and what the confessor learned, of course, his penitents also learned. Penitentials took the abstract teachings of the Church and concretized them at the level of practice, in this case the practice of the new penance introduced by the Celtic monks in the sixth century. They are sure guides for us as we explore the moral teaching of the Church at the time of their publication with respect to sexuality and marriage.

John McNeill's opinion is impossible to gainsay: "It is doubtful whether any part of the source literature of medieval social history comparable in importance to the Penitentials has been so generally neglected by translators. The difficulty of the texts and an unjust contempt on the part of some historians for the materials have probably contributed to this neglect."[125] Luckily, that neglect has been somewhat rectified since McNeill wrote, and we have plenty of material to choose from. Both the sins and the accompanying penances in the Penitentials are frequently curious and extreme, but for the purposes of this book we concentrate only on those sexual sins inside and outside marriage, what was sexually prescribed and proscribed in and out of marriage, and how seriously offences were punished.

The general rule for sexual behavior in the Penitentials is the ancient Stoic one and the one we have found in the Christian tradition from Clement onward: Sexual intercourse is permitted only between a man and a woman who are married and, even then, only for procreation. Every other sexual act is proscribed and, therefore, nonprocreative intercourse is prohibited. The sixth-century Irish Penitential of Finnian of Clonard prescribes that "if anyone has a barren wife, he shall not put away his wife because of her barrenness, but they shall both dwell in continence and be blessed if they persevere in chastity of body until God pronounces a true and just judgment upon them."[126] There is, however, no mention of any sin or penance if they do not remain continent. Both oral and anal sex are also prohibited, most frequently between male homosexuals but also between heterosexuals. The Anglo-Saxon canons of Theodore (ca. 690) prescribe that "whoever emits semen into the mouth shall do penance for seven years; this is the worst of evils,"[127] and "if a man should practice anal intercourse he must do penance as one who offends with animals," that is, for ten years.[128] Masturbation falls into the category of nonprocreative sexual behavior and is, therefore, prohibited.[129] The Celtic Penitential of Columban (ca. 600), closely related to that of Finnian, prescribes that "if anyone practices masturbation or sins with a beast, he shall do penance for two years if he is not in [clerical] orders; but if he is in orders or has a monastic vow, he shall do penance for three years unless his [tender] age protects him."[130] This is an interesting exception for those of tender age, though whether age protects from the sin or from the penance is not clear from the text.

Theodore also proscribes male homosexuality with severe penances: "A male who commits fornication with a male shall do penance for ten years"; "sodomites shall do penance for seven years"; and "he who commits this sexual offense once shall do penance for four years, if he has been in the habit of it, as Basil says, fifteen years."[131] There is some mitigation, however, for what may be seen as experimentation; if a boy engages in homosexual intercourse, the penance is two years for the first offense and four years if he repeats it. Payer notes that "for the writers of the Penitentials *adulterium* seems not to have been a univocal term but to have had a wider extension than the word *adultery* does today."[132] It can be understood in its modern meaning of sexual intercourse between two people, one of whom, at least, is married; it can also be understood in the modern meaning of fornication. It is prohibited but the penances, except for higher ecclesiastics, are relatively short. Finnian decrees that "if any layman defile his neighbor's wife or virgin daughter, he shall do penance for an entire year on an allowance of bread and water and he shall not have intercourse with his own wife."[133]

Besides the sexual sins enumerated, there are also concerns for ritual purity, the most widespread being concern for seminal emission other than masturbation, usu-ally named pollution. The early-sixth-century *Excerpts from a Book of David* pre-scribes that "he who *intentionally* becomes polluted in sleep shall get up and sing seven psalms and live on bread and water for that day; but if he does not do this he shall sing thirty psalms."[134] The Celtic Penitential of Cummean (ca. 650) has a similar canon: "He who is *willingly* polluted during sleep shall arise and sing nine psalms in order, kneeling. On the following day he shall live on bread and water or he shall sing thirty psalms." It adds a second canon: "He who desires to sin during sleep, or is unintentionally polluted, fifteen psalms; he who sins and is not polluted twenty four."[135] How one could sin during sleep is a question, but it need not detain us here. What concerns us is the idea of seminal pollution needing the remedy of penance. Sexual intercourse between a husband and a wife is not always a good thing. Cummean prescribes that "he who is in a state of matrimony ought to be continent during the three forty-day periods [prior to Christmas, prior to Easter, and after Pentecost] and on Saturday and Sunday, night and day, and in the two appointed week days [Wednesday and Friday], and after conception, and during the entire menstrual period."[136] A quick calculation reveals that few days remain avail-able for intercourse.[137]

Women's sexual purity also figures in the Penitentials. Theodore prescribes that "women shall not in the time of impurity enter into a Church, or communicate, neither nuns nor laywomen; if they presume [to do this], they shall fast for three weeks." He further prescribes that "in the same way shall they do penance who enter a Church before purification after childbirth, that is, forty days," and "he who has intercourse at these seasons shall do penance for twenty days."[138] Recall here Gregory the Great (d. 604), contemporaneous with the early Penitentials, who agreed with Augustine's judgment, that because of concupiscence, genital pleasure between spouses even in the act of procreation is sinful. He banned from access to the Church those who had just had pleasurable intercourse and required them to cleanse themselves by washing.

An obvious summary and conclusion emerges from this medieval analysis: a strong Catholic negativity toward sexuality, even between a husband and a wife in marriage. Gula's judgment is accurate. The Penitentials helped shape "a moral perspective which focused on individual acts, on regarding the moral life as a matter of avoiding sin, and on turning moral reflection into an analysis of sin in its many forms."[139] They also helped shape, in Catholic moral teaching, an immature focus on genitalia. That focus and the act-centered morality it generated were perpetuated in the numerous manuals published in the wake of the reforms of clerical education mandated by the Council of Trent. These manuals controlled seminary education well into the twentieth century and continued to propagate both an act-centered morality and a Catholic ambivalence toward both sexuality and marriage.[140]

Scholastic Doctrine

Augustine's teaching controlled the approach to sexuality and marriage in the Latin Church until the thirteenth century, when the Scholastic theologians made some significant alterations to it. The Scholastic sexual ethic remained an ethic for marriage, and Thomas Aquinas took over Augustine's three goods of marriage and transformed them into three ends of marriage. Aquinas shared Aristotle's view that humans, though sharing in the genus animal, were constituted by their reason a species apart from all other animals. This reason enables them to apprehend the ends proper to human animals, inscribed in the so-called natural law flowing from the design of the creator God. What were for the Neoplatonic Augustine goods of marriage therefore become for the Aristotelian Aquinas ends of marriage, and ends established in a "natural" priority.

"Marriage," Aquinas argues, "has as its principal end the procreation and education of offspring, . . . and so offspring are said to be a good of marriage." It has also "a secondary end in man alone, the sharing of tasks which are necessary in life, and from this point of view husband and wife owe each other faithfulness, which is one of the goods of marriage." There is another end in believers, "the meaning of Christ and Church, and so a good of marriage is called sacrament. The first end is found in marriage in so far as man is animal, the second insofar as he is man, the third is so far as he is believer."[141] As is customary in Aquinas, this is a tight and sharply delineated argument, and its terminology *primary end–secondary end* came to dominate discussion of the ends of marriage in Roman Catholic manuals for seven hundred years. But neither the sharpness of the argument nor the authority of the author should be allowed to obscure the fact that it is also a very curious argument, for it makes the claim that the primary end of specifically *human* marriage is dictated by humanity's generically *animal* nature. It was precisely this curious argument that would be challenged in the twentieth century, leading to a more personal approach to the morality of both sexual activity and marriage.

Aquinas, of course, wishes to insist that reason must have control. Not that there is any rational control *in* the act of sexual intercourse, for animals lack reason. But there is reason *before* human intercourse and, because there is, sexual intercourse between a husband and a wife is not sinful. Excess of passion, which corrupts virtue and which is, as in Augustine, sinful, is what not only impedes reason but also destroys it. Such is not the case with the intensity of pleasure in sexual intercourse for, "though a man is not then under control, he has been under the control of reason in advance."[142] Besides, nature has been created good by God, so that "it is impossible to say that the act in which offspring are created is so completely unlawful that the means of virtue cannot be found in it."[143] Some ambivalence toward sexual desire, activity, and pleasure remains. As in Plato and Aristotle, they are "occupations with lower affairs which distract the soul and make it unworthy of being joined actually to God,"[144] but they are not sinful at all times and in all circumstances. Indeed, within the ends of marriage they are meritorious,[145] and Aquinas asserts explicitly that to forgo the pleasure and thwart the end would be sinful.[146] This latter opinion leads Messenger to go beyond Aquinas and declare that "both passion and pleasure are natural concomitants of the sex act, and so far from diminishing its goodness, if the sex act is willed beforehand according to right reason, the effect of pleasure and passion is simply to heighten and increase the moral goodness of the act, not in any way to diminish it."[147] That is a defensible opinion within Aquinas's system, and a far cry from Augustine and Gregory. It is also a move toward the liberation of marriage, legitimate sexual intercourse, and sexual pleasure from any taint of sin and also toward their recognition as a sign and a cause of grace, that is, as a sacrament.

The early Scholastics did not doubt that marriage was a *sign* of grace. But because of their negative evaluation of sexual activity, they seriously doubted that it could ever be a *cause* of grace. They hesitated, therefore, to include it among the sacraments of the Church, defined in the categories of both sign and cause. "A sacrament, properly speaking," Peter Lombard teaches, "is a sign of the grace of God and the form of invisible grace in such a way that it is its image and its cause. Sacraments are instituted, therefore, not only for signifying grace but also for causing it."[148] He proceeds to list the sacraments of the New Law, carefully distinguishing marriage from sacraments properly so called. "Some offer a remedy for sin and confer helping grace, such as baptism; others offer a remedy only, such as marriage; others support us with grace and virtue, such as eucharist and orders."[149] Marriage is a sacrament for Lombard, as it was for Augustine, only in the general sense that it is a sign, "a sacred sign of a sacred reality, namely, the union of Christ and the Church."[150]

The Dominicans Albert the Great and Aquinas had no such hesitations and they firmly established marriage among the sacraments of the church. In his commentary on Lombard, Albert lists the various opinions about the sacrament of marriage and characterizes as "very probable" the opinion holding that "it confers grace for doing good, not just any good but that good specifically that a married person should do."[151] In his commentary on Lombard, Aquinas goes further, characterizing as "most probable" the opinion that "marriage, insofar as it is contracted in faith in Christ, confers grace to do those things which are required in marriage."[152] In his *Contra Gentiles*, he is even more positive, stating bluntly that "it is to be believed that through this sacrament [marriage] grace is given to the married."[153] By the time he achieved his mature thought in the *Summa theologiae*, he lists marriage among the seven sacraments with no demur whatever about its grace-conferring qualities and, by the Reformation, his opinion was held universally by theologians. A further scholastic teaching about marriage that was to become central to marriage discussions in the twentieth century should be noted here, namely, the personal relationship and equality between husband and wife. Both Aquinas and Bonaventure write about the importance of this relationship. Aquinas understood, at least inchoately, that the relationship between men and women should be one of friendship and that sexual intercourse enhances that friendship as well as being a means to procreation;[154] Bonaventure calls the friendship between spouses the sacrament of the relationship between God and the soul.[155] Sufficient proof that any claim that the mutual love between spouses is an exclusively modern concern is quite unhistorical.

The Modern Period

Albert the Great and Aquinas established marriage among the sacraments of the Church, and from their era onward the sacrament of marriage began to assume center stage in theological analyses. When Pietro Cardinal Gasparri codified Catholic law in the 1917 *Code of Canon Law*, book 3, title VII, on marriage was heavily inspired by his influential book on marriage, *Tractatus canonicus de matrimonio*, published in 1892. Three prominent notions were developed in that book: Marriage is a contract; the formal object of the contract is the permanent and exclusive right of the spouses to each other's bodies for sexual intercourse that leads to procreation; and the primacy of procreation over every other end of marriage. These three notions were not traditional in magisterial teachings but were all novel opinions in Gasparri's work and, therefore, in the code that his work dominated. With respect to the notion of marriage as contract, even Gasparri himself acknowledged that marriage was never considered a contract in either Roman or European law.[156] With respect to the right to the use of the other's body for procreative intercourse, Fellhauer demonstrates in a comprehensive analysis that there is no magisterial source "which presents the juridical essence of marriage as the *ius in corpus* (right to the body) for procreation or which identifies the object of consent in similar terms."[157] With respect to the ends of marriage, Navarette points out in an equally comprehensive analysis that, in the documents of the Magisterium and in the corpus of canon law itself, "we find hardly anything about the ends of marriage precisely as goals until the formulation of Canon 1013, 1."[158] He further points out that a preliminary version of Canon 1013 indicated no hierarchy of ends and concludes that the 1917 *Code of Canon Law* is the first official document of the Catholic Church to embrace

the terminology *primary end–secondary end*. Gasparri's three contributions, therefore, are hardly traditional Church doctrine, but they did control the Church's
approach to both marriage and the morality of marital sexuality from 1917 to 1964.

The 1917 *Code of Canon Law* yields the following reductionist definition of both
the contract and the sacrament of marriage, which are inseparable in the marriages
of baptized persons. Marriage is "a permanent society (Can. 1082), whose primary
end is procreation and nurture (Can. 1013), a society that is in species a contract
that is unitary and indissoluble by nature (Can. 1012 and 1013, 2), whose substance
is the parties' exchanged rights to their sexual acts (Can. 1081, 2)."[159] That definition articulates the essence of marriage that controlled the arguments in Catholic
tribunals up to the Second Vatican Council, when it was displaced. We call it a
reductionist definition because, though it carefully specifies what is included in the
essence of marriage, it equally carefully specifies, at least by implication, what is left
out. It was precisely on that basis that it was attacked and eventually displaced.

In December 1930, in response to the Anglican Lambeth Conference's approval
of artificial contraception as a moral action in certain situations, Pope Pius XI published an important encyclical on marriage, *Casti connubii*. In it, predictably, he
insisted on everything we have just considered as the juridical essence of marriage
but, unpredictably, he did more. He retrieved and gave a prominent place to a long-
ignored item from the *Catechism of the Council of Trent*: marriage as a union of
conjugal love and intimacy. If we consider only the juridical definition of marriage,
we could reasonably conclude that marriage has nothing to do with mutual love,
that a man and a woman who hated one another could be married as long as each
gave to the other the right over her or his body for procreation. By emphasizing the
essential place of mutual love in a marriage, Pius firmly rejected such nonsense and
placed the Catholic view of marriage on the track to a more personal definition.

Marital love, Pius teaches, does not consist "in pleasing words only, but in the
deep attachment of the heart [will] which is expressed in action, since love is proved
by deeds." This love proved by deeds "must have as its primary purpose that husband and wife help each other day by day in forming and perfecting themselves in
the interior life . . . and above all that they may grow in true love toward God and
their neighbor."[160] So important is the mutual love and interior formation of the
spouses, he continues, that "it can, in a very real sense, as the Roman Catechism
teaches, be said to be the *chief reason and purpose of marriage*, if marriage be looked
at not in the restricted sense as instituted for the proper conception and education
of the child, but more widely as the blending of life as a whole and the mutual
interchange and sharing thereof."[161] In these wise words, Pius directs us to see that
there is more to the essence of marriage than can be contained in the cold, precise
canonical categories of the reductionist definition. European thinkers were poised
to point in the same direction, most influentially two Germans, Dietrich Von Hildebrand and Heribert Doms.

Von Hildebrand and Doms

In the opening paragraph of his work on *Marriage*, written in 1939, Von Hildebrand states the problem precisely. The modern age, he suggests, is guilty of a terrible antipersonalism, "a progressive blindness toward the nature and dignity of the spiritual person." This antipersonalism expresses itself in all kinds of materialism, the most dangerous of which is biological materialism, which considers the human being as a more highly developed animal: "Human life is considered exclusively from a biological point of view and biological principles are the measure by which all human activities are judged."[162] The Catholic juridical approach to marriage, with its insistence on rights over bodies and their physiological functions, is wide open to the charge of biological materialism. So, too, is the centuries-old Stoic-cum-Christian doctrine that argues from physiological structure to human "nature" and to "natural" ends (recall the question we raised about this approach in the prologue). So, too, is Aquinas's position that founds the primary end of *human* marriage in the *biological* structure of men and women. In contrast to this biological approach, Von Hildebrand introduced a radical innovation in thinking about marriage, claiming that Pius XI and *Casti connubii* support his central thesis that marriage is for the building up of loving communion between the spouses. Conjugal love, he claims, is the primary meaning and ultimate end of marriage.[163]

In marriage, Von Hildebrand argued, the spouses enter an interpersonal relationship, in which they confront one another as I and Thou, as Ego and Other, and "give birth to a mysterious fusion of their souls."[164] This fusion of their innermost personal beings, not merely the fusion of their physical bodies, is what the oft-quoted "one body" of Genesis intends. This interpersonal fusion is the primary meaning of the spouses' mutual love and of their sexual intercourse, which is the symbol of that love, and intercourse achieves its end when it expresses and leads to such fusion: "Every marriage in which conjugal love is thus realized bears spiritual fruit, becomes *fruitful*—even though there are no children."[165] The parentage of such thought in modern personalist philosophy is as clear as the parentage of biological-natural thought in Stoic philosophy. Parentage or sociohistorical origin, of course, tells us nothing about the truth or falsity of a statement; to assume that it does is a genetic fallacy. More important than origin, however, is the deep resonance of such an interpersonal description of marriage and lovemaking with the lived experience of married couples.

Doms agreed with Von Hildebrand in that what is natural or unnatural for human animals is not to be decided on the basis of what is natural or unnatural for nonhuman animals. Humans are specifically spiritual animals, vitalized by a spiritual soul, and are not to be judged, as the Stoics and Aquinas judged them, on the basis of animal biology. Human sexuality is essentially the capacity and the desire to fuse, not merely one's body, but one's very self with an other person. Sexuality drives a human to make a gift of herself or himself (not just of her or his body) to an other, in order to create a communion of persons and of lives that fulfills them both. In such a perspective, marital intercourse is a powerful, interpersonal activity in which a woman gives herself to a man and a man gives himself to a woman, and in which they accept the gift of each other, to express and procreate, if you will, marital communion.

The primary end of sexual intercourse in this perspective is the loving communion between the spouses, a communion that is both signified and enhanced, or "made," in intercourse. Popular language is correct; in their sexual intercourse, spouses "make love." This primary end is achieved in every act of intercourse in which the spouses actually enter into intimate communion. Even in childless marriages, marriage and intercourse achieve their primary end in the marital communion of the spouses, their *two-in-oneness*, as Doms would have it. He summarizes his case in a clear statement: "The immediate purpose of marriage is the realization of its meaning, the conjugal two-in-oneness. . . . This two-in-oneness of husband and wife is a living reality, and the immediate object of the marriage ceremony and their legal union." The union of the spouses tends naturally to the birth and nurture of new persons, their children, who focus the fulfillment of their parents, both as individuals and as a two-in-oneness. "Society is more interested in the child than in the natural fulfillment of the parents, and it is this which gives the child primacy among the natural results of marriage."[166] Since Doms wrote, social scientific data have demonstrated that the well-being of the child is a function of the well-being of its parents,[167] suggesting that the relationship between the spouses is the primary natural result of marriage because all other relationships in the family depend on it.

The Church's immediate reaction to these new ideas, as has been so often the case in theological history, was a blanket condemnation, which made no effort to sift truth from error. In 1944, the Holy Office condemned "the opinion of some more recent authors, who either deny that the primary end of marriage is the generation and nurture of children, or teach that the secondary ends are not essentially subordinate to the primary end, but are equally primary and independent."[168] In 1951, as the opinions of Von Hildebrand and Doms persisted and attracted more adherents, Pius XII felt obliged to intervene again. The truth is, he taught, that "marriage, as a natural institution in virtue of the will of the creator, does not have as a primary and intimate end the personal perfection of the spouses, but the procreation and nurture of new life. The other ends, in as much as they are intended by nature, are not on the same level as the primary end, and still less are they superior to it, but they are essentially subordinate to it."[169] The terms of the problem could not be more precise. Some traditionalists, adherents to what is known as New Natural Law Theory, continue to bring forward these magisterial condemnations as proof that the traditional hierarchy among the ends of marriage is still the official magisterial position and, therefore, is to be followed.[170] They ignore the fact that the balance was seriously altered by the Second Vatican Council's document *Gaudium et spes*.

The Second Vatican Council

Before the Second Vatican Council opened in 1962, the bishops had been sent a preparatory schema on "Chastity, Virginity, Marriage, and Family." We consider the fate of this schema to introduce a contemporary Catholic approach to sexuality and marriage and conclude this chapter. The schema had been prepared by the Theological Commission chaired by Alfredo Cardinal Ottaviani, then prefect of the Holy Office, who explained that the schema laid out the "objective order, . . . which God himself willed in instituting marriage and Christ the Lord willed in raising it to the dignity of a sacrament. Only in this way can the modern errors that have spread everywhere be vanquished."[171] Among the many errors specified are "those theories that subvert the right order of values and make the primary end of marriage inferior to the biological and personal values of the spouses, and proclaim that conjugal love itself is in the objective order the primary end."[172] The schema highlights the primary end–secondary end terminology, the primary end being the procreation and nurture of children, the secondary end the mutual help of the spouses. The debate in the Preparatory Commission, and again in the council when elements of the schema made it to the floor for discussion on what became *Gaudium et spes*, centered on the hierarchy of the ends of marriage, specifically on the relative values of conjugal love and the procreation of children. For our purposes here, only the outcome of that debate, as it was promulgated in *Gaudium et spes*, need be discussed.

The debate was initiated in the Theological Commission itself, and its main direction may be summed up in the words of Cardinal Alfrink. "Conjugal love," he argued, "is an element of marriage itself and not just a result of marriage. . . . Conjugal love belongs to marriage, at least if marriage be not considered as merely a juridical contract. And, in the objective order, the primary end of this conjugal love remains offspring."[173] We have already highlighted the juridical essence of marriage as it is described in the *Code of Canon Law*, and Ottaviani's proposed schema replicated that juridical essence. Much of the debate in the commission was opposed to that merely juridical way of looking at marriage and marital love. Alfrink, a biblical scholar, pointed out that "the Hebrew verb *dabaq*, in Greek *kollao*, does suggest physical, bodily, sexual union, but it suggests above all spiritual union which exists in conjugal love. Sacred Scripture itself insinuates this when it compares conjugal union to the union between parents and children which is spiritual and presupposes love."[174] This, he continued, is the way modern women and men think, more spiritually, more humanly, and indeed more biblically and theologically.

Julius Cardinal Dopfner agreed. The entire section of the schema dedicated to marriage should be withdrawn, he suggested, because of the absence of any serious discussion of conjugal love which modern women and men take so much for granted: "Any constitution [on marriage] should speak persuasively to Christian spouses so that they would willingly assume the burden of a numerous family. . . . It is not enough to propose conjugal love as a virtue, or as an extraneous subjective end of marriage, and to exclude it from the very structure of marriage itself."[175] The battle lines were already clearly drawn in the Preparatory Commission; either the "traditional"[176] juridical approach to marriage or a renewed interpersonal approach in which conjugal love is of the essence of marriage. The latter approach began to win in the commission[177] and won, finally, in the council itself.

Gaudium et spes, into which the preparatory schema's section on marriage was inserted in its preliminary stage, opens its teaching on marriage by following Cardinals Alfrink, Dopfner, Suenens, and many other members of the Central Preparatory Commission in describing marriage as a "communion of love,"[178] an "intimate partnership of conjugal life and love."[179] The position of the majority of the Council Fathers could not be clearer. In the face of strident demands to relegate the conjugal love of the spouses to its customary secondary place in marriage, they declared conjugal love to be of the very essence of marriage, a clear rejection of an exclusively juridical approach. There was another explicit rejection of Gasparri. Marriage, the council declared, is founded in a "conjugal covenant of irrevocable personal consent."[180] Gasparri's word *contract* is replaced by the biblical word *covenant*, which has the same juridical outcomes as contract but also situates marriage in a biblical-theological and *interpersonal* context rather than in an exclusively *juridical* one. The insertion into the text of the biblical term *covenant* was explained in the commentary given to the Council Fathers along with the revised text in September 1965: "There is no mention of 'matrimonial contract' but, in clearer words, of 'irrevocable personal consent.' The biblical term 'covenant' (*foedus*) is added at the intuition of the Eastern Churches for whom 'contract' raises some difficulties."[181] The understanding of *covenant* as used by the council is dependent upon the intuition of the Eastern Churches and to this intuition, therefore, we must briefly turn.

The Orthodox intuition of marriage as covenant is located within the *oikonomia* of the biblical covenants of God with Israel and the Church. Covenantal election involves both God and people in a steadfast commitment, and in the Church the fullest expression of that commitment takes place in the sacrament of marriage. "The covenantal bond within which God works out our salvation is in essence a nuptial bond. And, conversely, the nuptial relationship achieves its true purpose and attains its true fullness only insofar as it is based upon an eternal covenantal commitment."[182] The purpose of marriage between a man and woman is to create between them "a bond of covenant responsibility and faithfulness that represents and reactualizes the eternal bond established by God with his chosen people,"[183] and so it is that marriage is "a great mystery" that refers to Christ and the Church (Eph 5:32). In such an expansive vision of marriage, it is little wonder that the narrow juridical vision of "contract" would create "some difficulties." The use of *covenant* rather than *contract* deliberately takes marriage out of its traditional, juridical sphere and situates it in the sphere of interpersonal, religious, steadfast commitment and responsibility. Its identification as a "biblical term" insinuates its connection to the eternal covenants between God and Israel and Christ and the Church. This interpersonal characteristic is underscored by the choice, again in the face of demands to remain with the traditional characterization, of a way to characterize the formal object of the covenanting. The council declares that the spouses "mutually gift and accept one another,"[184] rejecting the reductionist, material biological notion that they gift merely the right to the use of one another's bodies. In their mutual personal covenanting and gifting, a man and a woman create an interpersonal communion of love that is permanent and is to last for the whole of life.

The Second Vatican Council also teaches that "by its very nature the institution of *marriage* and *married love* is ordered to the procreation and education of children, and it is in them that it finds its crowning glory."[185] We have added emphasis to this citation to underscore not only the teaching of the council but also of the entire Catholic tradition prior to Paul VI's *Humanae vitae*, namely, that *marriage*, not *each and every marriage act* as Paul VI taught, is to be open to the procreation of children.[186] Once procreation has been mentioned, one would expect a recitation of the hierarchical ends of marriage but, again despite insistent voices to the contrary, the council Fathers rejected the primary end–secondary end dichotomy. To make sure that its rejection was understood, the Preparatory Commission was careful to explain that the text just cited "does not suggest [a hierarchy of ends] in any way."[187] Marriage and sexual love "are by their very nature ordained to the generation and education of children," but that "does not make the other ends of marriage of less account," and marriage "is not instituted solely for procreation."[188]

The intense debate that took place both in the Preparatory Commission and in the Second Vatican Council itself makes it impossible to claim the refusal to speak of a hierarchy of ends in marriage was the result of oversight or, as some New Natural Law Theorists argue, a mere avoidance of the primary–secondary terminology, leaving the concept in place.[189] It was the result of a deliberate, intentional, and explicit choice of the Catholic Church meeting in council. Any doubt was definitively removed in 1983 by the appearance of the revised *Code of Canon Law*, frequently called the last council document. "The *matrimonial covenant*, by which a man and a woman establish between themselves a partnership of the whole of life, is by its nature ordered towards the good of the spouses and the procreation and education of offspring" (Can. 1055, 1). Notice three things. First, it is the *matrimonial covenant* and not *each and every act of intercourse* that is ordered toward procreation. Second, there is no specification of either of these ends being primary or secondary. And third, as in *Gaudium et spes*, the good of the spouses or *conjugal love* is discussed before procreation and education of children or the fruitfulness of marriage. The Catholic Church changed its canon law to be in line with its renewed theology of marriage, moving beyond the narrow juridical essence to embrace in the very essence of marriage the mutual love and communion of the spouses. Toward the end of the twentieth century, the Church had come a long way from the negative approach to sexuality and marriage bequeathed to it in a long tradition going back to the struggles of the Fathers against dualistic Encratites, Gnostics, and Manicheans. It would be naive, and a complete ignorance of past conciliar history, to assume that the debate ended with the council.

Two theoretical models are available in the modern Catholic tradition for thinking about marriage, and each offers insight into the morality of sexual activity. One is an ancient one, a model of marriage as a procreative institution and of sexual intercourse within marriage as a primarily procreative action; the other is a modern model of marriage as an interpersonal union and of sexual intercourse within marriage as a primarily unitive action.[190] The model of marriage as procreative institution was thrust into center stage in the 1960s in a great debate about artificial contraception. We will provide a detailed analysis of that debate in chapter 5, and we mention it here only as it is connected to our discussion of Catholic models of marriage.[191] Rigali offers a useful category in which to consider that debate. He asks not what was the *outcome* of the debate in Pope Paul VI's controverted *Humanae vitae*, which is well known, but what was the *process* whereby that outcome was reached.[192] This process can be easily summarized.

The Papal Birth Control Commission

At the instigation of Leo Cardinal Suenens, archbishop of Malines, Belgium, whose ultimate intent was that an adequate document on Christian marriage be brought before the Second Vatican Council for debate, Pope John XXIII established a commission to study the issue of birth control. The commission was confirmed and enlarged by Pope Paul VI until it ultimately had seventy-one members, not all of whom attended its meetings or voted.[193] The final episcopal vote took place in answer to three questions. In answer to the question "Is contraception intrinsically evil?" nine bishops voted "No," three voted "Yes," and three abstained. In answer to the question "Is contraception, as defined by the Majority Report, in basic continuity with tradition and the declarations of the Magisterium?" nine bishops voted "Yes," five voted "No," and one abstained. In answer to the question "Should the Magisterium speak on this question as soon as possible?" fourteen voted "Yes" and one voted "No."[194] A preliminary vote of the theologians who were advisers to the commission, in response to the question "Is artificial contraception an intrinsically evil violation of the natural law?," had resulted in a count of fifteen "No" and four "Yes" answers.[195] Both a majority report and a minority report were then submitted to Paul VI, who—professing himself unconvinced by the arguments of the majority and probably also sharing the concern of the minority report that the Church could not repudiate its long-standing teaching on contraception without undergoing a serious blow to its overall moral authority—approved the minority report in his encyclical letter *Humanae vitae*.[196] The differential between the two groups is easily categorized.

The minority report, which became the controverted part of the encyclical, argued that "each and every marriage act [*quilibet matrimonii actus*] must remain open to the transmission of life."[197] As we have already noted, Paul VI was the first to state the Church's teaching in this way. The tradition had always been that it is *marriage* itself, and not each and every act of intercourse in marriage, that is to be open to procreation, and that is what the majority report argued. It judged that "what had been condemned in the past and remains so today is the unjustified refusal of life, arbitrary human intervention for the sake of moments of egotistic pleasure; in short, the rejection of procreation as a specific task of marriage." It went on to assert that "human intervention in the process of the marriage act *for reasons drawn from the end of marriage itself* should not always be excluded, provided that the criteria of morality are always safeguarded."[198] The differential in the two positions was precisely the differential created by adherence to two different models of marriage, the minority report being based on the traditional procreative institution model and the majority report being based on the emerging interpersonal union model that had its origins in the 1930s and was embraced by the Second Vatican Council. McCormick commented in 1968 that "the documents of the Papal Commission represent a rather full summary of two points of view. . . . The majority report, particularly the analysis in its 'rebuttal,' strikes this reader as much the more satisfactory statement."[199] This continues to be the judgment of the majority of Catholic theologians and the vast majority of Catholic couples, because they adhere to the same interpersonal model on which the majority report was based—so much so that Farley can offer the judgment that "in much of Catholic moral theology and ethics, the procreative norm as the sole or primary justification of sexual intercourse is gone."[200] Thirty-eight years after *Humanae vitae*, despite a concerted minority effort to make adherence to *Humanae vitae* a test case of genuine Catholicity, the debate between the procreative and interpersonal models perdures in the Church and is far from resolved, as we will see in the chapters that follow.

A summary of the approach to marriage and sexual activity in the modern period of Catholic theology and teaching is easy to present. The modern period represents yet one more development in Catholic theology and, to a lesser extent, in magisterial teaching. The major development in the Catholic theological approach to marriage is the recovery of the two purposes of marriage and sexual intercourse articulated in Genesis, the relational and procreational, and a rearranging of their relative priorities. Since Clement, Augustine, and Aquinas, the procreational became established in Catholic teaching as the *primary* purpose of sexual intercourse and the relational became relegated to a *secondary* purpose. Beginning with Pius XI's *Casti connubii* and culminating in the Second Vatican Council's *Gaudium et spes*, these two purposes of sexual intercourse have been equalized, so that neither is prior to the other. Marriage and sexual intercourse "are by their very nature ordained to the generation and education of children," but that "does not make the other ends of marriage of less account,"[201] and marriage "is not instituted solely for procreation."[202] Paul VI's *Humanae vitae* tried to change the terms of the debate over marriage and sexual intercourse by teaching for the first time in Catholic history that "each and every marriage *act* must remain open to the transmission of life,"[203] but that judgment is controverted by the vast majority of Catholic believers and, "in much of Catholic theology and ethics, the procreative norm as the sole or primary justification of sexual intercourse is gone."[204] With the reestablishing of the relational purpose for marriage and sexual intercourse, the judgment about the morality of any sexual act is now made by Catholic ethicists not on the basis of the *act* but on the basis of the place of the act with its *relational* context. We shall see as we proceed what difference that development makes to moral judgments.

Conclusion

This chapter has done two things. First, it has documented the origins and correctness of the claim we made at the outset: that traditional Catholic sexual morality is essentially *marital* morality. This morality is encoded in two magisterial statements: "Any human genital act whatsoever may be placed only within the framework of marriage,"[205] and "Each and every act [of sexual intercourse] must remain open to the transmission of life."[206] We traced the origins of these two claims from the ancient Stoic philosophy, through the early, medieval, and modern Catholic tradition, down to the present day, when they are being reevaluated. This reevaluation, which is taking place in both theological and magisterial circles, is the second thing we documented. It was provoked by a new historical-critical approach, approved by the Magisterium, applied first to the sacred scriptures and then to the teaching of the Magisterium itself.

Pope Pius XII, in his 1943 encyclical *Divino afflante spiritu*, approved the historical-critical approach to the study of the Bible and instructed Catholic exegetes that their prime concern was "to arrive at a deeper and fuller knowledge of the mind of [the author]."[207] Pius further taught that the way to arrive at that mind is "to discern and define that sense of the biblical words which is called literal."[208] When he wrote in 1943, it was boldly assumed that, at least in most instances, the mind of the author could be determined with "objective" exactitude using the tools of historical-critical analysis. In 1994, when the Pontifical Biblical Commission made the same claim about the importance of the literal meaning of the biblical text, it made it less boldly with the exigencies of a double hermeneutic in mind: "The Bible itself and the history of its interpretation point to the need for a hermeneutics. . . . On the one hand, all events reported in the Bible are interpreted events. On the other, all exegesis of the accounts of these events necessarily involves the exegete's own subjectivity."[209] Meaning is always sociohistorically constructed and, if an interpreter is to arrive at the meaning intended by an author, then he or she has to be aware of the objective sociohistorical situation of both the ancient writer and the contemporary interpreter. This means in the concrete, for our present concern, that the Bible is not a moral manual to be followed slavishly without careful consideration of the situation of the text and of the situation of the human subject seeking to arrive at a moral judgment on the basis of the text. If this is true of the biblical text, the meanings of which found the Christian religion in general, it is also true a fortiori of the patristic, medieval, and modern texts of the later ecclesiastical tradition. Textual historicity demands not unquestioning obedience but careful, attention, understanding, judgment, and decisions.

Because the Bible is not a manual of morality, neither is it a manual of sexual morality. It is concerned not with sexuality as such but with living a life according to the will of God. Neither biblical Hebrew and Greek nor medieval Latin had words for the modern concepts "sexuality" and "sex." There are allusions to sexual acts, some of them frank and explicit but none of them constituting laws to be followed without question. All of them, to repeat, suffer the limitations introduced by their sociohistorical context; some of them also suffer from a seriously inaccurate understanding of human "nature" and a deficient sexual anthropology. This latter is particularly true of what the Bible and the early Fathers of the Church understand about human biology and say, for example, about "spilling the male seed."[210] This seriously colors what the tradition has to say about human sexuality in general and about male homosexual activity in particular. It has almost nothing to say about female homosexual activity, but we shall withhold detailed discussion of this until chapter 7. We will present, in chapter 4, a revised but traditional, foundational sexual ethical principle in light of the historical development of sexual teaching in the Catholic tradition we have documented. Before we do that, however, we first investigate two Catholic schools of moral theology that have evolved in the wake of *Humanae vitae*, the traditionalists and the revisionists, together with the sexual anthropologies that each school offers.

Chapter Two

Natural Law and Sexual Anthropology

Catholic Traditionalists

"Traditionalist" is the general label given to moral theologians who support and defend absolute magisterial norms prohibiting certain types of sexual acts such as premarital sex, artificial birth control, artificial reproductive technologies, masturbation, and homosexual acts. The traditionalist school is contrasted with the revisionist school. "Revisionist" is the general label given to moral theologians who question many of these absolute norms. These two groups disagree on many specific sexual norms because they disagree, more fundamentally, on method and the sexual anthropology that either supports these norms or questions their legitimacy and credibility. After defining the complex term "nature," which is at the root of methodological and anthropological differences in sexual ethics, describing the Second Vatican Council's call for the renewal of moral theology, and explaining the correlation between natural law and sexual anthropology, we will investigate traditionalist and revisionist methods and sexual anthropologies in this chapter and the next.

"Nature" Defined

Because there will be much talk of "nature" in this and following chapters, we must first confront a difficulty with any argument from "nature." This difficulty was highlighted initially by David Hume, who asked whether we can deduce moral obligation from what exists in "nature" and answered that we cannot.[1] We cannot draw conclusions from what *is* to what *ought to be*, from the presumed biological structure of the sexual act—for example, to moral obligation—for even after determining what *is*, we still have to determine whether it is right or wrong. To draw such a conclusion is a logical fallacy—a "naturalistic fallacy," Moore calls it, or a "theological fallacy," Frankena calls it.[2] All we can understand from "nature" is the naked facticity of a reality, sexuality and sexual intercourse for instance; nothing else. "Nature" reveals to our attention, understanding, judgment, and decision only its naked facticity, not our moral obligation. Everything beyond "nature's" facticity is the result of interpretation by attentive, understanding, rational, and responsible human beings.[3]

In reality we have no access to the pure, unembellished experience of "nature;" we experience "nature" only as interpreted by rational, social beings.[4] When we derive moral obligations from "nature," we are actually deriving them from our human attention to and our interpretation and evaluation of "nature." It is, of course, inevitable that different groups of equally rational human beings may derive different interpretations of "nature" and moral obligation deriving from "nature," and that any given interpretation may be wrong. That fact has been demonstrated time and again in history, including Catholic history.[5] It is also something taken for granted in the social scientific enterprise known as the sociology of knowledge. One of the founders of this discipline, Alfred Schutz, presents its widely-taken-for-granted principle: "It is the *meaning* of our experiences and not the *ontological structure* of the objects that constitute reality."[6] "The potter, and not the pot," Alfred North Whitehead adds metaphorically, "is responsible for the shape of the pot."[7] The uninterpreted experience of "nature," as of every other objective reality, is restricted to its mere facticity and is void of meaning, a quality that does not inhere in "nature" but is assigned to it by rational beings in interpretive acts. The decisive criterion for the meaning of any human action, including any moral action, is the project of the actor.[8] Meaning is what is or was meant by the *actor*, who is always to be understood not as an Enlightenment radical *individual* but as an Aristotelian-Thomistic radically *social being*. Because "nature" is not pure uninterpreted "nature"—because it is, as philosophers and sociologists say, socially constructed—throughout this book we speak of it always within quotation marks, that is, as "nature."

If the decisive criterion for the meaning of any action, including any moral action, is the meaning assigned to it by social actors, an immediate question arises. Different social actors in different social groups may define the meaning of an action in radically different ways and, then, a question arises as to which definition is true. Common sense suggests that something is the "same" for each and every social and individual actor, but common sense cannot determine how that sameness is to be understood. Only critical research, interpretation, history, and dialectic can do that.[9] The entire world watched Nazis herd gypsies, homosexuals, and Jews into gas chambers. Committed Nazis interpreted the action as purification of the race; the rest of the world interpreted it as murder of innocent people; and we can only guess how the people waiting for the gas interpreted it. For all three groups the action was naturally the "same," the herding of people into gas chambers. For each group, however, the *meaning* of the action was far from the same. It was radically different, and it is utterly futile to point out to committed actors the "objective" meaning of the act, for the objective meaning is the meaning assigned to the act by social actors, not the naked, uninterpreted facticity of the act.

Object and Objectivity

Bernard Lonergan distinguishes two kinds of objects. There is the object in the immediate world, the reality that is there before anyone asks "What is it?" and before anyone answers with a name, "It is an apple" or "It is sexual intercourse." Such an object is "already, out, there, now, real." It is *already* for it is prior to any human attention to it; it is *out* for it is outside human consciousness; it is *there* for it is spatially located; it is *now* for it exists and is attended to in time; it is *real* for it is bound up with human living and acting "and so must be just as real as they are."[10] There is also the object in the world mediated by meaning. This object is what becomes socially understood, judged, and decided by the answer to the question What is it? "To this type of object we are related immediately by our questions and only mediately by the [intellectual] operations relevant to the answers."[11] There are, in short, objects independent of any human cognitive activity and objects that are the result of human cognitive activity. The two should never be confused. Not all "objects" are absolutely independent of human cognitive activity.

To these two meanings of the word *object* correspond two meanings of the word *objectivity*. In the world of immediacy, objectivity has one component; it is a characteristic of the object already, out, there, now, and real. In the world mediated by meaning, however, objectivity has three components. First, there is the experiential objectivity constituted by the facticity of objects that are already, out, there, now, and real. Second, there is the normative objectivity constituted by the human knowing and naming of these factual objects through attending, understanding, judging, and deciding about them. Third, there is the absolute objectivity that results from the combination of experiential and normative objectivity. Through experiential objectivity, the conditions for already, out, there, now, and real objectivity are fulfilled; and through normative objectivity, those conditions are truly linked by an attending, understanding, judging, and deciding subject to the object they condition. "The combination yields a conditioned [object] with its conditions fulfilled and that, in knowledge, is a fact and, in reality, is a contingent being or event."[12] This same conclusion is articulated in the philosophy of science as "all facts are theory-laden."[13] The eminent physicist Werner Heisenberg formulated this position as the Uncertainty Principle: Our knowledge of reality is never purely objective but is always conditioned by the knowing subject. Joseph Cardinal Ratzinger, now Pope Benedict XVI, comments, in an essay on the place of history in biblical exegesis, that "where human beings are concerned, or where the mystery of God makes itself visible, all of this [consideration of the impact of history] is even more important."[14]

The Sociology of Knowledge

Peter Berger and Thomas Luckmann, following Karl Mannheim, have codified this analysis of object and objectivity into a systematic sociology of knowledge.[15] They have highlighted one facet of the problem of social reality that has been in the background to this point, namely, that the individual and the society in which he or she lives are not two completely separate and independent realities. They are conjoined realities in an ongoing dialectic of interdependence. Human society, with its symbols, meanings, and values, is a human product and nothing but a human product. "Despite the objectivity that marks the social world in human experience, it does not thereby acquire an ontological status apart from the human activity that produced it."[16] And yet this humanly produced social world constantly acts upon its producers, conforming them to itself and controlling their understanding, judgment, and action. On the one hand, in their social life expressions, humans are social products that, on the other hand, act upon the society that produced them to modify it and give it new form. The relationship between men and women, the producers, and the social world, their product, is dialectical. Society is a product of human activity, and humans, in their social and personal reality, are products of society. Berger and Luckmann argue that the dialectic tension between individual and society has three moments: a moment of externalization, a moment of objectivation, and a moment of internalization.

Humans do not have a given relationship with the world that is already, out, there, now, and real; they must establish one. In the process of establishing this relationship, they simultaneously produce both a *human* world and themselves as social beings in this world. The world that is produced is called, broadly, culture— the totality of human products, both material and nonmaterial.[17] Men and women produce tools of every kind. They also produce language and via this language, complex constructions of meaning that permeate every aspect of their lives. They produce, in Schutz's terminology, complex and finite provinces of meanings; in Lonergan's terminology, they produce perspectives.[18] Society is part of that complex of meanings, the part that structures men's and women's ongoing relations with their fellow men and women. Humans define themselves, and are socially defined, through the opportunities and constraints others set before them as either socially appropriate and right or socially inappropriate and wrong. "It is human nature to grow real in the mirror of other people's eyes."[19] As an element of the cultural meaning complex, society fully shares in culture's character as a human product. Society and its citizens are both constituted as socially constructed and maintained by the activity of human beings, and they have no meaningful reality apart from such activity.

Social reality, then, is an externalized product of the human, symbolic animal. To speak, however, of an externalized product is already to imply that the product achieves a certain autonomy from its producer. The process of transformation of human products into a world that not only derives from humans but also confronts them as an objective reality apart from them is called objectivation. The product of human activity becomes something as already, out, there, now, and real as any physical object, something that has the status of objective reality. For the material products of human activity, this objectivity is readily grasped. Men and women construct cars, computers, houses, automobiles, and cakes, and by their actions increase the totality of physical objects that confront them as already, out, there, now, and real independent of them. So it is, too, with the human products they produce. They construct a language and then find that their verbal communication is controlled by that language and its rules of syntax. They construct values and then feel guilty when they contravene them. They fashion structures of meaning, institutions, that then confront them as powerful forces in the external world apart from their activities. These institutions—such as family, education, politics, economics, and religion—meaning structures—such as mythology, religion, philosophy, and science—and roles and identities—such as parent, child, theologian, and scientist—are all apprehended as already, out, there, now, and real phenomena in the social world apart from human activity. Yet both they and the social world are nothing but the products of creative human activity.

Voegelin states what we have been saying slightly differently, but no less firmly. Human society "is illuminated from within by the human beings who continuously create and bear it as the mode and condition of their self-realization. It is illuminated through an elaborate symbolism, . . . from rite, through myth, to theory. . . . And this symbolism illuminates it with meaning so far as the symbols make the internal structure of such a cosmion, the relations between its members and groups of members, as well as its existence as a whole, transparent for the mystery of human existence."[20] Persons embraced into a society that humans have socially constructed experience that society not as something merely convenient or accidental but as something that is of their human essence.

Human consciousness, then, is confronted by its own objectivated products, intellectual as well as physical. Internalization is the process of absorbing these objectivations into consciousness in such a way that the humanly created structures of the objectivated world become the objects of human consciousness. Human products, and they need not be enumerated again, act as formative elements of the consciousness of the humans who created them. Insofar as internalization has taken place, individuals apprehend the elements of the humanly objectivated world as phenomena both of the world already, out, there, now, and real and also of internal consciousness. Every society faces the problem of communicating its objectivated meanings to succeeding generations, a task accomplished through the broad process of education called socialization.[21] Berger advances the foregoing dialectic understanding of human and social reality as a synthesis of the theories of the two fathers of classical sociology, Max Weber and Émile Durkheim. Weber understood social reality as constituted by human meaning; Durkheim understood it as having the character of facticity over against the individual. They intended, respectively, the subjective origin and the objective facticity of social reality.[22] Berger's theory preserves both these ideas in dialectical tension.

Perspectivism versus Relativism

To many, such an approach to reality and truth raises the specter of relativism. With Lonergan, however, we prefer to speak of *perspectivism* rather than of relativism. "Where relativism has lost hope about the attainment of truth, perspectivism stresses the complexity of what the historian is writing about and, as well, the specific difference of historical from mathematical, scientific and philosophic knowledge."[23] Whereas relativism concludes to the falsity of a judgment, perspectivism concludes to its *partial* truth. According to Lonergan, perspectivism in human knowledge arises from three factors. First, human knowers are finite, the information available to them is incomplete, and they do not attend to or master all the data available to them. Second, knowers are selective, given their past socialization, personal experience, and the range of data offered to them. Third, knowers are individually different, and we can expect them to make different selections of data. The theologian-knower trained in the philosophy of Plato—for instance, Augustine—will attend to different data, achieve a different understanding, make different judgments, and act on different decisions from the theologian-knower trained in the philosophy of Aristotle—for instance, Aquinas. They produce different theologies, both of which will necessarily be incomplete explanations and partial portrayals of a very complex reality. They are like two viewers at the first-story and tenth-story windows of a skyscraper; each gets a different, but no less partial, view of the total panorama that unfolds outside the building.

Every judgment of truth—including, perhaps especially, every judgment of theological truth—is a limited judgment and commitment based on limited data and understanding.[24] "So far from resting on knowledge of the universe, [a judgment] is to the effect that, no matter what the rest of the universe may prove to be, at least *this* is so."[25] It is precisely the necessarily limited nature of human, sociohistorical sensations, understandings, judgments, and knowledge that leads to perspectivism, which is not, to repeat, a source of falsity but a source of partial truth. Though he said it on the basis of God's incomprehensibility, Augustine's restating of earlier Greek theologians is à propos and accurate here: "*Si comprehendis non est Deus*, if you have understood, what you have understood is not God."[26] Aquinas agrees: "Now we cannot know what God is, but only what God is not; we must, therefore, consider the ways in which God does not exist rather than the ways in which God does."[27]

True "objective" knowledge, therefore, is a *tertium quid*, a third thing, that results from the dynamic interaction of the already, out, there, now, and real object and the attending, understanding, judging, and deciding subject. It derives not from ontological structure alone but also from the interaction of an object and an intelligent human subject socially constructing reality, meaning, value, and truth. What is frequently called *objective* reality by uncritical common sense is more properly called *social reality* or reality humanly invested with *social existence, meaning, and truth*. Objective knowledge is like a mythology. It is "an arbitrary construct in which a given society in a given historical situation has invested its sense of meaningfulness and value."[28] Such an approach to the relationship of being, meaning, and truth in the human world precludes the absolute connection of meaning and truth with ontological being alone and explains why plural meanings and truth about the "same" reality abound in the human world. Plural meanings and truth, all of which are deemed objective by the actors who subscribe to them, derive inevitably from the plural sociohistorical perspectives that abound in the human world.

"Nature," Knowledge, and Norms

This epistemological overview of object and objective knowledge has profound implications for how we understand "nature" and the norms and principles we derive from that understanding. First, depending on the meaning derived from the dialectic of interdependence between object, individual, and society, "nature" includes a variety of meanings and partial truths. These meanings must be judged morally, as *Gaudium et spes* correctly notes, in light of the objective criterion of the human person who is a relational, incarnated, inculturated, historical subject.[29] These epistemological considerations caution against positing a one-size-fits-all morality deduced from "nature," and they have implications for the norms we formulate to guide sexual persons.

Second, Josef Fuchs allies our foregoing discussion of "nature" to moral norms in the following manner. He asks what is meant by the objectivity of moral norms, and he gives two answers. The first is a negative answer: "Objectivity does not derive from formal revelation, tradition, or the authentic documents of the Magisterium." The second is a positive one: "If the norms of moral rightness derive from a process of knowledge, evaluation and judgment [and with Lonergan he assumes they do], then it must be admitted that they are determined not only by the elements of the world-object but also by elements of the judging subject that necessarily enter into this process."[30] The human subject cannot make a genuinely moral judgment without careful hermeneutics, that is, without attention to, and understanding, judgment, and affirmation of both the world and himself or herself in the world. "It is only in this way that a norm is truly objective—whether it is discerned by society or by a single person."[31] This concept of objectivity is different from the one that calls a norm "objective" if it is generally accepted in a society, the Church for example, or is proposed by a social authority, the Magisterium for example. It is, however, the only concept of objectivity that takes account of the true "nature" of not only physical acts but also the rational subject who performs the acts.

We agree with the majority of Catholic moral theologians that absolute ethical norms exist and that these norms dispel all possible confusion. We agree also, however, with the Catholic moral theologian Dietmar Mieth that the only absolute norm is that "good is to be done and evil left undone," and that every other ethical judgment requires concrete, empirical judgment.[32] Fuchs also agrees. "There is no discrepancy of theories and opinions within Catholic moral theology about the one ethical *absolutum*, the translation of the ethical *absolutum* into the [concrete] *material plurality* of human reality is, however, a different matter."[33] The hermeneutic for that translation is controlled, as it is always in the Catholic moral tradition, by human reason seeking to be attentive, intelligent, rational, and responsible in the actual sociohistorical situation.[34] It cannot be otherwise for free persons who live in a world that is both physical and human and that is subject to historicity.

With regard to these matters, the Second Vatican Council taught that laypersons are not to imagine that their pastors "are always such experts that to every problem which arises, however complicated, they can readily give a concrete solution, or even that such is their mission." The clear acknowledgment is that they are not. The council goes on to advise laypersons, "enlightened by Christian wisdom and giving close attention to the teaching authority of the Church,"[35] to take on their own distinctive role. That distinctive role, it teaches with regard to the moral norms of married life, is to reach "objective" judgments based on the "nature" not only of the acts but also of the human person, "*ex personae eiusdem actuum natura.*"[36] Acknowledging the evident plurality of objective moral judgments in the modern world, the council enjoins "the entire People of God, especially pastors and theologians, to hear, distinguish, and *interpret* the many voices of our age, and to judge them in the light of the divine word. In this way, revealed truth can always be more deeply penetrated, better understood, and set forth to greater advantage."[37] These magisterial teachings suggest to us that the concept of objectivity we have proposed lies well within the Catholic tradition. That it does is already underscored by our prior consideration of historicity.[38]

The Revision of Catholic Moral Theology

The Second Vatican Council's *Gaudium et spes* marked a fundamental transformation in the Catholic Church's specific teaching on marital sexuality, but the council also called for a general revision of Catholic moral theology. The Declaration on Priestly Formation, *Optatum totius*, prescribes that "special attention needs to be given to the *development* of moral theology. Its scientific exposition should be more thoroughly nourished by scriptural teaching. It should show the nobility of the Christian vocation of the faithful, and their obligation to bring forth fruit in charity for the life of the world."[39] In response to this call both traditionalist and revisionist moral theologians continued the process, under way prior to the council, of revising the manual approach to moral theology that had predominated from the Council of Trent to the Second Vatican Council.

The commitment to renewal includes common ground between traditionalists and revisionists on seven main issues. First, each school accepts natural law as an objectivist or universalist meta-ethical theory. That is, both reject relativism or sub-jectivism.[40] Second, both define *right* or *good* as that which facilitates "integral human fulfillment," "authentic personhood," "the human person adequately con-sidered," "human flourishing," "human dignity," or some similar variant. The definition of "authentic personhood," however, and the norms that facilitate or frustrate it often differ in each theory. Third, both schools see shortcomings with traditional Catholic natural law theory as it was developed in the manualist tradition and seek to revise the implicit method that tradition used. Fourth, in reaction to the weaknesses of the manualist tradition, both emphasize the need to reintegrate spirituality or ascetical theology and moral theology. Fifth, they agree that faith *and* reason are essential in the revision of Catholic moral theology and, further, that reason and revelation are not diametrically opposed but complement one another in justifying normative claims for what facilitates authentic personhood. Sixth, they recognize the importance of four sources of moral knowledge for developing a nor-mative method—scripture, tradition, reason, and experience—though they priori-tize and assign different weight to these sources and frequently have a fundamentally different hermeneutic for interpreting them.[41] Seventh and finally, both schools draw from natural law but formulate very different sexual anthropologies and nor-mative ethics in light of that law.

The promulgation of Pope Paul VI's *Humanae vitae* in 1968 highlighted the urgency to renew Catholic moral theology and established a clear line of demarca-tion between traditionalist and revisionist ethical methods, for these two schools of thought were fundamentally divided on the issue of artificial birth control. Tradi-tionalists tend to be staunch advocates of the magisterial teaching affirmed in *Humanae vitae* that "each and every marriage act must remain open to the transmis-sion of life."[42] Revisionists adopt the position of the majority report of the Papal Birth Control Commission, arguing that "human intervention in the process of the marriage act *for reasons drawn from the end of marriage itself* should not always be excluded, provided that the criteria of morality are always safeguarded."[43] The two schools are divided on the issue of artificial contraception because, more fundamen-tally, they are divided on sexual anthropology and ethical methodology. Though both schools have heeded the call from Vatican II for the renewal of Catholic moral theology and share similar visions on some aspects of that renewal, they have devel-oped radically different sexual anthropologies and ethical methods.

The tendencies of these two ethical methods, and their relationship with the two models of human sexuality, are the following. Traditionalists tend toward a rule-based, act-centered, authoritarian, classicist approach to ethical method and sexual anthropology, which parallels the juridical approach reflected in *Humanae vitae*. Revisionists tend toward a person-based, relation-centered, historically conscious approach to ethical method and sexual anthropology, which parallels the interper-sonal approach reflected in *Gaudium et spes*.

Natural Law and Sexual Anthropology

Natural law, a foundation of Catholic moral teaching, indicates what it means to be fully human—our final end is friendship with God[44]—and provides guidelines for attaining this end. Before we can formulate norms to attain human fulfillment, however, we must first define human fulfillment; this definition is what contemporary theology refers to as theological anthropology. Natural law seeks, through reason guided by faith, to define a normative anthropology and to discern the acts and/or virtues that facilitate attaining authentic human fulfillment. The challenge with natural law, human "nature," and human sexuality is that the understanding of human sexuality—including the biological, emotional, psychological, relational, and spiritual dimensions—has developed and continues to develop. Contemporary natural law theory, therefore, must look not only to traditional sources for basic insight into natural law and human fulfillment but also to contemporary philosophical, theological, and scientific contributions to understand and construct a sexual anthropology.

Contemporary Catholic natural law discourse reflects a fundamental shift from "human nature" to "human person." That is to say, the biological and physicalist understanding of traditional natural law and human "nature" is in the process of being transformed into a contemporary personalist, relational understanding. The former defines the morality of acts based on the physical, biological structure of those acts; the latter defines the morality of acts based on the meaning of those acts for persons and relationships. Johnstone describes this shift as "a move from a 'physicalist' paradigm to a 'personalist' paradigm."[45] A challenge with paradigm shifts is that unless one is extremely attentive to history, context, and language, old wine can often be poured into new wineskins. The static and physicalist classicist anthropology with its attendant conceptual and theoretical baggage can be transposed into a historically conscious anthropology with the same or similar conceptual and theoretical baggage. When this happens, the terminology (human "nature" vis-à-vis the human person or classicism vis-à-vis historical consciousness) may have changed, but the same challenges and shortcomings of neoscholastic natural law interpretations remain. As will become clear, it is our position that, though traditionalists have attempted to renew Catholic moral theology, they have not substantially renewed their sexual anthropology, which continues to reflect many of the shortcomings of the neoscholastic manuals and a physicalist interpretation of the sexual human person.

Traditionalists and Sexual Anthropology

Although traditionalists appear to be united in their goal to defend the absolute sexual ethical norms of magisterial teaching,[46] there are different emphases in the natural law normative theories and sexual anthropologies they construct to justify these norms. In this chapter, we present and critically analyze traditionalist interpretations of natural law, the sexual anthropology that follows from these interpretations, and the norms that facilitate human dignity in light of this anthropology. In chapter 3, we do the same for revisionist moral theologians.

New Natural Law Theory: Basic Goods

The best-known traditionalist attempt to revise neoscholastic natural law is New Natural Law Theory (NNLT), developed by Germain Grisez, John Finnis, Joseph Boyle, and their colleagues.[47] According to NNLT, the person is essentially *homo rationalis*, a rational agent whose choices are to actualize and realize basic or intelligible goods. This theory draws from Thomas Aquinas and posits the self-evident first principle of practical reason—do good and avoid evil—as the foundation for moral judgment. According to Grisez, this first principle "articulates the intrinsic, necessary relationship between human goods and appropriate actions bearing upon them."[48] The human or basic goods are "aspects of our personhood, elements of the blueprint which tells us what human persons are capable of being, whether as individuals or joined together in community."[49] We come to an awareness of basic goods in and through our experience of a natural inclination toward them. Finnis summarizes: "By a simple act of non-inferential understanding one grasps that the object of the inclination which one experiences is an instance of a general form of good, for oneself (and others like one)."[50] There are two subdivisions constituting eight basic goods. The first three are "nonreflexive" or "substantive" goods (human life, including health, physical integrity, and safety; knowledge and aesthetic appreciation; and skilled performances of all kinds). These goods "are not defined in terms of choosing, and they provide reasons for choosing which can stand by themselves." The next four basic goods are reflexive (self-integration, practical reasonableness or authenticity, justice and friendship, and religion or holiness) "since they are both reasons for choosing and are in part defined in terms of choosing."[51] This list of basic goods has evolved, and marriage and its fulfillment through parenthood have recently been added.

The Basic Good of Marriage

NNLT's sexual anthropology is founded upon the basic good of marriage. Its argument for marriage as a basic good and the absolute norms that follow from that basic good develops in three steps. The first step defines heterosexual marriage as a basic good; the second defines marital sexual acts in terms of that basic good; and the third judges all other sexual acts to be nonmarital and, therefore, unnatural, unreasonable, and immoral.

First, then, marriage, a communion of "life and love,"[52] is a basic human good. Grisez explains: "The *communion of married life* refers to the couple's *being* married, that is, their being united as complementary, bodily persons, so really and so completely that they are two in one flesh."[53] As noted, marriage is NNLT's most recently identified basic good. This raises the question of the interrelationship between this good and the other basic goods. Did marriage derive from these other goods, is it a combination of them, or does it stand alone?

Grisez maintains that though marriage is related to friendship as interpersonal union and life in terms of parenthood, it cannot be reduced to these other goods; "marriage is one reality having a basic good proper to it."[54] This two-in-one-flesh reality is realized by both "marital consent which conjugal intercourse fulfills" and bodily communion between the spouses.[55] Marital consent and bodily communion are both required to realize a two-in-one-flesh communion between a man and a woman. For couples who are engaged and not yet married, sexual intercourse may realize bodily communion, but it lacks the public consent required for marriage and marital intercourse. Without that public, marital consent, bodily communion between male and female is not a real but only an illusory good; "such a choice always is unreasonable"[56] and, therefore, immoral.

Second, the marital act of sexual intercourse that realizes bodily communion is an essential aspect and actualization of marriage as a basic good. "This form of interpersonal unity is actualized by conjugal love when that love takes shape in the couple's acts of mutual marital consent, loving consummation, and their whole life together, not least in the parenthood of couples whose marriages are fruitful."[57] NNLT asserts that the marital act consists of two intrinsic and inseparable meanings, one procreative (parenthood), and the other unitive (friendship). Finnis explains: "The union of the reproductive organs of husband and wife really unites them biologically (and their biological reality is part of, not merely an instrument of, their *personal* reality); reproduction is one function and so, in respect of that function, the spouses are indeed one reality, and their sexual union therefore can *actualize* and allow them to *experience* their *real common good—their marriage* with the two goods, parenthood and friendship, which (leaving aside the order of grace) are the parts of its wholeness as an intelligible common good even if, independently of what the spouses will, their capacity for biological parenthood will not be fulfilled by that act of genital union."[58]

Finally, in light of the basic good of marriage and the twofold intrinsic meaning of marital acts, NNLT maintains that nonmarital sexual acts are absolutely prohibited because they cannot fulfill the intrinsic meanings of marital acts and, therefore, cannot activate and achieve the basic good of marriage. Such nonmarital acts include premarital sexual intercourse, artificially contraceptive sexual acts, homosexual acts, marital or nonmarital nonreproductive sexual acts, and masturbation. These acts are unnatural, unreasonable, and therefore immoral.

NNLT claims that nonmarital sexual acts are "unnatural" because they are not acts of a reproductive kind. Nonmarital acts, that is, are not open to reproduction because the organs are prevented from realizing their reproductive capacity (in artificial birth control) or their reproductive organs do not create a complementary biological unit (in homosexual acts). Though this statement may appear to fall prey to accusations of biologism or physicalism, to claim that an act is unnatural, and therefore immoral, does not mean that the act's immorality is assessed *purely* on its biological structure. Biological acts of a reproductive kind and personal friendship are both necessary for a truly human marital act and are, therefore, intrinsically linked. As Finnis claims, the biological union of the reproductive organs of a husband and wife is part of, not an instrument of, their personal reality.[59] Biological union is necessary to realize the marital act, but it is not sufficient by itself. To be a marital act, the act of biological union must also be an act of friendship.

Finnis summarizes: "Sexual acts are not unitive in their significance unless they are marital, . . . and . . . they are not marital unless they have not only the generosity of acts of friendship but also the procreative significance."[60] Because there can be no acts of a reproductive kind between a male–male or female–female couple, homosexual acts are unnatural. And because they are unnatural, they are also immoral because they cannot realize the other intrinsic meaning of marital acts, namely, friendship.

Nonmarital sexual acts are unreasonable. Because marriage is a basic good, and basic goods are "intelligible goods," to act against a basic good is to act unintelligibly and unreasonably. According to NNLT, a foundational moral principle is that "one may never *intend* to destroy, damage, impede, or violate any basic human good, or prefer an illusory instantiation of a basic human good to a real instantiation of that or some other human good."[61] By definition, nonmarital sexual acts cannot be marital acts and, therefore, to engage in such acts is to "destroy, damage, impede, or violate" marriage as a basic good. Although nonmarital heterosexual acts may be natural acts of a reproductive kind, they do not actualize the marital good of friendship. Nonreproductive-type sexual acts between a married heterosexual couple may seem to include the good of friendship, but they cannot actualize a truly human marital act because they are not acts of a reproductive kind. In all these cases, the acts are not marital acts; they destroy, damage, or impede the marital good, and are thus unreasonable and immoral. NNLT's explanation of the basic good of marriage, and of the norms deduced from this basic good that prohibit certain sexual acts absolutely, reveals its foundational sexual anthropology.

Sexual Anthropology, Marriage, and Absolute Norms

NNLT's anthropology recognizes that human "nature," natural inclinations to the basic goods, and the goods themselves are both stable and changing. They are stable "in that the givenness and fundamental unalterability of natural inclinations account for the unalterability of the principles of natural law; but also changing, in that the dynamism of the inclinations, their openness to continuing and expanding fulfillment, accounts for the openness of natural law to authentic development."[62] George affirms the historical and evolutionary nature of the goods as well, noting that many of "the possible intelligent purposes [of the goods] remain as yet unenvisaged."

Knowledge of these goods, and thus of human nature, arises from "practical inquiry, reflection, and judgment."[63] NNLT, then, recognizes a dialectic between classicism and the essential nature of human "nature," basic goods, and natural law, and historical consciousness and the historical, evolving nature of those same realities. Any authentic development in moral knowledge from a historically conscious perspective, however, is dependent upon maintaining the unity of each basic good. Though norms can change and develop on the basis of an "unfolding understanding of the human good," in the case where "aspects of the human goods . . . are already understood,"[64] no such development is possible.

The sexual anthropology that arises from NNLT's understanding of basic goods and their stable and changing characteristics can be summarized as follows. Basic goods are aspects of human personhood, and marriage is such a basic good, defined as a communion of life that requires consent and consummation and is actualized and realized through marital sexual acts that have two intrinsic meanings, parenthood and friendship. All nonmarital sexual acts, defined as acts that do not have these two meanings, are unnatural, unreasonable, and immoral. NNLT argues that the absolute norms of the Magisterium on sexual issues such as artificial contraception, homosexual acts, masturbation, and reproductive technologies are grounded in those aspects of the basic good of marriage already understood. Consequently, these norms are absolute, perhaps even infallible,[65] and cannot be changed.

NNLT's Sexual Anthropology: A Critique

There are some important questions for NNLT regarding its sexual anthropology, its theory of basic goods, and the absolute norms derived from these goods. These questions concern complementarity, Aquinas and generic natural law, the naturalistic fallacy, sexual orientation, heterogenital and personal complementarity, orientation complementarity, intentionality, and an act-centered anthropology. Let us briefly examine each one.

Complementarity. Johnstone notes the lack of an adequate definition of the person in NNLT. NNLT "lacks a profound account of the persons who elicit the acts, make the choices and are fulfilled by the goods."[66] In other words, while NNLT claims that certain choices to act, by definition, always entail a choice to directly destroy, damage, or impede a good or an aspect of that good,[67] it has failed to establish that such choices do in fact manifest a negative impact on the human person, human relationships, and human fulfillment. NNLT has failed to do so because it lacks a developed, personalist anthropology, and the anthropology it has developed is classicist; it emphasizes the biological over the personal dimensions of the sexual human person.

As noted, NNLT claims that sexual intercourse actualizes the good of marriage, and that it is an act of a reproductive kind that contains two intrinsic meanings, one procreative (parenthood), the other unitive (friendship). Though these two meanings are intrinsically related, there is a strict hierarchy prioritizing the biological

over the personal meaning of the sexual act. First, NNLT defines the good of marriage in terms of male–female "organic complementarity,"[68] what we refer to as
"heterogenital complementarity."[69] According to organic complementarity, in order
to reproduce, male and female must come together to "complete each other" and
become an "organic unit."[70] Thus, penis and vagina, biological genitalia, are the
foundational requirement, and in fact the sine qua non, for the personal meaning
of marital sexual acts. Without organic complementarity, one cannot even consider
the personal meaning of marital sexual acts.

Although biological genitalia are necessary for marital sexual acts, however, they
are not sufficient to realize such acts; they must also function properly, the second
biological requirement of marital sexual acts. If the genitalia are biologically present
but cannot function properly, as in the impotent, then there is no real organic
complementarity and marital acts of a reproductive kind cannot be realized. Third,
only "acts of a reproductive kind"—that is, where the penis is inserted into the
vagina and male orgasm takes place in the vagina—are suitable for marital sexual
acts. All other sexual acts that lead to orgasm—such as mutual masturbation, oral
sex, and anal sex, whether homosexual or heterosexual, even between a married
couple—are considered nonmarital acts and are thus unreasonable, unnatural, and
immoral. Thus, three biological criteria—genitalia, functioning genitalia, and spatial
location of orgasm—must be met before one can even consider whether a sexual act
can be a personal, relational, marital act. As Finnis states, acts of a reproductive
kind are "biologically *and thus* personally one."[71] Nonmarital sexual acts (including
nonmarital acts within a marital relationship) are merely acts of personal gratification.[72] In the case of marital acts, then, there is a strict hierarchy in the relation
between the biological aspects necessary to realize the sexual act and the personal
meaning of the act. The biological (organic complementarity) is the necessary foundation for the intrinsic personal meaning of the sexual act.

Aquinas and generic natural law. There are two basic concerns with NNLT's
focus on the biological dimensions over the relational dimensions of sexual anthropology. The first concern is that it is not truly personalist; it too closely reflects
Aquinas's generic natural law. Catholic moral teaching has relied largely upon natural law and has drawn predominantly from Aquinas to develop this teaching.
Though an in-depth discussion of Aquinas's natural law is beyond the scope of this
work, it is important to highlight one aspect of his teaching, for this aspect is relevant to NNLT's sexual anthropology. He provides the classic definition of natural
law: Eternal law is God's rational plan for creation and redemption. God has created
an orderly universe, and every created thing within that universe participates in the
eternal law according to its "nature." Natural law is the participation of humans in
the eternal law through reason.[73] It is a rational appetite that provides human beings
with knowledge of inclinations that direct them toward ends, including both the
final end, human fulfillment or friendship with God, and proximate ends, human
actions that facilitate attainment of the final end. Practical reason is concerned with
human actions and pursuing proximate ends that originate from our final end.[74]

Though the first principle of practical reason is to do good and avoid evil,[75] Aquinas distinguishes between three precepts of the natural law that correspond to humans' natural tendencies.

The first inclination humans share with all creatures is the inclination to preserve themselves in being. This inclination fosters the protection and defense of life, and it prohibits suicide, for example. The second inclination is sometimes referred to as "generic natural law" and includes what humans share with all animals, for example, the procreation and education of children. This inclination is frequently associated with physicalism, the idea that the moral meaning of an act is defined by its physical structure. For instance, the *telos* or end of sexual intercourse is reproduction, and to frustrate that end is to frustrate the natural *telos*. This strand of natural law is certainly emphasized in the traditional hierarchy of the ends of marriage; the procreative meaning of marriage is primary, the unitive meaning is secondary. Though all animals can procreate and educate their offspring, only human beings, through reason and will, have the natural inclination to experience relational union in marriage; this inclination constitutes "specific natural law," the third precept of natural law. Specific natural law pertains exclusively to human beings and includes inclinations guided by reason such as knowing truths about God, living in community, and striving to realize the common good.[76] The natural inclinations of specific natural law focus on the human capacity to reason and to pursue the good, a capacity unique to human beings.

Both generic natural law and specific natural law are related to our discussion of NNLT's sexual anthropology. Though NNLT emphasizes the importance of marriage as a communion of life, which reflects specific natural law, its emphasis on the biological components to realize this good more closely reflects generic natural law. If one focuses on generic natural law, the natural and biological meanings of the sexual act are emphasized. If one focuses on specific natural law, the personal and relational meanings of the sexual act are emphasized. Though NNLT posits an intrinsic relation between the biological and personal, it clearly prioritizes the biological over the personal in defining the marital act. For example, spousal rape violates the personal dimension of human sexuality but, prior to any determination of the immorality of the act on the basis of the violation of friendship, rape could potentially be a marital act because organic complementarity and freely given marital commitment are in place. Contrarily, regardless of the personal meaning of a sexual act between a gay or lesbian couple, for example, NNLT holds that the lack of organic complementarity precludes the possibility of the personal meaning of the sexual act. Finnis explains that acts of a reproductive kind are "biologically *and thus* personally one."[77] Generic natural law, the biological and physical, is emphasized over and above the specific natural law, the personal and relational. Though we agree with Aquinas and NNLT that the biological is essential in specific natural law, and genitalia are necessary to realize any marital sexual act, the evolving, historically conscious understanding of human sexuality in general, and sexual orientation in particular, which the Magisterium recognizes as something that is given and not chosen,[78] challenge this strict reliance upon male–female organic complementarity to define sexual anthropology and sexual ethics.

NNLT's claim to be "new" seems to be more a case of new wine in old wineskins. It is still plagued by the order of "nature" and biological reasoning reflected in Aquinas's application of natural law to *some* sexual ethical issues, the approach to human sexuality of neoscholastic manuals of moral theology, and contemporary magisterial sexual teaching. A personalist approach to natural law first asks questions about the *meaning* of sexual acts for human relationships before asking the biological question of genitalia or the spatial question of where orgasm takes place. Positing an intrinsic meaning to sexual acts on the foundational basis of physically functioning genitalia and the location of (male) orgasm prioritizes the physical and biological over the personal and relational.

The naturalistic fallacy. A second concern with NNLT's sexual anthropology that prioritizes the biological over the relational is that it seems to commit the naturalistic fallacy; it makes moral judgments based on factual claims. Finnis recognizes this concern in his defense of marital acts of a reproductive kind—including temporarily or permanently sterile reproductive acts, as the only natural, reasonable, and moral sexual acts—and he addresses the question of whether the position seeks to "make moral judgments based on natural facts." His response is yes and no: "No, in the sense that it does not seek to infer normative conclusions or theses from non-normative (natural-fact) premises. Nor does it appeal to any norm of the form 'Respect natural facts or natural functions'. But yes, it does apply the relevant practical reasons (especially that marriage and inner integrity are basic human goods) and moral principles . . . to the realities of our constitution, intentions, and circumstances."[79] We take issue with both Finnis's "no" and "yes" responses to whether or not NNLT commits the naturalistic fallacy with regard to anthropology and intentionality.

Finnis's "no" to whether or not NNLT commits the naturalistic fallacy claims too much. It seems that NNLT does commit the naturalistic fallacy. The fallacy is evident in its anthropology and principle of "organic complementarity," which claims that only acts of a reproductive kind are "biologically *and thus* personally one."[80] The natural fact of physically functioning male and female genitals and spatially located ejaculation allows NNLT to infer normative conclusions that only acts of a reproductive kind between a married couple are natural, reasonable and moral. Finnis's claim that NNLT "does not seek to infer normative conclusions or theses from non-normative (natural-fact) premises" seems inaccurate in terms of its own sexual anthropology.

Finnis's "yes" that NNLT "does apply the relevant practical reasons (especially that marriage and inner integrity are basic human goods) and moral principles . . . to our constitution, intentions, and circumstances" claims too little. The application of practical reasons and moral principles to our constitution is inadequate because NNLT's definition of "our constitution" is incomplete. NNLT posits inner integrity or self-integration as a basic good. It defines self-integration as "harmony among all the parts of a person which can be engaged in freely chosen action."[81] Self-integration is an important psychosocial dimension of the human person, and therefore of the sexual human person. To be truly human, and therefore reasonable and moral, a sexual act must be integrated with the whole self, biologically, personally, relationally, psychologically, emotionally, and spiritually. An essential part of the human person and of his or her constitution, and therefore an essential part of self-integration, a part that NNLT does not integrate into its sexual anthropology, is sexual orientation.

Sexual orientation. The meaning of the phrase "sexual orientation" is complex and not universally agreed upon.[82] NNLT provides this incomplete and tendentious definition: "The stable disposition of an adult toward sexually arousing and gratifying bodily contact with persons of the same sex."[83] This definition is incomplete because it totally ignores heterosexual orientation; it is tendentious because it focuses exclusively on the biological ("arousing") and physically pleasurable ("gratifying") dimensions of homosexual orientation, and it totally ignores the emotional and relational dimensions. The Magisterium offers a more complete definition of sexual orientation. It distinguishes between "a homosexual 'tendency,' which proves to be 'transitory,' and 'homosexuals who are *definitively* such because of some kind of innate instinct.'" It goes on to declare that "it seems appropriate to understand sexual orientation [heterosexual or homosexual] as a *deep-seated* dimension of one's personality and to recognize its *relative stability* in a person. A homosexual orientation produces a stronger emotional and sexual attraction toward individuals of the same sex, rather than toward those of the opposite sex."[84] We offer this definition of sexual orientation: a "psychosexual attraction (erotic, emotional, and affective) toward particular individual *persons*" of either the same-sex or the opposite sex, depending on whether the orientation is homosexual or heterosexual.[85]

Concerning the genesis of homosexual and heterosexual orientations, the scientific community generally agrees there is no single isolated cause.[86] The experts point to a variety of genetic, hormonal, psychological, and social "*loading*" factors, from which the orientation may derive.[87] There is growing agreement also in the scientific community that sexual orientation, heterosexual or homosexual, is an innate condition over which the person has no control and that she or he cannot change without psychosexual damage.[88] In addition, because homosexual orientation is experienced as a given and not as something freely chosen, it cannot be considered unnatural, unreasonable, and therefore immoral, for morality presumes the freedom to choose. Where ethical (and legal) theorists disagree is on the morality and reasonableness of homosexual acts.

Heterogenital and personal complementarity. NNLT theorists condemn homosexual acts as immoral because they violate both heterogenital and reproductive complementarity and, *because of this violation,*[89] they also violate the friendship or unitive meaning of the sexual act, what we refer to as personal complementarity.[90] Heterogenital complementarity, where the male penis penetrates the female vagina in an act of a reproductive kind, is established as *the* litmus test for determining whether or not a sexual act can fulfill personal complementarity, and thus be natural, reason-able, and therefore moral. There is no doubt that reasonable and moral sexual acts necessarily include personal complementarity but, for NNLT, personal complemen-tarity is not sufficient for a reasonable and moral sexual act. Heterogenital comple-mentarity is the necessary, foundational, sine qua non condition for what defines a reasonable and moral sexual act. Because homosexual acts clearly lack heterogenital complementarity as defined, they can never be reasonable and moral. All this would be true *if* NNLT had sufficiently grounded its definition of heterogenital comple-mentarity and defended its claims about the unreasonable and immoral nature of homosexual acts.

Although it consistently condemns homosexual acts on the grounds that they violate heterogenital and reproductive complementarity, NNLT does not explain why they also violate personal complementarity, other than to assert that homosex-ual acts between gay or lesbians, "since their reproductive organs cannot make them a biological (and therefore personal unit)," cannot fulfill what those couples "hope and imagine."[91] This statement, however, begs the question of whether or not homosexual acts can ever be natural, reasonable, and therefore moral on the level of personal complementarity. Though NNLT has made no effort to confront this ques-tion on the basis of the lived experiences of monogamous, loving, committed, homosexual couples,[92] these couples have confronted it experientially and they tell us that they do experience personal complementarity in and through homosexual acts. They add that these acts also facilitate the integration of their human sexuality, thereby realizing the basic good of self-integration.

Acknowledging that the question of same-sex relations remains in dispute, Mar-garet Farley notes this homosexual experience and comments that we "have some clear and profound testimonies to the life-enhancing possibilities of same-sex rela-tions and the integrating possibilities of sexual activity within these relations. We have the witness that homosexuality can be a way of embodying responsible love and sustaining human friendship." She concludes, logically, that "this witness alone is enough to demand of the Christian [and social] community that it reflect anew on the norms [and laws] for homosexual love."[93] Her judgment is in line with Courtney Murray's principle that practical, as distinct from theoretical, intelligence is preserved from ideology by having "a close relation to concrete experience."[94] The NNLT position with respect to the potential self-integration of gay and lesbian couples through sexual acts is very much theoretical intelligence divorced from prac-tical experience; ideology posing as practical intelligence; biological reasoning posing as normative reasoning.

Orientation complementarity. The relationship between biological and personal complementarity is not either/or but both/and. Natural, reasonable, and moral sex-ual acts require human genitals. In couples of heterosexual orientation, personal complementarity is manifested, nurtured, and strengthened through the just and loving use of their genitals; they use their genitals to "make love" or actualize friend-ship. In couples of homosexual orientation, personal complementarity is equally manifested, nurtured, and strengthened through the just and loving use of their genitals; they also use their genitals to make love or actualize friendship. Sexual orientation complementarity—that innate personal dimension directing a person's sexual desires and energies and drawing him or her into deeper and more sexually intimate male–male, female–female, or male–female relationships, depending on whether the orientation is homosexual, bisexual or heterosexual—fully integrates genital and personal complementarity. If one takes heterogenital complementarity as the *primary* principle for a natural, reasonable, and moral sexual act, one defines a person's potential for reasonable and moral sexual acts in terms of a single, physical dimension: the genitals. This monodimensional, truncated anthropology does not acknowledge the complexity of the human sexual person's constitution and refuses to acknowledge that the person is much more than his or her genitals. Our principle of sexual orientation complementarity embraces the entirety and complexity of the human person, and it understands genital complementarity to be in dialogue with and at the service of personal and orientation complementarity.

Natural, reasonable, and moral sexual acts can be defined only in the context of this complex orientation, this personal and genital interrelationship. Because it would be an unnatural, unreasonable, and immoral sexual act for a heterosexual person to engage in sexual acts with a person of the same sex, so also it would be an unnatural, unreasonable, and immoral sexual act for a homosexual person to engage in sexual acts with a person of the opposite sex. It would be unnatural, unreasonable, and immoral not because of the presence or absence of functioning genitals, which are by "nature" the same in all humans irrespective of their sexual orientation, but because of the individual's sexual orientation, integral sexuality, and personhood. Recognizing, embracing, and internalizing his or her sexuality facilitates a deeper realization and integration of self in relation to that other with whom he or she enters into intimate sexual acts. If we shift the sine qua non requirement for a natural, reasonable, and moral sexual act from heterogenital complementarity to a more real, experiential, and integrated orientation—personal and genital complementarity—the principle for what constitutes a natural, reasonable, and therefore moral sexual act can be formulated as follows.

We define a natural, reasonable, and moral sexual act as a just and loving act in accord with a person's innate sexual orientation that facilitates a deeper appreciation, integration, and sharing of a person's embodied self with another embodied self. Biological-genital complementarity is always a dimension of the natural, reasonable, and moral sexual act, and reproductive complementarity may be a dimension of it in the case of fertile, heterosexual couples who choose to reproduce. Reproductive complementarity will not be a possibility in the case of homosexual couples, but genital complementarity—understood in an orientation, personal, and integrated sense, and not just in a biological, physical sense—will be. This personalist interpretation of genital complementarity, which sees the physical genitals as organs of the whole person, including his or her sexual orientation, allows us to expand the definition of a natural, reasonable, and therefore moral sexual act to include both homosexual and heterosexual nonreproductive sexual acts. The foundation for this definition and its moral evaluation rest not on heterogenital complementarity but on the integrated relationship between orientation, genital, and personal complementarity. Given this complex dialogical relationship, it remains to ask whether or not a particular sexual act facilitates or frustrates the partners' human flourishing, their becoming more affectively and interpersonally human. We agree with Stephen Pope that "interpersonal love is here the locus of human flourishing."[95]

In summary, to posit organic complementarity between biological male and female human persons as the primary, foundational, sine qua non principle for marital acts and to define natural, reasonable, and moral sexual acts in terms of this complementarity seems to commit the naturalistic fallacy. In addition, Finnis's claim that NNLT "does apply the relevant practical reasons (especially that marriage and inner integrity are basic human goods) and moral principles . . . to the realities of our constitution" derives from an incomplete consideration of human constitution and is, therefore, not an application of all relevant practical reasons. Its incompleteness is grounded in a truncated and insufficient anthropology that prioritizes the biological and physical over the personal and relational, and its failure to recognize and integrate sexual orientation as a "natural" component of the human person. If the human constitution one is working with is incomplete, then the application of practical reasons and moral principles to that constitution is also incomplete. A personalist sexual anthropology must move beyond the physical and biological as foundational anthropological dimensions and explore the entire constitution of sexual human beings. Sexual orientation, and its implications for natural, reasonable, and moral sexual acts, is an essential dimension of both this exploration and the sexual human person.

Intentionality. NNLT also has an incomplete and classicist view of intentionality reflected in its anthropology. NNLT's sexual anthropology posits an intrinsic correlation between intentionality and the moral object of choice that is different from a historically conscious understanding of intentionality grounded in human experience. If a person chooses to perform a particular act, then NNLT posits an intrinsic intentionality to the particular object of choice, regardless of that person's *actual* intention. Regardless of a couple's actual intention for practicing artificial contraception, for example, the mere fact that they choose artificial contraception reflects, ipso facto, a contralife intention or will.[96] Similarly, regardless of a couple's actual intention for utilizing artificial reproductive technologies, the mere fact that they choose to utilize these technologies "is to will the baby's initial status as a product."[97] Positing such a correlation between the object of choice and a predetermined will or intention is a classicist approach to intention and the moral object. It does not recognize the unfolding meaning of an aspect of a basic good that can be realized in a variety of ways and the complexity of intentionality in relation to the object of choice. It posits a static, absolutist correlation between the object of choice and intentionality, which does not necessarily represent the intentionality of a couple in a particular historical, cultural, and contextual relationship; their reasons for choosing certain acts associated with human sexuality; and the *actual* intention behind their choices.

It is remarkable that NNLT would posit a definitive correlation between intentionality and the object of choice associated with the sexual acts mentioned and posit no inherent intentionality of the act of killing another human being. The intention to kill can be malevolent, in which case the killing is murder; or it can be to defend oneself, in which case the killing is self-defense and morally acceptable.[98] If there is not an inherent intentionality in the object of the choice to kill, it seems remarkable that NNLT would posit an inherent contralife intentionality in the choice to practice artificial birth control. We argue that the intentionality of human acts that do not have an inherent intentionality in the very term itself (killing vs. murder or artificial birth control vs. a contralife mentality) must be determined not a priori but a posteriori on the basis of the *actual* intentionality of a couple in their particular historical, cultural, relational, and socioeconomic context. It is logical and possible that both the intention to choose natural family planning (NFP) and the intention to choose artificial birth control reflect a contralife intention or an intention to practice responsible parenthood. There is not an inherent intentionality for the moral object of birth control, whether the form of control is NFP or artificial contraception. If the couple chooses to practice artificial contraception with a contralife intention or will (a contraceptive mentality), *then* that choice is intrinsically wrong. Intentionality, however, cannot be determined a priori; it can only be determined in the concrete lived relationship of two human beings.

NNLT posits what we designate a biologically grounded intentionality in the willing subject. This intentionality is evident in their moral distinction between NFP, periodic abstinence to avoid pregnancy, and artificial contraception. According to NNLT, when NFP is not used with a contralife will, it is morally distinct from artificial birth control.[99] When NFP is chosen responsibly, the couple abstains during fertile periods to avoid pregnancy, but their intention to abstain during these times does not preclude intercourse during infertile periods. In choosing to have intercourse during infertile periods, "their intention to do so plainly cannot be to impede the beginning of a new life, since the infertility is due to *natural conditions*, not to their marital intercourse."[100] Similarly, in the case of either temporarily or permanently sterile couples, the choice to engage in sexual intercourse "cannot involve a contralife will; thinking they are sterile, they cannot choose to do anything whatsoever to impede what they believe to be impossible—the coming to be of a possible person—and so they cannot choose to engage in intercourse with that intent."[101] In the cases of sexual intercourse between a couple practicing noncontraceptive NFP and a couple that is sterile, the reality that procreation is believed to be impossible in both cases precludes the possibility of a contralife will.

There are several concerns with this reasoning. First, as indicated above, NNLT seems to infer normative conclusions from nonnormative or natural fact premises. As Grisez states, the intention of a couple avoiding conception by periodic abstinence "plainly cannot be to impede the beginning of a new life, since the infertility is due to *natural conditions*, not to their marital intercourse."[102] The natural condition of infertility precludes a contraceptive intent. Surely, however, this does not logically follow. Consider the people in a couple who have practiced artificial birth control or NFP for their entire relationship with a contralife intent. When the woman reaches menopause and fertility is biologically impossible, the people in the couple continue to have sexual intercourse, but the fact that it is now impossible for them to procreate does not change the contralife intent. They can, and probably do, still have a contralife intent; they realize, however, that the infertility they ensured previously through either artificial or natural means is now provided by nature. This scenario is all the more compelling in NNLT, for it recognizes that a virtuous (or vicious) moral character is shaped by repeated choices.[103] The biological fact that a woman reaches menopause does not change a lifelong contralife intentionality to one that is virtuous or even morally neutral; nor is this intentionality determined by biological laws. There is no necessary logical correlation between what is biologically possible and intentionality unless one makes what is biologically possible a foundational determinant for what is possible in the realm of intentionality. One cannot deduce an intentional *ought* from a biological *is*, even when it suits one's ethical goals or agenda.

Second, notwithstanding the naturalistic fallacy, NNLT may respond to our concern about intentionality in relation to NFP and contraception in the following way. The couple that practices noncontraceptive NFP and abstains from sexual intercourse during fertile periods could not reasonably intend contralife sexual intercourse during infertile periods because fertility is reasonably believed to be a logical impossibility. Similarly, the infertile couple could not have a contralife intention when engaging in sexual intercourse because fertility is reasonably believed to be a logical impossibility. Following Aquinas, NNLT asserts that "the acts constituted by intentions are either good or evil by their conformity or lack of conformity to right reason, that is, to practical reason, unfettered by non-rational factors."[104] Those nonrational factors that may be significant but are "not morally determinative" include feelings, emotions, wishes, hopes, dreams, and so on.[105] For NNLT, intentionality as it pertains to choice is a purely rational endeavor. So, even though a couple that is by definition infertile, whether through the natural rhythm cycle or through sterility, may not desire to have a child, this desire is not morally determinative. The biological possibility of whether or not a woman is capable of becoming pregnant shapes the intentionality of a couple having sexual intercourse that practices NFP in a morally determinative way.

There are four concerns with this line of reasoning. First, it too narrowly defines the rationality and nonrationality of intentionality. Aristotle, Aquinas, magisterial teaching,[106] and modern psychology recognize the affective dimensions, desires, emotions, and passions of intentionality that must be factored into one's sexual and moral anthropology.[107] Second, it reflects a classicist approach to ethical theory, which attempts to draw a univocal correlation between intentions and acts that does not reflect a contemporary understanding of the human person and the complexity of that person, intentionality, and human acts.[108] Third, it raises the question of how a couple practicing noncontraceptive NFP engaging in sexual intercourse or an infertile couple engaging in sexual intercourse is actually open to the procreative meaning of the sexual act when the couple knows that fertility is a biological and logical impossibility.

Fourth, NNLT seems to posit a classicist view of the interrelationship between intentionality and the object of choice in its arguments against contraception and reproductive technologies. From a classicist perspective, one can posit a static and unchanging univocal correlation between intentionality and the object of moral choice. From a historically conscious perspective, which recognizes the complexity of intentionality and the lived relational experience between married couples, no such correlation exists. One could reasonably argue that, if a couple has a contraceptive mentality, then artificial contraception is morally wrong or, if a couple wills a child as a product, then artificial reproductive technologies are wrong. However, one cannot impose intentionality onto these realities a priori, without taking into consideration the actual relationship of a couple considering using artificial birth control or reproductive technologies. To do so is anthropologically classicist and methodologically deductive, and does not serve well sexual anthropology or ethical methodology.

From the critiques of NNLT's anthropology and intentionality developed above, in relation to Finnis's claim that NNLT applies "the relevant practical reasons (especially that marriage and inner integrity are basic human goods) and moral principles . . . to the realities of our constitution, intentions, and circumstances," it seems that the opposite is the case.[109] That is, NNLT does not apply practical reasons and moral principles to human constitution, intention, and circumstances; rather, human constitution, defined biologically, heterogenitally, and therefore reductively, is applied to, and in fact defines, practical reasons, moral principles, and indeed human intentionality on certain sexual issues. Through the marital sexual act, therefore, we are "biologically *and thus* personally one."[110] In addition, a permanently or temporarily sterile couple cannot engage in sexual intercourse during infertile times with a contralife intent. As we have demonstrated, however, neither conclusion logically follows unless, of course, one's ethical theory is grounded in biological determinations.[111]

An act-centered anthropology. Finally, NNLT sexual anthropology is act centered, tending to focus on the moral impact of individual acts on the formation of a person's moral character without looking at the total and evolving meaning of those acts for the person and his or her relationships. An act-centered sexual ethic emphasizes a classicist worldview of single, isolated acts that define the moral character of a person or couple, rather than a historically conscious worldview that recognizes the evolving nature of human beings and how individual acts shape this evolving nature in multifaceted ways. In other words, there is no univocal correlation between a single act and the moral character of a human being. The moral life is, as human experience clearly shows, an evolving process and unfolds in a series of acts that define the moral character of the human person.

Classicism and Historical Consciousness

What unites the anthropological dimensions of NNLT—the biological meaning over the personal-relational meaning in the sexual act, the view of intentionality, and its act-centered emphasis—is the prioritization of a classicist worldview over a historically conscious worldview. Classicist consciousness sees culture, knowledge, and human understanding as established realities. There is but one culture, one objective knowledge, and one possible understanding. Historical consciousness sees culture, knowledge, and human understanding as unfolding realities within the dialectic of sociohistorical experience, relationships, spirituality, and psychology. It is only through the prioritization of classicism that NNLT can posit biological or organic complementarity as the foundation for its sexual anthropology in light of the Magisterium[112] and contemporary sciences' understanding of the complexity of human sexuality, which involves the biological as well as the psychological, emotional, relational, and spiritual dimensions of the human person. From a historically conscious perspective, the biological is integrated into a holistic understanding of human sexuality and its multiple facets.

Basic Goods

Another set of questions for NNLT anthropology concerns the basic goods, their division into aspects, and how these aspects relate to one another. First, regarding the authentic development of aspects of basic goods and their particularity in light of historical consciousness, how are the basic goods divided into "aspects"? What constitutes an aspect of a basic good that is open to further understanding and an aspect of a basic good that is not? Why is it that an aspect of the basic good of justice and its unfolding that allowed slavery but now forbids it is an authentic development,[113] whereas the aspect of the basic good of life that prohibits contraception is not open to authentic development? This question is all the more pressing because there is substantial evidence indicating a direct correlation between higher birthrates and increased poverty leading to disease and death among developing-world populations.[114] These populations are least able to provide adequate nutrition, care, and basic needs for children born into poverty as a result of failed "natural" attempts to regulate reproduction. Hence, it could be argued that not using artificial birth control in the case of abject poverty is irresponsible and reflects a contralife intention. More than 20,000 people die every day due to extreme poverty.[115] It would seem, then, that in many cases artificial contraception would actualize and realize the good of life, not directly attack it, as NNLT maintains.

Second, if the development of one aspect of a basic good and the norm deduced from it have repercussions on another basic good, how can one determine whether or not the norm violates another aspect of the second basic good unless there is some basis for comparison between the basic goods and/or their aspects? The question is all the more perplexing because the basic goods are incommensurable, according to

NNLT.[116] It seems that integral human fulfillment, which "moderates the interplay" of reasons for acting that the basic goods provide,[117] requires criteria for establishing the precise "interplay" of the basic goods. Though NNLT's modes of responsibility ostensibly provide these criteria,[118] there seems to be a more fundamental criterion when it comes to specific absolute sexual norms deduced from the basic goods. From NNLT's perspective, the Magisterium is the definitive judge of whether or not an aspect of a basic good and the norm deduced from it can be revised.[119] This criterion is grounded in authority, however, and not necessarily in the particularity and existential reality of basic goods and how we come to discern their significance for human fulfillment through historical consciousness.

Third, the existential nature of the basic goods is subject to critique as well. NNLT has a narrow definition and interpretation of human experience in relation to the basic goods. It argues, for instance, that, in addition to violating the good of life, artificial birth control also attacks the basic good of marriage by severing the unitive and procreative meanings of the marital act. Thus, Grisez asserts that "by carrying out an intention to impede procreation, spouses who contracept *mutilate* their sexual intercourse so that it is not truly marital."[120] Does this statement accurately reflect the relational experiences of all married couples who practice some form of artificial birth control? Is it morally credible to assert that all couples who practice some form of artificial birth control are, ipso facto, not truly engaging in meaningful, loving, responsible, and committed marital acts? Could it be that marital stress associated with practicing NFP could damage the unitive dimension of the marital relationship and the marital act, and thus require the use of artificial contraception? As the only morally licit form of birth control in magisterial teaching, NFP presumes a fundamental relational equality between husband and wife. There are, however, very few cultures in the world that actually recognize gender equality; by far the vast majority of them are patriarchal.[121] In these cultures, the male dominates the marital relationship and often usurps the moral decision making within that relationship. This disparity between gender relations inhibits the relational equality envisioned by the proponents of NFP. To teach NFP as the only morally licit option for regulating reproduction in light of the lived experiences of the vast majority of married couples throughout the world is a classicist approach, and may be oppressive for women. All theology must be in dialogue with human experience. Theology that is not in dialogue with that experience is ideology masking itself as theology.

Absolute Norms

There seems to be a problematic relationship between the basic goods as fundamental aspects of personhood and absolute norms deduced from those goods. Jean Porter notes what seems to be a disconnect between, on the one hand, claiming that certain goods are self-evident to all persons and yet, on the other hand, providing specific and absolute content to those goods as a basis for practical reflection and moral judgment. For example, NNLT argues that life as a basic good can be expanded to procreation and argues that contraception is contralife. Porter notes, however, that "while a case can be made that the inclination to procreate is indeed an expression of a more fundamental inclination to live and flourish, this conclusion can hardly be said to be self-evidently contained in the apprehension of the goodness of life itself."[122] NNLT posits the basic goods as fundamental aspects of the human person but stretches the epistemological claim for the aspects of the goods that justify certain absolute norms.

Although NNLT claims to grant the full possibilities of authentic development in natural law,[123] it fails to do so. In relation to sexual anthropology *and* the formulation of specific absolute norms, NNLT focuses on the classicist and static nature of basic goods; the aspects of the good, and the norms deduced from them, are already defined. Though this emphasis on the goods' universality would certainly justify some absolute norms (e.g., the norms prohibiting rape and adultery), it is by no means clear that it justifies all the absolute norms that NNLT seeks to defend. This is especially the case regarding absolute sexual norms such as artificial reproduction, artificial contraception, masturbation for seminal analysis, and homosexual acts. The claim for absolute specific norms founded on the basic goods betrays the commitment to open-endedness in their fulfillment. In other words, though the claim to universal and unchanging natural law principles could certainly be justified based on NNLT's perception of human "nature," it is not self-evident that it would also justify all the specific, absolute sexual norms. In fact, the specific absolute sexual norms defended by NNLT rule out, by definition, the historical consciousness that it claims for the open-endedness and the ability to participate in the basic goods in multiple ways. To defend its position regarding absolute specific norms, NNLT necessarily focuses on the classicist understanding of human "nature," basic goods, and intentionality, and it slights the historically conscious and evolving understanding of these realities.

NNLT: Conclusion

On the basis of a reductive, underdeveloped and biologically centered sexual anthropology, a lack of clarity on the nature of the goods and their aspects, and how these goods serve as a foundation for absolute norms, NNLT is less than credible in its attempt to justify absolute sexual norms. Insights into human sexuality based on biological, relational, and spiritual dimensions, as well as the lived experiences of married couples, must be incorporated into both ethical discourse and the discernment of the unfolding understanding of the basic goods and the formulation of the norms guiding human sexual behavior. NNLT's a priori generalizations about goods, intentions, and acts betray a classicist worldview where an act has an intrinsic meaning regardless of the relational meaning of that act for human beings. Many relational, cultural, and even biological considerations challenge NNLT's interpretation of marriage as a basic good and the absolute sexual norms it deduces from that good. From a historically conscious perspective, these considerations both have an impact on and reflect the dynamic nature of the goods. Historical consciousness allows for the basic goods' development and realization reflected in more general norms—for example, responsible parenthood understood as applying to the marital and familial relationship in its entirety, and not just to each and every marital sexual act. From a classicist perspective, however, no such development is possible. By selecting, interpreting, and prioritizing certain sources of moral knowledge over others, NNLT is not attuned to the lived experiences of married couples. It defines the basic good of marriage from a closed, classicist perspective.

A strength of NNLT and its sexual anthropology is that because it recognizes the intrinsic interrelationship between the biological and personal in its sexual anthropology, it cannot be accused of biologism in the traditional natural law sense. The weakness of this argument is that the normative conclusions it does draw from its sexual anthropology are grounded in a prioritization of a biological understanding of human "nature" and basic goods over a relational and personal understanding. In addition, Porter notes that " 'pure reason' is no more promising than 'pure nature' as a basis for a theory of morality."[124] In other words, basic goods, which provide reasons for choices in NNLT, are more like generic goods or "Platonic ideas,"[125] detached from concrete reality, human persons, and interpersonal relationships. These goods are suspended from many of the contingencies and complexities that confront the human person in relationships, which require "ordering, comparative judgments, and preferential choices," which "are integral aspects of practical reasoning as we experience it."[126] Though NNLT focuses on basic goods as reasons for choices to illumine human "nature" and to justify absolute norms, another traditionalist natural law theory focuses on the interrelationship between goods, acts, and virtues to define the human person and to justify these norms.

Martin Rhonheimer

NNLT defines human "nature" in terms of the basic goods, and from these goods deduces absolute norms[127] prohibiting any nonmarital sexual acts. Rhonheimer's interpretation of natural law emphasizes the role and function of virtue to justify those same absolutes. Rhonheimer admits his indebtedness to Grisez and Finnis and accepts many of the basic tenets of NNLT developed in the preceding section.[128] His unique contribution is to develop an "intimate connection" between moral virtues and the precepts of the natural law.[129] His "integral/personal anthropology" is grounded in moral virtue.[130]

Rhonheimer develops the foundation for this interpretation of natural law and anthropology in his influential work *Natural Law and Practical Reason: A Thomistic View of Moral Autonomy*. In this work, he seeks to provide an alternative reading of Aquinas's theory of natural law that critiques, and diverges from, two predominant interpretations. The first interpretation derives from the neoscholastic natural law tradition that grounds natural law in the order of nature. The natural order contains intrinsic moral meaning, which practical reason merely reads to determine moral action. The legacy of this interpretation is all too familiar to Catholic moral theologians of all ideological persuasions in terms of its inherent biologism, physicalism, and essentialism. The second interpretation developed in reaction to neoscholasticism and is known as "autonomous morality." This natural law moral theory, developed largely through the works of Alfons Auer, Franz Böckle, Josef Fuchs, Bruno Schüller, and the like, reduces natural law to "an imperative to act reasonably and responsibly" and is summed up in a proportionalist calculation of premoral values and disvalues.[131] Rhonheimer judges that both these interpretations of natural law suffer from the "dualistic fallacy," a fundamental separation between the objective, nature, and the subjective, reason.[132] In the neoscholastic interpretation, nature is the moral order that imprints itself on the subject, "written in the heart." In the autonomous morality interpretation, "reason is *completely* divided from nature."[133] Though Rhonheimer supports an autonomous morality, the autonomy he proposes overcomes the dualistic fallacy by developing a "personal structure of practical reason" that integrates nature and reason.[134] This view of practical reason shapes his personal anthropology and extends to human sexuality.

Person as Autonomous-Virtuous Agent

The basic tenets of Rhonheimer's personal anthropology are the following. First, the human person is a "corporeal-spiritual unity."[135] There is no dualism between body and spirit; and the neoscholastic interpretations of Aquinas's natural law theory warrant the accusation of physicalism or biologism.[136] The person as a corporeal-spiritual unity overcomes this dualism. Rhonheimer recognizes that reason, the subjectivity of the person, is part of the objective "nature" of the human person. The natural law, then, exists in the rational person as knowing subject; in that sense it is "subjective." It is also "objective," in that the inclinations draw us to the good in its various manifestations as part of the eternal law we know in and through reason. The inclination toward the good emerges out of our corporeal-spiritual unity, which practical reason perceives as a reasonable good that must be respected as an aspect of the human person. We know the nature of the person only by first knowing the specifically human good.[137]

The human person possesses "real autonomy," what Rhonheimer calls "participated theonomy," which means that the person "will understand the good known by him not only as a 'good to be done' but also as the will of God."[138] He believes that this autonomy distinguishes his theory from the so-called autonomous ethics school of natural law, which claims that natural law essentially means to act reasonably and responsibly according to the principle of proportionate reason, that is, balancing the premoral values and disvalues of particular acts.[139] In his view, autonomy is grounded in the eternal law known through practical reason that guides specific choices and is intimately linked to the virtues, the central aspect of his theory.

Rhonheimer notes that the key to understanding Aquinas's natural law, one often overlooked by Aquinas scholars, is question 94, article 3, which provides a "conclusive explanation" of the natural law. Article 3 asks "is every act of virtue of natural law"? He summarizes Aquinas's response: "Insofar as any action can have the character (*ratio*) of moral virtue, so all virtuous actions belong to the natural law; for the natural law constitutes, in a universal way, that which makes a virtuous act virtuous."[140] Though the precepts of the natural law direct the human toward the good in specific acts, the moral virtues, "which are essentially a type of *ordinatio rationis*, . . . are the fulfillment of the natural law at the level of concrete acting since they are the *habitus* of choosing what is good for man at a concrete level."[141] This focus on the connection between the precepts of natural law and moral virtues allows Rhonheimer to argue that moral theology, even in its absolute normative prescriptions, is focused more on virtue than on law. Artificial contraception, therefore, is intrinsically wrong and absolutely prohibited, not because it is a violation of a prescriptive norm but because it is a violation of the virtue of chastity. To understand Rhonheimer's natural law theory of the rationally autonomous-virtuous person as it applies to human sexuality, we must first understand his view of human sexuality.

The Sexual Person, Inseparability Principle, and Virtue

Rhonheimer defines the "truth of human sexuality" as married love, "a free, mutual self-giving of indissoluble permanence between two persons of the opposite sex, in the totality of their body-soul existence."[142] At the core of human sexuality is freedom, an autonomy in the "nature" of the human being, to be drawn to the good of marriage. The truth of human sexuality is necessarily between male and female, without body/soul dualism, and this truth is dependent not on physical or natural functions but on the personal function of autonomous human beings in relation to one another. Rhonheimer argues that sexual acts that stand outside this truth contradict it and are objectively immoral, not because they are unnatural "but because they contradict the (practical) truth of the natural, as it appears on the horizon of apprehension and regulation by the reason."[143] In this way, he is consistent in arguing that we know human "nature" by the inclination toward the goods through practical reason. Humans are inclined toward the good of married love, and this inclination reveals the true "nature" of human beings and the truth of human sexuality. This objective truth is specified by the inseparability principle and is affirmed by chastity, the virtue of human sexuality.

Like NNLT, Rhonheimer accepts the inseparability principle, the "'object' of the marital act." This principle is the "indispensable anthropological background for any argument against contraception" and, one could reasonably posit, any other type of nonmarital sexual act.[144] Following *Humanae vitae*, he posits that the marital act has two meanings, a unitive meaning (spiritual love) and a procreative meaning, and he distinguishes between "meanings" and "functions" to clarify both his and

Humanae vitae's understandings of the conjugal act. Only fertile sexual acts have a "procreative function"; that is, only such acts are actually capable of procreation. He admits that, in reality, most sexual acts do not have the procreative function. As a meaning, however, procreation is part of the essence, along with spiritual love, of the marital act. If one separates one meaning (procreative) from the other meaning (spiritual love), one destroys the intrinsic meaning of the marital act. The inseparability principle alone, however, because it is a *principle*, does not justify the argument that each and every contraceptive *act* violates the meaning of the marital act. To justify this claim, he employs natural law, specifically the intimate connection between action theory and virtue in natural law.[145]

At the heart of Rhonheimer's natural law theory is the intimate connection between the precepts of natural law and the virtues. In the case of human sexuality and the natural law precepts that guide moral sexual behavior, chastity, defined as "mastery of one's own sexual drives so as to integrate them into the order of personal love,"[146] is the foundational virtue. Personal, conjugal, or married love arises from desire or sexual inclination. Chastity provides "*habitual* or *virtual* integration of this desire into the order of reason which is the order of human love."[147] Procreative responsibility is part of the virtue of chastity, and it is defined as "the morally upright and virtuous integration of sexual drives into the dominion of reason and will."[148] Acts of procreative responsibility must respect the virtue of chastity and the truth of human sexuality, a truth defined in acts of loving union as the unitive and procreative meanings of every such act. In this way, he establishes the connection in natural law between the virtue of chastity, procreative responsibility as part of the virtue of chastity, the inseparability principle, and marital acts of loving union, which allows the principle to condemn every contraceptive act: "For virtues are shaped by and aim at concrete performances of acts and their corresponding choices, and single acts and their corresponding choices are morally specified by their intentional contents which spring from the virtues to which they belong."[149] On the basis of the truth of human sexuality and the virtue of chastity, then, he condemns as objectively immoral all acts that contradict this truth, including homosexual acts, nonmarital sexual acts, and contraceptive acts.

The Truth of Human Sexuality and Contraception

Rhonheimer notes that, at the foundation of *Humanae vitae*'s teaching, there is a "philosophically relevant perspective" that represents "an important doctrinal development." This philosophical perspective emphasizes "the 'intentionalness of the thing one is doing' by contracepting."[150] This intentionality distinguishes periodic abstinence from contraceptive sexual behavior. In periodic abstinence, the couple intends to respect both the unitive and procreative meanings of the conjugal act. In addition, there are "two different, although closely correlated actions of 'sexual behavior'" included in periodic abstinence:[151] engaging in intercourse and periodic abstinence. Periodic abstinence is a "real conjugal act" that includes the two mean-ings of marital love, procreative and unitive.[152] It is procreative because the reason for practicing periodic abstinence is procreative responsibility—that is, the couple chooses to abstain from possibly fertile intercourse—and in so doing, "spouses relate to sexual acts, to themselves, and to each other as a possible cause of new life."[153] The reason or intentionality why the couple abstains from sexual intercourse is to respect their sexual activity as a cause of new life. Periodic abstinence is unitive because the spouses behave alike; their intentionality is grounded in procreatively responsible continence, which has "a proper *marital* and even *parental* meaning."[154]

Contraceptive intercourse, conversely, "*is not* an expression of *marital* love." It alters the objective meaning of the sexual act by intentionally removing its procre-ative meaning, and because the choice is no longer guided by reason and will, it is a falsification of the marital act. Rhonheimer summarizes: "Insofar as the contracep-tive choice involves intentionally rejecting procreative responsibility for one's sexual behavior, it also involves an anti-procreative volition."[155]

Rhonheimer's Sexual Anthropology: A Critique

Although Rhonheimer's attempt to defend the Magisterium's teaching against the use of artificial birth control and other sexual norms emphasizing the virtue compo-nent of Aquinas's natural law theory is admirable, there are some important ques-tions regarding his theory. His moral distinction between periodic abstinence and contraception reflects underlying questions regarding his sexual anthropology. These sexual, anthropological questions concern the univocal correlation between acts and virtues and the definitions of intentionality in relation to the human act and the procreative act. We consider each question in turn.

Interrelationship between acts and virtues. The first question asks whether one can claim, as Rhonheimer does, a necessary correlation between certain acts (abstaining from sexual intercourse) and certain virtues (chastity)? Aquinas makes a distinction in referring to acts of virtue. In the first case, all acts of virtue are of natural law. In the second case, however, there are acts, which, due to the particularity of individual conditions, may be virtuous to some people because they are right and proper and vicious to others because they are wrong and improper.[156] The distinction between the two sets of acts of virtue raises questions about the univocal correlation between certain acts and certain virtues. Grisez notes that "virtues are not concerned with specific kinds of acts."[157] Though abstaining from sexual intercourse *may* incarnate the virtue of procreative responsibility, it may also, if done with a contraceptive mentality, as Rhonheimer admits,[158] violate the virtue itself. This seems to indicate that there is not a necessary logical or causal correlation between specific virtues and specific acts. Rather, the *intentionality* behind the act indicates its relationship with virtue. If this is the case, then is it not possible to recognize the virtue of procreative responsibility in other types of acts, such as artificial birth control?

Just as it is possible, and logical, that the intentionality of a married couple practicing periodic abstinence can be associated with the vice of a contraceptive mentality,[159] it is also possible, and logical, that the intentionality of a married couple practicing artificial birth control can be associated with the virtue of procreative responsibility. Rhonheimer would respond that, in the case of periodic abstinence, the couple's intention is to respect the procreative meaning and, in the most extreme cases of contraceptive sterilization, the procreative dimension of marital love "is entirely 'off.'"[160] How is it, however, that couples that practice periodic abstinence during the wife's fertile period, couples that are infertile, or couples that have entered menopause, all of which know that procreation is not an option and "is entirely 'off,'" intentionally realize the procreative dimension of sexual intercourse? Rhonheimer asserts that "the intentional relation to naturally given and voluntarily produced sterility is different." Naturally given sterility "does not imply a choice of rendering needless the modification of sexual behavior," whereas voluntarily produced sterility does imply such a choice. It is the intentionality of the choice "which specifies and shapes further actions."[161] Thus, intentionality is an essential link between action-theory and virtue-theory.

Intentionality defined. The second question asks about Rhonheimer's definition of intentionality. In periodic abstinence the intention of the couple is defined as modifying their sexual behavior, which objectively embeds the procreative meaning of sexual intercourse in the chastity-related virtue of procreative responsibility.[162] In the case of artificially contraceptive behavior, however, the intention is both to reject procreative responsibility for one's sexual behavior and to involve an antiprocreative volition.[163] According to this definition, there are two different acts morally speaking, periodic abstinence and contraceptive behavior, because there are two different intentionalities. These could be formulated as follows: first, "abstaining from sexual intercourse to respect the procreative meaning of an act of loving union"; second, "having sexual intercourse while eliminating the procreative meaning of an act of loving union." Yet Rhonheimer admits that in the case of periodic abstinence, there are "two different, although closely correlated actions of 'sexual behavior,' . . . both the performance of engaging in intercourse and the performance of continence."[164] What correlates these actions of sexual behavior if not intentionality?

The intentionality of abstaining from a human act of loving union in periodic abstinence is a partial description of the total intentionality, which embraces the human act of engaging in unitive intercourse, in which the procreative meaning cannot be actualized. It is this fuller description of intentionality and the human act, at least in part, that specifies the object of choice for abstaining from the conjugal act at this particular time.[165] Why does one abstain from the conjugal act at this time? The answer: to engage in the conjugal act at a time when the procreative meaning will not be actualized. The relationship between the two acts is designated by the intention that links them and can define them as an intrinsically related sexual act realized over an extended period of time. The intentionality of periodic abstinence to prevent the actualization of reproduction, in its fuller sense, could be described as "having sexual intercourse while eliminating the procreative meaning of an act of loving union." The intentionality of an act of artificial contraceptive behavior can be described in the same way.

To avoid this logical conclusion of the relationship between intentionality and the human act, Rhonheimer makes the qualification that the two meanings of the sexual act are broken "on the level of single acts of contraceptive intercourse."[166] Such a vision of the human act (and intentionality) reflects a classicist worldview of the human act performed in strictly confined spatial and temporal parameters. A historically conscious view of the human act (and intentionality) recognizes its relational meaning and significance as a progressive reality. Elsewhere, we refer to this relational, progressive, holistic understanding of the human act as the human act adequately considered.[167] The human act adequately considered acknowledges the complexity of the act, including the fact that the intentionality of one act can carry over and define another act directly and intrinsically related to it. An act-description can encompass a variety of different types of acts. Interestingly, Rhonheimer allows for a historically conscious and holistic interpretation of the human act *in certain act-descriptions*.

Procreative act defined. A third question asks whether Rhonheimer expands the definition of the conjugal act in some situations and narrows it in others, depending on the point he is arguing. For example, he asserts that the conjugal act includes sexual intercourse, cooperating in parenting, and abstaining from sexual intercourse.[168] Periodic abstinence is a conjugal act that includes *both* its unitive and procreative meanings. Periodic abstinence has "a fully procreative meaning" because "it actually is, by its very intentional content and thus objectively, an act of procreative responsibility."[169] This claim for a broad definition of the conjugal act warrants comment.

For *Humanae vitae*, it is evident that the unitive and procreative meanings of the conjugal act are narrowly defined.[170] In the words of NNLT, these acts are acts of a reproductive kind and periodic abstinence does not constitute such an act. There is, however, an important insight in asserting that conjugal acts are diverse, and periodic abstinence as well as other acts within a marital relationship can be conjugal acts. If we espouse such a broad definition, however, it is unclear why the use of *some* artificial reproductive technologies would be morally prohibited. Certainly *some* such acts are conjugal acts and they include the procreative meaning of the sexual act. Because Rhonheimer denies that artificial reproductive technologies are morally acceptable, then is not his expanded definition of procreation merely eliding that meaning into the unitive meaning of the conjugal act? In other words, if the procreative meaning of the act of sexual intercourse does not have some *intrinsic* relationship to procreation as reproduction, then it is not clear what distinguishes it from the unitive meaning of the marital act. If there is no difference between the procreative meaning of the act of sexual intercourse broadly defined and the unitive meaning, there seems to be no clear moral distinction between periodic abstinence and artificial contraception. Rhonheimer notes that "the conjugal act is perfectly licit even if it is performed *only* for the reason of expressing mutual love."[171] Follow-ing the Catholic tradition's teaching on the ends of *marriage*,[172] rather than the meanings of the *conjugal act*, it is this broad definition of procreation in the marital relationship as a whole, rather than each and every marital act, that allows revision-ists to argue for the use of artificial birth control to help regulate fertility. If, how-ever, the intentionality of periodic abstinence is to not procreate, why cannot artificial contraception, which has the same intentionality, be considered a marital act as well?

To answer this question, Rhonheimer narrows the definition of the conjugal act. Unlike periodic abstinence, which is a conjugal act, artificial contraception as "an act of preventing sexual behavior from possibly procreative consequences is not in itself a *sexual act*; it is exclusively a 'method' which only *relates to* sexual acts by preventing their procreative consequences."[173] There are two points to address in this statement: the definition of a sexual act, and how artificial contraception relates to sexual acts.

Is it accurate to claim that contraception is not in itself a sexual act, given the broader definition of the conjugal act stated above? Grisez argues similarly that "a contraceptive act is distinct from any sexual act."[174] He does so on two accounts. First, one can practice contraception independently of a sexual act. For example, a man might be sterilized and yet not find a person with whom to engage in sexual intercourse. Second, a couple considering fornication has two choices to make: whether or not to fornicate and/or contracept. The contraceptive act does not entail the sexual act in either scenario.[175] Vacek challenges Grisez's claim that contracep-tion is a single act and not part of a sexual act. In the first case, the person sterilized intends the sterilization to be part of his or her sex life; otherwise, the sterilization would be simple self-mutilation. Because intention, *in certain act-descriptions*, is decisive for Grisez (and Rhonheimer) in determining what an agent does, the inten-tion to sterilize is necessarily part of one's sexual life. Applying the logic of the second scenario to the case of sex between spouses, one might be forced to conclude that sex in this case is not a marital act. This is so because some people have inter-course outside the marital relationship and others make two distinct choices in choosing to be married and choosing to make love.[176] It does not necessarily follow that contraception is not a sexual act or, at least, part of a sexual act. If it is the case that artificial contraception can be a sexual act or part of a sexual act, we must ask the further question of how this act relates to sexual acts.

We may ask whether it is the case, as Rhonheimer claims, that artificial contra-ception "only *relates to* sexual acts by preventing their procreative consequences." This statement is certainly biologically correct. Artificial contraception does prevent procreative consequences when a couple chooses to engage in sexual intercourse, just as periodic abstinence during fertile periods prevents procreative consequences when a couple chooses to engage in sexual intercourse. The real question, however, is whether or not Rhonheimer's statement is logically or morally correct. Can artifi-cial contraception be defined only in relation to the sexual act in this way, without remainder? There is no logical or moral necessity that requires such a definition; there is only a biological necessity. Rhonheimer must strip artificial contraception of its moral relationship to responsible parenthood and limit it to a biological description. Just as periodic abstinence entails a broader description of the conjugal act and a broader intentionality, artificial contraception can also entail a broader description of the conjugal act and a broader intentionality. Both methods of regulating conception can be "performed for reasons of procreative responsibility."[177] The premise that allows Rhonheimer to make such a correlation is to posit an essential intentionality and act-description between contraceptive behavior and the biological structure of the conjugal act. Having recourse to virtue theory to justify this correlation is insufficient as well.

Virtue, classicism, and conjugal acts. Rhonheimer posits a classicist view of virtue and its correlation to conjugal acts on three accounts. First, he emphasizes an intrinsic correlation between certain sexual acts and responsible parenthood as part of the virtue of chastity. It has long been acknowledged in reading Aquinas, however, that discussing the virtues in terms of paradigmatic actions is ambiguous.[178] If this venture is ambiguous, then it seems difficult to establish stable, let alone absolute, norms from the definition of the human good deduced from a sexual anthropology that reflects these paradigmatic act descriptions. Variations in history, culture, gender relationships and marriage, and socioeconomic considerations all warrant against the correlation between periodic abstinence and responsible parenthood as a part of chastity, which Rhonheimer posits. Second, to posit a predetermined moral meaning of the act and its interrelationship with chastity reflects a deductive approach to moral reasoning and the virtues, which discounts the inductive and experiential consideration of the meaning of the act for human relationships. If artificial contraception entails a contraceptive mentality, then it is a violation of chastity as procreative responsibility. This intentionality, however, cannot be deduced from the mere fact that a couple practices artificial contraception.

Third, Rhonheimer's view of virtue is classicist and posits chastity and its parts as the defining virtue of sexual anthropology. There is no doubt that chastity is an important virtue throughout Christian tradition. That history, however, shows an evolution in the understanding of virtues in themselves, and especially in relation to one another. This evolution is apparent in the interrelationship between justice and charity, for example.[179] Aquinas developed Augustine's understanding of the virtues in his use of Aristotle. Augustine argues that all real virtues are informed by charity, and without charity there is no real virtue; Aquinas argues that justice not informed by charity lacks perfection but is still virtue. In addition, Aquinas's view on the cardinal virtues that justice is supported by fortitude and temperance is often challenged by contemporary scholars. Paul Ricoeur argues that the virtues are distinct and even oppose one another at times.[180] The tension between the virtues in human sexuality is apparent in the tension between justice and chastity, for example, when the two cannot both be recognized in a single act. Recognizing a tension between the virtues can elicit responsible forms of behavior that neither of the virtues considered in themselves might elicit. Classicism limits the dialectic between the virtues, whereas historical consciousness recognizes that the virtues "challenge and define one another."[181] It is this ongoing dialectic between the virtues that shifts the focus from act-centered absolute prohibitions of specific sexual acts such as artificial birth control, homosexual acts, and reproductive technologies to a relation-centered, virtue based ethic, which emphasizes being a sexual human person in the world.

Rhonheimer: conclusion. Although Rhonheimer's attempt to develop a comprehensive and comprehensible explanation of the interrelationship between action-theory and virtue ethics to explain and defend Catholic sexual teaching is admirable, his attempt falls short. It falls short due to his claim for the absolute correlation between certain sexual acts and the virtue of chastity, the biological and essentialist underpinnings of his theory in terms of intentionality and the conjugal act, and a classicist anthropology. The sexual human person is not given his or her full due.

One important aspect of Rhonheimer's account of Aquinas's natural law theory, like that of NNLT, is that it serves as an apologetic ethical method for the Magisterium's absolute prohibition of specific sexual acts. As Schockenhoff points out, however, when Aquinas's theory is developed in light of subsequent doctrinal developments, "the open-ended list of *inclinationes naturales* is filled out with a substance corresponding anachronistically to this development—in contradiction of the conscious reserve employed in the original texts themselves."[182] In other words, traditionalist theorists tend to take great liberty in their hermeneutics of Aquinas to justify the absolute norms of the Magisterium. In the case of NNLT, it does so by positing a direct correlation between basic goods and the absolute prohibition of specific sexual acts. In the case of Rhonheimer, he does so by positing a direct correlation between the virtue of chastity and the absolute prohibition of specific sexual acts. We must analyze the arguments on their merits, not only as faithful interpretations of traditional texts but also as incorporating contemporary contributions of theology, philosophy, science, and reflections on human experience into that hermeneutics. Such an incorporation seems to be lacking in the natural law theories of those who defend absolute magisterial teachings on a variety of sexual issues. Though NNLT grounds its sexual anthropology in basic goods and Rhonheimer grounds his in the context of virtue, Pope John Paul II grounds his in the theology of the body.

John Paul II: Thomistic Personalism and the Theology of the Body

Before becoming Pope John Paul II, Karol Wojtyla developed "Thomistic personalism" as an ethical theory, combining, he claimed, Thomism, phenomenology, and scripture. Thomistic personalism recognizes the importance of basic goods and the human person;[183] phenomenology recognizes that these goods have an existential character, which is "bound up with the very existence of the human person;"[184]

scripture provides the theological basis for responsible love guiding all human activity and relationships. Out of this personalism, Wojtyla develops the "personalistic norm," which he relates to the love commandments and formulates both negatively and positively: "This norm, in its negative aspect, states that the person is the kind of good that does not admit of use and cannot be treated as an object of use and as such the means to an end. In its positive form the personalistic norm confirms this: the person is a good towards which the only proper and adequate attitude is love." According to him, the positive formulation is "precisely what the love command teaches."[185] Some defenders of NNLT claim that this personalistic norm is compatible with Grisez's first principle of morality.[186]

John Paul develops personalism in conjunction with scripture to explain his language or theology of the body as the foundation for norms guiding human sexuality.[187] This language, it is claimed, is grounded in the theological anthropology, developed from Genesis, of the communion between man and woman.[188] "This at last is bone of my bones and flesh of my flesh; she shall be called woman, because she was taken out of man" (Gen 3:23). Masculinity and femininity are "two 'incarnations' of the same metaphysical solitude before God and the world." These two ways of "'being a body' . . . complete each other" and are "two complementary ways of being conscious of the meaning of the body."[189] It is through the complementarity of male and female, where a "communion of persons" can exist, that the two "become one flesh."[190]

Complementarity

Though we find the term "complementarity" used in John Paul's earlier writings,[191] and though it has appeared only relatively recently in magisterial sexual teaching, it has become a foundational ethical concept in both John Paul II's theological anthropology and magisterial teaching on human sexuality. Consequently, we will have recourse to both sources in explaining, and critiquing, complementarity, though we will more fully develop the explanation and critique in chapters 4 and 7.

The idea of complementarity, if not the term itself, is used throughout John Paul II's writings and magisterial documents and applies to eschatological,[192] ecclesiological,[193] vocational,[194] and anthropological realities. Basically complementarity intends that certain realities belong together and produce a whole that neither produces alone. Though space does not permit an exploration of how complementarity is applied to all these realities, we can note the following characteristics of its use.

First, complementarity is nearly always classified along masculine and feminine lines, and this classification is used biologically, metaphorically, or in combination of both.[195] Commenting on the complementarity between man and woman and its relation to the "role and dignity of women," Charles Curran notes two reasons, one theoretical and one practical, which ground John Paul's theory of male and female complementarity. The theoretical reason is reflected in his sexual anthropology, which we further explain and critique below, whereby man and woman complement each other in marriage and create a unity of the two. John Paul develops this notion of complementarity theologically, anthropologically, and scripturally, especially in reference to Genesis.[196] Genesis serves as the foundational text for his theology of the body as well. Unfortunately, as Curran notes, because "there are different theologies of the body"—single people, widows and widowers, celibates, and homosexuals—it "cannot serve as a theology for all bodies."[197]

The practical reason supporting male–female complementarity is to defend the absolute prohibition of ordaining women to the priesthood. This focus on complementarity allows John Paul II "to claim to accept the fundamental equality of man and woman and oppose discrimination and marginalization while still maintaining that women cannot be ordained priests."[198] Such a claim is replete with inconsistencies, entails a logical sleight of hand, and need not detain us here.

Second, complementarity is often formulated as a "nuptial hermeneutics" in terms of bridegroom and bride.[199] So, God, Jesus, and husband are masculine and bridegroom; creation, church, and wife are feminine and bride. Third, in his theological anthropology John Paul II posits an "ontological complementarity" whereby men and women, though fundamentally equal and complete in themselves,[200] are incomplete as a couple.[201] Sexual complementarity completes the couple in marriage and sexual acts by bringing the masculine and feminine biological and psychological elements together in a unified whole.

"Natural Complementarity"

All three characteristics of complementarity—male/female, nuptial, and ontological—are evident in John Paul II and the Magisterium's treatment of sexual anthropological complementarity and serve as a foundation to formulate various types of this complementarity with subcategories within each type. First, in *Familiaris consortio*, John Paul II discusses "natural complementarity," lauding what we refer to as biological and personal complementarity that creates "an ever richer union with each other on all levels—of the body, of the character, of the heart, of the intelligence and will, of the soul—revealing in this way to the Church and to the world the new communion of love, given by the grace of Christ."[202] We note three important points in John Paul's explanation of "natural complementarity."

First, there is an intrinsic relationship between biological and personal complementarity, between body and person (heart, intelligence, will, soul). Second, biological complementarity can be divided into heterogenital complementarity and reproductive complementarity. Heterogenital complementarity is the physically functioning male and female sexual organs (penis and vagina). Reproductive complementarity is the physically functioning male and female sexual organs used in sexual acts to biologically reproduce. Heterogenital and reproductive complementarity, however, are to be carefully distinguished for, though John Paul maintains that a couple must complement each other heterogenitally, the Magisterium also teaches that, "for serious reasons and observing moral precepts," it is not necessary that they biologically reproduce.²⁰³ Infertile couples and couples that choose for serious reasons not to reproduce for the duration of the marriage can still enter into a valid marital and sacramental relationship. Though reproductive complementarity always entails heterogenital complementarity, heterogenital complementarity does not always entail reproductive complementarity. Heterogenital complementarity is distinct from and can stand alone from reproductive complementarity in the service of personal complementarity. Third, given that John Paul's theology of the body and magisterial teaching explicitly forbid homosexual acts, it is clear that both regard heterogenital complementarity as a sine qua non for personal complementarity in sexual acts. Without heterogenital complementarity, "natural complementarity" in the sexual act is not possible.

"Ontological Complementarity"

John Paul also discusses "ontological complementarity,"²⁰⁴ what is also referred to by the Congregation for the Doctrine of the Faith as "affective complementarity."²⁰⁵ This type of complementarity is at the crux of John Paul's teaching on the theology of the body and the sexual human person because it intrinsically links biological and personal complementarity between man and woman. He claims that "even though man and woman are made for each other, this does not mean that God created them incomplete."²⁰⁶ Each individual has the potential to be complete by integrating the biological, psychoaffective, social, and spiritual elements of affective complementarity. When considering the couple, even though man and woman are "complete" in themselves, he argues that "for forming a couple they are incomplete."²⁰⁷ He further notes that "woman complements man, just as man complements woman. . . . Womanhood expresses the 'human' as much as manhood does, but in a different and complementary way."²⁰⁸ We may reasonably ask, however, where the incompleteness and the need for complementarity are to be found in an individual that is complete in himself or herself, but is incomplete for forming a couple. Where in the human person does this incompleteness reside that needs completion by being complemented by the opposite sex?

John Paul responds that "womanhood and manhood are complementary *not only from the physical and psychological points of view,* but also from the *ontological.* It is only through the duality of the 'masculine' and the 'feminine' that the 'human' finds full realization."²⁰⁹ The masculine and feminine complement each other to create a "unity of the two,"²¹⁰ a "psychophysical completion,"²¹¹ not only in sexual acts but also in marital life.

For John Paul II, then, sexual intercourse between spouses is a language of the body in truth, which includes two dimensions. The first dimension pertains to the two intrinsic meanings of the sexual act, the unitive and the procreative meanings. To eliminate or suppress either the unitive or procreative meaning of the sexual act, whether in the case of contraception²¹² or reproductive technologies,²¹³ falsifies "the inner truth of conjugal love."²¹⁴ The second, and more fundamental, dimension pertains to an "honest anthropology"[215] based on "the nature of the subjects themselves who are performing the act."[216] Complementarity is a principle that explains this anthropology whereby, in marriage and the sexual act, the masculine and feminine biological and psychological elements are ontologically linked in a unified whole. These two dimensions by definition eliminate the possibility of moral homosexual acts and moral nonreproductive heterosexual acts, even between a married couple.

John Paul II's Sexual Anthropology: A Critique

John Paul II's personalistic norm is a good example of how paradigm shifts can change terminology, human "nature" vis-à-vis human person, and yet fall prey to the same conceptual and terminological baggage. While his works are laden with references to the person, personal dignity, and responsibility, these are frequently explained and defined in terms of "nature"[217] and more often than not ignore the lived human experience of married couples.[218] As he notes, "In the order of love a man can remain true to the person only in so far as he is true to nature. If he does violence to 'nature' he also 'violates' the person by making it an object of enjoyment rather than an object of love."[219] A violent act toward "nature," and therefore human love, is contraception, which has a "damaging effect on love."[220] Love and procreation are intrinsically linked in his theology of the body, but in this relationship there is a clear hierarchy of the natural over the personal and relational.[221] This prioritization is clear in his discussion of complementarity. Heterogenital complementarity is the sine qua non, and primary consideration for whether or not personal complementarity can be realized. If heterogenital complementarity is not present, as it is not present in homosexual acts, the act is by definition "intrinsically disordered,"[222] and there can be no personal complementarity in sexual acts, regardless of the *meaning* of those acts for human beings.

In a personalist-based theology, however, one must ask whether or not the biological and physical can serve as an adequate foundation for the personal and relational. Should not personalism begin with a holistic understanding of the human person in all his or her emotional, psychological, relational, spiritual, and biological complexity? If this is so, then the biological is only one aspect of the person, which should not be given inordinate import in the hierarchy of being or as a foundation for sexual anthropology. Authentic personalism takes the particular human person in his or her sexual complexity and formulates normative guidelines for sexual relationships out of a profound appreciation of that complexity, not on the primacy of heterogenital complementarity. John Paul's notion of complementarity lacks an appreciation and integration of sexual orientation complementarity.

Sexual orientation and complementarity. In considering the sexual human person, John Paul, like NNLT, fails to adequately consider sexual orientation in his theology of the body. As noted above,[223] there is no univocal definition of sexual orientation. The U.S. bishops note that "it seems appropriate to understand sexual orientation (heterosexual or homosexual) as a *deep-seated* dimension of one's personality and to recognize its *relative stability* in a person."[224] A person does not choose his or her sexual orientation. Because homosexual orientation is experienced as a biological, psychological, and social given and not as something freely chosen, it cannot be considered sinful, for morality presumes the freedom to choose. This judgment is not to be understood as a claim that, according to the Magisterium, a homosexual orientation is morally good or even morally neutral, for elsewhere it teaches that "this inclination . . . is objectively disordered" and homosexual acts that flow from the orientation are intrinsically disordered.[225] The distinction between a homosexual orientation, which is not chosen, and homosexual acts, which are chosen, is central to John Paul's and the Magisterium's teachings. Homosexual acts are intrinsically disordered because "they are contrary to the natural law. They close the sexual act to the gift of life. They do not proceed from a genuine affective and sexual complementarity."[226] Heterosexuality is the norm against which all sexual acts are judged.

John Paul II condemns homosexual acts because they do not exhibit heterogenital and reproductive complementarities and, because they do not exhibit these biological complementarities, they are *ontologically* incapable of realizing personal complementarity, regardless of the meaning of the act for a homosexual couple. Heterogenital complementarity is the primary, foundational, sine qua non condition for what defines a moral sexual act. Because homosexual acts lack heterogenital complementarity, they can never be moral.

Although John Paul consistently condemns homosexual acts on the grounds that they violate heterogenital and reproductive complementarity, he does not explain why they also violate personal complementarity. The Magisterium proffers a vague explanation, asserting that homosexual acts "do not proceed from a genuine affective and sexual complementarity."[227] This statement, however, begs the question of whether such acts can ever be moral on the level of personal complementarity. Though John Paul has made no effort to confront this question, monogamous, loving, committed, homosexual couples have confronted it experientially, and they tell us that they do experience personal complementarity in and through their homosexual acts. This claim is amply documented by scientific research and through anecdotal testimonies of homosexual couples.[228] On the basis of such testimonies, Farley concludes that "this witness alone is enough to demand of the Christian community that it reflect anew on the norms for homosexual love."[229] An essential part of this renewed reflection is a reconstruction of John Paul II's and magisterial understandings of types of complementarity in relation to homosexual persons and theological anthropology. On the basis of the Magisterium's own recognition of sexual orientation, and the scientific research and anecdotal testimonies that affirm the personal complementarity experienced by homosexual couples, we suggest that the complementarity defended in John Paul's theology of the body needs to be reconstructed to include orientation complementarity.

Holistic complementarity. Orientation complementarity is a foundational sexual anthropological dimension of the human person that draws the person physically, emotionally, psychologically, and affectively toward individual persons of the opposite or same sex, depending on whether the orientation is heterosexual or homosexual. As such, it integrates genital complementarity into personal complementarity. In couples of heterosexual orientation, personal complementarity is embodied, manifested, nurtured, and strengthened through the use of their genitals; in couples of homosexual orientation, it is equally embodied, manifested, nurtured, and strengthened through the use of their genitals. Though heterogenital complementarity is needed for reproduction, it is not needed for the sexual, affective, spiritual, and personal connection between two people that the recent Catholic tradition acknowledges as an end of marriage equal to procreation.[230] Though they cannot exhibit heterogenital complementarity for reproduction, homosexual individuals can exhibit what we refer to as holistic complementarity. Holistic complementarity is an integrated orientation, personal, and genital complementarity. We suggest that heterosexual or homosexual orientation as part of a person's "natural" sexual constitution requires adding orientation complementarity as a type of complementarity to complement John Paul II's theology of the body. This addition yields the conclusion that holistic complementarity—an integrated orientation, personal, and biological complementarity—is a more adequate theological anthropology of the human sexual person and foundational principle for comprehending human sexual relationships and morally assessing sexual acts.

Orientation complementarity, then, challenges us to reconstruct John Paul's definitions of ontological complementarity and heterogenital complementarity. First, orientation complementarity cannot espouse his heterogenital point of departure for ontological complementarity. As we have seen, for him the point of departure for ontological complementarity is an essential unity between the biological (heterogenital) and the personal that can find completion only in heterosexual marriage and conjugal acts. The definition of ontological complementarity is the "unity of the two" where the masculine and feminine affective elements (biological, psychoaffective, social, and spiritual), which for forming a couple are incomplete, find completion in heterogenitally complementary sexual acts. By integrating orientation complementarity into John Paul's ontological complementarity model, the point of departure is not heterogenital complementarity but the sexual human person of either a homosexual or heterosexual orientation. The definition of ontological complementarity in moral sexual acts is the "unity of the two," where the affective elements (biological, psychoaffective, social, and spiritual) complement one another. In the case of persons with a homosexual orientation, these acts will be genitally male–male or female–female; in the case of persons with a heterosexual orientation, these acts will be genitally male–female.

Orientation complementarity also requires us to redefine heterogenital complementarity in relation to ontological complementarity. Severing the male–female ontological complementarity of the affective elements includes the genitals. No longer is heterogenital complementarity the foundational sine qua non for personal complementarity. Genital complementarity, indeed, can be determined only in light of orientation complementarity. In a moral sexual act, the genitals are at the service of personal complementarity, and they may be male–male, female–female, or male–female, depending on whether the individual person's orientation is homosexual or heterosexual. Our principle of holistic complementarity, which includes sexual orientation complementarity as one of its types, embraces the totality and complexity of the human person and reconstructs genital complementarity to be in dialogue with, and at the service of, personal and orientation complementarity. The genitals may be said to be complementary when they are used in a moral sexual act that realizes the psychoaffective, social, and spiritual elements of ontological complementarity.

John Paul II: conclusion. All that can be claimed with certainty in John Paul's version of ontological complementarity is that heterogenital complementarity is necessary for reproduction. His failure to include orientation complementarity as an essential dimension of sexual anthropology qualifies his theory as a "heterosexual theology of the body for reproduction" but renders it incapable of adequately addressing the human sexual person. Though his theology of the body attempts to integrate Thomism, personalism, phenomenology, and scripture, it falls short of a full or compelling account of a personalist sexual anthropology that comprehends the complexity of the sexual human person. The emphasis on the "natural," that is biological, over the relational prioritizes Aquinas's generic natural law over specific natural law, and too closely resembles the old wine of biologism, physicalism, and classicism of the manuals of moral theology in the new wineskin of Thomistic personalism and a theology of the body. We agree with Böckle's conclusion regarding John Paul's "realistic phenomenology": It "appears to neutralize the relationship of person and nature, giving nature priority."[231]

Conclusion

Although traditionalist attempts to develop a revised ethical method with a unique sexual anthropology are admirable, these attempts, which are intrinsically linked to defending magisterial norms absolutely prohibiting specific sexual acts, are subject to the same four main critiques as the manuals of moral theology. First, though this school certainly recognizes the importance of the personal and relational in human sexuality, there is a clear prioritization of the biological and physical dimensions of the human person. These dimensions are the sine qua non for any moral assessment of sexual behavior.

Second, the traditionalist school prioritizes a classicist consciousness over a historical consciousness. In the case of NNLT the basic good of marriage and its aspects that absolutely condemn certain sexual acts, and in fact claim infallible authority for those absolutes in the case of artificial birth control, clearly illustrate the classicist interpretation of this good. In addition the claim that *Gaudium et spes* did not reflect a fundamental shift in the hierarchy of the ends of marriage testifies to this classicist interpretation and, in fact, misrepresents magisterial teaching.[232] In the case of Rhonheimer the correlation between specific sexual acts and the virtue of chastity reflects a static view of virtue and its correlation with human acts. John Paul's theology of the body ignores the different languages the historically incarnated, sexual person speaks.

Third, the attempt to construct a "one-size-fits all" sexual morality is classicist in that it largely ignores the complexity of history, culture, gender roles and definitions, and socioeconomic variables that have an impact on all human relationships, including sexual relationships. These variables are not peripheral considerations to sexual ethics and sexual anthropology; they form the very material of ethical reflection that must be given due consideration in developing a sexual anthropology. Though there is a certain universalism in human "nature," the particularity of sexual beings must inform our sexual anthropology to a greater extent than traditionalists acknowledge or allow. To focus primarily, if not exclusively, on the universality of human "nature" is to prioritize classicism over historical consciousness.

Fourth and finally, in the defense of sexual norms that absolutely prohibit specific sexual acts always and everywhere, the focus is on the act, not on the meaning of that act for human persons and their relationships. Even in traditionalist virtue ethics, the emphasis is on how single acts are tied to specific virtues and either facilitate or frustrate the development of virtue. Though there is some truth in this stance, acts *may* develop patterns of behavior that reflect a virtuous or vicious character, the traditional stance that each and every nonmarital sexual act consists of grave matter and is potentially a mortal sin reflects an act-centered morality and betrays virtue ethics and its focus on character and relationship. As Selling notes such an act-centered morality has "done tremendous damage to our understanding of human sexuality and any efforts to build a positive, human, integrated and community-building sexual ethics."[233] True virtue ethics must focus more on an ethics of *being* than on an ethics of *doing*; more on the meaning of human acts for human relationships and the formation of virtue than on the acts themselves; and more on the interrelationship between sexual anthropology, which includes sexual orientation, and virtue.

We believe that revisionist attempts at developing a sexual anthropology more adequately incorporate the personal and relational dimensions of the human person. To those attempts we now turn.

Chapter Three

Natural Law and Sexual Anthropology

Catholic Revisionists

CATHOLIC TRADITIONALIST sexual anthropology emphasizes classicism, the universality of basic goods and human "nature," absolute norms, and an act-centered morality. Catholic revisionist sexual anthropology emphasizes historical consciousness, the particularity of basic goods and the human person, norms that reflect this particularity, and a relational-centered morality. In this chapter, we present a revisionist critique of traditionalist sexual anthropology. We then explore various dimensions of revisionist, including feminist, sexual anthropologies.

Revisionist Critiques of Traditionalist Anthropologies

Revisionist critiques of traditionalist sexual anthropologies have parallels with the critique of the implicit moral method and anthropology used in the manuals of moral theology. The defining aspect of these manuals, which were used to train seminarians for their roles as confessors and were the authoritative source of moral theology before the Second Vatican Council, was probably their focus on individual acts and sins. In determining the nature of a sin and the corresponding penance, the manuals were preoccupied with the individual act and largely neglected the overall character, formation, and intention of the human person who performed the act. The manuals have been criticized, therefore, because they did not acknowledge the complexity of the human person who cannot be defined by a single act. The classicist worldview was the predominant worldview in the manuals, and it perceives penitents as doers of isolated deeds that define them at any given moment. Historical consciousness rejects this static view of the human person who is infinitely more complex than one single act can reveal. Acts are important, but they do not fully encapsulate the identity or character of a person. Though most theologians see this act-centered morality as an inherent weakness in the manual tradition, traditionalists continue to prioritize this approach to morality in their defense of absolute sexual norms.

What are the concerns with this act-centered morality with regard to human sexuality? Just as one act can never fully define the character of a person, neither can one act fully define the meaning and "nature" of human sexual relationships. The relationship between a man and woman is more profound than anything that can be expressed in a single act. A single act may, and indeed does, say something about the relationship, its meaning, nature, and depth, but it does not define that relationship without remainder. A concern with *Humanae vitae*, and with those who would defend its perception of human sexuality, is that conclusions about the meaning and nature of a couple's relationship as a whole are to be drawn from a single act of artificial contraception. One traditionalist goes so far as to say that an act of contraception is by definition contralife, analogous to homicide.[1] A single act, however, cannot encapsulate the meaning of a person created in the image and likeness of God; nor can it define the nature and totality of human relationships. Selling notes that the natural law method that supports this act-centered sexual morality "is a mechanistic image of the universe and of creation"; it represents a classicist worldview of the person and his/her sexuality.[2] It is, at best, an impoverished indication of morality, persons, and sexual relationships.

Although the manuals and traditionalists both espouse an act-centered approach to moral theology, the *justification* for that approach has evolved. Scientific rationalism distinguishes both the manual and the contemporary traditionalist approaches to natural law. The scientific discovery of the female ovum in the 1850s and the discovery of the female fertility cycle in the 1920s sanctioned and gave scientific evidence for the traditional account that sexual differentiation, male and female, is linked to procreation. With this knowledge one could prove and predict the connection between sexual acts and reproduction, which justified the "truth" of the Church's teaching that each and every sexual act was "destined" for procreation. "This natural law view of human sexuality became the prisoner of scientific rationalism."[3] In the previous chapter we saw how the focus on biology and the procreative meaning of the sexual act predominate in traditionalist natural law sexual anthropologies. There is an implicit prioritization, even an explicit prioritization in the case of New Natural Law Theory (NNLT), of the procreative meaning over the unitive meaning of the conjugal act. This prioritization is largely due to scientific rationalism.

It is certainly true that there is an intrinsic relationship between sexual differentiation and procreation, but from a personalist sexual ethical perspective this insight is too narrowly focused. *Gaudium et spes* insisted that sex is about much more than procreation. It did so by eliminating the traditional hierarchical language of the procreative and unitive ends of sexual intercourse, and by discussing conjugal love as human, dignified, graced, charitable, reciprocal, and virtuous, and it did this without ever mentioning procreation. When it does discuss procreation, it discusses it in the context of responsible parenthood. It is this integrated view of human sexuality that allows revisionists to develop a revised sexual anthropology, in which procreation has an important role in the marital relationship but is never the only or the predominant aspect of human sexuality. Understanding the procreative dimension of human sexuality in terms of the totality of interpersonal relationship allows for a shift from an act-centered morality to a value-oriented, relation-centered, virtuous morality. Such a holistic sexual anthropology finds its foundational roots in the anthropology of Karl Rahner.

Karl Rahner: Transcendental Freedom

Two essential dimensions of Rahner's theological anthropology are that the human person is both free and historical. These two "existentials" are instrumental in transforming moral theology from an act-centered to a relation-centered morality, and existentially grounding the understanding of basic goods or fundamental values. We consider each in turn.

Rahner accepts Kant's turn toward the subject and the implications this turn has on the shift from a cosmos-centered to a person-centered theology. With this shift comes the necessity to know the human person-subject in his or her totality and, for Rahner, the person-subject's essential "nature" is grounded in transcendental freedom. This freedom is first of all "the subject's being responsible for himself, so that freedom in its fundamental nature has to do with the subject as such and as a whole. In real freedom the subject always intends himself, understands and posits himself. Ultimately, he does not do *something*, but does *himself*."[4] This foundational freedom is not a freedom *from* but a freedom *for*; it is responsibility drawn toward, and realized in, the love of God and neighbor.[5] The experience of this freedom directs us toward the moral ideal and a corresponding sense of moral obligation.

Rahner distinguishes between transcendental freedom and categorical freedom. Categorical freedom is a choice of particular actions. We choose to go fishing, play with our children, or read a book. These choices pertain to the category of acts. Transcendental freedom, which is distinct from but intrinsically related to categorical freedom, is at the core of our being and pertains to our fundamental choice to be in relationship with God as subject. It is transcendental freedom in relation to the transcendental subject, God, that makes categorical choices possible. Categorical choices may be a manifestation of transcendental freedom, but unless such choices involve transcendental freedom, they do not define it. Modras notes that "free actions can arise from outside the inmost core which do not affect us as acts of transcendental freedom do."[6]

Rahner's notion of transcendental freedom has been developed into the theory of the fundamental option by Josef Fuchs,[7] and the Congregation for the Doctrine of the Faith (CDF) agrees that "in reality, it is precisely the fundamental option which in the last resort defines a person's moral disposition."[8] The fundamental option is often used to explain mortal sin (the negative fundamental option) and spiritual wholeness (the positive fundamental option). An ongoing debate in contemporary Catholic moral theology is whether or not one can commit a mortal sin, that is, exercise a negative fundamental option, in a single act. An act-centered morality is focused on determining which acts do, and which acts do not, constitute a mortal sin. Pope John Paul II and traditionalists support an act-centered morality; *Veritatis splendor* clearly states that "the fundamental orientation can be radically changed by particular acts."[9] Because, according to magisterial teaching, there is no parvity of matter in sexual sins—that is, the object of every sexual act is grave moral matter—every morally wrong sexual act is a potential mortal sin. A relation-centered morality that accepts the theory of the fundamental option denies the possibility of committing a mortal sin in a single categorical act. Revisionists support a relation-centered morality. Curran notes that "the fundamental option is not an independent act but the determination of the subject who is doing particular categorical acts. Mortal sin involves a fundamental option on the transcendental level and cannot be identified with a categorical act."[10] The basic core identity of a person cannot be defined in a single categorical act, because it reflects his or her identity as subject in relation to God as subject.

Part of the debate between traditionalists and revisionists on the nature of the fundamental option in relation to particular acts revolves around how one defines an act. Both schools would agree that adultery *may* be a mortal sin, but traditionalists define adultery as a single act and revisionists would define it as a series of acts expressing transcendental freedom. A series of acts—deceptions, infidelities, and selfishness—normally precede the actual act of adultery. Taken as a whole, these acts culminate in an act of adultery that may reflect a fundamental rejection of our relationship with God, neighbor, and self. Similarly, the confession of the good thief crucified with Jesus (Lk 23:39–43) represents an act of a total commitment to relationship that defines his identity. This act, however, is an act of transcendental freedom expressed in a particular time and space. Acts of adultery and the confession of the good thief can be described as single categorical acts, but to explain them as such is erroneous. Such acts reflect a basic commitment of the person as subject expressed in space and time, but they entail more radically either a negative or positive fundamental commitment toward the infinite subject.

The distinction between transcendental and categorical freedom and its application to mortal sin lays the groundwork for a shift from an act-centered morality to a relational-centered morality. The most important questions of morality are not what acts a person does or does not do. The fundamental question is, rather, how a person defines himself or herself in relationship to God, self, and others. Rahner notes that "precisely because man is a many-layered being, precisely because he is not the abstractly formalized person one may so easily conceive him to be in moral theology, precisely because he is constructed as it were in layers starting at an interior core and becoming more and more external, and because (even free) activations can spring from many different layers," his categorical choices reflect many, including peripheral, layers, and do not define who he is at his core.[11] Humans are finite beings, capable of inconsistencies, and their categorical choices do not necessarily reflect their fundamental stance. The core of human identity is defined by transcendental freedom in relationship to God and neighbor. A theology of transcendental freedom emphasizes relationship and the impact of concrete choices on relationships in toto. An act-centered morality, mechanistic and simplistic, cannot accommodate this theology.

Freedom, Historicity, and Basic Goods

Transcendental freedom, which "actualizes one thing, the single subject in the unique totality of his history," [12] and historicity existentially ground basic goods or fundamental values. It is human reflection on this moral experience of transcendental freedom that provides the content of natural law. Though human freedom constitutes the essence of human "nature," or more accurately of the human person, the definition, understanding, and normative implications of human freedom are radically grounded in the existential and historical. The interrelationship between essential human "nature," constituted by transcendental freedom, and the historicity of human knowing and understanding creates an anthropology of the unchangeable and changeable. It is the interrelationship between the essential and the contingent that allows Rahner to claim that human "nature" changes; "despite its *ultimate* unchangeableness, . . . it is not *simply* always the same."[13] This unchanging and changing in human "nature" has implications for Rahner's perception of fundamental values. Though they are realized in a historical context, some values are universal, transcendental, and unchanging; they define our essential being and make us human. Other values are particular, immanent, and changing; they arise historically and belong to the changing nature of human beings grounded in the historical and existential.[14] It is historically evolving and changing values, and their expression in specific norms, that are of particular interest to moral theology. They lead Rahner to assert the following: "Apart from wholly universal moral norms of an abstract kind, and apart from a radical orientation of human life towards God as the outcome of a supernatural and grace-given self commitment, there are hardly any particular or individual norms of Christian morality which could be proclaimed by the ordinary or extraordinary teaching authorities of the Church in such a way that they could be unequivocally and certainly declared to have the force of dogmas."[15]

Transcendental freedom is always embodied, and the knowledge of what that freedom requires in moral obligation and authentic development is subject to the contingencies of human understanding. The historical reality of transcendental freedom explains the development of doctrine in moral teaching and is particularly relevant to human sexuality. The scientific understanding of human reproduction, for example, has profound implications for how men and women understand and live out their sexuality, which is part of their essential "nature" as human persons. As Rahner notes, there is a real history and development of the understanding of humanity, and with it a real history and development of the values that facilitate authentic human fulfillment.[16] This historical dimension of the essential freedom of human beings allows for an ongoing development in the knowledge of human "nature," and a creative freedom that may require redefinition of the understanding of changeable human "nature," the existential values that constitute that "nature," and the acts that facilitate or frustrate attainment of those values.

Although Rahner's anthropology has shaped much of revisionist thinking, it has also been critiqued for being too individualistic. It does not adequately consider the social and political realities of human relationships.[17] Nor does the fundamental option adequately consider the historical, cultural, political, and socially constructed realities of our lives.[18] Revisionist moral theologians have developed and expanded Rahner's anthropology, particularly those dimensions he ignored or left underdeveloped.

Revisionists and Basic Goods: Universal and Particular

There is an ongoing dialectic in Rahner's theological anthropology between the essential and the existential, the universal and particular, classicism and historical consciousness. Rahner and revisionists focus on the existential, particular, and historically conscious dimensions of fundamental values or basic goods in relation to the moral life; traditionalists focus on the essential, universal, and classicist dimensions of those values or goods. The dimensions emphasized in a particular anthropology have a profound impact on the meaning and nature of those goods and the norms that facilitate or frustrate human dignity.

Following Rahner (and Lonergan) revisionist moral theologians give priority to historical consciousness over classicism in developing ethical method and anthropology. On more than one occasion, Richard McCormick endorsed NNLT's notion of basic goods.[19] Like many revisionists,[20] however, he critiques the NNLT focus on the universality of basic goods at the expense of their particularity.[21] To remedy this shortcoming, revisionists have made historical consciousness a foundational point, indeed a sine qua non, of their ethical method. Historical consciousness has profound implications for the meaning, knowledge, and particular instantiations of the basic goods. While recognizing the universal rational inclination of human beings toward the basic goods, historical consciousness also emphasizes their particularity. As aspects of authentic personhood and human fulfillment, the basic goods are universal. As the instantiation of goods that provide human beings with a rational basis for choice, the basic goods and their aspects are particularized in light of history, culture, context, relationships, conceptual schemes, and social structures. The basic goods are both universal and particular not only from a historically conscious worldview but also in anthropology.

Revisionist theologians recognize the role and function of the basic goods in attaining authentic human fulfillment or personhood. Their debate with traditionalists is about the meaning and "nature" of the basic goods as aspects of personhood, and their role and function in normative ethics. Like traditionalists, revisionists recognize the universal and particular in anthropology. Norbert Rigali summarizes well the relationship between the universal and particular in human nature: "Formally, [universal human nature] is a principle, in every human being, of embodied spiritual self-transcendence in culture; and in this respect it is universal and unchanging. Materially, however, it is a principle, in every human being, of a particular historical mode of embodied spiritual self-transcendence, possible within the limits of a particular culture; and in this respect human nature is particular, historical and variable."[22]

Rigali's distinction between the formal and material dimensions of human "nature" is helpful for distinguishing the universality and particularity of the basic goods as aspects of human "nature." It is the natural inclination of human beings toward the basic goods that constitutes them "as a realm of objective moral values and as a universal basis of morality." It is "the inculturation of these universal values in the shared meanings, values, and institutions of a particular culture [that] constitutes the universality-in-particularity of morality."[23] Formally, the basic goods are universal, unchanging, incommensurable, and constant; materially, they are particular, changing, commensurable, and evolving. Though the formal and universal dimensions of human "nature" and the basic goods provide the basis for universal principles such as "do good and avoid evil," the material and particular dimensions provide the basis for more specific norms of behavior and for determining whether or not the particularity of an ethical situation coincides with one or another specific norm. Thus, whereas traditionalists focus on the universality of human "nature" and the basic goods in formulating absolute specific norms, revisionists emphasize the particularity of human "nature" and the basic goods. From the revisionist perspective, there are no absolute material norms of *right and wrong actions* because the open-endedness of human freedom and the basic goods are granted their full significance. There are, however, "virtually exceptionless" norms, which presume "common and universal danger" if they are violated. Until the spectrum of premoral values and disvalues at stake in a particular situation are assessed, however, one can only assert that such norms are valid in most cases.[24]

Given the revisionist emphasis on historical consciousness and particularity over classicism and universality of basic goods or fundamental values, we posit ten dimensions as essential hermeneutical guides for discerning the meaning and nature of fundamental values for anthropology and developing a sexual moral theology that facilitates authentic personhood. The first dimension is *history*. Any credible interpretation of the basic goods must recognize the impact of history on human understanding. As the understanding of human fulfillment evolves and changes, so too does our perception of the basic goods that lead to human flourishing and fulfillment. Historical consciousness is an essential epistemological tool in this process. It recognizes that there is not a single perception of authentic personhood but many authentic perceptions that are shaped by an ongoing dialogue in the present, with the past, directed toward the future.

The second dimension is *development*. An essential component of historical consciousness is the recognition of how our understanding of the basic goods evolves and changes. The developmental nature of human understanding is evident within both communities and individuals. Human beings are communal beings who belong to, participate in, and are socialized by numerous communities.[25] There is a dialogical relationship between communities and individuals. Communities shape individuals and their understanding of basic goods; individuals, through their actions and character, shape communities.[26] Through this ongoing dialogue, communities are formed and reformed in the light of developing human understanding. Justice, for example, which once prohibited usury, now generally condones it. There still may be, however, certain communal relations—between developed and developing countries, for example—where justice might condemn usury.[27]

One profound insight that developmental psychologists such as Jean Piaget and Lawrence Kohlberg have contributed to our analysis and understanding of the basic goods is that their definition, recognition, and realization is very much contingent on the individual's level of psychological maturity. Four-year-olds, for example, will not immediately understand the basic good of human life when their parents tell them not to hit each other. As they grow and mature, hopefully, the nature and meaning of this good, as well as its normative implications for authentic personhood, will become apparent. The recognition and realization of the basic goods is very much dependent upon both one's psychological development and moral maturity and one's ability to understand the basic goods and their implications for facilitating human relationships and human flourishing. This reality precludes a universalist, one-size-fits-all perception of the basic goods.

The third dimension is *culture*. Basic goods are very much shaped by culture; they are inculturated-transcendent goods. Any authentic hermeneutic of the basic goods, therefore, must be in dialogue with culture and assess its impact on the human understanding of the number and nature of basic goods. The relationship of the basic goods and culture is as dialogical as that between humans and society. The basic goods often serve as a foundation for critiquing culture, but culture also shapes their understanding and certainly provides the context for their recognition and realization.

The fourth dimension is *social structure*. Social structures must be analyzed to determine their impact on the definition, recognition, and realization of basic goods, and this analysis is again dialogical. By naming structures of oppression, we may discern their impact on basic goods. By striving to realize basic goods in light of structural oppression, we may seek to transform the structures themselves. As social structures are transformed, so too may the potential for recognizing and realizing basic goods be transformed. Oppressive structures are grounded in socioeconomic, political, gender, sexual orientation, ethnic, religious, hierarchical, and age-based realities. It is a complex task to name, analyze, and delineate the interrelationship between social structures and their impact on the particularity of basic goods. Consequently, this analysis is ongoing and, in the present period of globalization, has become even more crucial.

The fifth dimension is *concepts and language*. Terms and concepts evolve and change and are unique to a particular history, culture, tradition, and ethnic group. The basic good of human life, for example, reflected in the norm "Thou shalt not kill," has evolved and changed over time in the Christian tradition. Up until Constantine, Christians predominantly followed a path of nonviolence and pacifism. After Constantine, with the conversion of many soldiers, allowances were made for a just use of violence that included killing in war. The just war doctrine clearly illustrates this conceptual and linguistic evolution of the human understanding and interpretation of basic goods.

The sixth dimension is *context*. Basic goods and their aspects are instantiated only in a particular context. Though NNLT has a narrow definition of what constitutes "morally relevant circumstances" that would mitigate the application of norms deduced from the basic goods in a particular context, revisionist and liberationist theologies, grounded in historical consciousness and inductive reasoning, allow a much broader consideration of such circumstances.

The seventh dimension is *relation*. As we have seen, the basic goods indicate what constitutes authentic personhood, which is ultimately about relationship, with God, others, self, environment, culture, social structures, and the like. To discern the nature of basic goods as relational realities, we reflect upon the complexity of human-being-in-relation and how it affects our being and acting in the world. Because each human being is a unique creation, his or her network of relationships is unique as well. Relationships are a universal dimension of being human; their particularity resides in the unique nature of those relationships and how they affect human understanding and human flourishing. This particularity has an impact on the ongoing definition, recognition, and realization of the basic goods.

The eighth dimension is *science and interdisciplinary studies*. Especially in the area of biomedical, environmental, and sexual ethics, the sciences can enable us to come to a deeper understanding of humanity and aid us in discerning what facilitates or frustrates authentic personhood.[28] How, for example, does the knowledge that sexual orientation derives from a combination of nature and nurture and is not freely chosen affect the basic good of human sexuality?[29] This revised knowledge suggests, revisionists argue, a corresponding revision of the norms guiding human sexual behavior. An ongoing dialogue with the sciences and other modern disciplines (languages, history, global economics, anthropology, etc.) is essential for developing our understanding of the basic goods and the norms that facilitate their realization.

The ninth dimension is *interreligious dialogue*. Religion is frequently recognized as a basic good, and the variety of particular religious traditions creates a vast wealth of insight and understanding into human existence. Religious traditions discover what it means to be authentically human, not only in themselves but also in dialogue with other traditions. Within the Catholic Christian tradition, for instance, much has been learned regarding spirituality and meditation (holiness is also a basic good) through Catholic–Buddhist dialogue. Such dialogue is essential in a multicultural and religious context to facilitate tolerance, understanding, and respect for those who do not espouse our particular religious tradition.

The tenth dimension is *theology*. Even within a particular religious tradition, there is no single "theology." Dialogue within a particular religious tradition, between the disciplines within the tradition (systematic theology, moral theology, biblical exegesis), is as important a task as dialogue with other traditions. Such dialogue can facilitate understanding of the nature of the basic goods and of the norms that facilitate their attainment. Given the plethora of literature in a particular theological discipline, such dialogue is a monumental, though fundamentally important, endeavor.

In his address to the United Nations, Pope John Paul II summarizes well a proper balance of the relationship between the universal and particular that is applicable to the basic goods: "To cut oneself off from the reality of difference—or, worse, to attempt to stamp out that difference—is to cut oneself off from the possibility of sounding the depths of the mystery of human life. The truth about man is the unchangeable standard by which all cultures are judged; but every culture has something to teach us about one or other dimension of that complex truth. Thus the 'difference' which some find so threatening can, through respectful dialogue, become the source of a deeper understanding of the mystery of human existence."[30] The unfathomable mystery of human existence demands an ongoing pursuit of a deeper understanding of, and appreciation for, the particularity of basic goods that facilitate an inculturated-transcendent authentic human fulfillment.

The Catholic natural law tradition has been clear on the universality of the basic goods and of human "nature's" rational inclination toward them. It has not been so clear, especially in recent magisterial documents, on their particularity. Revisionist and feminist theologians have contributed substantially to a sexual anthropology that recognizes the particularity of the basic goods, and this particularity provides the basis for norms guiding human sexuality. We now consider revisionist and feminist contributions to sexual anthropology.

Revisionists and Sexual Anthropology

From a historically conscious understanding of natural law and the universal goods or values that are always actualized in a particular person in a historical, cultural, and relational context, revisionist theologians explore the various dimensions of a personalist sexual anthropology. In this section, we investigate several of these dimensions that are crucial in constructing a holistic sexual anthropology. In the next chapter, we will develop our own foundational sexual ethical principle, relying upon *Gaudium et spes* and revisionist contributions to formulating a sexual anthropology.

Although being part of the same Catholic tradition as traditionalists, revisionists have a fundamentally different interpretation of the multifaceted dimensions of human sexuality. As noted above, *Gaudium et spes* advances an interpersonal model of human sexuality, expressing the marital relationship in terms of "an intimate partnership of life and love."[31] It also reflects corresponding shifts in the interpretation of natural law theory. We have noted the largely physicalist, biological, and act-centered foundation of the earlier natural law tradition of the manuals, *Humanae vitae*, and traditionalists. In *Gaudium et spes*, especially in the section on marriage and family, there is a fundamental methodological transformation from a biological to a personalist interpretation of natural law: "Therefore when there is question of harmonizing conjugal love with the responsible transmission of life, the moral aspect of any procedure . . . must be determined by objective standards. These [are] based on the nature of the human person and his acts."[32]

Louis Janssens: The Human Person Adequately Considered

In a frequently cited article Louis Janssens points out that the official commentary on *Gaudium et spes* applied this criterion not only to human sexuality but also to the entire domain of human activity, so that "human activity must be judged insofar as it refers to the human person integrally and adequately considered."[33] To answer the question of what precisely constitutes the human person integrally and adequately considered, Janssens develops eight dimensions of the human person that must be taken into consideration to determine the moral nature of an act and an intention. The human person is (1) a subject, (2) in corporeality, (3) in relation to the material world, (4) in relation to others, (5) in relation to social groups, (6) in relation to God, (7) a developmental historical being, and (8) fundamentally equal to all other human persons and yet uniquely original.[34] Janssens opts for the term dimensions rather than definitions of the human person to insinuate that our understanding of these dimensions, and of the list of dimensions, may evolve and develop as human understanding evolves and develops. Acts and intentions that facilitate the human person adequately considered are morally acceptable; acts and intentions that frustrate this are morally unacceptable. What is clear from the move to personalism in *Gaudium et spes*, specified by Janssens's principle of "the human person integrally and adequately considered," is that the static and absolutist traditionalist sexual anthropology is no longer adequate, because personalism is grounded in the existential, lived reality of human experience and human relationships. This personalist context is the point of departure for sexual anthropology and for morally evaluating dispositions and actions involving human sexuality.

The logical implication for sexual ethics of this shift to a more personalist, relation-centered natural law is that, while the Magisterium could, and indeed should, teach norms guiding sexual relationships, these norms cannot always be posited as absolutes because of the unique existential context of human relationships. This assertion is readily exemplified by reference to the question of birth regulation. The Church's only approved method of birth regulation, natural family planning, presumes a fundamental equality and mutual respect between the spouses within the marital relationship. The human reality is, however, that the majority of cultures throughout the world are patriarchal cultures in which the husband is the authority in the household and in the marital relationship, and the fundamental equality required to freely practice natural family planning is absent. In this existential context, it may be oppressive for the Church to prescribe an approach to regulating birth that is countercultural and creates an undue burden, especially for women. In a personalist sexual anthropology, then, morality is not one size fits all as it was in a natural law method grounded in a presumed universal human "nature" and the biological laws of reproduction. The complex "natures" of both human persons and human sexuality do not allow for such an abstract, absolutist, juridical method.

Although many revisionists have recognized Janssens's important contribution to the ongoing formulation of a historically conscious, personalist anthropology, some challenge his anthropology and the specific conclusions he reaches utilizing that anthropology. For example, in terms of sexual anthropology, it is not entirely clear how corporeality and relationship interrelate in addressing specific ethical issues. In the case of artificial insemination by donor (AID), Janssens posits relationship as the ultimate criterion for its moral legitimacy, without addressing the value of corporeality in this process.[35] Thus the interrelationship between love, sex, and procreation is left somewhat ambiguous, even for an ethical theory that is grounded in the recognition that morality is ambiguous. Greater clarity is needed in defining the interrelationship between the dimensions of the human person adequately considered and a justification for why one dimension is of greater import than another when considering a particular issue. Though proportionate reason is offered as this justification, it presumes an interrelationship between the dimensions rather than defining that interrelationship.

Richard A. McCormick

In his sexual anthropology, McCormick draws anthropological insights from both traditionalists and Janssens's human person adequately considered. McCormick recognizes the existence of basic goods.[36] In particular, he accepts marriage as a covenanted friendship "which offers us the best opportunity to humanize our sexuality and our selves."[37] Though he largely agrees with Finnis's list of basic goods, he disagrees fundamentally on the nature of those goods. For NNLT basic goods are moral and incommensurable. One cannot directly attack or impede a basic good and those goods cannot be compared to one another, which rules out, by definition, proportionalist reasoning. For McCormick and other revisionists, however, basic goods are *premoral* goods and commensurable and, in the case of conflicting premoral values and/or disvalues, proportionate reason judges the appropriate premoral value to be pursued or premoral disvalue to be avoided.

The human person adequately considered is what facilitates the assessment of which premoral values one should seek to realize or premoral disvalues one should seek to avoid in one's actions. In positing this principle as decisive for the calculation of proportion, we see clear parallels between Janssens and McCormick. As McCormick's thought evolved, he expanded his understanding of physical integrity, especially in sexual ethics, to include psychological health, and he gave greater consideration to the social impact of interpersonal relationships for realizing the human good.[38] Still, further development is required in McCormick's sexual anthropology regarding his definitions of parenthood and sexual orientation.

Although McCormick shares the revisionist camp with Janssens, he disagrees with Janssens's application to AID of the principle of the human person adequately considered; McCormick argues that AID is morally unacceptable. This disagreement reflects a more fundamental disagreement on the definition of parenthood in his sexual anthropology. For McCormick, conjugal exclusivity entails the "genetic, gestational and rearing dimensions of parenthood" (except in cases of adoption or fostering); separating these three dimensions "too easily contains a subtle diminishment of some aspect of the human person."[39] He argues that marital exclusivity should include these three dimensions of parenthood on two accounts. In the first account, he relies upon proportionate reason and a benefit/burden calculation: "Any relaxation in this exclusivity will be a source of harm to the marriage (and marriage in general) and to the prospective child." In the case of AID, "there is a genetic asymmetry in the relationship of husband and wife to the child, with possible damaging psychological effects."[40] It is not the genetic, biological connection, *in se*, that concerns McCormick, but the possible relational harm for the spouses, their relationship with the child, and the child's relationship with self and parents in the absence of that genetic connection.

The second account does not rely upon proportionate reason and a benefit/burden calculation but upon the intrinsic nature of the marital relationship: "Third-party involvement is itself violative of the marriage covenant independent of any potential damaging effects or benefits."[41] Many couples consider in vitro fertilization (IVF) "not as a *replacement* for their sexual intimacy, but as a kind of *continuation* or *extension* of it."[42] From this perspective, the sexual act is broadly defined to include all those acts that facilitate sexual intimacy, but the act of AID is a fundamental violation of the unitive relation between the spouses. McCormick admits, however, that other people, "including very responsible persons,"[43] can see this issue differently.

Janssens does see the issue differently. For him, parenthood is a dimension of the good of marriage that does not require a genetic connection between parents and offspring. He denies that third-party genetic involvement will necessarily be a burden or cause harm to marital, familial, or social relationships.[44] In addition, though he would presumably accept McCormick's argument that IVF is a continuation of sexual intimacy, he would deny that the use of third-party donors intrinsically violates marital intimacy. Whereas McCormick's moral assessment emphasizes the relational implications of corporeality, in this case genetic material from a donor, and considers third-party involvement an intrinsic violation of marital intimacy, Janssens's moral assessment emphasizes the relational dimension between the spouses and denies that third-party involvement is an intrinsic violation of marital intimacy.

The disagreement between McCormick and Janssens revolves around the interrelationship between the biological and relational dimensions in parenthood, and the moral assessment of this interrelationship. There are two comments to make regarding this disagreement. First, though McCormick and Janssens agree that, when married couples choose to reproduce, parenthood is a good within that marital relationship, they disagree fundamentally on the dimensions that define parenthood. For McCormick, the genetic connection of parenthood is essential; for Janssens, it is not. McCormick's claim regarding the essential link between "genetic, gestational and rearing dimensions of parenthood," however, needs further clarification. The possibility of adopting frozen embryos would seem to fundamentally challenge this definition of parenthood. If embryonic adoption is viewed strictly as a case of adoption rather than parental reproduction, at the very least, it challenges us to rethink the interrelationship between these three dimensions in light of technological developments and the complex relational issues they pose. Based on our principle to be developed in chapter 4, we believe that the possibility of adopting frozen embryos helps us to redefine the interrelationship between the three dimensions of parenthood, and we can allow for the morality of third-party gamete donations in reproductive technologies. This argument will be developed in chapter 8.

Second, both McCormick and Janssens rely upon the principle of the human person adequately considered to justify their positions on AID. McCormick views the genetic connection as an essential relational consideration. Utilizing donor gametes (or a surrogate) introduces a third party into the marital and parental relationships, which infringes on conjugal exclusivity.[45] Janssens does not see this third-party involvement as necessarily infringing on conjugal exclusivity. Such disagreements on the applicability of the human person adequately considered, however, do not discount the moral credibility or value of the principle. The variation in application recognizes and takes seriously all dimensions of the principle, especially the historical and fundamentally equal but uniquely original dimensions. The principle recognizes that, in light of each person's historical and relational context and his or her uniqueness, reasonable people can come to different conclusions on AID and other issues, depending upon the hermeneutics of the dimensions, their interrelationship, and prioritization. This particularity is a trademark of revisionist anthropologies.

McCormick's anthropology also requires a more thorough and consistent explanation of how it understands and incorporates sexual orientation. He posits heterosexual orientation as a normative sexual anthropological dimension, but there seems to be a tension between this assertion and his claim that some homosexual acts *can* be morally right. This tension is revealed in his discussion of premoral evil (disvalue), sexual orientation, and the morality of homosexual acts. He recognizes and accepts, though not without qualification, the premoral/moral distinction that we find in the foundational work of European revisionist theologians such as Janssens, Knauer, Schüller, and Fuchs. Building on Fuchs's distinction, McCormick approvingly cites Lisa Cahill's explanation of "premoral" in the context of homosexual acts. Such acts are "'premoral evils in that their sheer presence does not *necessarily* make the total act or relation of which they are a part 'morally' evil or sinful.'"[46] For McCormick, such acts can be considered premorally evil because "homogenital acts always depart from the ideal or the normative."[47]

The claim that homogenital acts depart from the ideal or normative presumes a definition of the normative. The ideal or normative is established based on a heterosexual anthropological norm. According to this anthropology, heterosexual orientation is the norm and anything that departs from this norm is, in the words of the Magisterium, "objectively disordered."[48] There is tension in McCormick's thought here. On the one hand, he resists labeling homosexual orientation an objective disorder. On the other hand, by labeling homosexual acts premorally evil, he implies not only that these acts are nonnormative but also that there is something normative in the human person that makes such acts nonnormative. Exploration of this tension will provide us with an essential anthropological insight.

McCormick presents and critiques the CDF's 1975 Declaration *Persona humana*, regarding human sexuality, homosexual orientation, and its moral correlation with homosexual acts. Regarding human sexuality, the CDF states: "The human person, present-day scientists maintain, is so profoundly affected by sexuality that it must be considered one of the principal formative influences of a man or woman. In fact, sex is the source of the biological, psychological and spiritual characteristics which make a person male or female and which thus considerably influence each individual's progress towards maturity and membership of society."[49]

McCormick notes the problematic between claiming, on the one hand, that one's sexuality as reflected in one's sexual orientation is "one of the principal formative influences in the person" and, on the other hand, that in the case of persons with a homosexual orientation this principal influence is disordered. Such a statement means, quite simply, "that the person is disordered."[50] McCormick responds to this by claiming that the CDF has drawn too close an association between the immorality of homosexual acts and the objective disorder of homosexual orientation, such that the orientation itself becomes morally decisive. In effect, he is resisting the CDF's moral method of moving from an established definition of homosexual acts as intrinsically evil to an anthropological claim that homosexual orientation is disordered. The latter claim has moral implications from the former for, so runs the argument, though a homosexual inclination is not a sin, it is a more or less strong tendency ordered toward an intrinsic moral evil. He resists this move to draw a moral correlation between homosexual acts and homosexual persons, and he asks "what is achieved by designating homosexual orientation as a 'disorder'?"[51]

We believe there is a similar correlation in revisionist thought, not between homosexual acts as *intrinsically* evil and homosexual orientation but between homosexual acts as *premorally* evil and homosexual orientation. We pose the following question to revisionist theologians: "What is achieved by designating homosexual acts as premoral evils?" Does this label not insinuate a negative judgment on homosexual orientation similar to that advanced by the CDF for, after all, is not a premoral evil or disvalue a "disordered" value? It seems to us that one could draw a similar conclusion on the disorderedness of the person's orientation from the revisionist statement that homosexual acts are a premoral disvalue and from the CDF's statement that homosexual acts are "intrinsically disordered."[52] Both presume the anthropological claim that heterosexual orientation is the norm for humans. We believe that labeling heterosexual acts as normative, and acts that depart from this ideal as premorally evil, does not give the human sexual person adequately considered due consideration. The interrelationship between a premoral value or disvalue and sexual anthropology requires further consideration.

By claiming that heterosexual acts are normative, one has already made a judgment about sexual anthropology, namely, that heterosexual orientation is a normative dimension of human sexuality and sexual anthropology. Any sexual expression that deviates from that norm is therefore, by definition at least, premorally evil. McCormick and other revisionists, however, leave room for the possibility that some homosexual acts, though they may be premorally evil, are not morally evil and may, indeed, be morally good. McCormick's resistance to labeling sexual orientation as disordered, and his further assertion that some homosexual acts can be morally right,[53] would seem to imply that homosexual acts are not premoral evils. What may be at the root of this dilemma, and a way out of it, is how we define sexual orientation in relation to sexual anthropology and determine premoral disvalue in light of this anthropology.

Homosexual acts, whether judged as intrinsically evil or premorally evil, are being measured against an already defined sexual anthropology that posits *heterosexual* orientation, rather than simply *sexual* orientation, as normative for human beings. Such a classicist and deductive approach to anthropology, however, betrays fundamental methodological commitments of revisionism. It is classicist, because it accepts heterosexual orientation as the anthropological norm. Though this may be true statistically, as the Magisterium realizes, there are people with a permanent homosexual orientation who do not choose that orientation, and for them a homosexual orientation *is* normative.[54] McCormick's sexual anthropology is deductive, because it accepts heterosexual orientation as normative and judges all homosexual activity as premorally evil in light of that acceptance. Revisionists typically utilize a historically conscious and inductive method, which looks at human beings in their particularity and draws out anthropological generalizations that reflect this particularity.

From a historically conscious worldview, defining anthropology is an ongoing venture,[55] and the definition of what constitutes a premoral value or disvalue must be in dialogue with anthropology. As an anthropology evolves, the definition of what constitutes a premoral value and disvalue must also evolve. What constitutes a premoral value or disvalue differs fundamentally for persons of heterosexual and homosexual orientation. The person's sexual orientation fundamentally shapes his or her relational capacity and worldview, together with the premoral values and disvalues of that capacity and worldview. This historically conscious and inductive approach to anthropology adequately considers the sexual person. The revisionist shortcoming of assessing the premoral status of homosexual acts does not dissipate the relevance of the premoral/moral distinction, nor the importance of applying the label of premoral disvalue to certain types of sexual activity. That application, however, must be made in light of a historically conscious anthropology.

Historical consciousness recognizes the givenness of sexual orientation and the need to incorporate it as an essential component of sexual anthropology. It further recognizes that heterosexual and homosexual orientation, as an integral part of the "biological, psychological and spiritual characteristics which make a person male or female," are normative for heterosexual or homosexual human beings, respectively.[56] Ethical theory that assesses sexual behavior must be founded on that anthropological insight, and formulate its (premoral) values and norms for assessing sexual persons and sexual acts in light of that insight.

We agree with McCormick and other revisionist theologians that sexual orientation is an essential anthropological dimension. We disagree with them, however, that heterosexual orientation is normative and should be the standard for determining a set of premoral values and disvalues for heterosexuals and homosexuals alike. *Homosexual* and *heterosexual* are *further* specifications of *sexual* orientation, and this further specification constitutes what is normative for homosexual or heterosexual persons. Premoral values and disvalues must be defined according to this specification. Otherwise, a premoral value or disvalue is defined against a truncated anthropology, a false sense of what is normatively human. We propose, therefore, the following definition of a premoral value and disvalue with regard to homosexual and heterosexual sexual acts: Sexual activity that is consonant with one's sexual orientation and that strives for sexual integrity in light of one's orientation is a premoral value; sexual activity that is not consonant with one's sexual orientation and that does not strive for sexual integrity in light of one's orientation is a premoral disvalue. Though this definition may seem to reflect the moral plane, rather than the premoral plane, it does not. Until all the variables of the human person adequately considered are assessed, one cannot make a moral judgment on whether or not a particular sexual activity *actually* integrates the sexual person and his or her human relationships and is, therefore, morally right, or *actually* disintegrates the person and his or her relationships and is, therefore, morally wrong.

Although McCormick's contribution to the revision of Catholic moral theology has been immense and invaluable, from our perspective, his revision does not go far enough in his sexual anthropology. His commitment to remain within the normative Catholic tradition on certain sexual ethical issues (homosexual acts and donor insemination), and yet to fundamentally challenge those teachings on pastoral grounds on which such acts can be justified in certain circumstances, has a curious effect. Traina notes that "the 'proportionate, but not ideal' label that results has the practical effect of approving the action without altering the content of the troublesome norm."[57] Other revisionist moral theologians, especially feminists such as Lisa Cahill, have developed a more sophisticated methodology, which allows for a more developed, credible, and consistent sexual anthropology.

Feminist Revisionist Theologians

Although revisionist moral theologians, in general, have attempted to reform and form a sexual anthropology that is more historically conscious, existential, experiential, relational, and inductive feminist revisionists, in particular, have had a profound effect on the evolution in sexual anthropology that is taking place in Catholic moral theology. Before addressing feminist contributions to sexual anthropology, however, we explore the interrelationship between natural law and feminist thought.

Natural Law's Contribution to Feminism

Margaret Farley states the historical tension between feminism and universal moralities such as natural law: "In the name of universality, of a total view of human nature and society, such theories have in fact been exclusive, oppressive, and repressive of women and of men who do not belong to a dominant group."[58] This summarizes the history of natural law ethics on some issues, especially on issues pertaining to human sexuality, but an authentic natural law ethic, grounded in human dignity, cannot be "exclusive, oppressive, and repressive." The challenge is to bring the particularity of the historically voiceless to the fore and to empower them to participate in ongoing dialogue around how to define, and how to realize, human flourishing in human (sexual) relationships. Though the historical exigencies of Catholic natural law ethics, with its domination by churchmen, have formulated a gender- and power-skewed vision of natural law, this does not eliminate the possibility of reconstructing a credible natural law ethic in light of various correctives. Feminist thought, drawing on liberation theology, is an essential corrective for many historical aberrations of traditional natural law theory.[59] Rather than abandoning a universalist ethic to a postmodernist, relativist, contentless ethic, we wish to correct the distorted visions of an oversimplified universalist ethic. Natural law theory, with anthropological correctives, is well suited for this task on several accounts.

Natural law includes methodological and anthropological dimensions that complement feminist ethics. The methodological dimensions include a dialectic between history, culture, and natural law; casuistry and inductive reasoning; and an ethic grounded in human flourishing. Natural law is entrenched in the Western tradition, and it has formed and continues to form this tradition, for good and ill, ethically, politically, legislatively, and socially. Throughout its history, natural law has always been in dialogue with history and culture. It is certainly correct to point out the historical abuses and weaknesses of natural law shaped by cultural (mis)understandings of human dignity, gender, and social relationships—its justification of slavery throughout much of history, for example. Natural law, however, has also had great successes calling all humanity to a deeper and more profound respect for human dignity, despite contrary historical and cultural perspectives, for instance, serving as a basis for the United Nations Universal Declaration on Human Rights. In a word, natural law has served both to foster abuses of human dignity and to alleviate such abuses in the struggle to define and recognize human dignity. The fact that natural law is so influenced by the particularity of history and culture, whether for ill or good, and is methodologically flexible enough to integrate and incorporate these variables, offers hope that it will continue to serve as a credible universalist ethic. The shortcoming is not in the project of developing a credible natural law sexual ethic per se, but rather in its traditional formulation. Its ongoing dialogue with history and culture is an essential methodological dimension that makes natural law open to reform, and feminism stands as an essential corrective in this ongoing process.

Natural law emphasizes an inductive approach to ethics. It also provides principles and norms as well as a method for managing, refining, reformulating, and applying those principles and norms. The method of juggling this interrelationship is known as casuistry.[60] Case reasoning is grounded in the existential particularity of lived human experience, and is inductive by its very nature. Therefore, it avoids the Platonic absolutism that plagues many of the traditionalist accounts of human flourishing and the absolute norms or paradigmatic acts that traditionalists claim facilitate human flourishing. Such particularity is at the core of feminist ethics. Though feminism can emphasize the particularity of human experience at the expense of a universal vision of the human, natural law is committed methodologically to a universalist anthropology. It insists that a holistic, comprehensive ethic requires a vision of "an all-encompassing *telos*," including "all the elements of women's genuine flourishing."[61] This *telos* must include a dialectic between a universal definition of human flourishing and the recognition of, appreciation for, and interconnectedness of, its particularity. For feminism and a sexual anthropology, this particularity can be stated thus: Human flourishing must be reformed and informed with clear and deliberate concern for integrating feminist insights into a holistic sexual anthropology.

Natural law shares essential anthropological insights with feminist thought. First, natural law espouses a positive anthropology; it sees the person as fundamentally good. Given the history of natural law reasoning on human sexuality, and the norms derived with that reasoning, this emphasis has often been distorted and has not always come to the fore. Second, Thomas Aquinas's virtue theory is key to natural law as well as to a feminist sexual anthropology. It is key in that it transforms the emphasis from an act-centered ethics of *doing* to a relation-centered ethics of *being and becoming*. This being and becoming recognizes the evolutionary nature of the virtuous life both in prudence, becoming a person who reasons well, and in charity, ongoing transformation of the unjust social structures that demean women and human sexuality. All these are central concerns of a feminist anthropological definition of human flourishing. Third, Catholic social teaching grounded in natural law provides both an existentially grounded analysis of social issues and a method for utilizing and applying the social sciences in critical reflection on social and structural sin. More important, it provides a positive vision of the common good, the communal nature of human flourishing, which seeks to define and embody human flourishing both individually and communally. Finally, it provides a recognition of embodiment as an integral component of human knowing and flourishing, an area in which natural law has been least effective.[62] Combined, these three insights—the dialectical interrelationship between history, culture, and natural law, casuistic reasoning, and human flourishing as a foundational principle—highlight common methodological and anthropological ground between natural law and feminist ethics.

Feminism's Contribution to Natural Law

Natural law complements feminism methodologically and anthropologically, and feminism contributes essential but underdeveloped anthropological insights to natural law anthropology. Feminism furthers the project of a holistic sexual anthropology by expanding the understanding of human flourishing and incorporating dimensions of that flourishing that are often neglected in traditionalist, magisterial, and revisionist accounts of sexual anthropology. Through systematic philosophical and theological reflections on women's and oppressed men's experiences, feminism contributes the following anthropological insights to natural law anthropologies: historically and culturally sensitive notions of family and kinship relations; an appreciation for the anthropological impact of gender and sexual orientation; positive assessment of the body, including the role and function of pleasure in human sexuality; appreciation for self-love and its relation to human flourishing; and an egalitarian-feminist interpretation of virtue that moves beyond traditionalist patriarchal accounts of virtue. We consider each of these in turn.

Family and kinship relations. In her foundational book on sexual ethics, Cahill notes that she writes from a feminist perspective, which she describes as "a commitment to equal personal respect and social power for women and men."[63] Her method is grounded in Aristotle and Aquinas and is realist, inductive, experientially based, and historically conscious. In addition, she uses social and cultural criticism to create a dialogue with other cultures in discerning substantive universal goods associated with embodied personhood, which include sex, gender, marriage, parenthood, and family.[64] Though she is committed to the Catholic natural law tradition, a universalist ethic grounded in human flourishing reflected in basic goods or fundamental values, she differs with traditionalists on the definition of the goods and their normative implications for human relationships.

Cahill's list of fundamental values or basic goods includes many of the goods recognized by NNLT. She has, however, a nuanced understanding of those goods grounded in a traditional, yet revised, ethical method. She draws on Jürgen Habermas's discourse ethics and Martha Nussbaum's feminist Aristotelianism to develop a revised, feminist, natural law ethic and, based on this method, she posits goods that are both universal and particular. The goods are universal or, more accurately, "shared framing experiences and moral common ground,"[65] in that there is a "shared human being in the world."[66] They are particular, in that the "'shared' is achieved not beyond or over against particularity but in and through it."[67] Particularity is discerned through social criticism and intercultural dialectic.[68] Though Cahill espouses Nussbaum's method, she disagrees with her on some aspects of what constitutes shared human experience. Specifically, Cahill critiques Nussbaum for treating kinship as like "affiliation" or freely chosen relationships and bodily realities while largely neglecting its fundamental social significance for marriage and family.[69] Cahill notes that marriage and family are "the institutional arenas in which sexuality is endowed with significance for the whole fabric of society."[70] They are, therefore, central to consideration of ethics in general and feminist ethics in particular. Much historical oppression has been institutionalized against women on the basis of distorted definitions of marriage and family, and the failure to admit the intrinsic link between kinship, marriage, and family is another disservice to the feminist social agenda. Feminist thought is challenged to confront traditional patriarchal distortions of marriage and family, and to redefine them in terms of more just and caring social structures and a more profound reflection on gender relationships.[71]

Although the emphasis on kinship (marriage and family) as a good is shared with traditionalists, Cahill provides an interpersonal model of marriage that goes beyond traditionalist emphasis on biologism and procreationism over relationship. She espouses an interpersonal model of human sexuality but argues that this model "should be placed in a deeper and more nuanced social context, with better attention both to the familial ramifications of sexual partnerships, and to differences and similarities in cross-cultural experiences of sex, gender, and family."[72] This cultural sensitivity fundamentally distinguishes her method and definition of the goods of marriage and family from traditionalist methods and definitions of these goods. She highlights the importance of children as an aspect of that good, but she also emphasizes the need to see marriage and family as a complex interrelationship between relational, sexual, and social dimensions. In light of this complexity and totality, some absolute magisterial norms, such as the prohibition of artificial birth control, must be refined and redefined.

Furthermore, basic goods must be analyzed and evaluated cross-culturally in light of women's experiences. These experiences include positive and negative dimensions that shape our understanding of both a good and the norms that facilitate the realization of the good. Though we can agree on common ground regarding marriage and the family, that common ground is always realized in the historicity and particularity of human relationships. An essential consideration of this universality-particularity, and one that is very narrowly defined by traditionalists, is the interrelationship between sex and gender, that is, between being biologically male or female and the social and moral implications of maleness or femaleness.

Gender. Gender is distinct from sex. The human animal is essentially dimorphic, divided biologically into male and female sexes. Gender concerns the historical and socially constructed structures that particularize that biological difference at different times and in different places. These social structures are frequently patriarchal and oppressive to women, and they are, therefore, a central concern of feminist social criticism and feminist ethics. Cahill utilizes Susan Parson's work on Christian feminist theologies as a framework to present three feminist paradigms of gender that are evident in Christian ethics: *liberal, social constructionist,* and *naturalist.*[73]

The liberal paradigm emphasizes freedom and equality as foundational values for preserving human dignity, and the common good is ensured by protecting autonomy, self-determination, and human rights. Gender roles are minimized and defined in terms of equality; all people should have an equal right to education, work, and pay. This paradigm has little or no tolerance for the traditional gender roles assigned to men and women based on sexual differentiation. The social constructionist paradigm recognizes and resists the social construction of moral values. It recognizes that most or all moral values are constructed by social and moral ideologies created and perpetuated by those in power, and it resists the rampant abuses of this social construction by giving a voice to the voiceless. Men and women must redefine their identities and patterns of relationship in dialogue with those who have been marginalized. The common good is defined and preserved by deconstructing oppressive, and reconstructing just, social structures in light of new views of identity and patterns of relationship. In this paradigm, gender is not "natural"; it does not have a legitimate right to define social and personal relationships.

Finally, the naturalist paradigm investigates whether or not there are certain universal experiences shared by all human beings regardless of cultural influence and socialization, and whether or not these universal values can serve as a foundation for normative standards. Cahill shares this paradigm with traditionalists. In this paradigm, one way of interpreting gender is in terms of the shared universal experience of the reproductive differences between male and female. From this shared universal experience, naturalists ask whether or not these differences yield normative guidance for relationships and institutions and, if they do, what is the extent and nature of this guidance. There are three possible responses to the interrelationship between biological differentiation and gender. First, one can claim there is no interrelationship between the two; second, one can claim that biological differentiation entails defining characteristics of human "nature," which determine intrinsic or divinely established masculine and feminine roles based on that "nature"; and third, one can claim there is an interrelationship and that it is defined by a variety of historical, social, cultural, political, and economic institutions and realities. Radical feminists defend the first position, and espouse Parsons's liberal paradigm; the second and third positions are reflected in the anthropologies of traditionalists such as Pope John Paul II and Cahill, respectively.

John Paul II attaches ontological meaning to the male and female sex, with corresponding (absolute) normative implications for gender in marriage and in the Church. Genesis' second creation story reveals "the fundamental *truth . . . concerning man* created as man and woman in the image and likeness of God."[74] This fundamental truth reveals the fundamental equality between man and woman,[75] but their distinct physical nature entails distinct gender roles both in marriage and in the Church. Marriage is defined in terms of male–female complementarity, by which women are called to bring full dignity to motherhood and the conjugal life. Though John Paul II admits that women's roles have been defined too narrowly in terms of wife, mother, and family relationships without adequate access or representation in the public sphere, he also notes the following: "On the other hand, the true advancement of women requires that clear recognition be given to the value of their maternal and family role, by comparison with all other public roles and all other professions."[76] Men, however, are never defined primarily in terms of their roles as husbands or fathers; more emphasis is given, rather, to their social roles. Arguing from sexual complementarity to gender role complementarity perpetuates imbalances in power and perpetuates social structures that limit women's creativity and contributions in the public realm. Such distinctions between the feminine and the masculine in marriage and family life are more historically and culturally, than ontologically, determined.

Ecclesially, biological sexual differentiation and gender complementarity are used to defend the argument that only men can be priests. Jesus was a male, the apostles were males, and throughout its two-thousand-year year history only males have been ordained to the priesthood in the Catholic Church.[77] Because Jesus is the bridegroom and the Church is the bride, the male represents Jesus as bridegroom, who complements the female Church as bride. And because only males can be bridegrooms, it is ontologically determined also that only males can be priests. This perspective is reflected in Novak's comment. "Why is the priest male? It figures. It fits. The priest's maleness is a reminder of the role played in our salvation by the sacramentality of human flesh—not flesh in general but male flesh."[78] Through gender complementarity, John Paul can both defend the fundamental equality of men and women and yet argue that gender complementarity includes role complementarity. There are clear social and ecclesial roles grounded in masculinity and femininity; true complementarity must not entail a masculinization of the feminine or a feminization of the masculine.[79] John Paul posits gender complementarity, grounded in biological differentiation, to justify clearly defined roles for men and women both in marriage and in the Church.

Such definitions of complementarity have led many feminists to argue that complementarity, even under the guise of equality and dignity, always entails women's subordination.[80] Cahill proposes a more balanced approach to the interrelationship between sex and gender. It is the subordination and oppression found in traditionalist naturalist accounts of this relationship that leads her, at least in part, to consider gender as a foundational anthropological dimension in her ethical theory, and to refine it in light of social and cultural critical analysis. For her, biological differentiation is an essential and universal component of human experience that affects how men and women are in the world. Because too much emphasis has been, and continues to be, placed on biological difference to subordinate the feminine to the masculine, this situation begs for redress: "Gender understood as moral project entails the social humanization of biological tendencies, capacities, and differences, including the social ties that they, by their very nature, are inclined to create."[81] This social humanization must take place both in the marital relationship and ecclesially, and it takes place by the deconstruction and reconstruction of traditional gender roles and hierarchies in light of this humanization. Such reconstruction challenges many of the absolute magisterial norms on sexual ethics. It also allows for the ordination of women as priests (and bishops).

Sexual orientation revisited. Though we agree in large part with Cahill's method and the dimensions of sexual anthropology on kinship and gender she discerns from her method, we take issue with the role and function of sexual orientation within her anthropology. She explores the interrelationship between body and sexual orientation, and she rightly notes the complexity of that interrelationship. She seems hesitant, however, to draw out specific normative conclusions in light of it.[82] As noted above in our discussion of McCormick, however, we believe Cahill is too cautious in her assessment of (homo)sexual orientation as an aspect of human sexuality and does not go far enough in integrating that aspect into the normatively human. For her, the sources of moral knowledge (scripture, tradition, human experience) "point unavoidably toward a heterosexual norm for human sexuality."[83] Though this is historically true, the undoubted historicity of the sources raises the question of whether it is normatively true for men and women of all times, especially for men and women of permanent homosexual orientation, about which modern science is learning so much. This orientation fundamentally defines the homosexual person's physical, psychological, emotional, and spiritual attraction to another human being. Just as being male or female fundamentally shapes one's worldview, perspective, and experiences as male or female, so too does being homosexual or heterosexual. This integral view of human sexuality will require a more thorough reflection on the experiences of gays and lesbians, and its normative implications both for sexual expression and parenthood. We take up both of these issues in later chapters.

Body and pleasure. The common view of classical antiquity is that the human is *animal rationalis.* What specifically distinguishes humans from other animals is their ability to reason. This emphasis on reason, especially when it is combined with the dualism explicit in Plato and implicit in Aristotle, brought negative consequences for sexual anthropology in the natural law tradition. The body, and especially the pleasure associated with it, was often seen as a threat to human rationality.[84] This view of the body and pleasure as suspect has shaped much magisterial theological reflection on sexual anthropology. Although there have been profound developments in magisterial perceptions of the human body and an appreciation of pleasure associated with human sexuality,[85] there is still a disconnect between these theoretical developments and the norms guiding human sexual behavior in light of them.

Although the Magisterium recognizes the fundamental goodness of sexual pleasure within a marital relationship, this recognition is too closely associated with procreation and the traditional hierarchy of the ends of marriage. According to magisterial teaching, male orgasm, one of the most intense forms of sexual pleasure, can occur morally only within the marital act. Willed orgasm outside this relational and spatial context, no matter how pleasurable or how much it contributes to the sexual intimacy and union between the couple, is morally prohibited. There are at least two fundamental problems with this stance toward sexual pleasure and marital intimacy. First, though sexual intercourse can be the climax of sexual pleasure, not all orgasm takes place within sexual intercourse. Oral sex, anal sex, and mutual masturbation can be forms of sexual pleasure and enhance sexual intimacy for marital couples. Second, the Magisterium virtually neglects female orgasm. Kinsey reported that between 56 and 70 percent of women do not have an orgasm from penile–vaginal intercourse alone; direct clitoral stimulation, through manual manipulation or cunnilingus, is required to reach orgasm.[86] Orgasm is by no means the exclusive purpose of sexual activity, but responding to the specific needs of women in sexual activity makes it more enjoyable and pleasurable for both them and their male partners.

Attention to enjoyment and pleasure may facilitate the unitive and relational meanings of human sexual activity and is an important contribution to a holistic sexual anthropology. What is lacking in traditionalist accounts of sexual anthropology is an appreciation of the role and meaning of foreplay. A more holistic anthropology would recognize, appreciate, and incorporate pleasure and its multifaceted manifestations in sexual intimacy as capable of facilitating the unitive, if not necessarily the procreative, meaning of human sexual intercourse. Christine Gudorf has made profound contributions to incorporating pleasure into sexual anthropology.[87] Her reflections on the role and function of pleasure as an essential sexual anthropological consideration in human sexuality stand as an essential corrective to an overly rationalistic, procreationist view of the human sexual person.

Self-love and human flourishing. Susan Parsons raises an important point regarding the correlation between the traditional devaluation, trivialization, and fear surrounding women's "nature" and issues of self-esteem, which make it difficult for women "to love themselves, to believe in themselves, or to value themselves."[88] This devaluation is a result of a lack of appreciation for the distinctiveness of women's experiences, perspectives, and insights, and occurs on physiological, relational, and sociocultural levels. Physiologically, this correlation is evident in the scriptural and traditional laws regarding women's menstruation and purification rites; women's bodies are "defiled" because of this natural process and need "purification" before engaging in ritual worship practices. Such traditional taboos were ways of controlling women and defining their "natures" from exclusively physiological considerations, without asking what those experiences contribute to what it means to be a woman and a sexual being. In sexual anthropology, these experiences are part of what it means to be a woman, but often they are assigned negative, if not sinful, sexual and religious connotations that historically have shaped and defined women's experiences and their self-identity, perception, and esteem. Feminism incorporates distinctively feminine bodily experiences into ethical discourse and celebrates those dimensions as an integral part of what it means to be a woman. It also inquires how this meaning can be incorporated into a sexual anthropology that does not demean such experiences but interprets them in a way that fosters integration rather than division, separation, and judgment.

Although there has been a lack of appreciation for enjoyment and pleasure in theological sexual anthropologies, as noted above, the *exclusive* definition of women as objects of enjoyment and pleasure is also widespread. Social and cultural forms of feminine dehumanization take the following forms. First, the rampant objectification of women in print and film advertising, in prostitution, and in pornography is grounded in a hedonistic sexual anthropology. These types of exploitation define women from a strictly biological, aesthetic perspective and reduce them to objects of pleasure. Women's perception of themselves as aesthetic objects of pleasure for men (or boys) is instilled in girls at a young age. In the United States, for example, it is by no means trivial that Barbie is a size "0" and has a 39–18–33 figure implanting in girls' subconscious what constitutes the "ideal body" at a very young age.[89] These commercialized portrayals of women are damaging to both women and men, because they portray a purely physiological image of beauty and separate human sexuality from the relational sexual being.

The second form of social and cultural dehumanization limits women's participation in the workforce. Though changes are taking place gradually, throughout much of the world women continue to have little or no opportunity to participate in administrative positions that shape socioeconomic policy or affect social development and change. In countries where there are such opportunities, there is often a "glass ceiling"[90] for women in business, politics, academia, sports, and certainly the Catholic Church. Women have been exploited in the workforce, and their unique insights and contributions have been largely unnoticed and unappreciated. Those who succeed often do so because they have embraced the masculine social structures that control the workplace. The message in such a situation is clear: If a woman wishes to succeed, she must sacrifice her feminine "nature" and espouse a masculine "nature" that will allow her to compete according to the masculine rules for success.

Finally, women's familial roles have traditionally been defined in terms of nurturer and homemaker. The ideal woman is one who maintains the household, nurtures the children, and meets the physical, emotional, and psychological needs of the father and husband. Women who fall outside this ideal type are seen as falling short of their familial role. A woman who does not conform to this model is not a good wife, mother, or even woman. For a variety of social, historical, cultural, economic, psychological, and ethical reasons, this model is gradually being deconstructed, and feminist anthropologies recognize the infinite possibility of women's roles, grounded in their unique way of being-in-the-world, with its distinct and shared experiences, insights, and wisdom. Recognizing this being-in-the-world celebrates those possibilities in terms not of gender stereotypes but of existentially lived human relationships that allow for infinite possibilities of defining women's human flourishing and their contribution to the common good.

Although Parsons limits her discussion to the distinctiveness of women and the importance of highlighting this distinctiveness in a positive direction to foster self-esteem, self-love, and self-acceptance among women, such distinctiveness applies to other disenfranchised and oppressed groups as well. Gays and lesbians, for example, suffer many of the same biological, relational, and social forms of oppression as women, and as a result suffer similar damage to self-esteem. Though feminism is particularly sensitive to the experiences of women, and takes these experiences seriously in reconstructing a holistic sexual anthropology, it also draws from a variety of experiences, including male experience, to inform its anthropology.

Although we have highlighted many anthropological contributions of revisionist and feminist theologians to traditional anthropological perspectives—including a historically conscious, relational-centered anthropology that takes seriously family and kinship relations, gender, sexual orientation, embodiment, pleasure, and self-love—perhaps the most profound and significant contribution to sexual anthropology is the centrality of virtue in both natural law and feminism. The virtues are "traditional teleological (i.e., end-oriented) guides that collectively aim for the right realization of the human person."[91] There has been a renaissance in work on virtue ethics, spawned largely through Alasdair MacIntyre's classic text.[92] Keenan describes virtue ethics as "the attempt to articulate the normative anthropology of natural law."[93] It is a central aspect of Aquinas's natural law ethical theory, and it complements well the shift in focus from traditionalist's act-centered, classicist morality to revisionist and feminist character- and relational-centered, historically conscious morality. Virtue ethics does not focus primarily on actions. It asks another set of questions: Who are we? Who are we striving to become? How do we get there?[94] We consider each of these questions in turn.

Virtue Ethics: A Shift in Focus

Virtue ethics seeks an answer to the question of who we are in terms of virtue and how we reflect virtuous living in our lives. Aristotle lists eleven different virtues that constitute a fully human person; Aquinas lists four cardinal virtues, prudence, justice, temperance, and fortitude, and three theological virtues, faith, hope, and charity. The first four we acquire through deliberately willed habitual right actions; the theological virtues are gifts from God. These virtues define what it means to be fully human, and they help us to answer the question of who we are in terms of self-understanding and reflection. Are we just, loving, chaste human beings?

This self-reflection enables us to answer the second question, Who should we become? In honest and humble self-reflection, we can analyze and evaluate our strengths and weaknesses in terms of living out the virtues. We see where we attempt to incarnate and live out justice and love in our lives, and where we fail to do so. In light of both the successes and failures, we discern a moral compass that directs us toward a goal or end of greater fulfillment of the virtues in our particular historical, cultural, relational context. Not only do the virtues provide an end or goal for what it means to be fully human; they also indicate a path to achieve that end or goal. Prudence, in dialogue with the other virtues, directs us toward our end and answers the question: How do we get there? According to Aristotle and Aquinas, prudence enables us to attain the end by correctly looking at our place in the world and seeking the means to humanize ourselves, our relationships, and the world we live in. This is not a one-size-fits-all process, and strict adherence to an act-centered morality betrays the creative, imaginative, and unique nature of this journey. The answers to all three questions that virtue ethics seeks to answer are united by a historical view of reality that sees the human person as a developmental being. It is through an ongoing striving, seeking, and even sometimes failing that we define ourselves, realize our end, and seek to reach that end. Virtue ethicists agree on a shift in focus in ethics, but there are different models of virtue ethics that have anthropological implications.

A Patriarchal Paradigm of Virtue

Anne Patrick notes that there are two conflicting Catholic paradigms of virtue, a patriarchal paradigm and an egalitarian-feminist paradigm.[95] The paradigm one espouses will have a profound impact on one's anthropology, and the sexual ethics one constructs on the basis of that anthropology. A patriarchal paradigm of virtue reflects an anthropological, theological, and social dualism that has long plagued Christian theology: mind over body, male over female, biological over relational, otherworldly over this worldly, domination and subordination over equality and relationship. Though this perspective in theory emphasizes the importance and supremacy of the virtues of charity and justice, in fact chastity, "the pinnacle of perfection,"[96] is the ultimate virtue in its sexual anthropology, and sexual behavior is dictated by physicalist interpretations of natural law. Virtue is often defined in relation to vice. Whereas there is parvity of matter in sins against charity and justice, there is no such parvity of matter in sexual sins against chastity. All sexual sins constitute "grave matter." This confirms the de facto view that chastity is the most important virtue in this paradigm; sexual sins are the most dangerous of sins that endanger human salvation. In the patriarchal paradigm, the tendency is to emphasize the correlation between certain acts and their intrinsic violation of chastity. Rhonheimer, Grabowski, and the Magisterium posit such a patriarchal paradigm.[97]

There are, however, signs that there is an evolution in the Magisterium's patriarchal paradigm of virtue. This evolution is reflected in the *Catechism*'s definition of chastity: "Chastity means the successful integration of sexuality within the person and thus the inner unity of man in his bodily and spiritual being."[98] A sign that this definition of chastity is another example of old wine in new wineskins, however, is the fact that the Magisterium continues to defend its absolute sexual norms based on the revised formulation of this virtue without establishing a clear correlation between chastity as virtue, the inseparability principle of the unitive and procreative meanings of the sexual act, and the absolute norms derived from this principle. In addition, the Magisterium continues to teach that, in the case of sexual sins, there is no parvity of matter.[99] Finally, the whole treatment of sexual sins in the *Catechism* is seen as a violation of chastity, with only indirect discussion of the other virtues.[100]

An Egalitarian-Feminist Paradigm of Virtue

The egalitarian-feminist paradigm overcomes the dualisms of the patriarchal paradigm. In contrast to the often-disembodied rationality of the patriarchal paradigm, the egalitarian-feminist paradigm *embodies* human reason and posits the fundamental equality of men and women in the human community. In this paradigm, power is redefined from control to respect; power is "the energy of proper relatedness."[101] There is no implicit or explicit hierarchy of virtue in this paradigm. Rather, there is an integration of, and dialectic between, the virtues that equally govern both sexes individually and socially. Given the distorted and unhealthy view of chastity in the patriarchal model, the egalitarian-feminist paradigm does not emphasize the virtue of chastity. Within this paradigm, however, a balance is sought between viewing sexuality as a concern of personal virtue and social justice. Love and justice are mutually reinforcing virtues guiding all human relationships. From this perspective virtue and sexual anthropology must be deconstructed in their anthropological, theological, and social dualisms and reconstructed according to an integrated model of the virtues grounded in a holistic, sexual anthropology. James Keenan, among others,[102] has begun to develop an integrated vision of virtue ethics in relation to sexual ethics. He begins by noting a basic insufficiency of traditional accounts of virtue that posit a hierarchy among the virtues. Such a hierarchy preempts the recognition of tension between virtues, the clash of values in moral decision making, and a transformed view of the person from one whose powers need perfecting to one who is a relational being and whose modes of relationality must be realized correctly. From this emphasis on relationship, Keenan proposes four cardinal virtues.

Three virtues, justice, fidelity, and self-care, guide human relationship to the common good, particular relationships, and relationship with self, respectively. The fourth virtue, prudence, guides the interrelationship between those three and facilitates their integration. Such an integrated vision of the virtues recognizes the tension in morality between the universal and particular, impartiality and partiality, other and self. These virtues are universal in that all people share these relationships. They are particular in that they are defined and realized in a particular historical, cultural, relational context. They are uniquely Catholic when that particularity is informed by the virtue of mercy, "the willingness to enter into the chaos of another so as to respond to their need."[103] Mercy enables us to seek the common good, especially for those who are most marginalized in a society. It guides us in our particular relationships where forgiveness and reconciliation are the cornerstones of growth and development in the virtuous life. Mercy heals us in relationship to ourselves and, through prudence, guides us in caring for ourselves, so that we can care for and nurture particular relationships and seek the common good. The ancient Latin aphorism is as pertinent today as ever: *Nemo dat quod non habet* (no one gives what he/she does not have).

Keenan then indicates the structure of a sexual ethic that arises from these virtues. Justice entails appreciating all people and their intrinsic dignity as creatures in the image and likeness of God. Realizing another's human dignity always entails treating the other as subject, never as object. Justice applies to all our relationships, but it applies particularly to our relationship with the common good. Justice, informed and prompted by mercy, invites us to seek out those who are most marginalized, to work toward a more just society in sexual relationships and to confront structures of sexual oppression such as homophobia, the commercialization and commodification of human sexuality in prostitution and pornography, sexism, and gender discrimination. Working toward justice and the common good in the realm of human sexuality enables us to recognize and realize this virtue in our specific sexual relationships as well.

Whereas justice and the common good demand impartiality, fidelity and our specific sexual relationships demand decided partiality. Given their spatial and temporal finitude, men and women must prioritize their relationships and respond to them in a manner appropriate to the relationship. Fidelity, tempered with mercy, calls us to faithful and honest sexual expression in intimate sexual relationships. Fidelity requires responsible and appropriate sexual expression in those relationships and requires abstaining from sexual expression in other relationships where it is inappropriate. The primary, but not exclusive, context for sexual expression is marriage, a committed, loving, honest, and, for Catholics, sacramental relationship. Within fruitful marriages, fidelity strengthens the bond of intimacy between partners and extends that bond to children.

Finally, the virtue of self-care calls for the emotional, psychological, biological, and spiritual integration of one's own sexuality, directed toward self-knowledge and the capacity to relate to others as sexual beings. One of the major difficulties with the virtue of self-care is that the biological maturity of the sexual drive and the psychological maturity to act on that drive are not always in sync. Hormones draw young people toward sexual activity long before they are capable emotionally or psychologically of realizing the full implications of sexual intimacy. Self-care can make us aware of the disconnect between biological and psychological sexual maturity, and it can also enable us to be merciful when we act in a way that does not seek to integrate these two aspects of human sexuality. Self-care tempered by mercy invites us to be patient with ourselves as we seek to become integrated sexual selves and, given that sexual integration is a lifelong process, that mercy-patience is limitless. Keenan acknowledges that this sketch of a Catholic sexual ethic provides an opportunity for the community of faith to have an open dialogue about basic character traits and dispositions that represent what it means to be a faithful Catholic in the world today. Eventually, these basic dimensions will be translated into appropriate practices and sexual choices that reflect the virtues.

There is a profound difference between an egalitarian-feminist account of virtue ethics, a hierarchical-patriarchal account of virtue ethics, and a traditionalist and magisterial act-centered ethics. Given the uniqueness of each person, his or her sexual orientation, the relationship between a given couple, and the historical and cultural context of their relationship, virtue ethics does not posit absolute material norms that prohibit certain acts as always morally wrong. Virtue ethics does, however, posit moral absolutes, *formal absolutes*, norms that pertain not to acts but to character and/or virtue. A formal absolute norm, for example, might state the following: a not truly human, unjust, unloving, abusive, dishonest, uncommitted, sexual act, heterosexual or homosexual, is morally wrong; a truly human, just, loving, caring, honest, committed sexual act, heterosexual or homosexual, is morally right. The discernment and integration of the virtues in the context of a sexual relationship determines whether or not a sexual act is truly human and moral or not truly human and immoral. The process of discerning what is and what is not a truly human sexual act is carried on through communal reflection.

Conclusion

On the basis of revisionist and feminist contributions to sexual anthropology, we can summarize what we posit as essential qualities of our sexual anthropology. The sexual end of human beings is to become fully integrated sexual human beings, and this may be accomplished in marriage, partnership, religious celibacy, or the single life. This integration requires an appreciation of the emotional, relational, bodily, spiritual, and psychological dimensions of ourselves and others. The virtues of justice, fidelity, self-care, prudence, and mercy, all informed by love, serve in the ongoing individual and communal integration. All this takes place within a particular history and culture with all the exigencies of that history and culture, and is ongoing and developmental. In the next chapter, we present and explain a traditional yet revised principle guiding human sexuality in light of revisionist and feminist insights into sexual anthropology. And in the following chapters, we apply this principle to specific ethical issues.

Chapter Four

Unitive Sexual Morality

A Revised Foundational Principle and Anthropology

THEOLOGIANS WHO ESPOUSE the *Gaudium et spes* tradition find in the document a foundational principle for judging all human activity, including human sexual activity, namely, the criterion of the human person adequately considered. A reasonable question immediately arises: What does it mean to consider the human sexual person adequately in order to respond to complex moral issues surrounding human sexuality? In response to this question we first formulate a foundational principle of human sexuality; we then expand on the morally significant dimensions of that principle; and finally we draw insight from these dimensions in our reconstructed definition of complementarity, a recently introduced term in Catholic sexual teaching, to formulate a comprehensive explanation of a "truly human" (*humano modo*) sexual act. In this process we hope to offer an alternative to the primarily procreationist, traditionalist sexual anthropology in a more adequately considered unitive sexual anthropology. We do so with some trepidation because sexuality is far from an unambiguous reality. Like all the human appetites, sexuality can be used for good, and then it is loving, beautiful, unifying, and perhaps procreative. Or it can be abused for evil, and then it is unloving, ugly, divisive, and destructive of life. As the American bishops have noted, "the gift of human sexuality can be a great mystery at times."[1] The acknowledgment of mystery, however, does not free theologians or the Magisterium from the ongoing task of attempting to discern the human as sexual being and of determining the "nature," meaning, and morality of sexuality and sexual acts in the context of human relationships.

Gaudium et spes and a Foundational Sexual Principle

Gaudium et spes articulates a fundamental principle with respect to the essential meaning of human sexuality and sexual acts. In this chapter, we utilize this principle, adding in brackets certain components of our own that are not contained in the document but are, we believe, faithful to the Catholic tradition's understanding of the role and function of human sexuality in a marital relationship. The principle is the following: "[Conjugal] love is uniquely expressed and perfected through the marital act. The actions within marriage by which the couple are united intimately and chastely are noble and worthy ones. Expressed in a manner which is truly human, these actions signify and promote that mutual self-giving by which spouses [immediately] enrich each other [and mediately enrich their family and community] with a joyful and a thankful will."[2]

Our exegesis of this principle proposes a developed theology of the unitive purpose of human sexuality and sexual acts in a marital relationship, and inquires about sexual possibilities for persons other than the married heterosexuals that *Gaudium et spes* and the tradition have in mind. The context of this latter consideration is not simply the physical acts themselves but also the meaning and "nature" of interpersonal relationship and the sexual acts that take place within this context. We also ask how sexual acts reach beyond the couple to have an impact on their extended family and community.

We note two preliminary considerations. The first is an important distinction between sexuality and sexual activity. This distinction is expressed well by the U.S. bishops: "*Sexuality* refers to a fundamental component of personality in and through which we, as male or female, experience our relatedness to self, others, the world, and even God. *Sex* refers *either* to the biological aspects of being male or female (i.e., a synonym for one's gender) *or* to the expressions of sexuality, which have physical, emotional, and spiritual dimensions, particularly genital actions resulting in sexual intercourse and/or orgasm."[3]

Given our discussion in the previous chapter, we regret the implied synonymous equivalence of sex and gender, but sexuality is correctly described as intrinsic to the human person, in whom there is no division between the physical and spiritual. This important recognition banishes the dualism that has plagued the Christian tradition regarding human sexuality. Humans are created by God as sexual beings, embodied subjects whose spiritual and physical dimensions merge into a single being that expresses itself in a profound and holy manner in intimate human relationship and sexual acts. *Sexual* is an adjective that describes not only the actions of human beings but also their essential reality. Humans can and may renounce sexual action; they can never renounce their intrinsic sexual being.

The sexual drive, which is a powerful physiological drive, has three equally powerful personal meanings: It is pleasurable, relational, and procreative. Scientific research has demonstrated that sexuality influences our personality, our brain activity, our understandings of self and other, and our relationships,[4] and it also provides us with a means of personal communication that is carried out intimately, profoundly, and bodily in sexual actions. For the past one thousand years, the Catholic tradition has insisted that just and loving marital relationships and the sexual actions that both express and nourish them are sacraments, symbols of the loving relationships between God and God's people and Christ and Christ's Church. A group commissioned by the National Conference of Catholic Bishops boldly asserts, indeed, that mutually pleasurable marital sexual acts are possibly the human experiences that most fully symbolize the loving communication within the divine Trinity, a statement that affirms the goodness of both human sexuality and fully human sexual acts.[5]

The second preliminary consideration is that we will refer to the "dimensions" of the principle we have enunciated to underscore that our understanding of the principle and its dimensions is subject to development, evolution, revision, and expansion as human understanding evolves and expands. Remember Bernard Lonergan's explanation that perspectivism in human knowledge arises from three factors. First, human knowers are finite, their information is incomplete, and they do not attend to or master all the data available to them. Second, knowers are selective, given their past and present sociohistorical context and the range of data offered to them. Third, knowers are individually different, and we can expect them to make different selections of data. It would be dishonest to pretend that the present, indeed any, authors are free from these constrictions.

The Relationship between Conjugal Love and Sexual Intercourse

The foundational principle we have advanced needs explication. First, sexual intercourse is a unique expression and perfection of conjugal love. An individual's sexuality is expressed in and through daily interactions with other human beings, not just spouses. Humans naturally relate as sexual beings. The term "intercourse," frequently used as a euphemism for sex, literally means "communication or dealings between or among people." In this sense, we have human intercourse with numerous people throughout the day. Sexual intercourse, however, is a unique and particular expression of the communication-intercourse of our very being with a special loved one.

Although Western culture and churches tend to give the sexual aspect of the marital relationship a disproportionate focus, studies show the following relationship between age and frequency per year of sexual intercourse of a married couple: from age eighteen to twenty-nine years, 110.2 times; from age thirty to thirty-nine, 86.2 times; from age forty to forty-nine, 70.6 times; from age fifty to fifty-nine, 54.5 times; from age sixty to sixty-nine, 33.4 times; and age seventy and above, 17.6 times.[6] As these statistics make clear, even at a couple's sexual peak, the time spent in sexual intercourse is proportionately minimal. These data are noted not to diminish the significance of sexual intercourse for the marital relationship but to situate it in a more realistic context. As *Gaudium et spes* teaches, the act of intercourse is the perfection of conjugal love. It expresses and strengthens the interpersonal union between a couple, which is why, going back to Saint Paul, the Church has recognized that abstaining from sexual relations for too long can be detrimental to the marital union.[7] The marital relationship finds an essentially nurturing component in just and loving sexual acts that *procreate*, occasionally in a physiological sense, always in the sense of creating life for the couple, their bonded relationship, their family, and their wider community. Just and loving sexual union creates and nurtures love, the very essence of Christian discipleship; it *makes love*, as we say in everyday language.

Multiple Dimensions of Human Sexuality

It is generally agreed that there is no Greek noun that articulates the specificity of either male or female sexuality, but in the Western tradition there are always two poles in the discussion: the subject (the male) and the object (the female), the agent (the male) and the patient (the female). Aristotle articulates clearly the two poles and their contributions in the sexual act: "The female as female is passive, and the male as male is active."[8] There is always also the conviction that the pleasures (*aphrodisiai*) of sexual intercourse are intrinsically harmful. Pythagoras responds to a questioner who asked him the best time for intercourse: "When you want to lose what strength you have." He further advises: "Keep to the winter for sexual pleasures, in summer abstain; they [*aphrodisiai*] are less harmful in autumn and spring, but they are always harmful and not conducive to health."[9] Aristotle agrees and advises intercourse only when there is a pressing need.[10] Michel Foucault isolates four sexual figures, "four privileged objects of knowledge," that emerged in the nineteenth century: "the hysterical woman, the masturbating child, the Malthusian couple, and the perverse adult."[11] We know from the *scientia sexualis* of the twentieth century and from feminist critique that these traditional assumptions about human sexuality are not entirely accurate, and we prefer to deal with sexuality in its five dimensions—*physical, emotional, psychological, spiritual,* and *relational*—and we consider each in turn.

Physical Sexuality

We deal first with physical union, the obvious joining of bodies. In their excellent treatment of human sexuality, Masters and Johnson explain four phases in the physical process of sexual intercourse. Phase one is the excitement phase, in which, for the man, the penis becomes erect due to the flow of blood into the penile tissues and, for the woman, there is moistening of the vagina, enlarged breasts, and tensing of the muscles with increased breathing and heart rate. Phase two is the plateau phase, the entry of the penis into the vagina, further quickening of the heart and breathing, mounting erotic pleasure, and the appearance of a flush on both bodies. Most frequently noted in this phase is the penetration of the female by the male; not so frequently noted, but true in every just and loving intercourse, is the welcoming envelopment of the male by the female. The male penetrates the female, not only physically but also psychologically and emotionally, and is physically enveloped by her who, in turn, enters emotionally and psychologically into the male. In their intercourse they become, in very deed, a two-in-one-bodiness.[12]

That a man and a woman become one body in marriage has been much too exclusively linked in the West to this physical dimension of sexuality. From what has been said so far in this book about the place of sexuality in a human life and of sexual intercourse in a married life, it will be clear that this dimension is certainly included in becoming one body, but it is far from all there is. In Hebrew culture "body" implies the whole person: "One personality would translate it better, for 'flesh' in the Jewish idiom means 'real human life.'"[13] In marriage a man and a woman enter into a personal union, not merely a physical or genital one. Before their union, they were two individuals; after their union, they are ever afterward a couple, one coupled, social person. Rabbis teach that it is only in marriage and the union of man and woman in one coupled person that the image of God may be discerned in them. An unmarried man or an unmarried woman is not a whole man or woman. The mythic stories, always interested in etiology, the origin of things, say that it was so "in the beginning," and that it was so by the will and creation of God.[14] For the believing Christian, as for the Fathers whose teaching we considered in chapter 1, there could be no greater foundation for both the human and the religious goodness of marriage, sexuality, and parenthood.

Phase three, the climax, discharge of semen by the male and a number of orgasmic muscle spasms by the female, is the moment of greatest pleasure and ecstasy, the moment sought in every act of intercourse. This pleasure is, of course, quite individual, and it is part of the ambiguity of sexuality and sexual intercourse that, in the climactic moments of orgasm, the act intended to be the giving of one person to the other throws each back on herself and himself in a solitude of pleasure. The act that is intended to be and is fully unitive, more conscious of the other and the other's pleasure than of the self or the self's pleasure, at its peak moment is actually also divisive. Foucault reminds us of the similarity the ancients saw between sexual orgasm and epilepsy, both moments of being most alone and vulnerable.[15] This is but one instance of the essential ambiguity of sexuality and sexual activity; we will call attention to others as this chapter unfolds. Phase four is the resolution phase, in which the couple relax and blood pressure and respiration return to normal.[16] Though these four phases are not to be "used as a 'check list' against which to measure sexual performance,"[17] every sexually active couple can, at least sometimes, identify them in their intercourse, a natural fact that offers profound evidence for sexual "nature" as God intended it and for the "natural" pleasure of the sexual act that has been so suspect in Christian history.

A unifying component of these various physical stages of the sexual act is pleasure. A comment by Foucault in his magisterial *History of Sexuality* is à propos here. He describes the development of sexual morality in the early Roman Empire as taking place in three directions. "A 'monopolistic' principle: no sexual relations outside marriage. A requirement of 'dehedonization': sexual intercourse between spouses should not be governed by an economy of pleasure. A procreative finaliza-tion: goal [of sexual intercourse] should be the birth of offspring. These are three fundamental traits marking the ethics of conjugal existence that certain moralists developed at the beginning of the imperial epoch, an ethics whose elaboration owes a great deal to late Stoicism."[18] These three traits took deep root in the Catholic tradition, to such an extent that sexual pleasure has always been morally suspect in the tradition, even though it is a natural and intrinsic part of sexual intercourse. Pleasure unites with the relational dimension of humanity to draw us toward another person in the most profound way through sexual activity. It is a good cre-ated by God and given as gift to humans. Like all gifts, it can be used for good or evil. The abuses of pleasure and the danger of a morality based purely on pleasure, hedonism, are fully evident in the sociohistorical past and present. Such abuses, however, cannot and do not diminish the valuable and essential role of integrating pleasure as a natural component of human sexual morality. The nonrecognition in traditional Catholic teaching of the value of sexual foreplay and/or intimacy apart from vaginal intercourse, in oral or anal sex, for example, and its condemnation as immoral, could be interpreted, at least in part, as a failure to appreciate sexual plea-sure as an intrinsic, "natural" component of human sexuality and sexual activity.

Thomas Aquinas insisted that human reason must always be in control of sexual intercourse. Not that there is any control *in* the act of intercourse, but there is reason *before* the act and, because there is, Aquinas teaches, sexual intercourse between a husband and a wife is not sinful. Excess of passion, which corrupts virtue (and which is, therefore, as in Augustine, sinful), not only impedes reason but also destroys it. Such, however, is not the case with the intensity of pleasure in sexual intercourse between a husband and a wife for, "though a man is not then under control, he has been under the control of reason in advance."[19] Besides, nature has been created good by God, so that "it is impossible to say that the act in which offspring are created is so completely unlawful that the means of virtue cannot be found in it."[20] There remains some ambivalence toward sexual desire and pleasure. They are "occu-pations with lower affairs that distract the soul and make it unworthy of being joined actually to God,"[21] but they are not sinful at all times and in all circumstances. They are, in fact, meritorious within the ends of marriage,[22] and Aquinas asserts explicitly that to forgo the pleasure and thwart the end would be sinful.[23] This latter opinion leads E. C. Messenger, a well-known Thomistic commentator, to declare that "both passion and pleasure are natural concomitants of the sexual act and, so far from diminishing its goodness, if the sex act is willed beforehand according to right rea-son, the effect of pleasure and passion is simply to heighten and increase the moral goodness of the act, not in any way to diminish it."[24] This conclusion is totally in line with Thomistic principles, is bolstered by Augustine's claim that the Fathers of the Old Testament took "natural delight" in sexual intercourse, and may be verified in every just and loving act of marital intercourse.[25]

An essential component of a revised sexual ethical principle, then, we suggest, must be a deeper understanding of pleasure and its function in human sexuality, and the development of parameters for its responsible and moral expression. Such an investigation will discuss foreplay and other types of sexual intimacy leading to orgasm as legitimate moral expressions of sexual intimacy, and expand the parameters of traditional teaching that limits orgasm to heterosexual and vaginal intercourse.[26]

Emotional Sexuality

A theology of the unitive must necessarily include the emotional dimension of human sexuality, which cannot be separated from the emotional dimensions of the human being. Emotions—strong, generalized feelings with both physical and psychological manifestations—can be either positive or negative, and both categories essentially characterize a human, sexual being. Positive emotions include love, joy, hope, anticipation, humor, trust, happiness, passion, and inquisitiveness; negative emotions include hatred, sadness, despair, anxiety, anger, resentment, hurt, dissatisfaction, and brokenness. These positive and negative emotions are further influenced and have unique expression and importance in light of culture, ethnicity, gender, history, and experience. In the act of just and loving sexual intercourse, there is a complex combination and expression of emotions that unite two separate persons into one coupled person, the *one body* of Genesis, in an act that can heal, comfort, and create wholeness or, on occasion, affirm and console woundedness, anxiety, or brokenness. Either way, the sexual act reveals the wide spectrum of human emotions and brings out total vulnerability in both the positive and negative emotions. Indeed, analyzing human sexuality and the sexual act in terms of its emotional dimension entails a glorious mystery of the wounded human in his or her ongoing search for wholeness in intimate relationship.

Psychological Sexuality

Emotions are a unique and particular expression of a person's basic and stable human identity, and the emotional and psychological dimensions of human sexuality are intimately related. The psychiatrist Jack Dominian presents an excellent synthesis of six psychological dimensions that illustrate the sexual act between a loving couple.[27] First, through sexual intercourse a couple affirms one another's identity. The sexual act is symbolic in that, when we become naked in front of another human person, we become totally and completely vulnerable. To make love in "a truly human manner" is both a mutual affirmation and a mutual unconditional acceptance of the other, warts and all, that is, with all her and his physical, emotional, psychological, and spiritual blessings and flaws. This affirmation and acceptance progresses through various stages. As we have indicated above, sexual intercourse is more frequent early in a marriage, and perhaps it is also more passionate. As the relationship develops and deepens over the years, the routine of sexual affirmation and acceptance may lose its novelty, attraction, and excitement, but this is not to be interpreted to mean that affirmation and acceptance cease. In reality they increase as the couple comes to know and accept one another more profoundly and intimately over time. Though the novelty and excitement of sexual intercourse may diminish, the affirmation and acceptance of the person, a unique self created in the image and likeness of God and affirmed, accepted, and loved unconditionally, becomes more profound. Repetition may breed familiarity and a sense of routine, but it also deepens unconditional appreciation and acceptance of the other as he or she is.

In a very real sense the sexual act and relationship become symbols—sacraments, the Catholic Church teaches[28]—of the embodied reality of God's unconditional love for human beings. God accepts us totally and unconditionally in our strengths and weaknesses, and spouses unconditionally accept one another in their strengths and weaknesses. Both these acceptances are symbolized in and through sexual intercourse throughout the duration of the relationship, no matter how routine it might become. As sacrament and symbol, the act of intercourse shares in the common characteristic of all symbols. It is "characterized not by its uniformity [as is a simple sign] but its versatility. It is not rigid or inflexible but mobile."[29] It is also opaque and difficult to discern, and this opacity, Ricoeur comments, "constitutes the depth of the symbol which . . . is inexhaustible."[30] That the act of sexual intercourse is symbolic and dense with opaque meanings is one more reason for its essential mystery and ambiguity.

Second, the sexual act reflects, affirms, and creates gender identity, a fundamental dimension of sexual identity. Gender is concerned with the socially constructed meanings of femininity or masculinity. It is determined not only by individual sexuality but also by culture, ethnicity, and experience, and it is expressed in actions, interactions, social roles, and their expression in sexual acts. Dominian describes this gender expression as a liturgy of exchange, a divine language, in which a couple communicates with each other through sexual desire.[31] In the formation and development of sexual identity through a recognition and embodiment of gender roles, it is crucial that sexual activity be a form of loving, open, honest, and authentic human communication. If it is, then the act becomes humanly communicative at the deepest level; if it is not, then the same act can cause future possibilities for the communication and formation of healthy sexual identity to stagnate, or even block them. This is yet one more example of the essential ambiguity of human sexual activity.

Psychological studies repeatedly indicate that one of the greatest threats to healthy human development, including sexual development, is poor self-esteem, the third psychological dimension of human sexuality.[32] The Christian tradition has not always done an adequate job of emphasizing healthy self-love. Jesus' great commandment is well known: "'You shall love the Lord your God with all your heart, with all your soul, with all your mind, and with all your strength.' The second is this: 'You shall love your neighbor as yourself'" (Mark 12:28–34; Matt 22:34–40,46b;

and Luke 10:25–28). Not so well known is the fact that there are *three* commandments in this latter text: love God, love neighbor, *and* love self. Typically, the Christian tradition has interpreted neighbor love as altruistic and agapaic and self-love as egocentric and antithetical to the love of the gospel. This certainly *can* be the case, and the cultures of many developed countries that emphasize radical individualism encourage egocentric love, but egocentric love is not the healthy self-love demanded by the gospel. Authentic self-love first affirms oneself as a self-in-God, good, valuable, and lovable, and then, in alliance with neighbor-love, turns toward the other and gives this good, valuable, and lovable self-in-God unconditionally to the other. As Aquinas might argue: *Nemo dat quod non habet* (no one gives what he does not have). If a man does not truly and fully accept himself, in both his wholeness and his brokenness, he can neither give himself fully to an other person nor fully accept the other person. So it is, too, with a woman.

This is precisely the type of self-giving to the other that is reflected in a most profound way through sexual intercourse, the giving of self that affirms the desired goodness and uniqueness not only of the other but also of the self, and thus affirms also the self-esteem of both the gifter and the recipient. It also creates communion. This is why it is so important that the other in sexual intercourse never be objectified, as is the case in promiscuous sexual encounters. Many people, unsure of themselves, seek affirmation of who they are and strive to build self-identity and self-esteem through casual sex, but because casual sex is not an unconditional giving of self to the other, the search is constantly frustrated and neither self-identity nor self-esteem is ever truly established or affirmed.

Fourth, sexual intercourse is therapeutic and relieves distress. The embodied human person is a psychosomatic unity, an intrinsic union of *soma* and *psyche*, body and spirit. The dualism between these two realities the Western Church learned from Gnosticism is false;[33] there is no dualism. There is distinction between body and spirit in the human being but there is no separation, and there is ongoing and constant dialogue between them. When a couple makes love, each person brings to that experience all the psychological burdens that accompany daily life including worries about the relationship, work, finances, children, and other responsibilities. The act of sexual intercourse makes possible the suspension of those anxieties and worries, at least for the moment, and has a healing effect on the individual. This relief of distress, however, depends on the nature of the relationship. If the relationship is just, loving, committed, and honest, relief of distress is often an intrinsic component of sexual activity. If, however, the relationship is promiscuous, inauthentic, or dishonest, while the physical act can still suspend distress for the moment, the aftereffects of that experience can cause greater distress in the form of guilt, a sense of inauthentic or dishonest intimate communication, or objectification of the other.

There is a strange paradox about human sexuality in the West in general and in the Catholic Church in particular. On the one hand, access to casual sexual activity is at an all-time high; on the other hand, so too is the occurrence of depression.

Though this correlation is purely descriptive and in no way prescriptive, it still seems reasonable to conclude that facile sex alone does not provide relief of distress or depression. Only sex within a just and loving human relationship does that. Sexual intercourse can be therapeutic in a healthy, just, loving, committed relationship; but in an unhealthy, unjust, unloving, uncommitted relationship, its psychic impact can be greater distress engendered by disappointment, guilt, and a sense of objectification. The intrinsic psychosomatic "nature" of the human person and, therefore, of human sexual activity underscores the potential of that activity for generating healing or distress, the discrimination between the two being the nature and meaning of the relationship.

Fifth, sexual intercourse is reconciling. There are no conflict-free relationships, not even in the most just and loving of marriages. Frictions, disagreements, misunderstandings are all inevitable aspects of any human relationship, and any and all of these experiences can create hurt, distress, and general distrust of the other in the relationship. One is not likely to find couples who desire sexual intimacy at the peak of such quarrels. Intimacy comes after the resolution of the quarrel and may be an intrinsic component of that resolution. Some couples claim that the best sex they have is after an intense argument. This is because sexual intimacy heals those wounds and reaffirms the bond and commitment that may have been threatened by a quarrel. It is difficult for a couple to have a fulfilling sexual experience if the other dimensions of the relationship are not in sync. Sexual intercourse affirms self, other, and the relationship through healing and reconciliation.

Sixth and finally, sexual intercourse is a profound act of thanksgiving or Eucharist. The embodied nature of the human person binds him or her to bodily expression, which is best exemplified, though by no means limited to, verbal language. Beyond verbal language there is body language, and beyond body language there is ritual language, symbolic actions filled with socially approved meanings. Couples can say to one another "I love you," "I thank you," or "I forgive you," and in the spoken words they are reaching to meanings far beyond the words. They can say the same things in socially approved actions, by looks, by touches, by gifts, and in all these actions they are similarly reaching far beyond the actions to express love, forgiveness, reconciliation, affirmation, and thanksgiving. In the physical action of sexual intercourse, an action as symbolic in the West as any spoken word, they express all these things in the most profound and total way available to an embodied human being, namely, through the completely unmasked and therefore totally vulnerable body. They say to one another, in the words of the ancient Anglican wedding ritual, "with this *body* I thee worship." They say, that is, in the etymological meaning of the word *worship*, I ascribe worth to you and to us, and for this worth I give thanks. The thanksgiving embodied in intercourse is yet one more profound affirmation of the self, of the other, and of their relationship.

Couples who are Catholic cannot help but link this moment of ritual, sexual thanksgiving for human relationship with that other ritual, liturgical thanksgiving for divine relationship they call Eucharist.[34] "This is my body which is given for you," Jesus says to his disciples at the Last Supper.[35] "This is my body given for and to you," lovers say to one another in the act of intercourse. In both the Last Supper and the sex, the body and the person synonymous with it are vulnerable, even broken, but both body and person are given in love to the other, trusting that they will be received in love and handled with care. In the Last Supper, both past and present, the Body of Christ is given to be eaten; so, too, are the bodies of the truly human lovers in sexual intercourse. Thatcher points out, legitimately, that "many of the intimacies of love-making are fairly literally an eating of the body of the person one loves. Kissing, especially deep kissing; the use of the tongue in caressing and stimulating; biting, sucking, and nibbling; these are all patently ways in which we eat the bodies of our lovers."[36] The central theological point here is a very Catholic one. The God incarnate in the Christ who gives his body in the Supper for the salvation of all is the same God incarnate in the lovers and their act of mutual self-giving for the salvation of their relationship. In Catholic theology, the one ritual is as sacramental of God as the other, which is why both are listed among the Catholic sacraments.

These six psychological dimensions that are communicated and experienced in just and loving sexual acts—affirm self and other, create and affirm gender identity, embody the "triple love-commandment," restore and reconcile persons, and embody thanksgiving—create, contribute to, and sustain the psychosomatic and spiritual well-being of sexual persons.

Spiritual Sexuality

For the Christian, sexuality, love, and spirituality are all intertwined. "Spirituality" is not an easy term to define, especially in relation to sexuality, where much of the Christian tradition restricted authentic spirituality to those who were celibate.[37] As the tradition has evolved, however, empowered by the Second Vatican Council's call of the whole Church to holiness,[38] so too has the understanding that all people, married and celibate, are capable of a spiritual life. Far from being an impediment to authentic spirituality, truly human sexuality and sexual acts, embraced and used as gifts of the creator God, can enhance, deepen, and develop one's spirituality. Christian spirituality is a person's foundational relationship with the triune God, Father, Son, and Holy Spirit, lived out in daily life. This foundational relationship shapes all other relationships, including sexual relationships, and is reflected in them, helping believers to grow in their relationship both with God and with other humans. Far from suppressing human sexuality, the foundational spiritual relationship with the creator God fully affirms it.

In the Christian story, Father, Son, and Spirit are all intimately related to human existence. The Father created 'adam, humankind, in God's own image and likeness, and judged this creation to be "very good."[39] Sexuality is an intrinsic part of both this creation and what it means to be human and, because humans are created in the image and likeness of God, it must also be somehow part of the divine mystery we name God. The Son became embodied, incarnated, in human reality, thereby affirming everything that is human, including sexuality. The available evidence indicates that Jesus was celibate, but he was still fully human and, therefore, a sexual being. The doctrine of the incarnation, therefore, is the most radical affirmation of the physical embodiedness of the human and of human sexuality, and of the goodness of both. Miles writes that the early Christians "cared for living bodies and dead bodies because they understood that the incarnation of Christ had once and for all settled the issue of the value of the human body."[40] The bishops of the United States agree. "The *incarnation* of God's Word," they write, "the divine becoming fully human, adds even greater dignity or divine approbation to our being corporeal, sexual beings."[41] The Spirit of God, who proceeds from the mutual, loving self-gift of Father and Son, continues to grace the truly human sexuality affirmed in the relationship between just and loving husbands and wives.

The relationship of communion between the three persons of the Trinity provides the model for every genuine human relationship, and the grace of the Spirit enables each and every believer to share this communion with a loved other through a multitude of actions, including sexual actions. *The* characteristic of marriage that distinguishes it from other forms of friendship is that it is expected to be an exclusive sexual relationship. From what we have explained in this section, it is not difficult to conclude that the communion between spouses expressed in the sexual intercourse that characterizes marriage is also a sacrament of the divine communion. That, of course, is precisely what the Catholic Church intends when it teaches that marriage is a sacrament.

The act of sexual intercourse allows humans a unique insight into the love shared within the Trinity. In intercourse there is the unconditional gift of self to the other and the unconditional reception of the other's gift of self in return. Such mutuality, reciprocity, and unconditional acceptance reflect the total self-surrender within the Trinity. "It is our capacity to love and be loved that *makes* us most God-like. It is that capacity that most reflects Him and we are called to develop."[42] The love, including the sexual love, shared by a couple in relationship draws them together into communion, and this shared communion reflects the communion of the Trinity, draws them closer to God, strengthens their relationship, and overflows into all their other relationships. Most profoundly, this sexual communion always procreates new life, just as the loving communion between the Father and Son yields the Spirit. Even in cases where biological procreation is neither possible nor desired for legitimate reasons, their sexual union procreates and enhances the couple's life in communion in imitation, and as sacrament, of the divine Trinity, the infinite source of gracious and loving communion.

Sexual intercourse is like throwing a rock into a small pond. The initial splash is the intimate union of the couple in the sexual act. The ripple effect extends to and affects all their other human relationships and experiences. When the ripples reach the shore, there is reverberation, and the ripples return to the point of initial splash. Genuinely just and loving sexual acts ripple out in a similar way to create and enhance virtues such as love, commitment, integrity, reconciliation, forgiveness, and justice that then have an impact on other social relationships. These virtues enable believers to live out their Christian vocation to neighbor-love and, in its turn, living out this vocation further shapes their knowledge and understanding of sexual intimacy. Spirituality, lived relationship with the triune God, and its manifestation in human relationships, including sexual relationships, is a central reason why the Church emphasizes the importance of sexual intercourse within the marital relationship. Sexual intercourse is the most profound source within that relationship for bonding the couple together, for participating in the life of the Trinity, and for sharing that participation and life with others.

Relational Sexuality

Spirituality is all about relationship. So, too, is human sexuality, grounded in relationship with God, with neighbor, and with self. Human sexuality is a gift from God that draws us toward interpersonal communion. It is an intrinsic, mysterious dimension of human beings that draws individuals out of self and toward another. "Sexuality is a dimension of one's restless heart, which continually yearns for interpersonal communion, glimpsed and experienced to varying degrees in this life, ultimately finding full oneness only in God, here and hereafter."[43] In and through human sexuality and relationships, humans seek to become whole and holy. This relational gift is at the core of human identity, and it allows humans to enter into communion with God and one another.

Relationship with the gospel "neighbor" takes several forms. First, and primarily, neighbor is the spouse or intimate other. In that most beautiful and sexual of Hebrew love songs, the Song of Songs, the male lover addresses his beloved nine times as *plesion*, neighbor (1:9, 15; 2:2, 10, 13; 4:1, 7; 5:2; 6:4), leading Sampley to comment that "the content of the occurrence of *plesion* in the Song of Songs confirms that *plesion* is used as a term of endearment for the bride."[44] Sexual acts are the most intimate communion between two people, where two individuals become physically and personally one couple. Catholic tradition refers to this relationship in terms of a covenant and a communion of persons, and it limits this covenantal communion to marriage between a man and a woman.[45] A second close neighbor is family. God's gift of sexuality provides women and men with the desire to unite as couple and to create, nurture, and educate new life out of their union, thereby creating family. The Catholic Church correctly describes family as the "original cell of social life,"[46] the "domestic church,"[47] a relational community of partnered life and love.

Neighbor also extends to the human family and community beyond the domestic church. Discipleship is an all-encompassing relational reality, embracing even enemies.[48] Too often in history, Catholic moral theology has focused on the individual's acts and their impact on the individual's relationship with God, while neglecting the broader social implications of those acts. For instance, whereas magisterial teaching has focused on the separation of the unitive and procreative dimensions of the sexual act as the basis for condemning artificial reproduction, some moral theologians have focused more on the social justice issues of using such technology in terms of cost and the use of limited medical resources.[49] We shall develop this point later in chapter 8. This shift in focus is especially relevant in sexual ethics. Too often, sexual and social ethics are seen in isolation from each other, each utilizing its own methodology and having its own point of reference. Whereas the Magisterium's sexual ethics tend to focus on acts and absolute norms that guide individuals and married couples, its social ethics tend to focus on the complex network of interrelationships that constitute a community and general principles to guide these interrelationships toward the common good. Sexuality as a relational concept challenges us to more fully integrate its individual and communal moral dimensions.

Finally, human sexuality is a unique gift to each individual that summons everyone to recognize, accept, appreciate, and integrate the gift in the Christian task of drawing closer to God in Christ and neighbor. History demonstrates beyond doubt that, with the exception of an intellectual and abstract acknowledgment that sexuality and sex are good because they are created by a good God, much of the Christian tradition has not appreciated the goodness of this gift practically and concretely. This lack of appreciation for the gift of human sexuality in its various forms has created a great deal of guilt and self-loathing, with the unfortunate consequence that people sometimes live out their sexuality in unhealthy ways. Perhaps this is truer nowhere than in the case of men and women with a homosexual orientation, who feel personally rejected by the Church in what Jordan refers to as the "rhetoric of moral management."[50] This rhetoric is grounded in exclusion and is evidenced in the Magisterium's designation of homosexual orientation as "objectively disordered,"[51] a category that inhibits many gay and lesbian Catholics from revealing their sexual orientation.[52] Negatively labeling them as "objectively disordered" does not facilitate homosexuals' integration of their sexuality. Sexuality is intimately related to our attraction to other persons, to love, and to committed relationships. For this natural attraction to be nurtured and manifested in responsible relationships, it must be accepted and integrated in a healthy manner. It may be true that no human person has fully integrated his or her human sexuality, but Christians still need to be conscious of and critically reflect upon perspectives that, consciously or unconsciously, frustrate the personal acceptance and integration of sexuality.

These dimensions of the sexual person—physical, emotional, psychological, spiritual, and relational—explain the foundational principle for human sexuality contained in *Gaudium et spes* and reflect a holistic sexual anthropology. Our final task in this chapter is to draw out the logical implications of this principle for morally evaluating *Gaudium et spes'* "truly human" sexual act. To do so, we will have recourse to the concept of complementarity and the virtues of chastity, love, and justice. Combined, our foundational principle, truly human sexual acts, complementarity, and the virtues expand the possibility of moral sexual acts, which is currently limited in magisterial teaching to reproductive acts between married heterosexuals, to include nonreproductive homosexual and heterosexual acts.

Truly Human and Complementarity

We begin our excursus on the truly human sexual act with a look at the virtue of chastity, the central virtue guiding human sexuality throughout the Christian tradition. We complement this virtue with justice and charity later in this section.

Chastity

Chastity is a virtue that facilitates the attainment, internalization, and integration of authentic human sexuality. The *Catechism of the Catholic Church* provides a succinct definition. Chastity is "the successful integration of sexuality within the person and thus the inner unity of [the hu]man in his [and her] bodily and spiritual being. Sexuality, in which [the hu]man's belonging to the bodily and biological world is expressed, becomes personal and truly human when it is integrated into the relationship of one person to another."[53]

Chastity, then, is the authentic integration of a person's sexuality into human relationship and the practical living out of that relationship in fidelity and commitment to another person. In our citation of the *Catechism*'s definition of chastity, we intentionally left out the final clause of that definition. As stated, the focus is on integrating one's sexuality bodily and spiritually. The final clause limits this integration to heterosexual relationships: "in the complete and lifelong mutual gift of a man and a woman." There is a tension between this final clause and the opening clauses. As is now accepted in the scientific community and stated in the *Catechism* and in other magisterial documents, homosexuals do not choose their condition or orientation; it is a result of physiological (nature) or social (nurture) factors, or most likely a combination of both.[54] As such, what does it mean for a homosexual person to integrate his or her sexuality? Does it require celibacy, or is there the possibility of a moral expression of sexual activity between two people of the same sex given the criteria for a theology of the unitive that we are developing? It is interesting to note that the *Catechism* does not equate chastity for the homosexual person with celibacy.[55] As we will discuss briefly below and expand in chapter 7, from our theological principle, persons of a homosexual orientation may live a life of chastity within a monogamous, just, loving, committed relationship subject to the same moral guidelines used to morally evaluate a heterosexual nonfecund relationship.

The above definition of chastity has profound implications for what it means to express our sexuality and sexual acts in a manner that is truly human. Sexuality is a gift from the creator God to facilitate men's and women's task of becoming fully human in and through interpersonal relationship with others. Humans seek both wholeness, sometimes called human flourishing, and holiness in their journey toward becoming fully integrated, relational, loving persons. This requires them to embrace sexuality, to seek to define, develop, and perfect those dimensions that facilitate its authentic development, and to resist whatever frustrates this development. In a world of original, personal, and social sin, this is not an easy project; its realization is fraught with difficulties. The world humans inhabit, however, is not only a world of sin; it is a world also of abounding grace. It is a world into which the Father of all has sent his Son to be incarnated, making it thereby essentially holy. It is a world into which the Son has sent the Spirit-Paraclete to lead it into all truth. It is a world in which that Spirit is abroad, freely giving gifts of all kinds to all men and women of goodwill.[56] It is a world in which the search for full humanity, and therefore also for God, is pursued sexually by both heterosexuals and homosexuals, and therefore any search for the truly human must include both these groups.

Truly Human

"Truly human" and "complementarity" have recently been introduced into the discussion of sexual morality in the Catholic tradition. *Gaudium et spes*, which Selling describes as "a manifesto for contemporary moral theology,"[57] declared that the sexual intercourse in and through which spouses symbolize their mutual gift to one another is to be *humano modo*, "in a manner which is *truly human*."[58] The sexual act, the Second Vatican Council intended, is to be *actus humanus*, a deliberated and intentional act, not just *actus hominis*, an act that a person does without any responsible discernment.

Unfortunately, the Second Vatican Council offered no definition of what it meant by "truly human" and, when the phrase was introduced into the specification of marital consummation in the revised *Code of Canon Law* in 1983, it was again added without definition. Ten years before the revision of the *Code*, in 1973, the subcommission drafting the revision of the canons on marriage recognized the difficulty of including *humano modo* in law without definition and noted the lack of a verifiable criterion "to prove that a consummating act has not been done in a human manner." Given that lack, the commission unanimously recommended that the words *humano modo* be included in the text within parentheses "so that their doubts on the matter may be on record."[59] The commission's recommendation was ignored, and the revised *Code of Canon Law* decrees that a marriage is "ratified and consummated if the spouses have *humano modo* engaged together in a conjugal act in itself apt for the generation of offspring."[60] The problem noted by the subcommission, the lack of a verifiable criterion for nonconsummation, remains unresolved today, leaving legislators with no sure criterion for verifying that a marriage has been truly consummated and is therefore indissoluble.

Efforts have been made to provide a canonical description of intercourse *humano modo*, but they have been minimalist. Beal and his colleagues suggest the act of intercourse must be "a natural and voluntary act"; Coriden and his colleagues argue that intercourse must be "willingly and lovingly on the part of each party."[61] Beal and his colleagues' concluding comment, however, remains true: "The precise determination of what constitutes sexual relations in a human fashion will have to be determined gradually in the jurisprudence of the Congregation for the Sacraments."[62] This judgment remains especially true for any *theological* reflection on *humano modo*, and what follows seeks to be a contribution to that reflection.

Sexual Complementarity

The Congregation for the Doctrine of the Faith's (CDF's) *Considerations Regarding Proposals to Give Legal Recognition to Unions between Homosexual Persons (CRP)* has recently sought to clarify the meaning of truly human sexual acts. It first states that homosexual unions lack "the conjugal dimension which represents the human and ordered form of sexuality," and it then articulates the principle that "sexual relations are human when and insofar as they express and promote the mutual assistance of the sexes in marriage and are open to the transmission of new life."[63] This is the unitive-procreative principle that, in the twentieth century, became the foundational principle for all Catholic sexual teaching. According to this principle, truly human sexual acts are acts within marriage that are simultaneously unitive of the spouses and open to procreation, and only such acts are judged to be truly human. *CRP* uses the term *sexual complementarity* in relation to this principle, which includes parenting and the education of children and, on this foundation, defends heterosexual marriage and condemns homosexual unions. The term *complementarity* has appeared only relatively recently in magisterial sexual teaching, in Pope John Paul II's *Familiaris consortio* (1981).[64] Its types and implications for defining truly human sexual acts have yet to be fully explored. In the next subsection we investigate and critique several types of complementarity to advance its understanding and its implications for the "truly human" sexual act.

Biological and Personal Complementarity

There are two general types of sexual complementarity in the CDF's document, biological and personal, with subtypes within each (table 4.1). The definition of what constitutes truly human sexual acts depends on how biological and personal complementarity are defined in themselves and in relation to one another. We consider each definition in turn.

Biological Complementarity: Heterogenital and Reproductive

Biological complementarity is divided into what we label *heterogenital* and *reproductive complementarity*. The CDF describes heterogenital complementarity this way:

TABLE 4.1
TYPES OF SEXUAL COMPLEMENTARITY IN MAGISTERIAL TEACHING

I. Biological Complementarity

Type	Definition
Heterogenital complementarity	The physically functioning male and female sexual organs (penis and vagina)
Reproductive complementarity	The physically functioning male and female reproductive organs (testes and sperm, ovaries and ova) used in sexual acts to biologically reproduce

II. Personal Complementarity

Type	Definition
Communion complementarity	The two-in-oneness within a heterogenital complementary marital relationship created and sustained by truly human sexual acts
Affective complementarity	The integrated psycho-affective, social, relational, and spiritual elements of the human person grounded in heterogenital complementarity
Parental complementarity	Heterogenitally complementary parents who fulfill the second dimension of reproductive complementarity, namely, the education of children

"Men and women are equal as persons and complementary as male and female. Sexuality is something that pertains to the physical-biological realm."[65]

Heterogenital complementarity pertains to the biological, genital distinction between male and female. The mere possession of male or female genitals, however, is insufficient to constitute heterogenital complementarity; genitals must also function properly. If they cannot function complementarily, as they cannot in either male or female impotence, neither heterogenital nor reproductive complementarity is possible, and in that case canon law prescribes that a valid marriage and sacrament are also not possible: "Antecedent and perpetual impotence to have intercourse, whether on the part of the man or of the woman, which is either absolute or relative, of its very nature invalidates marriage."[66]

Heterogenital complementarity is the foundation for reproductive complementarity and "therefore, in the Creator's plan, sexual complementarity and fruitfulness

belong to the very nature of marriage."[67] Heterogenital and reproductive complementarity, however, are to be carefully distinguished for, while the Magisterium
teaches that a couple must complement each other heterogenitally, it also teaches
that, "for serious reasons and observing moral precepts," it is not necessary that they
biologically reproduce.[68] Infertile couples and couples that choose for serious reasons
not to reproduce for the duration of the marriage can still enter into a valid marital
and sacramental relationship. In light of this teaching, Pope Paul VI's statement
that "each and every marriage act must remain open to the transmission of life" is
morally ambiguous in the cases of infertile couples, couples in which the wife is
postmenopausal, and couples who practice permitted natural family planning with
the specific intention of avoiding the transmission of life.[69] We may reasonably ask
in what way are sexual acts between such couples "open to the transmission of life"?

Biological Openness to the Transmission of Life

Magisterial teaching, following Aquinas, distinguishes between reproductive acts
that are essentially (per se) closed to reproduction and reproductive acts that are
accidentally (*per accidens*) nonreproductive.[70] Contraceptive nonreproductive heterosexual acts, including natural family planning with a contraceptive will, and
homosexual sexual acts are types of sexual acts that are essentially closed to reproduction. Sterile sexual acts, either permanently or temporarily during the infertile period
of a woman's cycle, and postmenopausal sexual acts are accidentally nonreproductive
and belong to the same type of reproductive acts. Accidentally nonreproductive
sexual acts are essentially of the same type as reproductive sexual acts and thus fulfill
sexual complementarity, the unitive and procreative meanings of the sexual act. We
ask, however, is it really the case that all such sexual acts are essentially the same
type of act?

Gareth Moore notes that whether or not two acts are the same type depends on
our interest. The interest here is reproduction ("open to the transmission of life").
We call vaginal intercourse and not anal intercourse a type of reproductive act
because we know that, under the right conditions, pregnancy can result from the
former but never from the latter. Scientific knowledge of the biological facts of
reproduction enables us to classify certain sexual acts as reproductive and others as
nonreproductive. If science is relevant in distinguishing between vaginal intercourse
that is open to reproduction and anal intercourse that is not open to reproduction,
it would seem that this consideration applies equally to the distinction between
potentially fertile and permanently or temporarily sterile reproductive acts. As
Moore correctly notes, "Vaginal intercourse which we know to be sterile is a different type of act from vaginal intercourse which, as far as we know, might result in
conception."[71] Koppleman agrees. The penis of a sterile man is still a penis in the
taxonomic sense, but it is "not reproductive in the sense of power or potential."[72]

If potentially fertile reproductive acts and permanently or temporarily nonreproductive acts are essentially of a different type in terms of the "openness to the transmission of life," then we must ask what distinguishes infertile heterosexual acts from

homosexual acts. The answer seems to reside in heterogenital complementarity. That is, heterogenital complementarity, not reproductive complementarity, seems to be the essential foundation for categorizing potentially reproductive and permanently or temporarily sterile nonreproductive heterosexual acts.

Grounding the essential act-type of heterosexual potentially reproductive and permanently or temporarily nonreproductive sexual acts in heterogenital, rather than reproductive, complementarity raises two sets of questions. First, it raises questions about the morality of other types of nonreproductive heterosexual acts, such as oral sex, which are permanently nonreproductive even though heterogenital complementarity is present. Second, the Magisterium's claim that homosexual acts are intrinsically disordered because they are closed to the transmission of life can be challenged. Permanently infertile reproductive acts are as biologically closed to the transmission of life as homosexual acts. From a strictly reproductive point of view, nonreproductive heterosexual acts *may* have more in common with homosexual acts in terms of personal complementarity and relationality than with infertile reproductive sexual acts in terms of reproductive complementarity. Homosexual acts do not exhibit heterogenital or reproductive complementarity, but it remains to be seen if they exhibit personal complementarity.

Metaphorical Openness to the Transmission of Life

Rather than arguing biologically and scientifically for an essential type classification of reproductive acts that are open to the transmission of life, one can argue metaphorically for this openness. James Hanigan, for instance, argues for metaphorical openness in terms of an "iconic significance of one's sexuality," whereby "one's maleness or femaleness in all its embodied reality must be taken with full seriousness."[73] Male and female sexuality are created to be spousal in that they are ordered toward interpersonal union. Furthermore, male sexuality is "paternal in its ordination to the maternal, to the female, and to the raising up of new life." Similarly, female sexuality is "maternal in its ordination to the paternal, the male, and to the birthing and nurturing of new life."[74] In their genital maleness and femaleness, their paternity and maternity, postmenopausal, and other infertile heterosexual couples represent this openness to the transmission of life to the community in the very reality of their relationship, and this symbolic representation has moral significance. Hanigan's claim has moral credibility by interpreting "openness to the transmission of life" in a metaphorical rather than a biological sense.

A question to be posed to Hanigan, however, is this: In what way is an infertile heterosexual couple's sexuality iconically significant in a way that a homosexual couple's sexuality is not? The most obvious answer is that a homosexual couple does not have the heterogenital complementarity necessary to reproduce. Aside from heterogenital complementarity and potential biological reproduction, however, it is not clear that a homosexual couple's sexuality cannot be iconically significant. Referring to Paul VI, Hanigan himself notes that marriage is "*one* way God has of realizing in human history the divine plan of love." Though there may be other ways to achieve this plan, "conjugal union is the way that *fully* enacts human sexuality."[75]

One response to Hanigan's claim of iconic significance of male and female sexuality is that, though we may agree that conjugal acts of a reproductive kind fully enact human sexuality, it does not follow that acts that fall short of that full enactment, such as nonreproductive heterosexual or homosexual acts, are immoral and, therefore, impermissible. To say that an act is inferior is not to say that it is immoral.[76] One must demonstrate this immorality in terms of personal complementarity and the affective, relational, and spiritual dimensions of the human sexual person. Many would deny that nonreproductive heterosexual or homosexual acts violate personal complementarity and are, therefore, immoral.

Such an interpersonal response in the case of homosexual acts, however, too easily concedes heterogenital complementarity as normative and bypasses the moral significance of bodiliness to argue on the interpersonal significance of homosexual acts within a homosexual relationship. David McCarthy takes a different approach, arguing theologically for a nuptial metaphor of *both* homosexual *and* heterosexual unions grounded in the human body. He does so in four steps. First, the beginning of all theological reflection is "God's reconciliation with the world, which, in the gathering of the Church, constitutes a body."[77] Second, the Church or Body of Christ generates a relationship of bodies to create a network of communion or common life. Within this network there is a "desire of the body" to enter into permanent unions, "which is drawn to God's faithfulness and patterned in mimesis of God's enduring love." Third, this desire is "matched by a thoroughgoing hermeneutics of the body" whereby, "through marriage, the body is given an identity that does not merely bring its agency to fulfillment but also locates the communicative acts of the body at the axis of a community's whole life."[78] Up to this point, McCarthy and Hanigan agree.

Fourth, McCarthy argues that, although the hermeneutics of the body and the nuptial metaphor it justifies is limited to heterosexual marriage in the Catholic tradition, as it is in Hanigan's position, it can be extended to homosexual unions as well. It can be so extended by integrating an adequate definition of sexual orientation into a theology of the body to develop a "nuptial hermeneutics of same-sex unions."[79] The Magisterium defines heterosexual orientation as normative, the "natural" explanation of the nuptial metaphor, and defines homosexual orientation as objectively disordered in its *desire* for a person of the same sex ("A homosexual orientation produces a stronger emotional and sexual attraction toward individuals of the same sex, rather than toward those of the opposite sex"),[80] and because it creates a "strong tendency" toward homosexual *acts* that are intrinsically evil.[81] This emphasis on desire and act highlights the underlying disparity in magisterial teaching regarding the term "orientation." Its discussion of heterosexual orientation focuses on the affective complementarity of two embodied persons, biologically, psychoaffectively, socially, and spiritually,[82] but its discussion of homosexual orientation focuses on desire and acts.

McCarthy, however, provides a definition of homosexual orientation, which, aside from heterogenital complementarity, is consistent with the Magisterium's understanding of heterosexual orientation: "Gay men and lesbians are persons who encounter the other (and thus discover themselves) in relation to persons of the same sex. This same-sex orientation is a given of their coming to be, that is, *the nuptial meaning of human life emerges* for a gay man in relation to other men and a woman when face to face with other women."[83] In a steadfast interpersonal union, then, homosexual couples give their bodies to one another and are "theologically communicative"; that is, they are witnesses to the community of God's "constancy and steadfast fidelity."[84] It can be argued that in their witness, homosexual couples have "iconic significance" in their sexuality through embodied interpersonal union, just as heterosexual couples, both fertile and infertile, have "iconic significance" in their sexuality in their embodied interpersonal union. Heterogenital complementarity is not a determining factor. Rather, two genitally embodied persons, heterosexual or homosexual, in permanent interpersonal union, who reflect God's constant love and steadfast fidelity are the determining factor.[85] In the case of fertile heterosexual couples, embodied interpersonal union is potentially procreative; in the cases of infertile heterosexual couples and of homosexual couples, embodied interpersonal union is not potentially procreative. Embodiment and the nuptial metaphor, however, are essential to all three interpersonal unions.

To summarize: If one explores "openness to the transmission of life" in biological terms, then potentially reproductive and permanently or temporarily nonreproductive heterosexual acts are essentially different types of acts, and heterogenital complementarity becomes the essential difference that distinguishes nonreproductive heterosexual acts from homosexual acts. If one explores "openness to the transmission of life" in metaphorical terms, following McCarthy, both homosexual and heterosexual couples can exhibit "iconic significance" in their embodied interpersonal unions and sexual acts. For Hanigan, heterogenital complementarity becomes the essential difference that distinguishes iconic significance in heterosexual and homosexual interpersonal unions, allowing iconic significance to be morally determinative in the sexual act for heterosexual unions but not for homosexual unions.

It is to be noted that, although reproductive complementarity always entails heterogenital complementarity, heterogenital complementarity does not always entail reproductive complementarity. Heterogenital complementarity is distinct from and can stand alone from reproductive complementarity in the service of personal complementarity. Reproductive complementarity can also stand alone from parental complementarity, for a couple may choose to adopt rather than to produce offspring.

Personal and Communion Complementarity

The CDF also refers to sexuality on the "personal level—where nature and spirit are united." We refer to the personal level of sexuality as *personal complementarity*, which can be divided into several subcategories. First, there is *communion complementarity* in the marital relationship, "a communion of persons is realized involving the use of the sexual faculty."[86] The male and female genitals, the penis and vagina, contribute to the realization of a communion of persons in marriage expressed in truly human sexual acts. The CDF implies, however, that without heterogenital complementarity, communion complementarity is not possible: "There are absolutely no grounds for considering homosexual unions to be in any way similar or even remotely analogous to God's plan for marriage and family. Marriage is holy, while homosexual acts go against the natural moral law. Homosexual acts 'close the sexual act to the gift of life. They do not proceed from a genuine affective and sexual complementarity. Under no circumstances can they be approved.'"[87]

Affective Complementarity

Second, there is "natural,"[88] "ontological,"[89] or *affective complementarity*. This type of complementarity is at the crux of magisterial teaching on sexual complementarity because it intrinsically links biological and personal complementarity. Citing the *Catechism of the Catholic Church*, the CDF notes that affective complementarity is lacking in homosexual acts and, therefore, these acts can never be approved. It does not clarify here what it means by affective complementarity, but we can glean some insight from other magisterial sources. The Congregation for Catholic Education teaches that "in the Christian anthropological perspective, affective-sex education must consider the totality of the person and insist therefore on the integration of the biological, psychoaffective, social and spiritual elements."[90] Because affective sex education seeks to integrate the biological, psychoaffective, social, and spiritual elements of the human person, affective complementarity must similarly integrate these elements in a truly human sexual act. Important questions for the magisterial understanding of affective complementarity are how it understands these elements in the individual person, in the person in relationship, and in a truly human sexual act.

First, John Paul II claims that "even though man and woman are made for each other, this does not mean that God created them incomplete."[91] Each individual has the potential to be complete by integrating the biological, psychoaffective, social, and spiritual elements of affective complementarity. Claiming that men and women are complete in themselves seems to respond to the concerns expressed by some theologians that the idea of complementarity implies that celibate religious or single people are somehow not complete and lack something in their humanity.[92] Second, when he moves from individual to couple, even though man and woman are "complete" in themselves, the pope argues that "for forming a couple they are incomplete."[93] He further notes that "woman complements man, just as man complements woman. . . . Womanhood expresses the 'human' as much as manhood does, but in a different and complementary way."[94] We must ask, however, where the incompleteness and the need for complementarity reside in an individual that is complete in himself or herself but is incomplete for forming a couple. Where in the human person does this incompleteness exist that needs complementing by the opposite sex? John Paul responds that "womanhood and manhood are complementary *not only from the physical and psychological points of view,* but also from the *ontological.* It is only through the duality of the 'masculine' and the 'feminine' that the 'human' finds full realization."[95]

Kevin Kelly accurately notes that "ontological complementarity maintains that the distinction between men and women has been so designed by God that they complement each other, not just in their genital sexual faculties but also in their minds and hearts and in the particular qualities and skills they bring to life, and specifically to family life."[96] The masculine and feminine complement each other to create a "unity of the two,"[97] a "psychophysical completion,"[98] not only in sexual acts but also in marital life. Finally, beyond heterogenital complementarity for the purpose of reproduction, John Paul's claim of affective complementarity leaves ambiguous and undeveloped *how* these elements are integrated in a truly human sexual act. To summarize: In magisterial teaching on affective complementarity, the affective (biological, psychoaffective, social, and spiritual) elements are strictly divided according to gender and comprise essential male and female human "natures"; only when they are brought together in marriage and sexual acts is the human couple complete.

There are two important points to note in John Paul and the Magisterium's explanations of affective complementarity. First, there is an intrinsic relationship between heterogenital and personal complementarity, between body and person (heart, intelligence, will, soul).[99] Second, given the Magisterium's teaching on the immorality of homosexual acts, it is clear it regards heterogenital complementarity as a sine qua non for personal complementarity in truly human sexual acts. Without heterogenital complementarity, the other elements of affective complementarity in the sexual act cannot be realized.

Several points need to be made regarding the claims that God created individuals complete in themselves but incomplete when they come to form a couple and that this incompleteness is made complete through the (biological, psychoaffective, social, and spiritual) affective complementarity of male and female. First, to claim that a person is complete in himself or herself indicates that the person is complete biologically, psychoaffectively, socially, and spiritually, at least when the person is in relationship with God and neighbor. Second, though it is clear that male and female complete one another biologically in terms of genitalia for reproduction, it is not clear how they are incomplete and complete each other psychoaffectively, socially, and spiritually. John Paul II claims that "it is only in the union of two sexually different persons that the individual can achieve perfection in a synthesis of unity and mutual psychophysical completion."[100] The biological, psychoaffective, social, and spiritual elements of the human person are ontologically divided along masculine and feminine lines, however, without justification, save that these are God given from the very beginning.[101] It is reasonable to question, however, whether the psychoaffective, social, and spiritual elements are intrinsically divided along masculine and feminine lines and find completion only in male–female unity.[102] Besides genitalia, what "feminine" affective elements does a man lack and what "masculine" affective elements does a woman lack?

One finds certain gender stereotypes in magisterial documents where femaleness is defined primarily in terms of motherhood, receptivity, and nurturing and maleness is defined primarily in terms of fatherhood, initiation, and activity.[103] With the exception of biological motherhood and fatherhood, the ontological claim of gendered psychological traits does not seem to recognize the culturally conditioned and socially constructed "nature" of gender and does not adequately reflect the complexity of the human person and relationships. Within individuals and relationships, the psychoaffective, social, and spiritual elements are not "natural" to either gender per se but may be found in either gender, may vary within a relationship, and may express themselves differently depending on the relational contexts.[104] Psychoaffective, social, and spiritual traits are variously distributed among males and females and are not intrinsic to either's "nature" prior to socialization. For instance, some males are more nurturing than females and some females more dominant and analytical than males. These traits also vary within relationships, in which there may be two dominant people or two nurturing people. In these cases, do we want to claim that these two people do not complement each other? The "masculinity" and "femininity" of the nonbiological elements are largely conditioned and defined by culture,[105] and they are not "essential" components of masculine and feminine human nature mysteriously creating a "unity of the two."

All that can be claimed with certainty in the Magisterium's version of affective complementarity is that heterogenital complementarity is necessary for reproduction. For infertile couples where reproduction is physically impossible, even heterogenital complementarity is of only relative importance, and for fertile couples it may become increasingly insignificant as they age.[106] The further claim of intrinsic difference between male and female—whereby the male and female find psychoaffective, social, and spiritual completion in one another only in marriage—is entirely unsubstantiated by any scientific evidence.

Because there are reasonable grounds for questioning the Magisterium's claim that affective complementarity entails certain psychoaffective, social, and spiritual elements intrinsic to the male and female and strictly divided on gender lines and, further, that these can be realized only in heterosexual marriage and heterosexual acts, the absolute claim prohibiting homosexual acts because they lack affective complementarity is substantially weakened. Though homosexual persons cannot realize the biological element of affective complementarity (heterogenital and reproductive complementarity), it remains a question whether or not they can realize its personal elements. Granted, there is an important sense in which affective complementarity integrates the biological and personal elements in a truly human sexual act. We believe, however, that the Magisterium's account relies primarily on heterogenital complementarity; entails an incomplete, if not distorted, vision of gender; and neglects an adequate consideration of the experiential and relational dimensions of human sexuality.[107]

Parental Complementarity

Third, the CDF refers to *parental complementarity*. It argues against same-sex unions based on the claim that, "as experience has shown, the absence of sexual complementarity in these unions creates obstacles in the normal development of children who would be placed in the care of such persons. . . . Allowing children to be adopted by persons living in such unions would actually mean doing violence to these children."[108] The CDF, however, provides no scientific evidence, here or elsewhere, to substantiate its claim that homosexual union is an obstacle to the normal development of children. There is, however, abundant evidence to the contrary, as we shall elaborate in chapter 7. These social scientific data support the established claim that communion and affective complementarity between parents greatly facilitate both parental complementarity and the positive nurturing of children.[109] Given this evidence, the question whether parental complementarity is as intrinsically linked to heterogenital complementarity as the CDF claims is unavoidable. Parental complementarity, however, does serve to remind us that truly human sexual acts have public implications beyond a couple's private act of sexual intercourse, and that intercourse that leads to conception and adoption both demand long-term caring, nurturing, and authentic familial and social relationships.

The Interrelationship between Heterogenital and Personal Complementarity

Though heterogenital complementarity is necessary in magisterial teaching to realize a truly human sexual act, it is not sufficient. Heterosexual rape and incest take place in a heterogenitally complementary way, but no one would claim they are also personally complementary. Truly human complementarity is not either/or—either heterogenital complementarity alone or personal complementarity alone—but both/and, heterogenital and personal complementarity together. The Magisterium posits an intrinsic relationship between biological (heterogenital and possibly reproductive) and personal (communion, affective, and parental) complementarity, but there is a misplaced prioritization of heterogenital over personal complementarity in the absolute moral prohibition of homosexual acts. In addition, there is a misplaced emphasis on reproductive complementarity in the absolute moral prohibition of nonreproductive sexual acts between heterosexuals.

For the Magisterium, male and female genitals and their "natural" functioning in reproductive sexual acts are always the point of departure for personal complementarity in truly human sexual acts. Heterogenital complementarity, of course, must always be situated within the appropriate marital, interpersonal, and relational context. But if heterogenital complementarity is not present, as it is not present in homosexual acts, the act is by definition "intrinsically disordered."[110] For the

Magisterium, there is no possibility of personal complementarity in sexual acts that either do not exhibit heterogenital complementarity or are nonreproductive.

Important questions for the theological understanding of truly human sexual acts are whether or not there can be such acts without heterogenital complementarity and whether or not there can be such acts that are nonreproductive sexual acts. First, is heterogenital complementarity the primary, foundational, and sine qua non component of truly human sexual acts, or must genital and personal complementarity be more thoroughly integrated to found a truly human sexual act? If the latter is the case, then might a just and loving homosexual act fulfill the criteria for a truly human sexual act? Second, even though nonreproductive heterosexual acts may not fulfill reproductive complementarity, does that mean that, ipso facto, they violate personal complementarity, cannot fulfill the criteria for truly human sexual acts, and are thus morally wrong? We approach these questions via what we call *sexual orientation complementarity* and *holistic complementarity*.

Holistic Complementarity: Sexual Orientation Complementarity and Truly Human Sexual Acts

An important psychosocial dimension of the human person, and therefore of the sexual human person, is the person's integrated relationship to self. To be truly human, a sexual act must be integrated with the whole self. The Congregation for Catholic Education asserts what is widely taken for granted today: Sexuality "is a fundamental component of personality, one of its modes of being, of manifestation, of communicating with others, of feeling, of expressing and of living human love. Therefore it is an integral part of the development of the personality and of its educative process."[111] The congregation goes on to cite the CDF's *Persona humana* and its teaching that it is "from sex that the human person receives the characteristics which, on the biological, psychological, and spiritual levels, make that person a man or a woman, and thereby *largely condition his or her progress towards maturity and insertion into society.*"[112] If it is true that a person's sexuality and sexual characteristics largely condition her or his insertion into society, and we agree that it is true, then the question naturally arises about the "nature" and meaning of what is called today sexual orientation, the dimension of human sexuality that directs a person's sexual desires and energies and draws him or her into deeper and more sexually intimate human relationships. To define "truly human" sexual acts, we must first understand sexual orientation.

As noted above, the meaning of the phrase "sexual orientation" is complex and not universally agreed upon.[113] Following Nugent, we define sexual orientation as a "psychosexual attraction (erotic, emotional, and affective) toward particular individual *persons*" of the opposite or same sex, depending on whether the orientation is heterosexual or homosexual.[114] There is a growing agreement in the scientific community that sexual orientation, heterosexual or homosexual, is a psychosexual attraction that the person does not choose and that she or he cannot change.[115] In addition, because homosexual orientation is experienced as a given and not as something freely chosen, it cannot be considered sinful, for morality presumes the freedom to choose. The Magisterium recognizes the distinction between homosexual orientation, which is not chosen, and homosexual acts, which are chosen. Though the homosexual inclination is "objectively disordered" though not sinful, homosexual acts are "intrinsically disordered" and sinful.[116] The Magisterium teaches that homosexual acts are intrinsically disordered because "they are contrary to the natural law. They close the sexual act to the gift of life. They do not proceed from a genuine affective and sexual complementarity."[117] Heterosexuality is the norm against which all sexual acts are judged.

The Magisterium condemns homosexual acts because they do not exhibit heterogenital and reproductive complementarities, and because they do not exhibit these biological complementarities, they are ontologically incapable of realizing personal complementarity, regardless of the meaning of the act for a homosexual couple. Because the sexual act is frequently closed to reproductive complementarity—sometimes essentially and sometimes accidentally, even for fertile heterosexual couples, as we have already explained—heterogenital complementarity is established as *the* litmus test for determining whether or not a sexual act can fulfill personal complementarity and thus be "truly human." There is no doubt that truly human sexual acts necessarily include personal complementarity but, for the Magisterium, personal complementarity is not sufficient for a truly human sexual act. Heterogenital complementarity is the primary, foundational, sine qua non condition for what defines a truly human sexual act. Because homosexual acts lack heterogenital complementarity, they can never be truly human.

We suggest that the needed complementarity for a truly human sexual act is *holistic* complementarity that unites people bodily, affectively, spiritually, and personally under the umbrella of a person's sexual orientation. Heterogenital complementarity is needed for reproduction, but it is not needed for the sexual, affective, spiritual, and personal connection between two people that the recent Catholic tradition acknowledges as an end of marriage equal to procreation.[118] Though they cannot exhibit heterogenital complementarity, there is extensive anecdotal and empirical evidence that homosexual individuals can exhibit this holistic complementarity. We shall explore this evidence in detail in chapter 7.

Orientation Complementarity and Its Impact on Magisterial Complementarities

As we have already noted, the relationship between biological and personal complementarity is both/and. Truly human sexual acts require human genitals, whether fertile or infertile. In couples of heterosexual orientation, personal complementarity is embodied, manifested, nurtured, and enhanced through the use of their genitals; in couples of homosexual orientation, it is equally embodied, manifested, nurtured, and enhanced through the use of their genitals. Orientation complementarity embodies and judges genital complementarity within the context of personal complementarity.

Orientation complementarity reconstructs the Magisterium's definitions of affective complementarity and heterogenital complementarity. First, orientation complementarity cannot espouse the Magisterium's heterogenital point of departure for affective complementarity. As we have seen, for the Magisterium the point of departure for affective complementarity is an ontological unity between the biological (heterogenital) and the personal that can find completion only in heterosexual marriage and conjugal acts. The definition of affective complementarity is the "unity of the two" where the masculine and feminine affective elements (biological, psychoaffective, social, and spiritual), which are incomplete for forming a couple find completion in heterogenitally complementary reproductive type sexual acts. In our model, the point of departure for affective complementarity is not the *genital* but the *sexual human person* of either a homosexual or heterosexual orientation. The definition of affective complementarity in truly human sexual acts is the "unity of the two" where the affective elements (biological, psychoaffective, social, and spiritual) complement one another.[119] In the case of persons with a homosexual orientation, these acts will be genitally male–male or female–female; in the case of persons with a heterosexual orientation, these acts will be genitally male–female; in the case of persons with a bisexual orientation, these acts may be genitally male–male, female–female, or male–female.[120]

Second, orientation complementarity also requires us to redefine heterogenital complementarity in relation to affective complementarity. Severing the male–female ontological complementarity of the affective elements includes the genitals. No longer is heterogenital complementarity the foundational sine qua non for personal complementarity. Genital complementarity, indeed, can be determined only in light of orientation complementarity. In a truly human sexual act, the genitals are at the service of personal complementarity, and they may be male–male, female–female, or male–female, depending on whether the individual person's orientation is homosexual or heterosexual. Our principle of holistic complementarity, which includes sexual orientation complementarity as one of its types, embraces the entirety and complexity of the human person, and reconstructs genital complementarity to be in dialogue with, and totally at the service of, personal and orientation complementarity. The genitals may be said to be complementary when they are used in a truly human sexual act that realizes the psychoaffective, social, and spiritual elements of affective complementarity.

Holistic Complementarity and Truly Human Sexual Acts

Truly human sexual acts can be morally evaluated not simply as isolated acts but only in the context of this complex orientation, personal, and genital interrelationship. When we shift the foundation for a truly human sexual act from heterogenital complementarity to holistic complementarity—an integrated orientation, personal, and genital complementarity—the principle for what constitutes a truly human sexual act can be formulated as follows.

A truly human sexual act is an *actus humanus* in accord with a person's sexual orientation that facilitates a deeper appreciation, integration, and sharing of a person's embodied self with another embodied self. Genital complementarity as understood within the context of orientation, personal complementarity is always a dimension of the truly human sexual act, and reproductive complementarity *may* be a part of it in the case of fertile, heterosexual couples that choose to reproduce. Reproductive complementarity will not be a possibility in the case of homosexual couples (or infertile heterosexual couples), but genital complementarity, understood in an integrated, embodied, personal, orientation sense, and not just in a biological, physical sense, will be. This personalist interpretation of genital complementarity, which contextualizes the physical genitals as organs of the whole person, allows us to expand the definition of a truly human sexual act to embrace both heterosexual and homosexual nonreproductive acts.

Truly Human and Nonreproductive Sexual Acts

The magisterium teaches that only marital, reproductive sexual acts are truly human sexual acts. In explaining its condemnation of masturbation, for example, it notes the following: "The deliberate use of the sexual faculty outside normal conjugal relations essentially contradicts the finality of the faculty. For it lacks the sexual relationship called for by the moral order, namely the relationship which realizes 'the full sense of mutual self-giving and human procreation in the context of true love.' All deliberate exercise of sexuality must be reserved to this regular relationship."[121] Mutual masturbation, anal sex, and oral sex all lie outside the parameters of this definition, do not realize the finality of the sexual faculties, and therefore cannot be truly human or moral. This statement invites comment and critique and, on the basis of this critique, we expand the concept of a truly human sexual act to include nonreproductive sexual acts, both heterosexual and homosexual.

First, masturbation, both individual and mutual couple masturbation, and other nonreproductive sexual acts, "[contradict] the finality of the faculty." In this statement there is a clear parallel with Aquinas, who comments that some external acts are disordered in themselves, "as happens in every use of the genital organs outside the marriage act." "The end of the use of the genital organs," he continues, "is the generation and education of offspring, and therefore every use of the aforementioned organs which is not proportioned to the generation of offspring and its due education is disordered in itself."[122] What are we to make of Aquinas's and magisterial statements on the finality or end of the genital organs? The first point to note is terminological. As Moore comments, there is little difference in this discussion between the *purpose* (or finality) of our sexual organs, sexual acts, and sexual faculties.[123] The second point is that Aquinas's emphasis on the primary end of the genital organs for the procreation and education of children, since the promulgation of *Gaudium et spes*, no longer holds true. The procreation and education of children *and* the union between the spouses are equal ends of marriage; there is no longer a Catholic hierarchy of ends. The Magisterium defines the "finality of the faculty" of the sexual organs in terms of *both* the procreation and education of children *and* the union between the spouses in every sexual act.

The third point to note is Aquinas's limited understanding of human biology in relation to human sexuality and reproduction. The female ovum was not discovered until the 1850s. Before its discovery, the commonly held belief was that the male seed was solely responsible for generation; the female merely provided the fertile ground or field for the male seed, a true *homunculus* or little man, to develop into a fully fledged human being.[124] To spill the seed anywhere it could not develop properly, on the earth, in a mouth, or in an anal orifice, for instance, was regarded as murder, and murder was always judged to be a serious moral evil. This traditional teaching we would label, along with Ratzinger, a "distorting," as compared to a "legitimate," tradition that we must consider critically.[125] As we know now, both the male sperm and the female ovum are necessary to provide the forty-six chromosomes that make up the human genome. The tradition's erroneous understanding of human biology and reproduction allowed it to make claims about what is "natural" that were inaccurate. Though magisterial teaching now recognizes human reproductive biology, it continues to assert exclusively the natural finality of the sexual organs, and reproductive complementarity is considered such a natural finality.

Is it the case, however, that reproduction is the natural finality of the sexual organs? Moore distinguishes between the *purpose* (or finality) of our sexual organs and the *achievement* of our sexual faculties.[126] To claim that there is a purpose to our sexual organs overlooks this distinction. Reproduction is achieved via a human activity, but it is not itself a human activity. Though humans achieve reproduction through a sexual act, that act itself is not an act of reproduction. If reproduction were the purpose of the sexual act, then all reproductive-type sexual acts would have the possibility of realizing this purpose. Women who have had a hysterectomy, however, or infertile men continue to have and to use sexual organs, but they are without reproductive organs. All sexual human beings have *sexual* organs, but not all sexual human beings have *reproductive* organs. That an organ is sexual does not necessarily mean that it is also reproductive. As noted above, the Thomistic distinction between sexual acts that are essentially (per se) closed to reproduction and sexual acts that are accidentally (*per accidens*) closed to reproduction does not help us out of this quandary, because the common denominator distinguishing the two types of acts is the biological consideration of the openness of the act to the transmission of life. Clearly, with permanently infertile couples, the term "open to the transmission of life" is morally ambiguous at best and morally meaningless at worst. It is far from clear, therefore, that the sexual organs have the "natural finality" assigned to them.

There are three senses in which one could claim a natural finality for the sexual organs. The first is the purpose given them by "nature"; the second is the purpose given them by human beings' use of those organs; and the third is the purpose given them by the "moral order" or divine law. The first purpose we have already addressed. Though "nature" can be interpreted in a purely biological sense, in the sense of Aquinas, tradition, and current magisterial teaching, it is more accurately understood in terms of what facilitates human well-being or human flourishing. To claim that nonreproductive sexual acts are "unnatural" or "against nature," one must prove that such acts by definition frustrate human well-being or human flourishing. This leads to the second claim of the finality of the sexual organs: the meaning human beings give to this finality. Sexual organs do not have a single purpose; they have many purposes. The penis, for example, is responsible for both the evacuation of liquid waste and sexual intercourse that may or may not achieve reproduction. In sexual acts, it may also serve other purposes, the giving of pleasure, for instance, the relieving of tension, the celebration and enhancement of intimacy between two lovers, whether or not the particular sexual activity is capable of achieving reproduction. All these purposes have meaning for human beings and may or may not facilitate human flourishing depending on the meaning of this particular sexual act for this particular couple.

To counter these humanly assigned finalities of the sexual organs, one may respond with the third argument for finality; namely, even if people attach different meanings to the sexual activities, an order established by God determines the correct finality of the sexual organs, and this finality is reproduction. Reproductive complementarity, therefore, is an intrinsic meaning of the sexual act. Numerous questions may be posed to this claim. Why do we need to claim that God created a particular body part for a particular purpose? Cannot a particular body part have multiple purposes, as indicated above? If we do accept a God-given purpose, what are the reasons we may not act against it? Is to act against this God-given finality always morally wrong, or simply less than ideal? If it is simply less than ideal, is it accurate to claim that, although reproductive sexual acts are ideal sexual acts, nonreproductive sexual acts cannot facilitate human flourishing? There are many acts we do that are less than ideal—such as eating, sleeping, or exercising too much or too little—but we do not, on that account alone, judge them immoral. Is a "truly human" sexual act synonymous with the ideal sexual act? This would seem to set an unreasonably high standard for any act of reproductive sexual intercourse that must necessarily entail a reciprocal "total personal self-giving" between the couple.[127] This total self-giving would entail in each and every sexual act all those dimensions of human sexuality explored above—biological, emotional, psychological, relational, and spiritual—and any experienced married couple will tell you that the requirement of total personal self-giving in each and every sexual act is simply not real. It is nothing but ideology posing as reality. Is it possible that what was judged traditionally to be the single God-given purpose of sexual organs can be expanded to include other God-given purposes discerned on the basis of human experience and conscientious and faithful reflection on that experience?

All these are important questions that need to be investigated. If after such an investigation, however, we were to come to the (unlikely) conclusion that there is undoubtedly a single God-given purpose for sexual organs, would we then have to conclude logically that the God-given purpose is exclusive of all other sexual activity, or could it be inclusive of other sexual activity? Could we not, in other words, claim that on occasion the sexual organs could still be used for other purposes? Indeed, these organs are frequently used for other purposes deemed perfectly moral, for instance, among infertile couples. There is no possibility of achieving the reproductive finality of the organs in these infertile acts, but the acts always still have the capacity to acknowledge, celebrate, and enhance personal complementarity and human flourishing. The same is true with regard to nonreproductive acts. Though they cannot realize reproductive complementarity, nothing precludes them per se from realizing personal complementarity. Marital experience shows that such sexual acts, rather than being destructive of human flourishing, may facilitate human flourishing. Marital experience shows that it is never a question of either successful reproduction and, therefore, human flourishing or nonreproduction and, therefore, human diminishment. Reproductive complementarity is morally ambiguous or meaningless for infertile heterosexual couples. Human sexuality makes possible a variety of sexual acts with multiple meanings for sexual relationships. The judgment of whether or not a particular sexual act is moral, whether it be a reproductive or nonreproductive sexual act, is to be determined, as all moral judgments are to be determined, on the basis of its impact on human flourishing within the context of a particular interpersonal relationship. We have outlined this basis as a truly human sexual act that evinces holistic complementarity.

The Principle of Holistic Complementarity

The foundation for our definition of a truly human sexual act and its moral evaluation rest, then, not primarily on heterogenital or reproductive complementarity but on the integrated relationship between orientation, personal, and genital complementarity. Given this complex dialogical relationship, it remains to ask whether or not a particular sexual act facilitates or frustrates the partners' human flourishing, their becoming more affectively and interpersonally human and Christian. We agree with Stephen Pope that "interpersonal love is here the locus of human flourishing,"[128] and we are now able to offer a definition of complementarity. Complementarity is a multifaceted quality—orientational, physical, affective, personal, and spiritual—possessed by every person, which draws him or her into relationship with an other human being, including into the lifelong relationship of marriage, so that both may grow, individually and as a couple, into human well-being and human flourishing.

In light of the various types of complementarity explored in the foregoing, a truly human sexual act must be an authentic integration and expression of holistic complementarity, as set forth in figure 4.1. Holistic complementarity includes orientation, personal, and biological complementarity, and the integration and manifestation of all three in just and loving, committed sexual acts that facilitate a person's ability to love God, neighbor, and self in a more profound and holy way.

Just and Loving Sexual Acts

The careful reader will have noticed our consistent specification that, to be truly human, sexual activity, heterosexual or homosexual, must be not only in accord with holistic complementarity but also *just and loving*. This "just and loving" must be explained. The search for moral judgment in sexual matters today frequently ends with the vapid claim that sexual activity is moral when it is loving. That judgment is vapid because it is usually devoid of content. We agree with Margaret Farley: "Love is the problem in ethics, not the solution,"[129] and it is the problem to the extent that it is contentless. Our task here is to give it content. We begin with an ancient definition: *Amare est velle bonum*, to love is to will the good of another.[130] Love is an activity of the will, a decision to will the good of another human being. True love, as every lover knows, is ec-static; that is, in love a person goes out of herself or himself to another self who is absolute and unique in herself or himself. That there are two absolutely unique and yet like selves in any loving relationship introduces the cardinal virtue of justice, "the virtue according to which, with constant and perpetual will, someone renders to someone else her or his due rights."[131] The ancient author of *Economics*, said to be Aristotle, speaks obliquely of justice in marriage. A husband "must do her [his wife] no wrong, for thus a man is less likely

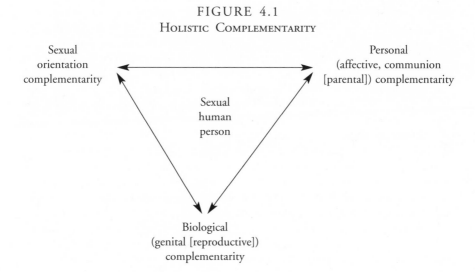

FIGURE 4.1
HOLISTIC COMPLEMENTARITY

Sexual
orientation
complementarity

Personal
(affective, communion
[parental]) complementarity

Sexual
human
person

Biological
(genital [reproductive])
complementarity

himself to be wronged. This is indicated by the general law, as the Pythagoreans say, that one least of all should injure a wife as being 'a suppliant and taken from her hearth.'"[132] If asked what does justice, rendering to someone her or his due rights, have to do with sexual acts, we respond that, because sexual acts are between two equal personal selves, justice has everything to do with them.[133]

One modern characteristic, perhaps the greatest characteristic, of a person is her or his equality with every other person. For Christians, that equality takes on a deeply religious character because it is believed to be the very plan of the God who created 'adam male and female, blessed them, and named them together 'adam.[134] A sexual act that is just and loving will seek the good of equality for, and will render all the rights flowing from equality to, both partners. Any sexual act that is achieved through inequities—of power, social or economic status, or level of maturity, for example—will be ipso facto not truly human. Flowing from the personal character of equality is the related personal character of freedom. A sexual act that is just and loving will render the rights associated with freedom to the other partner and will seek the good of freedom for both partners, in the act. This means, in concrete terms, that a loving and just sexual act requires the free consent of both partners and that any sexual act that subverts free consent is ipso facto not truly human. The use of power, violence, or rape against an unwilling partner will therefore never be truly human. With the modern "discovery" that a woman is as free as a man, free consent may be seriously interfered with, or even precluded, by any sexual activity that is marked by socially constructed male domination or female subordination. The same reasoning applies to anyone of diminished capacity—the immature, the dependent, the drugged, or the drunk, for example—for diminished capacity will automatically mean diminished consent.

A consistently recognized end of sexual activity, heterosexual or homosexual, is both the expression and enhancement of interpersonal relationship, love, or friendship; sexual activity is, in the common phrase, a way to make love. To express and enhance relationality, however, sexual activity must be *mutual*; it must be wanted by and participated in freely by both partners. Both Aristotle and Aquinas teach that love happens not when I love another but only when my love is reciprocated by the other. "Friendship requires mutual love," Aristotle teaches, "because a friend is a friend to a friend."[135] True love, truly willing the good of an other, is never one-sided; there is no true love until love is mutual. It is the mutual love between lovers that creates between them the communion that characterizes lovers. That leads us to a further specification of the mutuality between lovers: mutual, long-term commitment. The Christian tradition has always required some form of long-term commitment, some kind of solemn promise or covenant, from the partners for sexual intercourse to be moral. That this covenant always was linked to marriage, and that marriage was primarily linked to procreation, is no reason not to retain commitment as a reasonable and moral norm for sexual activity, heterosexual or homosexual. We believe long-term commitment is required for a just and loving relationship, including truly human sexual acts, to mature into fruitfulness for both marital and common good. This fruitfulness—which may include any or all of the goods of the love and communion between the partners, children, and the common good of the community in which the partners and any children live—requires a long-term commitment to be nourished into maturity.[136] To be loving and just, therefore, any sexual act requires commitment to be truly human.

Holistic Complementarity, Truly Human Sexual Acts, and Norms

Three immediate implications for Catholic sexual ethics follow if we espouse holistic complementarity—including the virtues of chastity (discussed above),[137] justice, and love—as our foundational principle for truly human sexual acts. The first is that the Magisterium's absolute moral norm prohibiting all homosexual acts must, at least, be reexamined. Without a prior consideration of one's sexual orientation, a sexual act that violates heterogenital complementarity can no longer be considered ipso facto intrinsically or objectively disordered. Genital complementarity is relevant in determining the morality of truly human sexual acts, but it is not the primary factor. The morality of the use of the genitals in sexual acts must be determined primarily in light of orientation and personal complementarity.

The second implication for Catholic sexual ethics, which follows from the first, is that the foundation for sexual moral norms may need to be redefined. Current magisterial teaching posits, for both homosexuals and heterosexuals, an intrinsic relationship between biological and personal complementarity in which heterogenital complementarity is primary and foundational. On this foundation, certain sexual acts are ipso facto immoral because they violate heterogenital complementarity, regardless of sexual orientation and the relational meaning of the act for personal complementarity. In holistic complementarity, an integrated relationship between orientation, personal, and biological complementarity serves as the foundation for sexual norms. In this relationship, for both heterosexuals and homosexuals, orientation and personal complementarity are primary, and they determine what constitutes authentic genital complementarity in a particular sexual act. If orientation complementarity indicates that a person is of heterosexual orientation, then personal complementarity would indicate that authentic genital complementarity would be male–female. If orientation complementarity indicates that a person is of homosexual orientation, then personal complementarity would indicate that authentic genital complementarity would be male–male or female–female. In current magisterial teaching, heterogenital complementarity is the primary foundational dimension for the essential relationship between biological and personal complementarity. In our holistic complementarity model, orientation and personal complementarity are the foundational dimensions for the integrated relationship between orientation, personal, and biological complementarity.

The third implication is that nonreproductive sexual acts cannot be absolutely morally prohibited. Although such acts violate reproductive complementarity, they do not ipso facto violate personal complementarity and diminish human flourishing. The truly human sexual act in our sexual anthropology is one that facilitates holistic complementarity, which may or may not include reproductive complementarity in any given act. Though one may reasonably argue that reproductive sexual acts are the ideal expression of human sexuality, this does not logically justify the judgment that any sexual act not evincing that ideal is morally wrong. Other types of sexual acts that lead to orgasm but are nonreproductive can facilitate personal complementarity and human flourishing. Such acts can also realize reproductive complementarity in the case of reproductive technologies, as we will see in chapter 8.

In light of these three considerations, we advance the following with regard to sexual moral norms and truly human sexual acts. Sexual moral norms must be formulated, and truly human sexual acts must be defined in light of a revised theological anthropology grounded in holistic, not heterogenital, complementarity. A person's sexual orientation is a fundamental dimension of the concretely and normatively human dimension of her or his being, and sexual norms that prescribe or proscribe specific sexual acts must be formulated and applied in light of that orientation. Sexual moral norms must seek to facilitate the integration of holistic complementarity—orientation, personal, and biological complementarity. This integration does not allow for the absolute condemnation of particular sexual acts without due consideration of a person's sexual orientation and the meaning of this sexual act for these persons in relationship—that is, in personal complementarity—which is expressed in and through genital complementarity. The Magisterium's model posits absolute norms forbidding homosexual acts and all nonreproductive-type sexual acts. Our model cannot justify these absolute norms, but it does posit a formally absolute norm in relation to truly human sexual acts.

Formal absolutes are norms that emphasize character and/or virtue in relation to acts. A formal absolute norm, for instance, might state the following: a not-truly-human, abusive, dishonest, uncommitted, unjust, unloving sexual act, heterosexual or homosexual, is morally wrong; a truly human, caring, honest, committed, just, loving, sexual act, heterosexual or homosexual, is morally right.[138] The integration of holistic complementarity—that is, the integration of orientation, personal, and biological complementarity—determines whether or not a sexual act is moral or immoral. In the case of a person with a homosexual orientation, a truly human, caring, honest, committed, just, loving, sexual act will be expressed personally with male–male or female–female genitalia. In the case of a person with a heterosexual orientation, a truly human, caring, honest, committed, just, loving, sexual act will be expressed personally with male–female genitalia. Some theorists have proposed this shift to formal absolutes in terms of a virtue-based sexual ethic in which the cardinal virtues of prudence, justice, fortitude, and temperance, always allied with the theological virtues of faith, hope, and charity, would be the guiding "norms" for what constitute truly human sexual acts.[139]

The challenge presented by this shift from predominantly act-centered norms to formal, holistic relation-centered norms is that the latter may not always be as clear as we would like. They may not always give clear guidelines for what we may or may not do. Especially when it comes to morality, humans often desire clear, simple, and unambiguous answers to complex questions. Unambiguous answers, unfortunately, sometimes oversimplify complex human relationships and the questions they raise. They may also be achieved at the expense of preempting the responsible discernment required for every *actus humanus*, every truly human moral act. In fact, responsible discernment in the area of sexual activity, and not the naked fact of "nature," is what makes possible the mature integration of a person's sexuality, heterosexual or homosexual, and the living out of that sexuality in a manner that facilitates a truly human flourishing in relationship with those we love, including the God who created all people as sexual in the first place.

Conclusion

For any sexual act to be truly human, it must exhibit holistic complementarity, equality between the partners, equal freedom for both partners, free mutuality between the partners, and the mutual commitment of both partners. The Christian tradition will add that those characteristics are all to be informed by the love of God and neighbor enjoined by Jesus. That neighbor-love is concretized by willing the good of the neighbor, compassion, mercy, forgiveness, and reconciliation, extending even to those neighbors who may be characterized as "enemies."[140] Considerations like these lead Farley to a conclusion with which we are comfortable and with which we will conclude this chapter: "Sex between two persons of the same sex (just as two persons of the opposite sex) should not be used in a way that exploits, objectifies, or dominates; homosexual (like heterosexual) rape, violence, or any harmful use of power against unwilling victims (or those incapacitated by reason of age, etc.) is never justified; freedom, integrity, privacy are values to be affirmed in every homosexual (as heterosexual) relationship; all in all, individuals are not to be harmed, and the common good is to be promoted."[141]

This sums up nicely what we have been arguing, and it leads us to our ultimate conclusion. On the basis of our revised foundational sexual ethical principle, *some* homosexual and heterosexual acts, those that meet the requirements for holistic complementary, just, and loving sexual acts, are truly human; and *some* homosexual and heterosexual acts, those that do not meet the requirements for holistic complementary, just, and loving sexual acts, are not truly human. Whether any given sexual act, heterosexual or homosexual, is truly human is determined, as is every moral judgment in the Catholic tradition, not by the naked application of abstract moral principles but by a careful, hermeneutical analysis of how these principles apply in real, concrete human relationships.

Chapter Five

Marital Morality

I N THE PREVIOUS CHAPTER we advanced a theoretical foundational principle for making judgments about the morality of sexual actions. This principle was articulated as follows: Sexual actions within marriage by which a couple is united intimately and chastely are noble and worthy. If expressed in a manner that is truly human and justly loving, these actions signify and promote that mutual self-giving whereby spouses enrich each other, their family, and their community with a joyful and thankful will. We also introduced into the discussion of complementarity, initiated by Pope John Paul II, a definition, the notion of orientation complementarity and, especially, of holistic complementarity, comprised of orientation, personal, and biological-genital complementarity. In this and the following chapters, we apply the theoretical discussion of the previous chapter to clarify the morality of the practical sexual questions about marital sexuality (chapter 5), cohabitation and premarital sexuality (chapter 6), homosexuality (chapter 7), and artificial reproductive technologies (chapter 8). As we do so it is important to keep in mind the two hermeneutical provisos we introduced in chapters 1 and 2: the questions of "historicity" and "nature." These two provisos are vital to the following discussions.

Marital Intercourse and Morality

In his influential 1951 speech to Italian midwives, as we have already seen, Pope Pius XII argued, on the one hand, that it was not immoral to avoid procreation in a *marriage*[1] and, on the other hand, that it was immoral to artificially prevent procreation in the marital *act.*[2] No discussion of the morality of marital intercourse can take place in the Catholic tradition without a serious consideration of these two claims. We consider each in turn.

The Catholic tradition has consistently followed Augustine, Trent, and Pius XII in the claim that procreation is not a *necessary* good in a marriage. New Natural Law Theory (NNLT) agrees, arguing that actual reproduction is not essential for a genuinely marital act. In the cases of married sterile couples, couples that are postmenopausal, and couples that choose not to reproduce for serious and morally acceptable reasons, they argue, "their will to engage in true marital intercourse is the only intention they must have to make what they do a marital act."[3] John Finnis adds that, though a couple must always be open to the transmission of life, the *actual* transmission of life does not have to occur for their intercourse to be genuinely marital intercourse and, therefore, moral.[4] The claim that the actual transmission of life is not necessary for marital intercourse to be moral is an eminently reasonable claim in light of the reality of human physiology, which opens sexual intercourse to procreation only a limited number of days per month. The second claim—that, although procreation is an intrinsic meaning of the marital act, sterile, postmenopausal couples and couples choosing not to procreate for serious moral reasons can realize this meaning through their *intention* to make what they do a genuinely marital and, therefore moral, act—does not seem equally reasonable. Germain Grisez and Finnis have been seriously challenged on this second claim.

NNLT and Marital Morality

The NNLT argument that, although procreation is an intrinsic meaning of marital sexual intercourse and that couples must always be open to it in their intercourse, actual procreation need not occur for their act to be moral, appears to us a strange and unconvincing argument. Grisez explains that sterile couples need only *intend* to engage in true marital intercourse for their intercourse to be moral. If that is the case with sterile and postmenopausal couples, the question raised by Stephen Macedo seems reasonable. What is the difference between those sterile couples for which marital intercourse is deemed moral, even though their openness to procreation is known to be a fantasy, and homosexual men and women for whom marital intercourse is deemed to be immoral *because* their intention to be "open to procreation" is known to be impossible? Finnis quotes Macedo's judgment ("Gays can have sex in a way that is open to procreation and to new life. They can be, and many are, prepared to engage in the kind of loving relations that would result in procreation—*were conditions different.* Like sterile married couples, many would like nothing better."), and declares it "fantasy."[5] We agree with Finnis that Macedo's judgment is "fantasy [that] has taken leave of reality." Macedo's point, of course, is to call attention not so much to the fantastic intentions of homosexuals as to the equally fantastic judgment of NNLT about sterile couples and their openness to procreation. Macedo's point is well made; why the double standard with respect to intention and fantasy?[6]

George and Bradley defend NNLT by suggesting that Macedo has not fully articulated their position. He has missed, they insinuate, its complexity. Marriage, they point out, considered "as a *two-in-one-flesh communion* of persons that is *consummated and actualized* by sexual acts of *the reproductive type*, is an intrinsic (or in our parlance 'basic') human good; as such marriage provides a *non-instrumental reason* for spouses, whether or not they are capable of conceiving children in their acts of genital union, to perform such acts."[7] This formulation is carefully chosen to present the NNLT position in its full complexity; it deserves to be given the careful consideration its writers claim Macedo did not give it. It is this nuanced position that enables NNLT to conclude that "in choosing to perform non-marital orgasmic acts, including sodomitical acts—irrespective of whether the persons performing such acts are of the same or opposite sexes (and even if those persons are validly married to each other)—persons necessarily treat their bodies and those of their sexual partners as *means* or *instruments* in ways that damage their personal (or interpersonal) integrity; thus, regard for the basic human good of integrity provides a conclusive moral reason not to engage in sodomitical and other nonmarital sex acts."[8] This NNLT position is complex, and it demands complex analysis. To make this analysis more orderly, we have underscored what we take to be the key phrases in George and Bradley's formulation, and we now consider these phrases in turn.

Two-in-One-Flesh-Communion

Marriage, NNLT believes, with the Catholic tradition, is "a two-in-one-flesh communion of persons." The resonance with Genesis 2:24 and the tradition that flows from it is obvious. Unfortunately, the Genesis text is better known than understood. That man and woman become one flesh in marriage has been exclusively linked in the Western tradition, and in NNLT, to one facet of marriage, namely, the physical and the heterogenital. The physical dimension is undoubtedly part of what it means to become one flesh, but it is far from all there is, for the Hebrew *basar*-body implies the entire person: "One person would translate it better, for 'flesh' in the Jewish idiom means 'real human life.'"[9] In the sociohistorical circumstances in which Genesis emerged, a man and a woman enter into a fully social-personal, and not just a physical, union. They become so socially and personally unified that they become again, as in the mythical beginning, male and female created, blessed, and named by God *'adam* (Gen 5:1–2). Rabbis go so far as to teach that it is only after the union of male and female in marriage that the image of God that Genesis insinuates (1:27) may be detected in them. The unmarried man or woman is not, they teach, a whole human person. The mythic stories, interested as always in etiology, the origin of things, proclaim that it was so "in the beginning" and that it was so by the express design of God. There could not be, for Jew or Christian, a greater foundation for the human and religious goodness of sexuality, marriage, and fertility. In such a context, to assert, as does NNLT, that marriage is a basic human good is a reasonable assertion. To assert, as they also do, that marriage is a two-in-one-flesh communion is reasonable, too, but only when the phrase is understood in its full personal meaning. To restrict it to a physical, heterogenital, sexual meaning is a mistake.

As we have pointed out several times, NNLT appears to read "two-in-one-flesh" in a restricted physical and heterogenital sense. We have already demonstrated that NNLT perspective in the previous chapter when we showed that they believe heterogenital complementarity to be the sine qua non of personal complementarity. It appears here again in the assertion that the two-in-one-flesh marriage is "consum-mated and actualized by sexual acts of the reproductive type." Sexual acts of the reproductive type, concretely and exclusively the insertion of a male penis into a female vagina, are clearly physical acts. NNLT argues that "the union of the repro-ductive organs of husband and wife really unites them biologically (and their biolog-ical reality is part of, not merely an instrument of, their *personal* reality)," and that judgment is partially accurate.[10] The union of the reproductive organs of husband and wife unites them physically and may unite them also personally. That is not to say, however, that the union of their reproductive organs is the *only* act that unites them biologically and personally or to deny that their genital union is an instrumen-tal actualization and symbol of their already existing personal union. We approach the question via the claim that the two-in-one-flesh communion that is marriage is "consummated and actualized by sexual acts of the reproductive kind."

Consummation Adequately Considered

The ancient Roman answer to the question "What makes marriage?" was that the free consent of the marrying couple makes marriage; the ancient northern European answer was that sexual intercourse between the couple makes marriage. In the twelfth century, the Catholic Church was embroiled in a debate over what makes a marriage valid and indissoluble, and Gratian, the master of the Faculty of Law at University of Bologna, proposed a compromise position between the Roman and northern European opinions: "It should be known that marriage is initiated by betrothal [consent], perfected [consummated] by sexual intercourse. Therefore, between spouses there is marriage, but only initiated; between spouses who have engaged in sexual intercourse, there is ratified marriage."[11] That compromise was, and continues to be, enshrined in the law of the Catholic Church,[12] and only the marriage that is both sacramental and consummated is held to be indissoluble in the Church.[13] NNLT claims that marriage is consummated by acts of the reproductive kind, that is, by sexual intercourse between spouses; this was the unchallenged Cath-olic position for a millennium. It is no longer unchallenged today.

The concrete reality and conscious experience of marriage has led spouses to suggest that the claim that a marriage is consummated, perfected, and actualized in their first marital intercourse is overly simplistic, grossly physicalized, and unrealis-tic. Spouses have learned that, because marriage is rooted in and sustained by marital love that is a life work, marriage itself is a life work. The fullness of marital love, they have learned, is not achieved in their courtship, or in their wedding ceremony, or in their first act of intercourse; it is achieved only in a life of mutually actualized commitment. The consummation or perfection of marital love, and therefore the consummation of the marriage rooted in it, happens only when love has reached such a fullness that the spouses judge they could not turn their backs on either their love or their marriage. This kind of thinking was given great impetus by the Second Vatican Council's definition of marriage as an "intimate partnership of life and love," and its further teaching that this intimate partnership "is rooted in the [spouses'] conjugal covenant of irrevocable personal consent."[14] Before the council, it was taken for granted in the Catholic tradition that marriage was a *contract*, and the only marital act that fell under the contract was sexual intercourse. When it is taken for granted that marriage is a *covenant*, marital acts that fall under the covenant are much more inclusive and varied, and no one act can be the consummation or perfection of such a covenant.[15]

We must demur, therefore, from NNLT's assertion that marriage is "consummated and actualized" in sexual acts of the reproductive kind, not because the assertion is completely false but because it is only partially true. The intimate partnership of life and love that is marriage is actualized in every act of just and loving sexual intercourse, and it is also actualized in every other just and loving marital act. It is actualized in what the ancient canonists called *consortium vitae*, the communion of life. Each and every just and loving marital act makes its own contribution to the manifestation and actualization of the developing fullness and ultimate consummation of a marriage. Each and every just and loving marital act, that is, in Catholic theological language, is both a sign and an instrumental cause, that is, a sacrament, of marital love and of the marriage rooted in it. That is why the specific teaching of the Catholic Church about marriage is that it is a sacrament.[16] The reader will have noted our specification of every *just and loving marital* act. That characterization, which we explained in the previous chapter, is critical to our judgment about marital acts that fulfill and consummate marriage, and it eliminates from discussion unjust and unloving marital acts. It is illogical to conclude, as NNLT sometimes does, that because all unjust and unloving heterosexual or homosexual acts are not moral all nonreproductive sexual acts are not moral.[17]

From one perspective, of course, we can easily grant that homosexual acts, no matter how just and loving, are not *marital* acts, for the homosexual couple is not married in any legal meaning of the word.[18] Whether justly loving, committed, stable homosexual partners are married or not, however, is not the question here. The question is whether nonreproductive sexual acts, heterosexual or homosexual, can be as intimately just, loving, and personally unifying for the partners as are sexual acts of a reproductive kind for heterosexual partners. Finnis insists they cannot be. "Their reproductive organs cannot make them a biological (and therefore personal) unit;" they can do no more than "provide each partner with an instant gratification," and such conduct "*dis-integrates* each of them precisely as acting persons."[19] That assertion falls under the scholastic axiom: *Quod gratis asseritur gratis negatur*, what is gratuitously asserted may be gratuitously negated; and we negate it as something not absolutely true. A consideration of Finnis's judgment about *dis-integration*, and George and Bradley's similar judgment about the damage caused to "personal (and interpersonal) *integrity*" by nonmarital orgasmic acts, heterosexual or homosexual,[20] gets us to the root of the issue.

Self-Integrity and Sexuality

Self-integrity, which results from the organization of the physiological, psychological, and social traits and tendencies of a personality into an organic whole, is undoubtedly a core characteristic of the mature person. Here we focus only on sexual integrity and recall an earlier discussion. The Congregation for the Doctrine of the Faith points to the root of a person's sexual integrity: her or his sexuality. It teaches what is now universally accepted, that it is "from sex that the human person receives the characteristics that, on the biological, psychological, and spiritual levels, make that person a man or a woman, and thereby largely condition his or her progress toward maturity."[21] If this is true, and it is virtually universally agreed that it is true, then any analysis of sexual integrity must give serious consideration to sexual orientation, a "psychosexual attraction (erotic, emotional, and affective) toward particular individual *persons*" of the opposite or same sex, depending on whether the orientation is heterosexual or homosexual.[22] Sexual orientation is produced by a mix of genetic, hormonal, psychological, and social "loading."[23] NNLT, though always insisting on its contact with reality, pays no attention whatsoever to sexual orientation and its implications. Indeed, Grisez readily concedes the naturalness of homosexual orientation, but "only in the sense that any handicap for which an individual is not personally responsible is natural."[24] Homosexuality, for Grisez, is nothing more than a handicap.

NNLT arrives at its conclusions on the unreasonableness, unnaturalness, and immorality of nonreproductive homosexual or heterosexual acts on the basis of an abstract philosophical analysis that totally ignores empirical human experience. It argues from what the Scholastics called "pure nature," which in their analysis seems to lead to seeing, hearing, heterosexual humans beings; from this perspective, blind, deaf, homosexual human beings are handicapped with respect to pure "nature." Catholic systematic theology, however, is in virtually universal agreement that pure human "nature" never existed and does not now exist. The only "nature" that real human beings ever had and continue to have is the empirical human "nature" that exists in the present, concrete economy created by God. Theologians call this "nature" "contingent or empirical nature." In his discussion of empirical "nature," Karl Rahner argues that "for an ontology that grasps the truth that man's concrete quiddity [nature] depends utterly on God, is not his binding disposition [such as the homosexual orientation] *eo ipso* not just a juridical decree of God but precisely what man *is*."[25] NNLT argues from pure human "nature" and derives its natural law from this nature; this enables it to treat homosexual orientation as an objective handicap or an objective disorder. We argue from empirical human "nature"; this enables us to take the experiential reality of homosexual orientation seriously as what a person *is* and, therefore, how she or he might act personally, sexually, and morally. Because marital acts of a heterosexual and reproductive kind—that is, the insertion of a male penis into a female vagina—are *naturally* beyond the capacity of homosexuals, they cannot be bound to them morally.

The theological implications for sexual integrity—and, therefore, self-integrity—are clear and profound. If what a person *is* unalterably by "nature" and the design of God is homosexual, then both sexual integrity and self-integrity require that the homosexual orientation be embraced and integrated into the personality, and they allow expression in just and loving acts. For a natural homosexual to behave as a heterosexual is as unnatural, dis-integrating and, therefore, immoral as for a natural heterosexual to behave as a homosexual. Ignoring what we called in the preceding chapter orientation complementarity, NNLT condemns homosexual acts as immoral because they violate heterogenital and reproductive complementarity and, therefore, also personal complementarity. Our principle of holistic complementarity embraces sexual orientation as its natural starting point and leads to a different series of questions and answers about what is natural, reasonable, and therefore moral in sexual activity. Our argument is that empirical human "nature" includes both heterosexual and homosexual orientation, and therefore empirical natural law dictates homosexual acts that, when they lead to just and loving human flourishing, are thoroughly moral. The genuine differentiation of approach to what is and is not natural, and therefore what is natural law, suggests that our position and not that of NNLT may be a *New* Natural Law Theory.

Instrumentality and the Sexual Act

Something that is truly new in the NNLT approach is its claim that neither marriage nor sexual intercourse in marriage "can legitimately be instrumentalized, that is, treated as a *mere* means to any extrinsic end, including procreation."[26] That marriage is a basic good in human lives can easily be conceded. That sexual intercourse is not a *"mere* means" to some other good but a basic good in itself can also be readily conceded. That intercourse may never be an instrumental means to some higher good intrinsic to the interpersonal relationship we cannot concede, for that claim contradicts a broad Catholic tradition which, despite Grisez's subtle argumentation to the contrary,[27] continues to be the Catholic Church's ongoing tradition. Finnis's judgment that Grisez has "brilliantly illuminated"[28] the development of doctrine that has taken place in the Church on this matter up to and including the Second Vatican Council is a sound judgment if he means that Grisez has presented a brilliantly subtle *interpretation* of the development that has taken place. If he intends a brilliant *exposition* of the reality of the theoretical development that has taken place, he is seriously mistaken. We have explained that historical theoretical development in detail in chapter 1, but it bears repeating briefly in response to NNLT's claim.

The early Christian understanding of sexuality, if not dictated by the Stoic understanding, at the very least closely resembles that understanding. It may be represented in a statement by Lactantius, a Christian African: "Just as God gave us eyes, not that we might look upon and desire pleasure, but that we might see those actions that pertain to the necessity of life, so also we have received the genital part of the body for no other *purpose* than the begetting of offspring, as the very name itself teaches."[29] This was the common early Christian teaching, which led to several conclusions. First, the *purpose* of sexual intercourse, by its very nature, is for the procreation of children; second, any sexual intercourse for *purposes* other than procreation is a violation of nature; third, any intercourse when procreation is impossible, when a wife is already pregnant, for example, is also a violation of nature. The Church Fathers will continue to offer that argument into the twentieth century. The instrumentality of sexual intercourse for a higher good, good though intercourse is in itself, is a long-established position in the Catholic Church.

For Augustine, marriage, which is a human good, even a basic human good, is also instrumentally good for two purposes. Marriage itself is instrumentally good for the companionship of the sexes, the medieval *consortium vitae*; sexual intercourse in marriage is instrumentally good for procreation, the propagation and nurture of offspring, and the loving community that results from propagation. Grisez asserts that these two goods "manifest a certain tension in Augustine's thinking."[30] We do not agree. There is no tension in Augustine, who easily accepts the instrumentality of both marriage and sexual intercourse in marriage. If there is tension, it is between Augustine's position and the NNLT's tortured denial of the same. For Augustine, there is one good that is procreation; there is another good that is *consortium vitae*; and there is no tension between the two. From the Augustinian goods of marriage, procreation and companionship between the spouses, medieval canonists will eventually fashion the Catholic tradition about the two *ends* or *purposes* of marriage: one primary, procreation; the other secondary, *consortium vitae* or *mutuum adjutorium*. This tradition is consistent in teaching that marital sexual intercourse is *instrumental* to both.[31]

Isidore of Seville is usually credited with first setting out the standard Catholic way for treating the ends or purposes of marriage. He distinguishes three purposes or ends (*causae finales*) for marriage: first, offspring; second, the mutual help spouses provide to one another; and third, a remedy for incontinence.[32] It was not Isidore, however, but Thomas Aquinas and his followers, who firmly established the Catholic approach to the purposes or ends of marriage. "Marriage has as its principal end [*finis*]," Aquinas taught, "the procreation and education of offspring. . . . It has a secondary end in man alone, the sharing of tasks which are necessary in life. . . . There is yet another end in believers, namely, the meaning of Christ and Church, and so a good of marriage is called sacrament. The first end is found in marriage in so far as man is animal, the second in so far as he is man, the third in so far as he is believer."[33] As is usual in Aquinas, this is a sharp and sharply delineated argument, and its primary end–secondary end terminology came to dominate discussions of the ends or purposes of marriage in Catholic manuals for seven hundred years. By the twentieth century, when it was articulated in the first *Code of Canon Law* (1917), its dominance was beyond doubt and the instrumentality of marriage and sexual intercourse in marriage equally beyond doubt: "The primary end of matrimony is the procreation and education of offspring; its secondary end is mutual help and the remedying of concupiscence" (Can. 1013, 1). This hierarchy of ends, and the subordination of ends it also implies, controlled every Catholic discussion of marriage up to the Second Vatican Council—and beyond.

Grisez offers an argument, purportedly drawn from the Catechism of the Council of Trent, to show that Trent did not deal with *ends* or *purposes* of marriage, but with what he calls *reasons*. This argument leads him down a tortuous path to the conclusion he wants to establish, namely that "Augustine [and Aquinas and the entire Catholic tradition that followed them] was mistaken in classifying marriage as an instrumental good."[34] This is the argument Finnis classifies as "brilliant." We classify it, rather, as "specious," that is, according to Webster, "having the ring of truth or plausibility but actually fallacious." This judgment we now explain.

Grisez's argument hinges on the implied differentiation in meaning between the Latin *finis* (end, *telos*) and *causa* (cause, "that by, on account of, or through which anything takes place or is done"[35]), which Grisez translates as *reason* and treats as if it has a meaning different from *finis*. It does not, certainly not in the Aristotelian philosophy followed by Aquinas. In that philosophy, which came to dominate Catholic philosophical and theological reasoning from, at least, the fifteenth century and on, there are four kinds of causes: a material cause that causes by sustaining the formal cause; a formal cause that causes by actuating the material cause; an efficient cause that causes by effecting the reality constituted by the material and formal cause; and a final cause that causes by drawing the reality toward some other reality, toward, that is, some end or purpose.[36] *Finis* and *causa finalis* are different words, but in the Catholic tradition from the Council of Trent to the Second Vatican Council, their meaning is the same, namely, the *end* or *purpose* for which some thing, good in itself, is done. To differentiate *finis* and *causa* (*finalis*) betrays, at best, ignorance of that tradition or, at worst, deliberate obfuscation of it as final cause for a predesired end.[37] Had Grisez read the paragraph that immediately precedes the segment he chooses to cite, he would have found the council teaching that "the words *increase and multiply*, which were uttered by the Lord, do not impose on everyone an obligation to marry but only declare the *cause* (*causa* [*finalis*]) of the institution of marriage."[38] The end point of this discussion is, of course, a logical one: If the premise is wrong, as it clearly is, then the conclusion drawn from the premise is also wrong. This wrongness is underscored by further consideration of the historic Catholic tradition.

Modern Catholic Thought and Marital Morality

In his important 1930 encyclical on marriage, *Casti connubii*, Pius XI underscored the established Catholic tradition on the ends or purposes of marriage, and he also introduced a new perspective consonant with the personalist philosophy of the times. The partnership of the spouses, Pius taught, can "be said to be the *chief reason [ratio] and purpose [causa]* of matrimony, if matrimony be looked at not in the restricted sense as instituted *for* [that is, for the purpose of] the proper conception and education of the child, but more widely for the blending of life as a whole and the mutual interchange and sharing thereof."[39] We provided in chapter 1 a detailed exposition and explanation of the development of this ends-of-marriage element of the Catholic tradition from Pius XI to the Second Vatican Council, and we see no need to repeat it here. There is a need, however, to examine the specific development of this element in the council.

The Second Vatican Council debate, both the preliminary one in the Preparatory Commission and the definitive one in the council itself, centered on the hierarchy of ends, specifically on the relative values of conjugal love and the procreation of children. We do not need to detail that debate here, but only its outcome in *Gaudium et spes*.[40] The council describes marriage as "a communion of love,"[41] an "intimate partnership of conjugal life and love."[42] In the face of loud demands to consign the conjugal love of the spouses to a secondary end, the council declares it to be of the essence of marriage. Both marriage and conjugal love "are ordained for the procreation and education of children [*ad procreationem et educationem prolis ordinantur*], and find in them their ultimate crown,"[43] but again there is no primary end–secondary end hierarchy. Indeed, lest this latter text be misrepresented in a hierarchical way, the Preparatory Commission included a note that explains that it "does not suggest [a hierarchy of ends] in any way."[44] We include the Latin text of *Gaudium et spes* (48), in which the Latin *ad* clearly indicates the *end* or *purpose* for which, by nature, marriage and marital intercourse are ordained, namely, *ad procreationem et educationem prolis*. Those who understand Latin know that the text cannot be manipulated to say anything other than what it clearly and intentionally states.

The Preparatory Commission's discussion of Ottaviani's schema and the Second Vatican Council's debate leading to the approval of *Gaudium et spes* negate Grisez's opinion that "it is often said that Vatican II deliberately set aside the traditional hierarchy of the primary and secondary ends of marriage. But it is more accurate to say that the Council avoided the terminology of primary and secondary ends."[45] Such spin is far from the picture documented in the *Acta Synodalia*. Grisez's decision to ignore the amply documented debate frees him to conclude that "the Council refrains from speaking of primary and secondary ends of marriage, thus avoiding the suggestion, associated with that terminology, that marriage is instrumental to ends extrinsic to it."[46] Here we come up against the core of NNLT's problem with instrumentality, which appears to equate *instrument* and *extrinsic*. If that equation is true, then we agree with its argument about instrumentality. Neither the good called *consortium vitae* nor the good called *procreation* is a good extrinsic to marriage; both are intrinsic goods. That, however, in no way negates the long Catholic tradition that they are also instrumental goods, for even intrinsic goods can be used instrumentally for higher goods, *ad bona maiora*.

The refutation of the claim that "marriage and marital intercourse are *only* instrumental goods"[47] is a refutation of one of the core points of NNLT argumentation. This claim, however, is a straw man that neither the Catholic tradition nor any Catholic theologian has ever held. Of course, marriage and marital intercourse are human goods, even *basic* human goods, but they are not absolute human goods that can never be subordinated to other goods. Human experience shows that, under normal human circumstances, they are both modes and *instruments* of human relationship; they express, enhance, or diminish human relationship depending on the concrete circumstances. To claim that marriage and marital intercourse are instrumental goods does not denigrate them in any way. The human actors in marriage and marital intercourse, the Aristotelian-Thomistic efficient cause(s), are evidently the spouses; marriage and marital intercourse are clearly not actors or efficient causes. It is the spouse-persons who effect friendship-love and procreation, using marriage and marital intercourse as instruments. Neither marriage nor intercourse comes into being by itself; each is brought into being by the free decision of the free spouses, marriage by their exchange of consent,[48] intercourse by the mutual sharing of their bodies.

The Catholic tradition is a thoroughly sacramental tradition. Good things, sacraments, can be and are used as instrumental causes by a higher efficient cause, God in Christ, for the purpose of effecting other good realities, grace or the effective presence of God in Christ. So it is in marriage. Good things (marriage and marital intercourse) are used by a higher efficient cause (the spouses) as instruments to achieve other goods (e.g., friendship-love or children). This scheme, which appears eminently reasonable to us and in line with human experience, does not denigrate marriage and marital intercourse; it does not make them any less good. It does, however, make them *instrumental* goods. The NNLT argument asserting that marriage and marital intercourse are not instrumental goods argues against a straw man and is not compelling. The overall NNLT argument, as articulated at the beginning of this present consideration, is that marriage is a two-in-one-flesh communion of persons that is consummated and actualized by sexual acts of the reproductive kind; that, as such, marriage provides a noninstrumental reason for spouses to perform such acts; and that, in choosing to perform nonmarital orgasmic acts, spouses treat their bodies and those of their sexual partners as instruments that damage their personal and interpersonal integrity.[49] The bases for this complex position, we believe, are now sufficiently rebutted.

Marital Morality and Contraception

We began to confront the lengthy and passionate debate occasioned by Pope Paul VI's encyclical letter *Humanae vitae* in chapter 1. Tentler has recently and comprehensively examined the history of this debate, and Rubio has recently pleaded for the transcendence of the divide created by the debate.[50] We agree with Rubio that the divide is "unnecessary and unhelpful."[51] She complains, however, of the silence of Catholic theologians on the topic of contraception since *Humanae vitae* in 1968, and Tentler shows that the silence has been progressively deafening since Pius XI's *Casti connubii* in 1930. Therefore, though Farley is correct in her articulation of the opinion of the vast majority of Catholic moral theologians that "in much of Catholic moral theology and ethics, the procreative norm as the sole or primary justification of sexual intercourse is gone,"[52] we judge continuing silence as unhelpful to both the Church–People of God and the Church-Magisterium and also grossly unfaithful to the theologian's task of "interpreting the documents of the past and present Magisterium, of putting them in the context of the whole of revealed truth, and of finding a better understanding of them by the use of hermeneutics."[53] In this section, therefore, we raise again the question of contraception within marriage, though we are convinced that the terms of the argument have neither much changed nor advanced since the publication of the encyclical *Humanae vitae* in 1968. The encyclical left the debate about contraception still open by choosing, as we shall see, to ignore the arguments and recommendations of the Papal Birth Control Commission that preceded its publication rather than to refute them. We propose to take a road less traveled in the debate, namely, a road that examines the sociohistorical *contexts* of the Catholic Church's teaching on the immorality of artificial contraception, in the hope that the moral principles involved in the debate will be illuminated to enable Catholic spouses to choose the "responsible parenthood" to which they are called.[54]

Contraception and Sociohistorical Contexts

We use *contexts* in the plural, because there have been, at least, three different sociohistorical contexts in which the Church's theoretical teaching has been construed, and different consequences for praxis may be drawn from each of these different contexts. In the 1960s, the Second Vatican Council sought to discern the "signs of the times" with respect to Catholic reality, including the reality of marriage and family. One outcome of the council, achieved by diocesan bishops and theologians over the insistent objections of Vatican functionaries,[55] was a re-reception of the Catholic theology of marriage that altered the Church's teaching on marriage as surely as the reception of capitalist theories altered its teaching on usury, the reception of personalist theories altered its teaching on slavery, and its re-reception of religious theories altered its teaching on religious freedom. An examination of the sociohistorical path to that re-reception is illuminating. First of all, however, we issue a plea.

In November 1988, a selective conference, "*Humanae Vitae*: Twenty Years After," was convened in Rome. Pope John Paul II spoke at the conference, focused his talk on the issue of authority, and argued, much as the Minority Report and Paul VI had argued, that theological challenges to the Church's ban on contraception lead to challenges "of other fundamental truths of reason and of faith." He added that to withhold submission from the teaching of the encyclical "is equal to refusing to give God himself the obedience of our intelligence."[56] In January 1989, the official Vatican newspaper *L'Osservatore Romano* warned against creating "great

error and confusion in the minds of the faithful" by challenging magisterial pronouncements. The central question, *L'Osservatore* argued, is "the position of the
Magisterium of the Church."[57] That, of course, is the traditionalist position; we and
all revisionists disagree. The central question is not the position of the Magisterium,
however much that is to be respected. The central question is the relevant rational
arguments that may either sustain or disprove the noninfallible magisterial position
on contraception and other sexual issues. Perhaps, more precisely, the central question is the search for moral marital intercourse that will "foster the marriage in its
broadest sense" and "favor that love and harmony that are so basic to mutual fidelity
and so necessary for raising children."[58] Our opening plea in this section is that the
search for relevant arguments be conducted with justice and love and not with the
dismissal, anger, and sarcasm that have so often characterized them since the publication of *Humanae vitae*.

No Catholic theologian has ever denied that, before the appearance of *Humanae
vitae*, the Catholic Church's condemnation of artificial contraception was recurrent
and consistent. No Catholic theologian aware of history ever could. In his masterful
history of contraception, John T. Noonan outlines the universal agreement:

> Since the first clear mention of contraception by a Christian theologian, when
> a harsh third-century moralist accused a Pope of encouraging it, the articulated
> judgment has been the same. In the world of the late Empire known to St.
> Jerome and St. Augustine, in the Ostrogothic Arles of Bishop Caesarius and the
> Suevian Braga of St. Martin, in the Paris of St. Albert and St. Thomas, in the
> Renaissance Rome of Sixtus V and the Renaissance Milan of St. Charles Borro-
> meo, in the Naples of St. Alphonsus Ligouri and the Liege of Charles Billuart,
> in the Philadelphia of Bishop Kenrick, and in the Bombay of Cardinal Gracias,
> the teachers of the Church have taught without hesitation or variation that
> certain acts preventing procreation are gravely sinful. No Catholic theologian
> has ever taught, "contraception is a good act." The teaching on contraception
> is clear and apparently fixed forever.[59]

That judgment was delivered in 1965 but, even then, Noonan hinted that a
development may be forthcoming and that his study "may provide grounds for
prophecy."[60] Noonan himself contributed to that development through his participation in the Papal Commission appointed by Pope John XXIII to consider the
question of the Catholic Church and contraception in the twentieth century.[61] The
activity of that commission and Paul VI's publication of *Humanae vitae* in 1968
ruptured forever the pacific Catholic agreement Noonan articulates in the above
paragraph.

The Procreative Model of Marriage

One model of marriage dominated the Catholic theological tradition from the second to the twentieth centuries. That model presented marriage as a *procreative institution*, a socioreligious, stable structure of meanings in which a man and a woman

become husband and wife in order to become mother and father; in order, that is, to procreate children. That model has its origin in the Genesis command to "be fruitful and multiply" (Gen 1:22), and it was solidified, as we noted in chapter 1, in the early Christian struggle to legitimate marriage as something good against Greek dualist theories. The dominance in the early Church of the procreative argument as a primary purpose of marriage was not, however, without contrary voices. The Orthodox theologian Paul Evdokimov shows that both Chrysostom and Basil offered contrary arguments. Chrysostom, he writes, argued that marriage was instituted for two reasons, "to lead a man to be contented with one wife and to give him children, but it is the first which is the principal reason." Marriage does not absolutely include procreation, "the proof of which is in the number of marriages that can not have children." Basil, Evdokimov writes, offers an interesting comparison. The creation of the world adds nothing to God's plenitude, except that it makes God God, for God is God, "not for himself but for his creatures." So it is with marriage. It has its own plenitude and children add nothing to that plenitude, except that they make the spouses father and mother. Children are added to marriage as "a *possible* not an *indispensable* consequence of marriage."[62] Even Augustine, whose procreative emphasis was mentioned above, hinted at another good of marriage, which "does not seem to me to be good *only* because of the procreation of children, but also because of the natural companionship of the sexes. Otherwise, we could not speak of marriage in the case of old people, especially if they had either lost their children or had begotten none at all."[63] This is a clear linking of marriage, sexual intercourse, and the relationship of the spouses apart from procreation. Consideration of this relationship in the different sociohistorical context of the twentieth century, as we will see, will yield a quite different model of marriage.

In the thirteenth century, Aquinas gave the priority of procreation its most reasoned argument: "Marriage has its principal end in the procreation and education of offspring." It has also "a secondary end in man alone, the sharing of tasks which are necessary in life, and from this point of view husband and wife owe each other faithfulness." There is a third end in believers, "the meaning of Christ and Church, and so a good of marriage is called sacrament." For Aquinas, marriage has three ends: a primary end, procreation; a secondary end, faithful love; and a third end, sacrament. "The first end is found in marriage in so far as man is animal, the second in so far as he is man, the third in so far as he is believer."[64] This is a tightly reasoned argument, as is customary in Aquinas, and its *primary end–secondary end* terminology dominated Catholic marriage manuals for the next seven hundred years. The validity of a model is determined, however, not only by its intelligibility, the authority of its author, or its age but also by the fact that it explains all that it purports to explain. Aquinas's authority cannot obscure the fact that his argument is a curious one, for the primary end of specifically *human* marriage is dictated by the human's generically *animal* nature. It was on that basis that his argument was challenged in the twentieth century. Before that challenge, however, it had been enshrined for the first time in an official Catholic document in the *Code of Canon*

Law in 1917.[65] "The primary end of *marriage* is the procreation and nurture of children; its secondary end is mutual help and the remedying of concupiscence" (Can. 1013, 1). Note here something that is generally overlooked, namely, that in Aquinas and the 1917 *Code* procreation is the primary end of *marriage*, not of *sexual intercourse*, as it would become in twentieth-century Catholic debate. This theologico-canonical fact will be important in a later context.

The procreative institution is the result of a contract in which, according to the 1917 *Code of Canon Law*, "each party gives and accepts a perpetual and exclusive right over the body for acts which are of themselves suitable for the generation of children" (Can. 1081, 2). Notice that the procreative marital contract was about *bodies* and their *acts* and the procreative institution was only secondarily and reluctantly about persons and their mutual love. From this perspective, couples whose members hated each other could consent to the procreative institution as long as they exchanged legal rights to each other's bodies for the purpose of the procreation of children. At the beginning of the third millennium, sociological research shows sexual intercourse is no longer viewed exclusively as being for biological procreation: A total of 82 percent of young adult Americans now see it as for *making love*, not necessarily for making babies.[66] That meaning is replicated in the contemporary American Catholic scene via another research datum: A total of 75 to 85 percent of Catholics, who consider themselves good Catholics, approve a form of contraception forbidden by the Church.[67] The situation is the same elsewhere. Speaking of the situation in England, for example, the sociologist Michael Hornsby-Smith notes that "the evidence we have reviewed suggests . . . that lay people . . . have largely made up their own minds on this matter, and now regard it as none of the business of the clerical leadership of the Church."[68] The theologian seeking factual judgment founded in experience has to ask whether or not such data tell us anything about, if not the truth of human experience, at least its relevance for Catholic theory and practice.

The model of marriage as procreative institution was thrust on to center stage in the 1960s with the appearance of the female-cycle-regulating anovulant pill. In 1962, the Jesuit theologian John Lynch wrote in *Theological Studies* that "since theological discussion of the anovulant drugs began some four or more years ago, moralists have never been less than unanimous in their assertion that natural law cannot countenance the use of these progestational steroids for the purpose of contraception as that term is properly understood in the light of papal teaching."[69] Three years later, in the same journal, Richard McCormick wrote that "contraception continues to be . . . the major moral issue troubling the Church," and that "the literature on contraception in the past six months would be voluminous."[70] At that time, McCormick declared that "the effect of repeated authoritative Church pronouncements on a matter of this importance is a presumptive certitude of their correctness. . . . Because there is a presumptive *certitude*, prudence demands the acceptance of the conclusion in defect of prevailing contrary evidence. But because this certitude is *only* presumptive, circumstances can arise which will create a duty for the theologian to test it in the light of changing fact, increasing understanding of ethical theory, etc."[71] Two years later McCormick had apparently been convinced to change his judgment of presumptive certitude by what is known as "The Majority Rebuttal" from the Papal Commission examining the question of the Catholic Church and contraception in the twentieth century: "The documents of the Papal Commission represent a rather full summary of two points of view. . . . The majority report, particularly the analysis in its 'rebuttal,' strikes this reader as much the more satisfactory statement."[72] By 1967, McCormick's earlier suggestion for theological testing was well under way in the Catholic theological community.

Humanae Vitae *and Contraception: Challenges to the Procreative Model*

The debate on contraception was definitively focused in 1968 with the publication of Pope Paul VI's encyclical *Humanae vitae*. This document emerged from the traditional procreative model of marriage and prescribed that "each and every marriage act (*quilibet matrimonii actus*) must remain open to the transmission of life."[73] The process by which *Humanae vitae* came to be is an important part of its history, and that process can be quickly summarized. At the instigation of Leo Cardinal Suenens, Archbishop of Malines, whose ultimate intent was that an adequate document on Christian marriage be brought before the Second Vatican Council for debate, Pope John XXIII established a commission to study the issue of birth control. The commission was confirmed and enlarged by Pope Paul VI until it ultimately had seventy-one members.[74] The final vote took place in answer to three questions. In answer to a first question, "Is contraception intrinsically evil?" nine bishops responded "No," three responded "Yes," and three abstained. In answer to a second question, "Is contraception, as defined by the Majority Report, in basic continuity with tradition and the declarations of the Magisterium?" nine bishops responded "Yes," five responded "No," and one abstained. In answer to a third question, "Should the Magisterium speak on this question as soon as possible?" fourteen responded "Yes" and one responded "No."[75] A preliminary vote of the theologians who were advisers to the Papal Commission, in answer to the question "Is artificial contraception an intrinsically evil violation of the natural law? resulted in a count of fifteen "No" and four "Yes."[76] Both an official majority report and an unofficial minority report from the four dissenters[77] were then submitted to Paul VI who, professing himself unconvinced by the arguments of the majority and sharing the concern of the minority that the Church could not repudiate its long-standing teaching on contraception without undergoing a serious blow to its overall moral authority, approved the minority report in his encyclical letter *Humanae vitae*.[78] The differential between the two groups is easily categorized.

The minority report, which became the controverted part of the encyclical, argued that "each and every marriage act (*quilibet matrimonii actus*) must remain open to the transmission of life."[79] The majority report argued that it is marriage itself (*matrimonium ipsum*), not "each and every marriage act," that is to be open to the transmission of life. It asserted that "human intervention in the process of the marriage act *for reasons drawn from the end of marriage itself* should not always be excluded, provided that the criteria of morality are always safeguarded."[80] The differential in the two positions was caused by adherence to two different models of marriage. The minority report was based on the traditional procreative institution model that focused on the "natural" meaning of the *act* of sexual intercourse; the majority report was based on the new interpersonal union model that emerged from the Second Vatican Council that focused on the total meaning of *marriage* and of sexual intercourse within marriage. The question of contraception had been pre-empted from council debate by Pope John XXIII and reserved to the pope and the Papal Commission he had set up to study it. It was exempted, therefore, from the discussion of the meaning and ends of marriage from which the interpersonal model of marriage emerged as an established Catholic model. McCormick's judgment already cited—that "the documents of the Papal Commission represent a rather full summary of two points of view; . . . the majority report, particularly the analysis of its rebuttal, strikes this reader as much the more satisfactory statement"[81]—continues to be the judgment of the majority of Catholic theologians and the vast majority of Catholic couples, because they adhere to the same interpersonal model on which the majority report was based. Thirty-five years later, despite a concerted minority effort, led by John Paul II, to make adherence to *Humanae vitae* a standard of authentic Catholicity, the debate between the procreative and interpersonal models perdures as a source of "unnecessary and unhelpful"[82] divide in the Church called to communion.

The debate over *Humanae vitae*, specifically over its claim that "each and every marriage act must remain open to the transmission of life," has raged since the moment of its publication. One month after the publication of the encyclical, Bernard Haring could write: "No papal document has ever caused such an earthquake in the Church as the encyclical *Humanae vitae*. Reactions around the world . . . are just as sharp as they were at the time of the *Syllabus of Errors*, perhaps even sharper. There is the difference [this time], of course, that anti-Catholic feelings have been rarely expressed. The storm has broken over the heads of the curial advisors of the Pope and often of the Pope himself."[83] The storm was occasioned by several factors.

A first factor, following the leaking of the appendices from the Papal Commission, was a frustrated expectation that there was going to be a change. Longley comments, for instance, that "in some circles, apparently including Archbishop's House, Westminster, change in the Catholic line on birth control was coming to be anticipated."[84] The occupant of Archbishop's House, Westminster, was Archbishop John Heenan, who had served on the Papal Commission and had evolved from being a staunch advocate of the traditional teaching to abstaining in the final bishops' vote. A second factor was more theoretically important, namely, the fact that the Majority Report, the Minority Report, and the encyclical itself did not provide compelling reasons for their various positions. This lack of reasons inevitably opened the door to the theologian's task, namely, "interpreting the documents of the past and present Magisterium, of putting them in the context of the whole of revealed truth, and of finding a better understanding of them by the use of hermeneutics."[85] What that "better understanding" is, in the sociohistorical circumstances of our time, continues to divide the majority of Catholics from the minority.

The Majority Report can serve as an exemplar of the problem that ensues from only partial discussion of the problems. Attached to it was a long "Pastoral Introduction," written in French, which may indicate its origin, setting out what the majority thought the new approach to contraception should be and how it was to be resolved with what had been consistently taught before. This introduction explains: "What has been condemned in the past and remains so today is the *unjustified refusal of life*, *arbitrary* human intervention for the sake of moments of egotistical pleasure; in short the rejection of *procreation as a specific task of marriage*. In the past the Church could not speak other than she did, because the problem of birth control did not confront human consciousness in the same way. Today, having clearly recognized the legitimacy and even the duty of regulating births, she recognizes too that human intervention in the process of the marriage act *for reasons drawn from the end* [*finalité*] *of marriage itself* should not always be excluded, provided that the criteria of morality are always safeguarded."[86]

The theological problem here is only half the story. The other half, the half that swayed both the minority of the Papal Commission Report and Paul VI, is that this suggestion seems so contrary to the traditional position of the Catholic Magisterium that it might undermine the entire moral tradition and authority of the Magisterium. The inability or simple refusal to recognize this problem, we believe, is at the root of the divide that continues to separate minority and majority today. Before we confront that problem, however, we must complete our look at the sociohistorical background.

The Personal Procreative-Union Model of Marriage

The unprecedented horrors of World War I transformed the context of human affairs in Europe, where the horrors were localized. This period of "bereavement" and "national trauma" gave birth to a variety of philosophical movements,[87] including the movement that came to be known as personalism. This personalism gradually affected theology and made its first, tentative Catholic appearance in December 1930, in Pope Pius XI's *Casti connubii*, his response to the Anglican Lambeth Conference's approval of the morality of artificial contraception. That encyclical initiated the expansion of the procreative model of marriage into a more personal model of conjugal love and intimacy. *Casti connubii* began timidly to give way to an interpersonal *union model*, in which procreation remained an important facet of marriage but did not encompass all that marriage is. Pius insisted that marriage had as its primary end procreation and that the mutual love and life of the spouses was also an end.

This mutual love, expressed by loving acts, has "as its primary purpose that husband and wife help each other day by day in forming and perfecting themselves in the interior life . . . and above all that they may grow in true love toward God and their neighbor." So important is the mutual love and life of the spouses, Pius argued, drawing on the *Catechism of the Council of Trent*, that "it can, in a very real sense, be said to be *the chief reason and purpose of marriage*, if marriage be looked at not in the restricted sense as instituted for the proper conception and education of the child but more widely as the blending of life as a whole and the mutual interchange and sharing thereof."[88] If we do not focus in a limited way on procreation, Pius taught, but broaden the scope of the model to embrace also the marital life and love of the spouses, then that life and love is the primary reason for marriage. With this authoritative teaching, Pius introduced a new, transitional model of marriage, a procreative union model, which, after thirty-five years of growing pains, eventually blossomed into an entirely new and previously unheard of Catholic model of marriage, a model of *interpersonal union*.

Pius XI suggested there is more to marriage than the biologically rooted, act-focused, procreative institution model can explain. He suggested a personal procreative-union model, a suggestion that was taken up by European thinkers, most influentially two Germans, Dietrich Von Hildebrand and Heribert Doms, whose work we have already explained. In marriage, spouses enter an interpersonal relationship in which they confront one another as "I" and "Thou" and initiate a mysterious fusion of their very beings. This fusion of their personal beings, and not merely the physical fusion of their bodies, is what the oft-quoted "one body" of Genesis 2:24 intends. It is this interpersonal fusion that the bodily fusion of sexual intercourse both signifies and instrumentally causes, and intercourse achieves its primary end when it actually does signify and cause interpersonal union. "Every marriage in which conjugal love is thus realized bears spiritual fruit, becomes *fruitful*—even though there are no children."[89] The parentage of this interpersonal model of marriage in modern personalist philosophy is as clear as the parentage of the traditional procreative model in Greek Stoic philosophy. We underscore again, however, that a demonstration of parentage is not *eo ipso* a demonstration of either truth or falsity. We must always be on guard against the genetic fallacy. More important, and clearer, is the resonance of an interpersonal description of marriage and marital lovemaking with the lived experience of modern married couples.

In this model, then, the primary end of sexual intercourse in marriage is the marital union between the spouses, and this primary end is achieved in every act of intercourse in and through which the spouses actually enter into intimate communion. Even in childless marriages, which sociological data show to be increasingly common today, marriage and sexual intercourse achieve their primary end in the marital union of the spouses, their *two-in-oneness* in Doms's language. "The immediate purpose of marriage is the realization of its meaning, the conjugal two-in-oneness. . . . This two-in-oneness of husband and wife is a living reality, and the immediate object of the marriage ceremony and their legal union." The union and love of the spouses tends naturally to the creation of a new person, their child, who fulfills both parents individually and as a two-in-oneness. "Society is more interested in the child than in the natural fulfillment of the parents, and it is this which gives the child primacy among the natural results of marriage."[90] Contemporary sociological data, however, demonstrate the fallacy in assigning primacy to the child, for the relational well-being of the parents is the key to the well-being of their child.[91]

The Catholic Church's reaction to these new ideas was, as so often in theological history, a blanket condemnation that made no effort to sift truth from error. In 1944, the Holy Office (now the Congregation for the Doctrine of the Faith) condemned "the opinion of some more recent authors, who either deny that the primary end of marriage is the generation and nurture of children, or teach that the secondary ends are not essentially subordinate to the primary end, but are equally primary and independent."[92] In 1951, after yet another world war of even greater horror, as the ideas of Von Hildebrand and Doms persisted and gained more adherents, Pius XII felt obliged to intervene again. "Marriage," he taught, "as a natural institution in virtue of the will of the creator, does not have as a primary and intimate end the personal perfection of the spouses, but the procreation and nurture of new life. The other ends, in as much as they are intended by nature, are not on the same level as the primary end, and still less are they superior to it, but they are essentially subordinate to it."[93] The terms of the question of the ends of marriage could not have been made more precise. Another question, however, was seriously clouded.

For twenty years after *Casti connubii*, the Catholic Church struggled with a paradox. Because, on the basis of its reading of natural law whose author was assumed to be God, the primary end of sexual intercourse in marriage is procreation, every act of intercourse should be open to procreation. But a moral question arose. Is it moral for a couple to practice periodic continence with the explicit intention of avoiding conception, that is, is it moral for a couple intentionally to limit their sexual intercourse to the wife's monthly period of infertility? This question raged for twenty years until Pius XII, in a famous speech to Italian midwives in 1951, ruled that such action was moral as long as there are "serious reasons" of a "medical, eugenic, economic, or social kind,"[94] with no specification of what such serious reasons might be. The obligation to procreate, the pope argued, rests not on individual couples but on the entire human race. An individual couple can be excused from adhering to this obligation, even for the lifetime of a marriage, if they have sufficient reason. This ruling, later validated by Paul VI in *Humanae vitae*, introduced a strange paradox into Catholic teaching about sexuality and marriage. On the one hand, God, the author of natural law, determined that the end of each and every act of sexual intercourse is open to procreation; on the other hand, the Catholic Church determined that a couple may be sexually active and intentionally avoid this end if they have sufficient reason. Selling's comment is apposite: "Although it has never been admitted by the Magisterium, with the teaching on periodic continence the natural law approach to sexual morality had reached a cul-de-sac."[95] The Second Vatican Council would attempt to resolve this and other paradoxes in ecclesial doctrine about marriage by rejecting the model in which this papal argument is based.

Though the council did not deal in detail with marriage and the sacrament of marriage, *Gaudium et spes* did provide material intimately related to our present discussion. Marriage, it taught, is a "communion of love, . . . an intimate partnership of life and love."[96] In spite of insistent demands from a small Vatican minority to repeat the centuries-old tradition of marriage as procreative institution, thus consigning spousal love to its traditional secondary place, the council declared the mutual love of the spouses and their passionate desire to be best friends for life to be of the very essence of marriage. It underscored its preference for an interpersonal model by making another important change in the received tradition. When faced with demands to describe the consent that initiates marriage in the traditional way as legal *contract*, the council demurred and chose to describe it as interpersonal *covenant*, explaining its choice of "covenant" in only one terse explanation in the commentary given to the Fathers along with the revised text in September 1965: "There is no mention of 'matrimonial contract' but, in clearer words, of 'irrevocable personal consent.' The biblical term 'covenant' [*foedus*] is added at the intuition of the Eastern Churches for whom 'contract' raises some difficulties."[97] The council's understanding of *covenant* is dependent upon the intuition of the Eastern Churches, and to that intuition, therefore, we must briefly turn.

Marriage, then, is founded in "a conjugal covenant of irrevocable personal consent."[98] Though in truth "contract" and "covenant" share many of the same meanings, there is one major difference: Contracts have people as witnesses, covenants have God as witness. Covenant is ineluctably related to God in a way that contract is not. Covenant is also a biblical word, saturated with overtones of divine, personal, mutual, steadfast love, characteristics which are now applied to the marriage between a man and a woman. The description of the object of the marital covenant places the interpersonal character of marriage beyond doubt. The spouses, the Council teaches, "mutually *gift and accept one another*,"[99] the focus on animal bodies and their acts is replaced by a focus on persons. In their marital covenant, spouses create not a procreative institution but a loving interpersonal union, which, because covenanted love is steadfast, is to last as long as life lasts and may or not be procreative.[100]

The Second Vatican Council devotes an entire section to the love that is the foundation of marriage and sacrament. It interprets the Song of Songs as a canticle to human-genital rather than to divine-mystical love, the reading that had long been prudishly traditional in Jewish and Christian hermeneutics.[101] This marital love is "eminently human," "involves the good of the whole person," and is "steadfastly true." It is singularly expressed and perfected in genital intercourse, which signifies and promotes "that mutual self-giving by which the spouses enrich one another."[102] Marriage and the marital love of the spouses are still said to be "ordained for the procreation of children,"[103] but that "does not make the other ends of marriage of less account," and "*[marriage] is not instituted solely for procreation*."[104]

The intense, and well-documented, debate that took place in the Second Vatican Council makes it impossible to claim, as Grisez wishes to claim,[105] that the refusal to sustain the received marital tradition was the result of a simple avoidance of the language. It was the result of deliberate and hotly deliberated choice, a choice replicated and given canonical formulation twenty years later in the revised *Code of Canon Law* in 1983. Marriage "is ordered to the well-being of the spouses and to the procreation and upbringing of children" (Can. 1055, 1), with no suggestion that either end is superior to the other. Notice that, once again in the Catholic tradition, it is *marriage* and not *sexual intercourse* that is ordered to procreation. Marriage is "brought into being by the lawfully manifested consent of persons who are legally capable" (Can. 1057, 1), and that consent "is an act of the will by which a man and a woman by irrevocable covenant mutually give and accept *one another* for the purpose of establishing a marriage" (Can. 1057, 2). The Catholic Church revised its laws about marriage in the twentieth century to bring them into line with a newly received and developing theology of marriage, moving beyond the model of marriage as exclusively procreative institution to embrace a model of interpersonal union in which the mutual love and communion of the spouses is as important as procreation.

The judgment of the majority of the competent faithful on the Papal Commission continues to be the judgment of the majority of Catholic theologians and Catholic couples. They do not receive the prescription that every act of sexual intercourse must be open to new life, because they do not receive the biologically procreative model of sexuality and marriage on which it is based. Rather, they re-receive the procreative model as an interpersonal procreative model on which the majority report was based. Their nonreception does not make the traditional teaching necessarily false; it does, however, make it irrelevant to the life of the whole Church, a theological fact that has been abundantly documented by sociological research. Thirty-five years after the publication of *Humanae vitae* and its underscoring of the inseparability of the unitive and procreative significances of sexual intercourse, despite a concerted and powerful minority effort to make adherence to the biologically procreative model a litmus test of authentic Catholicity, the dialectic between the biologically procreative and interpersonally procreative models persists tenaciously in the Church. Magisterial efforts to silence key voices in the theological debate, efforts that totally ignore the documented majority *sensus fidelium*, have not succeeded in silencing the debate. They have, however, succeeded, as sociology again shows, in creating a loss of respect for Church law about sexuality in general.[106] There is what might be called a silent schism in the Church over the question of contraception.[107] Authority can dictate truth, but it cannot impose it. In the constant authentic Catholic tradition, dictated or ruled truth becomes effective only when it is received by those under authority.

The scientifically documented nonreception of *Humanae vitae* and the nuanced re-reception of the procreative model in its interpersonal form, among both those expert in theology and those expert in marriage, suggest a contemporary example of re-reception and dramatic development of doctrine in the Church, in line with the developments that took place in the doctrines on usury, slavery, religious freedom, and membership in the Body of Christ.[108] Sociological research suggests that dramatic development is now well under way. It shows that the assertion that "the Church believes that each and every marriage act must be open to the transmission of new life" is not true today for the vast majority of Catholics who make up the People of God on whom the Second Vatican Council placed such emphasis.[109] Theologians can never be comfortable with any statement of belief that can be shown empirically to be untrue. At the very least, the social scientific data suggest a development that the whole Church, "from the Bishops to the last of the faithful,"[110] is called to discern in order to judge whether it is or is not an authentic example of re-reception of the apostolic truth toward which the Spirit of truth is constantly impelling the Church.

A Renewed Principle of Human Sexuality and Contraception

We turn now to our renewed principle and its concomitant further principle to ask what light they may throw on the debate over contraception. The renewed principle, to refresh your memory, is articulated as follows: "[Conjugal] love is uniquely expressed and perfected through the marital act. The actions within marriage by which the couple are united intimately and chastely are noble and worthy ones. Expressed in a manner which is truly human, these actions signify and promote that mutual self-giving by which spouses [immediately] enrich each other [and mediately enrich their family and community] with a joyful and thankful will."

The further principle is that, to be moral, sexual acts must be just and loving. The consideration of both principles leads to the conclusion that *some* heterosexual and *some* homosexual acts, those that are holistically complementary, just, and loving, are moral; and that *some* heterosexual and *some* homosexual acts, those that are not holistically complementary, just, and loving, are immoral. The question here is do these principles have any contribution to make to the discussion of the morality of artificially contraceptive acts. We shall argue that they do.

The love relationship between a man and a woman is transformed into a marriage, an "intimate partnership of life and love,"[111] by the valid legal ritual of their wedding. The wedding transforms the man and the woman into husband and wife. If their shared love is matched by their shared faith in the God revealed in Christ, their wedding can also be a religious ritual that transforms their relationship into a sacrament of the relationship between Christ and Christ's Church.[112] The root relationship or bond of these three, the relationship or bond that requires constant nurture for the support of the other two, is not the legal bond arising from wedding or the religious bond arising from sacrament. It is the relationship or bond arising from the mutual love in which the spouses affirm one another as good and equal selves, the very love that leads them in the first instance to commit to join their love and their life for as long as life lasts in marriage.[113] Though *"marriage and married love* are by nature ordered to the procreation and education of children, . . . marriage is not merely for the procreation of children. Its nature as an indissoluble covenant between two people and the good of the children demand that the mutual love of the spouses be properly shown, that it should grow and mature."[114]

In the contemporary Catholic tradition, *pace* Grisez and his colleagues, marriage has two equal, nonhierarchical ends, the mutual love of the spouses and the procreation of children. Any doubt about the Second Vatican Council's intentions with respect to the equality of the ends of marriage—and *Acta Synodalia Concilii Vaticani II*, as we have already demonstrated, shows that there is no possibility of legitimate doubt—was removed by the revised *Code of Canon Law*: "The *marriage covenant*, by which a man and a woman establish between themselves a *consortium* of their whole life, and which of its very nature is ordered to the well-being of the spouses and to the procreation and upbringing of children."[115] Marriage has two equal ends, the mutual love of the spouses and the procreation of children, with no hierarchical distinction between them. The equality of the ends in *Gaudium et spes* and in the *Code* necessarily changes the traditional argument about the morality of contraception. Our principle for the hermeneutics of sexual acts in marriage is focused on these two equal ends.

When a man and a woman are wedded, their human "nature" is transformed by the ritual; it is specified as definitively wedded. The partners are no longer the individual man and individual woman they were prior to the ritual; they have been made, rather, ritually and definitively coupled spouses, the biblical two-in-one-flesh.[116] Spouses are humans who have given themselves in loving intention to one another, have taken mutual responsibility for their separate and communal lives, and have promised to be permanently faithful to the covenant responsibilities they have pledged one to the other for the whole of life. It is in the context of that mutual, covenantal, spousal, just, and loving self-gift that the morality of their marital acts, including the acts of sexual intercourse, have meaning.

In their real historical, as distinct from some ideal and ahistorical, experience, human beings are fallible, prone to sin, and live their lives within variously sinful structures. Their concrete "nature," the Catholic tradition universally teaches, is a sinful, wounded "nature," always in need of salvation. Though spouses can *intend* their love and mutual self-gift to be total and indissoluble, in the concrete reality of their woundedness they cannot *make* them total and indissoluble at any given moment of their life, for love and self-gift reach out into the unknown, unpredictable, and uncontrollable future. All they can do, in Margaret Farley's wise words, is "initiate in the present a new form of relationship that will endure in the form of fidelity or betrayal." This they do by their ritual consent at their wedding, and their covenantal commitment to one another "is [their] love's way of being whole while it still grows into wholeness."[117] In Catholic theological language, marital love, like the love of God and love of neighbor, is essentially eschatological; that is, it reaches its totality only in the eschaton or end of marital life, not during and certainly not at the beginning of it. This eschatological quality of human love, allied to the sinful human structures that constantly threaten it, makes marital love "naturally" unfinished, imperfect, and fragile.

Totality and the Conjugal Act

The above discussion raises a question about the position on totality adopted, for instance, by Pope John Paul II and the traditionalists who uncritically follow him. The pope writes that "sexuality, by means of which man and woman give themselves to one another through the acts which are proper and exclusive to spouses, is by no means something purely biological, but concerns the innermost being of the human person as such. It is realized in a truly human way only if it is an integral part of the love by which a man and a woman commit themselves *totally* to one another until death. The *total* physical self-giving would be *a lie* if it were not the sign and fruit of a *total* personal self-giving. . . . This *totality* which is required by conjugal love also corresponds to the demands of responsible fertility."[118]

We agree with Lisa Cahill that "the cumulative effect of such rhetoric is to hit married couples over the head with an unattainable norm for their conduct—one which, moreover, is hardly left at the level of ideal, being translated into rules for action of the most concrete and absolute sort."[119] There is no problem offering a moral ideal to spouses; there is a major problem offering absolute, concrete rules that take no account of historical circumstances that can modify the ideal.

Cahill is correct in identifying the problem with this papal and traditionalist argument. It is not conducted on the level of abstract principle to be interpreted and specified according to concrete circumstance, as the abstract principle "Thou shall not kill," for example, is interpreted in the Catholic moral tradition. The tradition interprets "Thou shall not kill" to mean "Thou shall not directly kill an *innocent* person," but you can morally kill an aggressor in proportionate self-defense or in a just war. The pope's traditionalist argument about the meaning of sexual intercourse is conducted not on the level of principle but on the level of absolute concrete rule that applies in each and every circumstance and admits of no exception. We have already pointed out in this book the difficulty of translating absolute moral principle into concrete moral norm. We agree with Cahill that, in keeping with their interpretation of human "nature" as "pure nature" and their total ignoring of concrete human experience, traditionalists read human experience "through the lens of the advocated teaching, and assume an ideal and abstract character little reflective of the give-and-take of enduring sexual relationships, especially marriage."[120] Our approach interprets human "nature" as the concrete, socially constructed "nature" persons share in the less than ideal and frequently wounded and messy circumstances of their real, historical lives. In the concrete "nature" of love and marriage, Cahill's "give-and-take of enduring sexual relationships," the "nature" of human love, and of the marriage that is intended to serve its growth to fullness, is unfinished, imperfect, fragile, and far from total.

Although it is not possible for humans to emulate fully the total love of God and to love totally, there is a totality involved when that love is covenanted between two free and equal human beings in marriage. This totality is the totality of the couples' relationship as it is personalized, legalized, and covenanted in marriage and the totality of the family they create together. The totality of the marriage embraces the good of each partner, the good of their relationship, and the good of any children who may be born from their marital intercourse. Any decision about the morality of any marital act, including but not restricted to the act of marital intercourse, has to consider not only the so-called objective act but also how and where that act fits in the totality of these various goods. Once it is conceded, as *Gaudium et spes* and the *Code of Canon Law* concede, that marital love and relationship and procreation are equal ends of marriage, then the judgment about the morality of artificial contraception cannot be made on the exclusive basis of pure "nature" and the interpretation of its relatively rare biological outcome.

The Inseparability Principle Revisited

Paul VI argues in *Humanae vitae* that God has established an inseparable connection between "the unitive significance and the procreative significance which are both inherent to the marriage act."[121] John Paul II cites this claim with no further elaboration.[122] No proof is offered by either pope in support of this claim, Paul VI simply opining that "we believe our contemporaries are particularly capable of seeing that this teaching is in harmony with human reason."[123] This lack of proof or reason and the fact that many of our educated contemporaries do not see this teaching in harmony with human reason has been a major cause of the debate over Paul VI's claims. It can be argued that Paul himself promoted the debate via an apparent internal contradiction in his argument. In the paragraph immediately preceding his claim of the inseparable connection between the unitive and procreative significances of marital intercourse, he appears to have argued the contrary. Marital intercourse does not cease to be "legitimate even when, for reasons independent of their will, it is foreseen to be infertile. For its natural adaptation to the expression and strengthening [sign and cause] of the union of husband and wife is not thereby suppressed."[124] Here Paul is approving the act of intercourse even when it is known that there is no possibility of procreation, and the basis for his approval seems to be precisely that the act is still directed toward signifying and causing marital love and union.

In these infertile acts, the unitive and procreative aspects are not only separable but also actually separated by the pope. The encyclical, at this point, seems to imply a factual separation of the unitive and procreative aspects of individual acts of sexual intercourse during the infertile period. Paul VI even ascribes this separation of unitive and procreative significance to the wise plan of God: "God has wisely disposed natural laws and times of fertility in order that, by themselves, they might separate subsequent [or the succession of] births." Genovesi judges that the pope might just as well have written that "God has wisely disposed natural laws and rhythms of fertility that, by themselves, cause a separation in *the two meanings of the conjugal act as procreative and unitive.*"[125] With such evidence in support, and lack of compelling proof in nonsupport, it is no wonder that the claim of the inseparable connection between unitive and procreative meanings of marital sexual intercourse has been widely and convincingly challenged.

It appears that by "nature" and the wise design of God, widely verified in worldwide human experience, there are two kinds of natural sexual intercourse, one that is conceptive and one that is nonconceptive. We deny the truth of the proposition that the unitive meaning of sexual intercourse is a universally natural meaning of the sexual act. The unitive meaning is "natural" only as socially interpreted in Western culture. We have no doubt that the procreative and unitive dimensions of marital intercourse are intimately related, particularly in the sense that they are both good for children, the one to procreate a new child, the other to ensure the successful nurture and education of that child. That they are absolutely inseparable, however, is far from demonstrated, especially because it can be argued legitimately that procreation is a "natural" *physiological* outcome of only *some* intercourse and that union of the spouses is a "natural" Western *cultural* outcome of *every* just and loving intercourse.

Accepting without debate Paul VI's unproven assertion of the inseparable connection between the two ends of marriage and the two intrinsic meanings of sexual intercourse in marriage, John Paul II judges "natural" and artificial birth control on the basis of his "totality" argument:

> When couples, by means of recourse to contraception, separate these two meanings that God the Creator has inscribed in the being of man and woman and in the dynamism of their sexual communion, they act as arbiters of the divine plan and they manipulate and degrade human sexuality—and with it themselves and their married partner—by altering its value of *total* self-giving. Thus the innate language that expresses the *total* reciprocal self-giving of husband and wife is overlaid, through contraception, by an objectively contradictory language, namely, that of not giving oneself *totally* to the other. This leads not only to a positive refusal to be open to life but also to a falsification of the inner truth of conjugal love, which is called upon to give itself in personal *totality*.[126]

Again, this totality argument, which we would not challenge as an *ideal* for couples, founders on the rock of concrete circumstances where ideals get concretized as moral rules. The argument John Paul offers here against contraception is equally applicable to natural family planning, in which couples clearly act as "arbiters" of their marital intercourse and "alter" its value of total self-giving by *intentionally* deciding to have intercourse at a time when they judge that the wife is infertile. Indeed, in the face of the evidence, both scientific and experiential, that women in general experience the peak of their sexual desire and responsiveness immediately before, during, and after ovulation,[127] it is arguable that the decision not to have intercourse at that time is acting against total self-giving and nature, at least as much as any act of artificial contraception.

Recalling what was argued in chapter 2 about "nature"—that the reality of "nature" is always interpreted by human reason in particular historical contexts—we contend that our argument for the morality of marital intercourse using artificial methods to prevent the conception of a child is an argument from "nature" every bit as much as the traditionalist argument. The difference is that we argue from the "nature" of marriage and the "nature" of not *human beings* in general but *spouses* and *parents* in particular, the nature of husband and wife and of father and mother. All these common terms are essentially relative terms; that is, they have meaning only in relation to some other term and reality. "Husband" is a term that refers to a man's relationship to a woman who is his "wife"; "wife" is a term that refers to a woman's relationship to a man who is her "husband." "Father" is a term that refers to a man's relationship to another human called his "child"; "mother" is a term that refers to a woman's relationship to another human called her "child"; "child" is a term that refers to a person's relationship to a man called "father" and a woman called "mother." Our argument focuses on two of those relationships, that between spouses and that between parents and their child(ren).

Moral judgment that has to be made on contraception, whether natural or artificial, has to be made on a basis that includes what is good for the couple, their marriage, and any children previously born of their marital intercourse. Adhering to the Catholic tradition that the generation of children and parenthood are defining characteristics of marriage that deserve to be both respected and preserved, our argument is that it is *marriage itself* and not *each and every marital act* that is to be open to the transmission of life and parenthood. This argument is akin to the judgment already convincingly advanced by the majority of the Papal Commission in 1967, though we offer a different foundation for it. Human intervention in the process of the marriage act *for reasons drawn from the end of marriage itself*—that is, from the good of the spouses, their marital relationship, and any children born of their marital intercourse—should not always be excluded, *provided that the Catholic criteria of morality are always safeguarded*. The two phrases we have underscored are at the heart of this principle.

We hold, with NNLT, that marriage is a basic human good in the abstract and also a basic human good in the concrete for every committed and covenanted couple. We hold also that the marital act of sexual intercourse is a basic human good in the concrete but, as we have already explained, we do not agree with NNLT that marital sexual intercourse is a good that can never be instrumentalized for the sake of some other good. The Catholic tradition, as we have demonstrated and need not repeat again, is a thoroughly sacramental tradition. This means that one human good can be and is used as sacrament, that is, as sign and causal instrument, of a higher good. With *Gaudium et spes*, we embody this sacramental tradition in our overarching principle in the words "expressed in a manner which is truly human, these actions *signify and promote* [*or cause*] that mutual self-giving by which spouses immediately enrich each other and their marriage," and we apply it in our approach to the question of the morality of sexual marital intercourse.

Our argument is clear. Procreation is undoubtedly a good of *marriage* but, in the Catholic tradition advanced by Pius XII and Paul VI, it is not an essential good without which marriage could not exist. It can be avoided for "serious reasons,"[128] "just reasons,"[129] "worthy and weighty reasons,"[130] even "probable reasons."[131] The covenanted union of life and love, the traditional *consortio vitae*, that is the very essence of marriage and that is scientifically documented as necessary for the education and nurture part of procreation to be successful is, conversely, a necessary good of marriage. The loving and just union of the spouses is a necessary good of marriage, for the spouses, their children, and the communities, civil and religious, in which they live. It is not difficult to see why the not-necessary marital good of procreation can on occasion give way to the necessary goods embodied in marriage itself, not because it is a lesser good *in se* but because, on this specific occasion and for these just, serious, and weighty reasons, it is for the good of the spouses and the good of any children they may have. We argue that, to be moral, both conceptive and natural and artificial contraceptive intercourse must take place within the context of these various marital and familial goods. The demands of the good of marriage, the good not only of the couple but also of their children, can on occasion take priority over the good of procreation. A compromise may be needed between the good of the spouses and the good of procreation, the now-equal goods of marriage according to Catholic teaching. Not every married couple need procreate, or even be open to procreation, every time they have intercourse; indeed, as Pius XII taught, not every couple need procreate at all.

There is virtually no debate among Catholic theologians about the foregoing. The debate is about the *means* that may be taken to prevent procreation. The Catholic moral tradition is unanimous: Not only must a chosen end be moral but also the means chosen to achieve that end must be moral. The end of supporting my family is a perfectly moral end; working as an accountant for a construction company is a perfectly moral means to achieve that end, but stealing from the construction company is not a moral means to achieve that end. Our question here is what means may be used to achieve the perfectly moral end of precluding procreation. Our answer is that, when spouses have a serious, just, and weighty marital or familial reason to preclude procreation in a specific concrete circumstance, procreation can be precluded by any means that does not damage their complementary, just, loving marital or parental relationship, and is not otherwise immoral. The rational basis for such a judgment, to repeat, is the nature of both the marital and familial relationship and the necessary goods associated with them, which, when a serious, just, and weighty reason is present, take precedence, as we have explained, over the good of procreation.

Conclusion

This chapter has been about marital morality and, of necessity in the Catholic tradition, about birth control as an important issue in that morality. It has situated marital morality within our foundational principle, namely, that sexual acts within marriage by which a couple is united intimately and chastely are noble and worthy and, when expressed in a manner that is truly human and justly loving, signify and promote that mutual self-giving whereby spouses enrich each other, their family, and their community with a joyful and thankful will. It has situated marital morality, therefore, in a context not of individual marital *acts* but of the overall marital *relationship*. In this context, it has argued and concluded that *some* intentionally conceptive and *some* intentionally nonconceptive marital acts, whether achieved "naturally" or artificially, are moral, namely, those that promote the complementary, just, and loving marital relationship between the spouses and/or the just and loving relationship between parents and their children. It argued further that *some* intentionally conceptive and *some* intentionally nonconceptive acts, whether achieved "naturally" or artificially, are immoral, namely, those that damage the complementary, just, and loving relationship between the spouses and/or the just and loving relationship between parental spouses and their children. The morality of any act of marital intercourse is determined, as it is always determined in the Catholic moral tradition, not only by the act of intercourse itself but also by the intention of the spouses following a conscientious and integral examination of the marital and familial circumstances in which the act is performed. We conclude similarly regarding homosexual and nonreproductive heterosexual sexual acts. *Some* homosexual and nonreproductive heterosexual sexual acts are moral, namely, those that promote the complementary, just, and loving relationship between the spouses or couple and/or the just and loving relationship between parental spouses or a couple and their children. *Some* homosexual and nonreproductive heterosexual sexual acts are immoral, namely, those that damage the complementary, just, and loving relationship between a couple and/or the just and loving relationship between a couple and their children.

Chapter Six

Cohabitation and the Process of Marrying

EMMANUEL NTAKARUTIMANA EXPRESSES the Central African experience of marrying in the following words. "Where Western tradition presents marriage as a point in time at which consent is exchanged between the couple in front of witnesses approved by law, followed by consummation, the tradition here recognizes the consummation of a marriage with the birth of the first child. To that point the marriage was only being *progressively realized*."[1] Four years of field experience in East Africa taught us the same thing. We offer three points of clarification. First, the Western tradition to which Ntakarutimana refers is the Western tradition of only the past four hundred years; it goes back neither to Jesus nor to the New Testament. Second, even in this Western tradition, indissoluble marriage is not defined by a specific point in time and a specific act that consummates it. Rather, in the received Western tradition, as in the African traditions, becoming validly and indissolubly married is a process, which begins with the exchange of consent and ends with subsequent consummation. Third, two ongoing questions arise: What are we to make of the differences between the Catholic, Western tradition of marrying and other cultural traditions and how long can the Catholic Church continue to insist that the historically recent Western tradition is *the* universal tradition for all?

This chapter reflects on these points. In it we try, in Kevin Kelly's words, to make "faith-sense of experience and experience-sense of faith"; that is, we come to the contemporary experience of cohabitation with a Catholic faith and we attempt to bring that faith into conversation with the experience of cohabitation and how that experience affects the lives of cohabiting couples.[2] We engage in this exercise conscious of the fact that human experience is a long-established source for Catholic moral judgments. This chapter is about both cohabitation and marriage, and their possible connectedness. It is specifically about the process of becoming married in the living Catholic tradition of past and future. Because it reflects on the history of marriage in the West, it necessarily uncovers two facts about the phenomenon contemporary society calls cohabitation. First, despite the current concern, cohabitation is nothing new in either the Western or the Catholic traditions; second, as practiced both in the past and in the present, Western cohabitation is not unlike the

African cohabitation of which Ntakarutimana writes. This chapter, then, develops in three cumulative sections. The first section considers the contemporary phenomenon of cohabitation; the second unfolds the Western and Christian historical tradition as it relates to cohabitation and marriage; the third formulates a moral response to this phenomenon in light of theological reflection and our foundational sexual ethical principle.

Before embarking on this exploration, however, it is important to define precisely what is meant by the term *cohabitation*. The word derives from the Latin *cohabitare*, to live together. It applies literally to all situations where one person lives with another person: marriage, family, students in a dormitory, roommates in an apartment. An added specification is necessary to distinguish the meaning of the word in contemporary usage and, therefore, in this chapter. Cohabitation names the situation of a man and a woman who, though not husband and wife, live together as husband and wife and enjoy intimate sexual relations.

Roussel offers a useful typology based on the reason given for cohabitation: "*idealist* cohabitation, where the couple look on marriage as something banal; *anticonformist* cohabitation, where they seek to express their opposition to society; *prudent* cohabitation, where they live a sort of trial marriage; *engaged* cohabitation, where the couple anticipates by several months a marriage for which they are already engaged."[3] Whitehead also offers a four-point typology. *Prenuptial cohabitation* describes the living together of couples whose members have already publicly declared their intention to marry; *courtship cohabitation* is one in which the members of a couple are "passionately involved sexually before they have gone through the slower process of gaining trust, familiarity, and knowledge of each other and of each other's families"; *opportunistic cohabitation* is that of romantically involved couples that are not thinking of marriage; and *nonnuptial cohabitation* describes a union which is an alternative to marriage.[4] We prefer a simpler typology, which highlights the relation of cohabitation and marriage. "Engaged cohabitation" and "prenuptial cohabitation" we call simply *nuptial* cohabitation, because marriage is consciously intended to follow it; all other types of cohabitation we call *nonnuptial* cohabitation because there is no conscious intention of marriage. It is important to understand from the outset that everything we say about cohabitation in this chapter is said only of nuptial cohabitation and cohabitors, that is, those who are already committed to marry each other.

Cohabitation in the Contemporary West

The sharp increase in cohabitation is one of the most fundamental social changes in Western countries today. More than half of all first marriages in the United States are preceded by cohabitation.[5] Studies find a similar trend in Europe,[6] Britain,[7] Norway,[8] Sweden,[9] the Netherlands,[10] France,[11] Belgium and Germany,[12] Canada,[13] and Australia.[14] Surveys in France, the Netherlands, Austria, and Britain indicate that cohabitation before first marriage reached levels between 40 and 80 percent for recent marriages.[15]

What the Sciences Tell Us

Two social scientific facts about cohabitation are well known and frequently mentioned by Catholic theologians. The first is that unmarried heterosexual cohabitation increased dramatically in the United States, and elsewhere in the Western world, in the last quarter of the twentieth century. For couples marrying in the United States in the decade between 1965 and 1974, the proportion of marriages preceded by cohabitation was 10 percent; for couples marrying between 1990 and 1994, that proportion dramatically quintupled to 50 percent.[16] Between 1987 and 1995, there was an equally striking increase for the number of women reporting that they had cohabited at least once. In 1987, 30 percent of women in their late thirties reported they had cohabited; in 1995, 48 percent reported they had cohabited. These increases did not leave the social climate in which cohabitation flourished untouched. Rather, as cohabitation cohorts become more and more homogenized, cohabitation itself becomes more and more conventional and socially endorsed.

The second fact often mentioned is that premarital cohabitation tends to be associated with a heightened risk of divorce,[17] a fact on which there is consensus from a large variety of different researchers, samples, methodologies, and measures. This second fact has become beloved of Catholic commentators on unmarried heterosexual cohabitation and its implications for subsequent marriage,[18] which leaves both them and their pastoral responses at risk of being uninformed and outdated. More recent studies on more recent cohorts report more nuanced data about the relationship of cohabitation and marital instability.

As early as 1992, Schoen showed that the inverse relationship between premarital cohabitation and subsequent marital stability was minimal for recent birth cohorts, a result that he linked to the growing prevalence of cohabitation: "As the prevalence of cohabitation rises sharply, the instability of marriages preceded by cohabitation drops markedly."[19] In 1997, McRae demonstrated the common negative association between premarital cohabitation and marital stability when she analyzed her British sample in toto. When, however, she analyzed her sample by age cohort, her findings supported Schoen: "Younger generations do not show the same link between premarital cohabitation and marriage dissolution." She agreed with Schoen's conclusion that "as cohabitation becomes the majority pattern before marriage, this link will become progressively weaker."[20] This majority pattern, as noted above, has now arrived. When they analyzed their results in toto, Woods and Emery uncovered much the same data as McRae: "Premarital cohabitation had a small but significant predictive effect on divorce." When they controlled for personal characteristics, however, premarital cohabitation had no predictive effect on divorce.[21]

In a sophisticated study of an Australian sample that controlled for age at union formation, educational level, importance of religion in the relationship, parental divorce, and having a child before marriage (all strong predictors of divorce), De Vaus and his colleagues found the link between cohabitation and marital instability was apparent only for earlier cohorts.[22] When cohabitation alone, without any control variables, was considered, the greater risk of marital separation of couples that cohabited before marriage than couples that did not was 11 percent for those that married in the 1970s and only 2 percent for those that married in the early 1990s. When control variables were added to the analysis, those that cohabited before marriage in the 1970s had a 6 percent higher risk of divorce than those that did not, and those that cohabited before marriage in the early 1990s actually had a 3 percent *lower* risk of divorce than those that did not, though that difference was not statistically significant. Teachman recently replicated that result, showing that when a woman has cohabited only with her husband, cohabitation is not associated with increased likelihood of divorce.[23]

Two of America's most respected marriage researchers, Scott Stanley and Linda Waite, endorse the thesis that all cohabitors and all cohabiting relationships are not equal. Stanley writes that "those who are particularly at risk from premarital cohabitation are most likely those who have not already decided, for sure, this is who they want to marry before cohabitation, . . . while not all couples are at greater risk for cohabiting prior to marriage, it's surely a very great and unwise risk for those who are not sure they have found who they want to marry."[24] Waite states that "couples who live together with no definite plans to marry are making a different bargain than couples who marry or than engaged cohabitors,"[25] and she adds that "those on their way to the altar look and act like already married couples in most ways, and those with no plans to marry look and act very different. For engaged cohabiting couples, living together is a step on the path to marriage, not a different road altogether."[26] Waite's conclusion from her data is of the utmost importance: "Compared to marriage, *uncommitted cohabitation*—cohabitation by couples who are not engaged—is an inferior social arrangement."[27] On the basis of her data, Whitehead concludes minimally that prenuptial cohabitation is somewhat successful.[28]

There are at least two kinds of cohabitors,[29] those uncommitted to marriage and those already committed to marriage, perhaps even engaged, and it is only uncommitted cohabitation that is linked to an increased likelihood of divorce after marriage. Empirical research clearly shows that commitment is a distinctive determinant in relationship stability, whether that relationship be cohabitation or marriage.

Recent social scientific research, therefore, suggests that the generalization that cohabitation, without distinction, is linked to subsequent marital instability is far too unnuanced to be accepted uncritically. Careful consideration of these data should precede any pastoral considerations. We align with Stanley and Waite and all the other researchers who demonstrate recently that not all cohabitors are alike. Furthermore, we suggest the restoration of a betrothal ritual, which is grounded in the historical practice of betrothal in the Christian tradition.

The Meaning and Nature of Commitment

Before we consider betrothal, however, we must discuss the commitment that distinguishes both married couples and nuptial cohabitors. John Paul II teaches that conjugal love "aims at a deeply personal unity, a unity that, beyond union in one flesh, leads to forming one heart and soul; it demands indissolubility and faithfulness in definitive mutual giving; and it is open to fertility."[30] Kelly contends that this describes the situation of those cohabitors who have committed to a loving relationship with one another and who later come to him to be married. He refuses to consider them as "living in sin," because that would be "a denigration of something they had experienced as sacred and from God." They come to the Church "to celebrate the gift of their love for each other and to give it new permanence through the solemn commitment of their marriage vows to each other and to God."[31] Their growing *commitment* in love to one another and, ultimately, their grown commitment to marriage is not just an abstract, anonymous concept; it has a very concrete and recognizable face. Stanley has brilliantly analyzed this commitment.

Stanley distinguishes two kinds of commitment: commitment as *dedication*, defined as "an internal state of devotion to a person or a project," and commitment as *constraint*, which "entails a sense of obligation."[32] Those who lose the sense of dedication and retain only the sense of constraint "will either be together but miserable . . . or come apart."[33] Our brief consideration here is only of the more important sense of commitment, namely, commitment as dedication, which we define as "a freely chosen and faithful devotion to a person or project." Applied to relationships, including marriage, commitment as dedication is twofold: commitment to the partner and commitment to the relationship. Commitment to the partner entails those characteristics that John Paul lists or implies, namely, fidelity, loyalty, and fortitude in the vicissitudes and messiness of the relationship. Commitment to the relationship entails exclusivity, indissolubility, and potential fertility as fruitfulness.[34] The members of couples that share this double commitment manifest it in various ways. They give evidence of a strong couple identity, "a strong orientation toward 'us' and 'we.'" They "make their partner and marriage a high priority." They "protect their relationship from attraction to others." They are willing to "sacrifice for one another without resentment." They take a long-term view, "they invest themselves in building a future together."[35] Such double commitment, Stanley and others show, is the surest path to the marital intimacy that all partners and spouses seek.

The members of couples with such a double commitment report that they feel comfortable revealing their deepest desires, failings, and hurts to one another.[36] They do not think about possible alternatives to their partner, they are more satisfied with their marital life in general and their sex life in particular, and they have no need to consider adultery.[37] They are more willing to give up things important to them for the sake of their relationship, and they report higher levels of happiness and stability than do partners who do not regularly sacrifice for the sake of their relationship.[38] These couples have a strong sense of their future together and are more likely to speak of that future and of their dreams for it than of their past conflicts, failures, and disappointments[39] It is such commitment, we suggest, that nuptial cohabitors exhibit, albeit in seed at the beginning of their cohabitation together but in full flower when they come to be married. It is precisely the seedling love and commitment becoming flower that needs to be ritually realized and celebrated in the betrothal to which we now turn.

Betrothal and the Christian Tradition

All theology, perhaps especially the theology of the secular reality of marriage, which may or may not become also religious sacrament, must be attentive to social change, especially dramatic social change. It must also be attentive to the wealth of information provided by the social sciences because, as the Christian tradition demonstrates, human experience, which includes social change, informs and influences Christian theology.[40] Because theology is and must be rooted in reality, the relationship between the social reality of cohabitation and the theology of marriage must be carefully explored in light of and informed by all available and appropriate sources of wisdom.

Contemporary Christians, especially fundamentalist Christians, both Protestant and Catholic, easily assume that the nuclear family of early-twentieth-century America, the so-called traditional family, is both biblical and natural. It is always a surprise to them to discover that it is neither.[41] There is a similar problem with the contemporary phenomenon of cohabitation. Again, it is easily assumed to be a new phenomenon; and, again, it is not.

Historical Considerations

Two imperial Roman definitions have dominated the Western discussion of marriage. The first is found in Justinian's *Digesta* (23, 2, 1) and is attributed to the third-century jurist Modestinus: "Marriage is a union of a man and a woman, and a communion of the whole of life, a participation in divine and human law." The second is found in Justinian's *Instituta* (1,9,1) and is attributed to Modestinus' contemporary, Ulpianus: "Marriage is a union of a man and a woman, embracing an undivided communion of life." These two "definitions," which are no more than descriptions of marriage as culturally practiced in imperial Rome, controlled every subsequent discussion of marriage in the Western tradition. They agree on the bedrock: Marriage is a union and a communion between a man and a woman embracing the whole of life.[42]

Marriage, therefore, in both the Christian theological and the Western legal traditions, is the union of a man and a woman. But how is marriage effected in the eyes of these two traditions which, up to the Reformation, were identical? Already in the sixth century, Justinian's *Digesta* (35, 1, 15) decreed the Roman tradition: The only

thing required for a valid marriage was the mutual consent of both parties. The
northern European custom was different; there, penetrative sexual intercourse after
consent made a valid marriage. This different approach to what made marriage valid
provoked a widespread legal debate in Europe. Both the Roman and the northern
opinions had long histories, sound rationales, and brilliant proponents in twelfth-
century Europe. The debate was ended in midcentury by Gratian, master of the
Faculty of Law at the ancient Catholic University of Bologna, who proposed a
compromise solution. Consent *initiates* a marriage or makes it *ratum*; subsequent
sexual intercourse completes it or makes it *consummatum*. This settlement continues
to be enshrined in the *Code of Canon Law*: "A valid marriage between baptized
persons is said to be merely ratified (*ratum*) if it is not consummated; ratified and
consummated (*ratum et consummatum*) if the spouses have in a human manner
engaged together in a conjugal act in itself apt for the generation of offspring" (Can.
1061).

To be underscored here is the *process* character of valid, indissoluble marriage,
matrimonium ratum et consummatum, in the Catholic Church, for that process character is central to the argument presented in the third section. The present law
requires for valid, indissoluble marriage two distinct acts, the mutual free consent
of the couple and their subsequent, penetrative sexual intercourse.[43] How the law
was followed in practice is a part of the historical marital tradition of both the
Catholic and the Western worlds that has been long ignored. It is grossly ahistorical
to assume that the current practice and understanding of marriage is what has always
been.

Gratian's compromise—mutual consent makes a marriage *ratum* and sexual
intercourse makes it *ratum et consummatum*—ended the debate between the Romans
and the northern Europeans over what effected marriage. Consent could be given
in either the future tense (*consensus de futuro*) or the present tense (*consensus de
presenti*). When it was given in the future tense, the result was called betrothal, and
the process from cause (consent) to effect (betrothal) was known as *sponsalia* or
spousals; that is, the members of the couple became spouses. When consent was
given in the present tense, the result was called marriage, and the process from cause
(consent) to effect (marriage) was known as *nuptialia* or nuptials; that is, the members of the couple became wedded. The first sexual intercourse between the spouses
usually followed the betrothal, and this is a fact of both the Western and the Catholic traditions that has been obscured by the now-taken-for-granted sequence of wedding, marriage, sexual intercourse, and possible fertility. It was not, however, until
the Council of Trent in the sixteenth century that the Catholic Church prescribed
that sequence and decreed that marriage resulted from the nuptials or ceremonial
wedding. For more than half of contemporary Catholic couples in the modern West,
the sequence has reverted to the pre-Tridentine sequence: cohabitation, sexual intercourse, possible fertility, and wedding.

The pre-Tridentine sequence has been well documented in sociohistorical
sources. Remy describes the situation in France, where sexual relations regularly

began with *sponsalia* or betrothal: "In the sixteenth century, the Churches began to lead a campaign against premarital sex. Previously the engagement or betrothal carried great weight. If the Church frowned on the unblessed marriage she did not forbid it. Very often, above all in the country, the Church marriage took place when the woman was pregnant, sometimes towards the end of her pregnancy."[44] He also points out that, in a society in which fertility was central to the meaning of marriage, sexual intercourse took place as a test of the required fertility. His statement justifies the pre-Tridentine sequence against the backdrop of its cultural context. It holds equally true for African cultures today.[45]

A host of commentators describe the situation in England and its Empire, which for some time included colonies on the Eastern Seaboard of what became the United States. Lawrence Stone writes: "Before the tightening up of religious controls over society after the Reformation and the Counter-Reformation in the mid–sixteenth century, the formal betrothal ceremony seems to have been at least as important, if not more so, than the wedding. To many, the couple were from that moment "man and wife before God."[46] The Church recognized this situation, Stone points out, and in the Deanery of Doncaster in 1619 betrothal was a successful defense in the courts against an accusation of premarital sex. Macfarlane emphasizes that "the engaged lovers before the nuptials were held to be legally husband and wife. It was common for them to begin living together immediately after the betrothal ceremony."[47] "In Anglo-Saxon England," he adds, "the 'wedding' was the occasion when the betrothal or pledging of the couple to each other in words of the present tense took place. This was in effect the legally binding act; it was, combined with consummation, the marriage."[48]

Later, a celebration of the marriage, an occasion for relatives and friends to bring gifts and to feast, was held but, up to the Council of Trent in the Catholic tradition and up to the Hardwicke Act in mid-eighteenth-century England, the central event of the *sponsalia* or betrothal was held separate from the ceremonial event of the *nuptialia* or wedding. After the betrothal, "the couple saw themselves as man and wife, and therefore sexual intercourse was a natural consequence."[49] This meant, of course, as Quaife points out, that "for the peasant community, there was very little premarital sex. Most of the acts seen as such by Church and State were interpreted by the village [the cultural community] as activities within marriage—a marriage begun with the promise and irreversibly confirmed by pregnancy."[50] Parker underscores something central to our argument, namely, that the marital process from betrothal through pregnancy to marriage "was located in a general belief in the ability of public opinion to command obedience to community values."[51] For the peasant community, there was little premarital sex, for acts seen as such by Church and state were seen and enforced by the local community as acts within marriage, made irreversible by pregnancy. In what continued to be the broader northern European tradition, long after Gratian's compromise, pregnancy consummated a marriage.

Neither Church nor state was satisfied with this marital process, but neither had any choice but to recognize the validity of marriages thus effected. Church law, accepted by European states as binding in marital affairs, was clear. Free consent to marry, whether articulated publicly or privately, initiated marriage, and sexual intercourse after consent, with or without subsequent pregnancy, consummated marriage and made it indissoluble. In the eyes of the Church, marriages, however private and secret, which were the result of free consent and subsequent consumma- tion had to be held as valid marriages and, therefore, when the spouses were bap- tized, as also valid sacraments. Genuinely secret or clandestine marriages, however, became the scourge of Europe and provoked a change in both canon and civil law.

Clandestine marriages took place for all sorts of reasons. A couple, Romeo and Juliet, for instance, could not marry publicly because their families would not allow it, or class distinction would not allow it, or the fact that one of them was illegiti- mate would not allow it. Clandestine marriages, because of their very clandestinity or secretiveness, were difficult to verify and frequently ended in clandestine divorce, with charge and countercharge of concubinage, fornication, illegitimacy, and big- amy. That a marriage made valid by mutual free consent, made indissoluble by sexual intercourse, and made sacrament of the union between Christ and his Church would cease to be at someone's unsubstantiated whim was intolerable for the Catho- lic Church, and in the sixteenth century the Council of Trent moved to preclude forever the possibility of clandestine marriage.

The council's decree *Tametsi* (1563) prescribed the marriage the Church would recognize as valid and sacramental and, when consummated, indissoluble: that mar- riage, and only that marriage, which was publicly celebrated in the presence of a duly appointed priest and two witnesses .[52] Only if celebrated in this canonical form, as it came to be called, would a marriage between Catholics be recognized by the Church as valid and sacramental. *Tametsi* transformed the ritual celebrating mar- riage, namely, the wedding, from a simple contract between families, one not cir- cumscribed by any legal formalities, into a solemn contract, one in which certain legal formalities had to be observed for validity. That canonical change was within the power of the Church to make; it is, of course, equally within its power to unmake. In addition to transforming the contractual nature of marriage, *Tametsi* transformed also the *how* and the *when* of marriage. No longer could anyone claim that marriage was effected at betrothal; it could be effected only at a public Church ceremony called a wedding. The modern era of marriage had begun. It took another two hundred years, however, for the new marital process to become established in the English-speaking world.

By the middle of the eighteenth century, the marriage custom that had been common practice in England was giving way to competing practices. In the preced- ing one hundred years, the betrothal, sexual intercourse, fertility, wedding sequence had become a subject of controversy, not around religion or sexuality but around social class. As Gillis explains, "The ideal of the nuclear family, something that had divided the middle class from the aristocracy in the seventeenth century, now united them in common opposition to their social inferiors. From the mid–eighteenth century onward sexual politics became increasingly bitter as the propertied classes attempted to impose their standards on the rest of society."[53] Among the upper and aspiring middle classes, betrothal lost its public character and became an internal family affair called *engagement*, a prelude to marriage which was never to be confused with marriage, and which did not confer the rights of marriage, including the right to sexual intercourse. An engaged couple could never be confused with the married couple they would become after their wedding.

This development in the process of marriage, and in the success of the English upper class in imposing its practice on everyone in England, reached its apogee in 1753 when Lord Hardwicke introduced an act to prohibit clandestine marriages. The Hardwicke Act, which became law on May 1, 1754, prescribed that no marriage in England would be valid other than the one performed by an ordained Anglican clergyman, on premises of the Church of England, after the calling of banns for three successive weeks or the purchase from the local bishop of a license not to call banns. The act exempted the marriages of Jews and Quakers from its provisions, and it underscored the seriousness of its intentions by prescribing fourteen years transportation for any Anglican minister who attempted to conduct any wedding apart from the provisions of the law.

The present process of marriage in the West, specifically the focus on the wedding ceremony as the beginning of marriage, has been in effect only since the sixteenth century. The present practice of the English-cum-American civil law has been in effect only since the mid–eighteenth century. In both institutions, the present procedure was enacted not for some grand theological or legal reason. It was enacted to put an end to the scourge of clandestine or secret marriage and the misery it brought to people. Because the process of marriage was otherwise prior to Trent and Hardwicke, it is not unthinkable that it could be otherwise again.

Sociotheological Considerations

Before 1564, when the papal bull prescribing compliance with the decisions of the Council of Trent became Catholic law, Catholics needed no wedding ceremony to be married. Before 1754, the citizens of England and its empire needed no wedding to be married. That historical reality can never be erased. The process of becoming validly married in the Catholic and Western traditions has not always been as it currently is. That this is so, that Catholic marriage practice was adapted and greatly transformed within historical memory, leads easily to the conclusion that it could adapt and change again. That possible change in Catholic marital practice will be the focus of this section of this chapter.[54] We emphasize from the outset that there is nothing new in the change we will propose; rather, the change is a reversion to something old, something that was part of the Catholic tradition of marriage for centuries before Trent introduced the change that established the present received tradition. A Thomistic principle is in play here: *Ab esse ad posse valet illatio*, the conclusion from actual being to possibility is valid. From the actual historical being of the marital sequence betrothal–sexual intercourse–possible fertility–wedding, the conclusion that it could be so again, albeit in changed circumstances, is logically legitimate. This section will show that it is also theologically legitimate.

The parallel between premodern, pre-Tridentine, and pre-Victorian practices and modern or postmodern practices is striking. Premodern betrothal led to full sexual relations and pregnancy, which in turn led to indissoluble marriage; modern nuptial cohabitation leads to full sexual relations and in turn to indissoluble marriage, with or without pregnancy. We underscore here, again, that in this chapter we are focused only on *nuptial cohabitation*, cohabitation premised by the intention to marry. Nothing we say refers to nonnuptial cohabitation. "The full sexual experience practiced by betrothed couples [in pre-Tridentine and pre-Victorian times] was . . . *emphatically premised by the intention to marry*."[55] Only those cohabitors with an emphatic intention to marry are our concern.

Our proposal is straightforward: a return to the processual marital sequence of betrothal (with appropriate ritual to ensure community involvement), sexual intercourse, possible fertility, and ceremonial wedding to acknowledge and to mark the consummation of both valid marriage and sacrament. This is not a new proposal; it has been made with different nuances before. The first detailed proposal was made in 1977 by the Canadian moral theologian Andre Guindon; he was followed independently in 1978 by the French theologian M. Legrain.[56] Guindon seeks to respond theologically and canonically to the growing prevalence of cohabitation in Canada. He argues that the contemporary marital situation has been transformed by the socioeconomic changes that have taken place over the past two hundred years; the new roles accorded to women; the desire, especially of women, for an adult and satisfying sexuality; and the centrality of mutual love in the marital relationship. He notes that the human sciences have shown that sexuality is a language to be progressively learned in an ongoing apprenticeship subject to all the laws of human development. Reflecting these social scientific data, he seeks a renewed canonico-theological understanding of consummation, founded not automatically on a first act of sexual intercourse but on the personal, spiritual, and physical union established between the partners. This leads him to propose the consummation of a marriage before its ratification, *matrimonium consummatum et ratum* rather than the traditional-since-Gratian *matrimonium ratum et consummatum*.

Legrain reflects a different perspective, that of customary African marriage, where "even among Christians, . . . only those who have followed all the customary tribal requirements, including the performance of the required rituals, are held to be truly married."[57] He, as Guindon, is concerned with the processual character of *matrimonium consummatum et ratum*, particularly with the Roman claim that consummation follows from the first sexual intercourse. That is not the case in African custom. Echoing Ntakarutimana, Legrain states what is obvious to all cognizant of the African context: "The marriage of Christians would never be accepted as *ratum et consummatum* until the birth of a child."[58] The birth of a child stamps a union as marital, marking the union in African eyes as a truly consummated marriage.

In Legrain's and African eyes, marriage is not just a wedding ceremony—not a moment in time when a couple give publicly witnessed consent, however dear such precision might be to canon lawyers—but also a process from betrothal through human, including sexual, intercourse to the consummating birth of a child. Could African customary marital rituals be Christianized? Of course they could, just as imperial Roman and northern European tribal rituals were Christianized to yield the present received tradition. That they have not yet been Christianized is due to the imposition of a Roman canonico-theological form based on the assumption that a compromise twelfth-century European form is *the* unique Christian model for marriage. They could be Christianized by accepting the processual character of African marriages as a human value and adapting, yet once again, legislation, liturgy, and pastoral practice to highlight human, marital, and sacramental value. If what Legrain argues is possible for an African cultural context, and we see no theological reason why it is not, it is also possible for a Western cultural context once again in the full flower of change.

What Guindon and Legrain propose, each in his own way, is an adaptation of Christian, sacramental marriage to diverse cultural realities. They abandon the received Catholic model of becoming married as synonymous with becoming wedded, of marriage taking place at a moment in time, the moment of mutually given public consent, and they seek to replace it with a developmental model, in which marriage takes place in stages.[59] They reject the received, legalistic, reductionist model of Christian marriage as being incapable of responding to the processual nature of interpersonal love, sexuality, and marriage in new, postmodern cultural manifestations.[60] They agree in recognizing a real marriage, *matrimonium ratum*, from the moment of betrothal, and in recognizing a consummated and indissoluble marriage, *matrimonium ratum et consummatum*, when the members of the couple have fully expressed in their marital life the marital values of their culture. Above all, and this is to be underscored for the argument of this section, they agree in condoning sexual intercourse only between members of couples who have seriously committed themselves to becoming married. For Legrain, those are African Christian couples living out the required customary stages of a marriage; for Guindon, and for us, those are Western Christian couples nuptially cohabiting with an already-given firm consent to marry.

The most recent and most detailed treatment of the relationship between contemporary cohabitation and marriage is provided by the English theologian Adrian Thatcher, whose concern is "to *preserve the ancient link between betrothal and marriage* while acknowledging that betrothal is not yet marriage and so does not yet preclude the possibility of revoking the multiple intentions which end in marriage."[61] He rehearses the history reported in this chapter, which leads him to the same conclusion we reached earlier: *Ab esse ad posse valet illatio*: "Christians who think *all* preceremonial sex is wrong have wrongly assumed that the ceremonial requirement of a wedding, in fact a requirement of modernity, has always been normative. It has not."[62] History shows that betrothal as entry into marriage, with all the rights of marriage including sexual intimacy, was a premodern institution recognized by the Catholic Church and, therefore, also the Western tradition. "Since it is part of the Christian tradition *already*, conservative orthodoxies can hardly continue to ignore it."[63] The argument that cohabitation presents "'a threat to the institution of marriage and the family' assumes that there are fixed, not changing institutions of marriage and family, and so 'defending' marriage entails defending a peculiar inherited version of it."[64] The version widely received in the Christian marital tradition is that of marriage as a procreative institution.[65]

The stumbling block to granting moral legitimacy to any premarital sexual activity in the Catholic tradition, and in all the Christian traditions, is the exclusive connection the traditions see between sexual intercourse and marriage. "Every genital act must be within the framework of marriage."[66] Outside marriage, genital activity always constitutes a grave sin and excludes one from sacramental communion. This teaching certainly appears to be a major stumbling block to the claim of this chapter that *some* prewedding sexual activity is morally legitimate. There can be no way forward until the traditional and exclusive connection between sexual activity and marriage—which is, in fact, the exclusive connection between sexual activity and procreation—is severed. To get really real about sexuality and sexual activity in the modern world, the exclusive connection between sexual intercourse and procreation has to be abandoned.[67]

At the beginning of this chapter, we suggest that different circumstances and different premises, perhaps learned from a close study of the contemporary social, psychological, and theological situation, would lead to different conclusions. That suggestion is true for sexuality, procreation, and marriage, the connection of which has a long history in the Catholic Church. The earliest Christian theologians learned it from the ancient Stoic philosophers who, basing their explanations of sexuality on their observations of animal behavior, argued that the sexual organs were only for procreation, only to perpetuate the species.[68] This argument, exclusively based on physical structure, organs, and functions, might be a good argument for nonhuman animals whose sexual activity is limited by instinct and fertile periods ("heat"). Is it a good argument, however, for human animals whose sexuality is not exclusively instinctual but is under the control of social, psychological, and personal factors, whose fertility is restricted to a few days a month, and whose normal sexual feelings, desires, and activities occur more frequently than, and do not always coincide with, their fertile periods?[69] Many Catholic and Christian theologians, taught by the insights of the human sciences, believe it is not. They believe that the bodily act of sexual intercourse between humans has a surplus of meaning beyond the physical; they believe it is multivalent in meaning and value. They see it as much more than an animal activity. They see it as a language celebrating personal love, two-in-oneness, and mutuality; a language proclaiming, affirming, and realizing the value of an other; a language in which a couple, mutually committed to one another, "make love." They acknowledge that, like any language, the language of sex must be learned with the utmost care, honesty, and ongoing fidelity. It is hardly surprising that with these changed premises, they would come to conclusions quite different from those drawn from a traditional approach.

The Stoic approach to sexual activity and its exclusive connection to marriage canonized marriage in the Western tradition as a *procreative institution*, an institution whose primary end was procreation. Other ends of marriage related to the spouses were acknowledged but they were secondary to procreation, and the primary end–secondary end hierarchy dominated the Catholic approach to marriage for centuries. Karl Barth once complained that the traditional Christian doctrine of marriage, both Catholic and Protestant, situated marriage in juridical rather than in theological categories.[70] The Roman Catholic Church corrected that imbalance in 1965. The history of marriage in the Catholic tradition has progressed from a model of *procreative institution*, in which procreation is everything, to a model of *interpersonal union*, in which the relationship and love between the spouses is the foundation of both the marriage and the sacrament of marriage. There is no evidence that this theological shift was in any way influenced by the human sciences, but almost forty years later the socioscientific evidence is overwhelming.

The genuine procreation of children, which always intended and continues to intend their education and nurture beyond mere biological generation, which intends human motherhood and fatherhood beyond biological maternity and paternity, depends on the happiness and stability of the relationship between the spouses/parents. Divorce is a result of the breakdown of the relationship between the spouses, and it is now beyond debate that divorce is bad for children.[71] For those parents who successfully progress beyond maternity and paternity to genuine motherhood and fatherhood, thus successfully nurturing children into functioning adults, in thirty years their children are grown up and they still have twenty to thirty years to live together. That living together will be successful only if the relationship between the spouses has been a loving and faithful one for the whole of life. If for no other reason than that, it is time for the Church's exclusive preoccupation with the act of intercourse and procreation to yield to interpersonal reality; it is time for the Church to preoccupy itself with the positive marital relationship.

It is time to return our discussion to the claim that the sexual act must always take place exclusively within marriage. It is not a claim that anyone who knows the social scientific evidence would challenge; inductive experience shows that, for most human beings, all that is expected and desired from a total and mutually self-giving relationship is best delivered in that stable relationship we call marriage.[72] A question arises, however: Why is it that the sexual act must always take place exclusively within marriage? We submit that sexual intercourse so radically involves all the potentials of a human person that it is best expressed and safeguarded in *a stable and lasting relationship* between two people. This stable, lasting, and legally guaranteed relationship has traditionally been called marriage.

What has happened in the modern age is that those couples whom we have called nuptial cohabitors are beginning their stable marital, including their sexual, relationship before their wedding ceremony. They are committed to one another, though they have not articulated that commitment in legal, public ritual; they fully intend to marry when the psychological and, especially, the economic restrictions modern society puts upon their right to marry are removed. Their nuptial cohabitation, perhaps even their betrothed or engaged cohabitation, is the first "little step" in their journey toward marriage.[73] In the canonico-legal words of the received tradition, their engagement or betrothal *initiates* their marriage; their subsequent ceremonial wedding, before or after the birth of a child, *consummates* their marriage and makes it indissoluble. Since their betrothal, however expressed, and we would prefer that it be expressed in a public ritual,[74] initiates their marriage, their cohabitation is no more premarital than that of a pre-Tridentine and pre-Harwicke couple. Their cohabitation and intercourse are certainly preceremonial or prewedding, though that could be easily remedied by the introduction of a public betrothal ceremony, but they are far from premarital.

A major change in the approach of Catholic ethicists to sexual sin parallels the change in the approach to marriage.[75] The majority of Catholic ethicists have agreed for years that decisions of morality or immorality in sexual ethics should be based on *interpersonal relationship* and not simply on *physical acts* like masturbation, kissing, petting, premarital, marital, and extramarital sexual intercourse, both heterosexual and homosexual.[76] Cahill argues that "a truly humane interpretation of procreation, pleasure and intimacy will set their moral implications in the context of enduring personal relationships, not merely individual sexual acts. If human identity and virtue in general are established diachronically, then this will also be true of sexual flourishing."[77] Serious immorality, what is traditionally called mortal sin, is not decided on the basis of an individual act against "nature," that is, the biological, physical, natural processes common to all animals. It is decided on the basis of human goods and human relationship built upon them. Cahill suggests such human goods as "equality, intimacy, and fulfillment as moral criteria."[78] We would add the virtues of love and justice, to make more fully explicit what she clearly intends. Sexuality has three bodily meanings: intimacy of bodily contact, even bodily interpenetration; pleasure; and reproduction or procreation. All these meanings are realized and developed over time and in the social institutions that a given society recognizes. Immoral or less-than-moral behavior is defined not exclusively by any sexual act related to these three but rather by any less-than-loving, just, equal, compassionate, and mutually fulfilling act.

In the case of nuptial cohabitors, for a man and a woman who are deeply committed to one another and already betrothed to marry, and whose preceremonial but nuptial sexual intercourse takes place in this context of personal commitment to a future marriage, the moral theological argument proceeds along these lines. A man and a woman have a fundamental freedom to marry. Modern society has established socioeconomic structures for marriage that the couple are presently unable to achieve. These circumstances surrounding the intercourse of this couple who are deeply committed to each other, who are in right relationship with both one another and God, and who fully intend to marry "may render their premarital intercourse an ontic evil but not a moral evil." That such intercourse is not a moral evil would appear to be true especially, Keane argues, "when the committed couple whose rights are unreasonably prejudiced by society do not experience themselves as genuinely free to take the more ideal route of abstaining from that intercourse that cannot be publicly proclaimed as part of a marriage."[79]

We accept the probative value of this argument. In the proposal we are presenting, however, the members of the mutually committed nuptial cohabiting couple are already, if inchoately, married, and their intercourse, therefore, is not strictly premarital but inchoately marital, as it was in the pre-Tridentine Catholic Church and pre-Hardwicke England. Our proposal envisages a marital journey that is initiated by mutual commitment and consent, is lived in mutual love, justice, equality, intimacy, and fulfillment in a nuptial cohabitation pointed to a wedding that consummates the *process* of becoming married in a mutually just, human, and public manner. In such a process, we believe, sexual intercourse meets the legitimate Catholic and social requirement that the sexual act must take place exclusively within a stable marriage.

The notion, and reality, of relationship, commitment, and interpersonal union as *process* is emphasized throughout this book, and it is framed in terms of historical consciousness in contrast to classicism. Historical consciousness emphasizes particularity and views relationship, commitment, and interpersonal union as processes and evolving realities; classicism emphasizes universality and views relationship, commitment, and interpersonal union as static and demonstrable in single acts. With regard to nuptial cohabitation, historical consciousness has important implications for the concept of complementarity and marriage as sacrament. We consider each of these in turn.

Complementarity and Nuptial Cohabitation

As we have already seen, complementarity has recently emerged as a foundational concept for Catholic sexual teaching. Though we critiqued John Paul II's and the Magisterium's sine qua non, foundational heterogenital complementarity, and posited an alternative "holistic complementarity"—the integration of orientation, personal, and biological complementarity—we did not explicitly comment on the evolving nature of complementarity. The issue of nuptial cohabitation and its relationship to the sacrament of marriage provides us with an occasion to do so.

Complementarity: Classicist and Historically Conscious

There are both classicist and historically conscious views of complementarity in the writings of John Paul II and the Magisterium. The classicist view of complementarity, which defines the essence of human "nature," is reflected in the Genesis accounts whereby God creates humans male and female from the beginning. Male and female are "two ways of being a body" that "complete each other." They are complementary in "self-consciousness," "self-determination," and "being conscious of the meaning of the body."[80] This complementarity between male and female is labeled elsewhere "ontological complementarity"; that is, "it is only through the duality of the 'masculine' and the 'feminine' that the 'human' finds full realization."[81] Kelly accurately notes that "ontological complementarity maintains that the distinction between men and women has been so designed by God that they complement each other, not just in their genital sexual faculties but also in their minds and hearts and in the particular qualities and skills they bring to life, and specifically to family life."[82] Man and woman "communicate in the fullness of humanity, which is manifested in them as reciprocal complementarity *precisely because* they are 'male' and 'female.'" Masculinity and femininity, and the psychological and biological elements that constitute the masculine and feminine, are part of the essential nature of human beings. In the ontological order, "it is only in the union of two sexually different persons that the individual can achieve perfection in a synthesis of unity and mutual psychophysical completion."[83] In the ontological "givenness" of male and female human "nature," complementarity is essentialist and classicist.

At the same time, man and woman "*become* a gift for each other,"[84] forming an "interpersonal relationship" in marriage "that has to be *continually developed.*"[85] This *becoming* a gift and *continually developing* an interpersonal relationship through reciprocal complementarity is a historically conscious progressive, evolving, interpersonal reality, realized in both marriage and conjugal acts.[86] We refer to the historically conscious dimension of complementarity as *existential complementarity*, because it recognizes the specific corporeality of ontological complementarity in the particularity of an evolving corporeal and interpersonal relationship. For John Paul II and magisterial teaching, ontological complementarity is classicist in defining essential human nature and existential complementarity is historically conscious in defining its evolving nature in an interpersonal relationship.

These two conceptual notions of complementarity are summed up by the Pontifical Council for the Family: "That man and woman are called upon from the beginning to live in a communion of life and love and that this complementarity *will lead to strengthening* the human dignity of the spouses, the good of the children and of society itself."[87] In this statement, there is a tension between two notions of complementarity, the ontological and existential, that have a bearing on defining the sacrament of marriage in light of the historical practice of betrothal in the Christian tradition and the contemporary cultural practice of nuptial cohabitation, which can be posed as follows. What is the relationship between the ontological complementarity of male and female human "nature" and its existential realization and manifestation in the interpersonal relationship between two people in history? What effects the transformation of the universality of complementarity in its essential "nature" to the particularity of complementarity shared between two people in an interpersonal relationship? Investigating the sacrament of marriage from a classicist and an historically conscious perspective sheds light on these questions.

Marriage as Sacrament

The Catholic Church has long suffered from what Guindon referred to as a "sacramental automatism,"[88] and this is especially apparent in the sacrament of marriage with regard to both consent and to consummation. Marital sacramental automatism is the idea that "the initiation of marriage is a single event," which "tacitly sanctions a vertical, external, and mechanical version of grace, . . . which descends on the couple once the formulae of consent and blessing have been heard."[89] According to this view, in Catholic tradition the sacrament of marriage and the grace the couple receives from the sacrament begin *only* at the moment the sacrament is celebrated.

This automatism is also apparent in current Catholic canonical teaching that requires two distinct acts for a valid, indissoluble marriage, the mutual free consent of the couple[90] and their subsequent, penetrative sexual intercourse.[91] Mutual consent in the sacrament of marriage is posited at a specific time, directed toward the future, but with insufficient appreciation for, and ritual celebration of, its past. In this view, the grace of the sacrament of marriage originates at the moment of consent, and in a sense, is discontinuous from the grace experienced by a couple during the period of betrothal. The grace present in the previous period is defined sacramentally in terms of baptism, confirmation, reconciliation, and Eucharist. There is a discontinuity in sacramental theology between marriage as sacrament and its relationship to the couple's premarital relational journey that brought them to this point. The moment of consent in the wedding is the current canonical definition for when sacramental grace in the sacrament of marriage begins. As such, consent, which effects the beginning of the sacramental grace in marriage, takes on a "quasi-magical significance." This significance is reflected in John Paul II's statement that "once a commitment has been made and accepted through consent, love *becomes* conjugal and never loses this character."[92] Consent is explained elsewhere as "the formula" in which "the spouses will always remember the personal, ecclesial and social aspect gained from this consent for all their life, as a gift of one to the other even unto death."[93] Though the exchange of consent at the wedding is certainly an important point in time to remember—sacramentally, theologically, historically, and experientially—an exclusive focus on it overlooks the evolving nature of consent that is "exchanged gradually" from the beginning of the couple's relationship.[94] Marital consent cannot be encapsulated in a single moment.

Similarly, in Canon Law, consummation is a single act that ratifies a marriage and makes it indissoluble. This understanding of consummation gives a single act of sexual intercourse the "power to achieve a crucial transformation in the relationship in the sight of God," and consummated relationships cannot be undone.[95] The notion of consent and consummation in *The Code of Canon Law* and the sacramental theology there represented highlight the differential between canon law and the juridical and theology and the interpersonal and experiential. There is a tension, if not a disconnect, between canon law, theology, and human experience. It is incomplete and misleading, experientially, interpersonally, and therefore theologically, to claim that a sacramental marriage begins only at this specific point in time. From the canonical perspective, both consent and consummation are single acts given a definitive significance for defining the nature of the relationship between two human beings. This emphasis on the single act and its singularly important meaning is classicist; it posits what initiates a sacramental marriage in terms of two single acts, and transforms the sacrament of marriage from a process to two acts. Marriage and sacrament, however, are an interpersonal event, an unfolding of human relationship more adequately reflected from a historically conscious perspective.

"Catechumenate for Marriage"

To combat sacramental, consensual, and consummational automatism, Thatcher proposes a "Catechumenate for Marriage,"[96] which helps to elucidate a historically conscious view of marriage as sacrament. A catechumen is a person receiving religious instruction in the Christian faith with a view to being baptized, and the catechumenate is the body of catechumens awaiting baptism and full initiation into the Church. Historically, catechumens preparing for baptism in the Christian community were considered already Christians, in the sense that they had already made their commitment in faith to Christ. A catechumen who died before baptism would still be given a Christian burial.[97] Though the sacrament of water baptism had not been administered, baptism of desire had been, and the grace of God was already offered to the catechumen in the inchoate but not completed journey of the catechumenate. Sacramental rituals are undoubtedly channels of grace in the Catholic tradition, but equally undoubtedly they are not the only channels.

According to Thatcher, the term "catechumenate," when used in relation to marriage, "is intended to emphasize the parallels between the 'in-between' state of believing Christians seeking baptism, and the 'in-between' state of persons who are no longer single and who wish to bind themselves to one another unreservedly in marriage."[98] This in-between state is reflected in the interpersonal relationship of betrothed couples. Implementing the catechumenate for marriage "requires a paradigm shift, from treating the ceremony as the beginning of marriage, to treating it as the confirmation, celebration, and blessing of it."[99] In our terms, this is a paradigm shift from the discontinuity of classicism between engagement and marriage as a single event to the continuity of historical consciousness between nuptial betrothal and marriage as a process. Bressoud argues, and we agree, that it is the maturation of both their relationship and their faith during their nuptial cohabitation that permits a couple's relationship to attain to the fullness of marriage and, therefore, also sacrament. This point of view makes the sacrament of marriage an important and "privileged stage" in the journey toward marriage.[100]

This paradigm shift also helps us to make sense out of John Paul II and the Magisterium's understandings of the interrelationship between the ontological complementarity of men and women in their essential human "natures" and the existential complementarity between man and woman in a marital relationship. The papal teaching asserts that the existential complementarity and the unity of the two in marriage is legitimated and embarked upon only at the moment of consent in marriage, and is subsequently consummated in a reproductive sexual act. The proposed catechumenate for marriage views the transformation from ontological to existential complementarity as a gradual process that begins with betrothal and is confirmed, celebrated, and blessed in the wedding ceremony. This process includes the complementarity between two people in all their human dimensions—biological, psychological, affective, emotional, spiritual—that begins with betrothal and is expressed in sexual acts as well as an infinite number of other act types that constitute an interpersonal relationship. Furthermore, in our model of holistic complementarity, this process is extended to both heterosexual and homosexual couples, depending on whether a person's sexual orientation is heterosexual or homosexual.[101] We defined complementarity as "a multi-faceted quality, orientational, physical, affective, personal, spiritual, possessed by every person, which draws him or her into relationship with another human being, including the life-long relationship of marriage, so that both may grow, individually and as a couple, into human well-being and human flourishing." We specify here that existential complementarity is an evolving reality that precedes the wedding and extends far beyond it.

Historical consciousness as it pertains to both existential complementarity and the sacrament of marriage emphasizes their becoming as a process. The history of betrothal in the Catholic tradition, the contemporary cultural practice of nuptial cohabitation, and the lived, evolving experience of two people who become self-gift to one another together reflect more a historically conscious than a classicist view of the sacrament of marriage. In light of history, culture, and experience, we propose the following as a tentative model for the catechumenate and sacrament of marriage.

Conclusion

We can summarize the argument we have been developing in this chapter via the presentation of a schematic proposal. We propose that an option for the process of marrying in the Catholic Church revert to a four-step process accepted in the Church before the Council of Trent.

The first step is *betrothal* or, in the pre-Tridentine language, *sponsalia*. The betrothal, for which a ritual highlighting free consent to wed in the future should be developed, would be witnessed and blessed on behalf of the church community, preferably, though not necessarily, by a parish priest. The betrothal ritual would differ from the present wedding ceremony only in the fact that the consent would be *consensus de futuro*, a consent to wed in the future. Such betrothal, as it did before, would confer on the couple the status of committed spouses with all the rights that the Church grants to spouses, including the right to sexual intercourse. The betrothal ceremony would function also as public enrollment in the catechumenate for marriage. Theologically, this marriage catechumenate would be as much a time of grace as the baptismal catechumenate; as baptismal catechumens are already-inchoate Christians, so also marriage catechumens are already inchoate spouses.

The second step is *nuptial cohabitation*. In this period, the members of the couple would live together as spouses; would have marital intercourse, including sexual intercourse, with one another in a community-approved, stable environment; and would continue the life-long process of establishing their marital relationship as one of love, justice, equality, intimacy, and mutual fulfillment. This inchoate marriage period would be a perfect time for the Church community to assist the couple in honing both their relationship and their faith with an ongoing marriage preparation program aimed precisely at this maturation.[102] This prewedding period of marital instruction is the marriage catechumenate, analogous to the established prebaptism period of doctrinal instruction required of catechumens before their baptism. It is theologically unthinkable that either catechumenate could happen without the grace of God. Given the expected lifelong character of Christian marriage, the marriage catechumenate is vitally important, for social scientific data indicate that relationship is both the core of long-term spousal and parental success and a reality that can be dangerously flawed by both the self-selecting factors that directed the couple to cohabitation in the first place and the experience of cohabitation itself.

The third step is *fertility*. We are fully conscious that this is the part of our proposal that can cause the most unease among Christians of all denominations. Sexuality and sexual activity have been treated with suspicion in the Catholic Church since the days of the early, Stoic-influenced Christians. That suspicion led to the exclusive focus on procreation that once characterized the Church and continues to characterize it even now when moral approaches among many of its leading thinkers have changed. We have argued, in concert with other Catholic scholars, that this focus on procreation needs to yield to another focus, namely, the focus on the interpersonal relationship that is at the very root of all spousal and parental success in marriage and family. We stand by what we argued earlier: The moral implications of sexual intercourse, sexual pleasure, and procreation leading to parenthood are best set in the context of interpersonal relationship and not in the context of mere sexual acts. The context of the nuptial cohabitors with whom we are concerned in this chapter is a context of committed, stable, and intentionally lifelong relationship. It is a context that meets the Catholic requirement that sexual intercourse be exclusively within the stable relationship of marriage. It is also a context in which the three dimensions of sexual activity we have mentioned—personal and not just bodily intercourse, mutual pleasure, and procreation leading to not only the biological birth of children but also long-term motherhood and fatherhood—might intersect to the benefit of the relationship. Parenthood, particularly maternal and paternal shared parenthood, expresses and realizes the union of the spouses as much as intercourse and pleasure. In our proposal, it can be the task of nuptial cohabitors as much as of married couples in the received tradition.

The fourth step is *wedding*. There will come a time when the committed nuptial cohabitors have overcome the socioeconomic restrictions imposed on them by society. There will come a time when their relationship has reached such a plateau of interpersonal communion that they will wish to ceremonialize their loving, just, and symmetrical relationship. That time is the time for their wedding when, with their families, friends, and Christian community, they will renew their consent *de praesenti* and celebrate their union for what it has inchoately become, namely, a symbol or sacrament of the loving union between God and God's people, between Christ and Christ' Church. Their wedding can then be considered the consummation of their marriage, the consummation of a relationship that they have sought to make as humane and as Christian as possible. The process of marrying would then be complete; *matrimonium ratum* would become *matrimonium ratum et consummatum*.

Chapter Seven

Homosexuality

ONE SEXUAL ISSUE is today causing anguish to some Christians and confusion and anger to others and is tearing the churches apart as never before. It is the issue of homosexuality. In this chapter we consider this issue in the context of scripture and the Catholic moral tradition interpreted in the contemporary sociohistorical context. Our approach is that mapped out by Pope Benedict XVI when he was Professor Joseph Ratzinger: "Not everything that exists in the Church must for that reason be also a legitimate tradition; in other words, not every tradition that arises in the Church is a true celebration and keeping present of the mystery of Christ. There is a distorting, as well as legitimate, tradition, . . . [and] . . . consequently tradition must not be considered only affirmatively but also critically."[1] The approach is an empirical theology that examines traditional norms not as moral facts for uncritical and passive acceptance but as bases for active and critical understanding, pondering, and evaluating that leads to reasoned, conscientious judgments and decisions in the contemporary sociohistorical context.

The theological tools for this approach draw from four sources of moral knowledge: scripture, "tradition" and "Tradition,"[2] reason, and experience. Traditionally, Catholic moral theology has relied upon these four sources of moral knowledge in developing its natural law method and formulating norms to guide human behavior. Both traditionalists and revisionists have recourse to these four sources. What distinguishes them fundamentally in their ethical methods in general, and in the issue of homosexual acts in particular, is their hermeneutic or interpretation and prioritization of those sources. Traditionalists use a hierarchical approach to the sources of moral knowledge and tend to interpret Tradition in the narrow sense of magisterial teaching, especially as this teaching pertains to moral absolutes. Scripture, reason, and experience, in that order, are all subject to the Magisterium's interpretation. One could say that traditionalists espouse an apologetical ethical method defending the moral absolutes of the Magisterium. Revisionists, while assigning a very important role to Tradition, understanding it in a broad sense to include the Magisterium and the other aspects that make up a universal, ecclesiastical Tradition, use a dialectical approach between the four sources of moral knowledge. Though there is a presumption of truth in favor of magisterial teaching, that teaching is to be critically reflected upon in light of theologically sound scriptural exegesis, the reasonable input of the sciences in areas where it has competence, and the cultural, historical, and relational experiences of the faithful, not necessarily in that order. When there is a conflict between these sources, a process of research, dialogue, and discernment must be undertaken to determine right understanding of divine law. This is a complex and involved process, which takes time, patience, and a commitment to dialogue.

The received tradition of the Catholic Church condemns homosexual acts as "intrinsically disordered"[3] and gravely immoral and does so on the basis of three foundations. The first is the teaching of scripture, in which such acts "are condemned as a serious depravity and even presented as the sad consequence of rejecting God"; the second is "the constant teaching of the Magisterium"; and the third is "the moral sense of the Christian people."[4] This theological tradition is not, and cannot be, in question in any contemporary discussion. Following Ratzinger, however, and the scientific and experiential insights available to us, the tradition can be and must be approached critically, to clarify its foundation, rationale, and continued meaningfulness in the changed sociohistorical circumstances of the contemporary world. It is the clarification of each foundation that is sought in this chapter. Though we respect the theological tradition on this issue, on the basis of empirical theology and a dialectical hermeneutic of the sources of moral knowledge, we maintain that the teaching on the intrinsic immorality of homosexual acts represents a distorting tradition. We conclude by defending our principle of holistic complementarity and argue that *some* homosexual acts *may* be morally right.

The Bible and Homosexuality

Because Christianity is a religion of the book, Christians automatically turn to their Bible, believed to be the Word of God, for guidance in ethical matters. The issue of homosexuality is no exception. The Congregation for the Doctrine of the Faith (CDF) turns to the Bible in its discussion of the "problem of homosexuality" and rhetorically asserts that "there is . . . a clear consistency within the sacred scriptures for judging the moral issue of homosexual behavior. The Church's doctrine regarding this issue is thus based not only on isolated phrases taken out of context, from which could be developed uncertain theological arguments, but rather on the solid foundation of a constant biblical testimony."[5] It lists the texts on which this "solid foundation" is built: Genesis 19:1–11; Leviticus 18:22, 20:13; Romans 1:26–7; 1 Corinthians 6:9; and 1 Timothy 1:10.[6] Interestingly, when the *Catechism of the Catholic Church* lists the biblical texts that present "homosexual acts as acts of great depravity,"[7] it omits the Leviticus text. Lawler, Boyle, and May, none of whom is a Catholic biblical scholar, all accept this "solid foundation" without question and assert that "there are specific biblical passages referring to homosexual acts, and in each of these passages such acts are unambiguously condemned."[8]

In the light of contemporary biblical scholarship, Catholic included, it is impossible to agree that the texts on which this Catholic tradition of the immorality of homosexual acts is based are "unambiguous" and provide "solid foundation." We believe that, when read as the Magisterium itself requires they be read, that is, in the "literary forms" of the writer's "time and culture,"[9] "contextually" as Coleman puts it,[10] the texts that are advanced as a solid and unambiguous foundation of the Catholic teaching on homosexual acts are far from clear and unambiguous. They are, rather, complex and sociohistorically conditioned literary forms that demand careful historical analysis that raises questions in the informed and inquiring theological mind. Those questions are not as easily dismissed as Lawler, Boyle, and May dismiss them, as "not well founded."[11] Three questions are central to this issue. First, does the Bible say anything about homosexuality as we understand it today? Second, if it does say something, what does it say and what does it mean? Third, can the Bible speak to and enlighten the confusion that characterizes contemporary Christian dialogue about homosexuality? Ultimately, the real issue in this section is one we have already confronted in our opening chapter. It is the issue, not of homosexuality and what the Bible says or does not say about it, but of how to read the Bible in order to inform our contemporary Christian lives. This issue is central as we confront our three questions in turn.

Homosexual Orientation and the Bible

The first question, does the Bible say anything about homosexuality as we understand it today, is a question of definition. What do we mean today by the words *homosexuality* and *homosexual*? The answer to that question is embedded in what the sciences and the Magisterium of the Catholic Church now take for granted, namely, the distinction between homosexual *orientation* and homosexual *behavior*.[12] In contemporary scientific and theological literature, the noun *homosexuality* and the adjective *homosexual* are used to refer to a person's *psychosexual condition*, produced by a mix of genetic, psychological, and social "loading,"[13] not to refer to a person's sexual behavior. Sexual orientation, in general, is defined as "the sustained erotic attraction to members of one's own gender, the opposite gender, or both—homosexual, heterosexual, or bisexual respectively."[14] Homosexual orientation, specifically, is "a *condition* characterized by an emotional and psycho-sexual propensity towards others of the same sex,"[15] and a homosexual is "a person who feels a most urgent sexual desire which *in the main* is directed towards gratification with the same sex."[16] In its modern, scientific connotation, homosexuality is a way of *being* before it is a way of *behaving*. Stephen Donaldson, president of the organization Stop Prisoner Rape, was therefore correct in 1994 to challenge the *New York Times*'s characterization of rape within American prisons as "homosexual rape" and to point out that prison rape is predominantly "heterosexual rape," that is, rape committed by those who share the heterosexual *condition*.[17] The homosexual actions of heterosexuals do not make them genuine homosexuals any more than the occasional homosexual tempta-tions of some 37 percent of the American male population reported by Kinsey in 1972 make them homosexual.[18]

Neither the Bible nor the Christian tradition rooted in it prior to the twentieth century ever considered the homosexual condition; they took for granted that every-one was heterosexual. To look for any mention in the biblical texts of what today is called "homosexual orientation" is simply anachronism. One might as well search the Bible for advice on buying a car or a computer. The biblical passages most frequently cited as condemning *homosexuality* actually condemn homosexual *behav-iors*, and they condemn these behaviors specifically as a *perversion* of the heterosexual condition they assume to be the natural condition of every human person. In its modern meaning, homosexuality is not and cannot be a perversion of the heterosex-ual condition because homosexuals, by natural orientation, do not share that condi-tion. Homosexuality is, rather, an *inversion* of the heterosexual condition that psychosexual homosexuals, by no choice of their own, do not naturally share, and they cannot be held morally accountable for something they did not choose.[19] The context in which both the Old and New testaments condemn homosexual acts is a false assumption, shaped by the sociohistorical conditions of the times in which they were written, that all human beings naturally share the heterosexual condition and that, therefore, any homosexual behavior is a perversion of "nature" and immoral. Because that biblical assumption is now scientifically shown to be incorrect, the Bible has little to contribute to the discussion of genuine homosexuality and homo-sexuals as we understand them today. This conclusion will become clearer when we consider our second question: What does the Bible say about homosexual behavior and what does it mean when it says that?[20] We might add, with Vacek, what is obvious, namely, that the Bible contains many questionable moral teachings—on sex during menstruation, stoning adulterers, women's role, slavery, and a host of others—all of which have been rejected by modern Catholic moral theology.[21]

Interpreting the Bible on Homosexuality

The single most influential strand in the Western tradition leading to the condemna-tion of homosexual acts is probably the *interpretation* given to the biblical story of Sodom, at least since the Jewish historian Josephus and the Hellenistic philosopher Philo.[22] Western churches have taught that the fiery destruction of Sodom was caused by the immoral male homosexual behaviors practiced there, and understand-ably Christians have uncritically believed what their churches taught. Sodom has even given its name to one form of male homosexual activity, *sodomy*. Two reason-able questions may be raised with respect to this widespread interpretation, the first about its accuracy, the second about its basis in the biblical text. Our contextual exegesis shows that the homosexual interpretation of the Sodom story is not accurate and is not supported by a reading of the text in its sociohistorical context.

The biblical story is not as straightforward as it appears to the untrained reader. The context of the story and its meaning begins not with Lot and the men of Sodom in chapter 19 but with the story of Abraham's hospitality to "three men," one of whom is soon identified as "the Lord,"[23] in chapter 18. Three "men" pass by Abraham's tent on their way to Sodom, and Abraham offers the strangers the hospitality required by the Levitical law: "When a stranger sojourns with you in your land, you shall not do him wrong. . . . You shall love him as yourself."[24] Abraham invites the strangers to his tent. "Let a little water be brought and wash your feet, and rest yourself under the tree while I fetch a morsel of bread that you may refresh yourselves."[25] In fact, Abraham does more than offer the strangers bread and water. He has his wife, Sara, bake cakes for them; he kills a calf "tender and good" for them; and he serves them himself. His goodness is established by his hospitable reception of the three strangers, and so too will his nephew Lot's goodness be established in the sequel. After they were fed, two of the men left for Sodom, while the Lord remained behind to have with Abraham the famous discussion about how many righteous men would be required to save Sodom from destruction.

"Two angels came to Sodom in the evening and Lot was sitting in the gate of Sodom."[26] Lot offered the two angels the required hospitality, bringing them to his house and feeding them, but before they retired for the night the men of Sodom surrounded the house and called for Lot to bring the two men out "that we may know them (*yadha*)."[27] That word *yadha* is critical for understanding what the men of Sodom were asking. *Yadha* is the ordinary Hebrew word for the English *know*, as it is translated in the Revised Standard Version, but it is also used on occasion to mean specifically sexual intercourse. The question then is which meaning is intended in this text. The Hebrew-English Lexicon of the Old Testament notes that *yadha* is used 943 times and in only 10 of those instances is it used with any sexual connotation. Taking his stance on this datum, Barton argues that in this text it is not clear that *yadha* is to be interpreted in its sexual connotation and that it could just as easily mean that the men of Sodom simply wished to get to know the two strangers.[28] We do not find Barton's interpretation convincing. The sexual meaning of the word seems, at least, to be insinuated by two facts. First, if all the men of Sodom wanted to do was to learn the identity of the strangers, why would Lot beg them "do not act so wickedly";[29] second, the same word *yadha* is used in a clearly sexual sense when Lot offers his two daughters to the crowd: "Behold I have two daughters who have not known man (*yadha*), let me bring them out to you. . . . Only do nothing to these men *for they have come under the shelter of my roof*."[30] We believe there is clear insinuation of homogenital intent against the two strangers at Sodom, which does not mean that the sin of the men of Sodom was the sin of homosexual behavior.

The clearer sin in both the Hebrew text and context is the sin of inhospitality. That Lot is concerned about that hospitality is made evident in the phrase we have underscored above, "do nothing to these men for they have come under the shelter of my roof," that is, under the shelter of my hospitality, which embraces protecting them against the wrongful designs of the crowd. The men of Sodom are as bound by the law of hospitality as is Lot, but they demonstrate their wanton sinfulness by not living up to the law. If *yadha* is to be understood in its sexual connotation, and we believe it is, then the men of Sodom demonstrate the extent of their inhospitality by seeking violent rape of the strangers. If any action is condemned in the text, it is the crime of wrongful, violent, and inhospitable *homosexual* rape carried out by perverted *heterosexual* men. Moore's rational principle for argument about the morality or immorality of homosexual behavior is à propos here: "Argue with the best of homosexual practice, not with the worst. The Church wants to show that homosexual practices are *as such* contrary to the will of God, and so contrary to human well-being, not simply that the worst excesses of homosexuality are contrary to human well-being."[31] Even if the act of male homosexual rape perpetrated by perverted heterosexuals is condemned in this text, that is a long way from a clear and unambiguous condemnation of the loving homosexual acts of people with a homosexual orientation.

The interpretation of the text we propose is supported by the fact that in the rest of the Old Testament, where Sodom is regularly mentioned, not once is its crime said to be homosexual behavior. Ezekiel describes it as "pride, surfeit of food, and prosperous ease, but did not aid the poor and the needy; they were haughty and did abominable things."[32] Isaiah advises the rulers of Sodom, insinuating the standard Old Testament equivalence between God and the poor,[33] to "seek justice, correct oppression, defend the fatherless, plead for the widow."[34] The Book of Wisdom explicitly charges both the men of Sodom and the Egyptians with inhospitality: "Others [the men of Sodom] had refused to receive strangers when they came to them, but these [the Egyptians] made slaves of guests who were their benefactors."[35] For Christians, a prime argument in support of our interpretation that the sin of Sodom is inhospitality is Jesus' mention of Sodom in the same breath as the inhospitality accorded his disciples: "Whenever you enter a town and they do not receive you, go into the streets and say 'Even the dust of your town that clings to our feet we wipe off against you.' . . . I tell you it shall be more tolerable on that day for Sodom than for that town."[36] Jesus also makes hospitality or inhospitality a major cause of salvation or damnation in the great judgment scene in Matthew.[37] Lawler, Boyle, and May opine that Jude 1:7 "refers to Sodom and Gomorrah, and indicates their sin as unnatural vice,"[38] but the Greek text *ekporneusasai kai apelthousai opiso sarkos heteras*—especially *sarkos heteras*, "other flesh"—simply does not support that tendentious reading.

If the Sodom story is ultimately about inhospitable and not homosexual acts, no such reservation can be made about the prescriptions of the Holiness Code in Leviticus. "You shall not lie with a male as with a woman; it is an abomination";[39] and "If a man lies with a male as with a woman both of them have committed an abomination; they shall be put to death."[40] What the Holiness Code says could not be clearer: *Male homosexual behavior* is an abomination. It is important we realize it is *male* acts that are prohibited in these texts; lesbian acts are not part of the prohibition. The word *you* in "you shall not lie" can be misleading. In English *you* applies indiscriminately to both males and females; in Hebrew the word that is used is used only of males. It is male homosexual acts that Leviticus says are an abomination, and that restriction yields some insight into both the sociohistorical context in which Leviticus says what it says and what it might mean when it says it.

The first thing to be noted about the Hebrew context is bad biology. The ancient Hebrew, Greek, and Roman understanding was that the male gave "seed" that contained the whole of life; the female simply provided the "ground" or the "field" in which the "seed," a true *homunculus*, was sown to develop into a fully fledged human.[41] To spill that seed or nascent *homunculus* anywhere it could not develop properly, on the ground or in a male body, for instance, was regarded as tantamount to murder, and murder was always held as an abomination. Those guilty of murder suffered the same penalty as our present text prescribes for male homosexual acts, namely, death.[42] Because they waste no life, perhaps also because women in a patriarchal society simply do not count, female homosexual acts are not considered worthy of consideration in the Holiness Code or anywhere else in the Old Testament. The fact that only male homosexual acts are declared an abomination introduces another contextual consideration, that of male honor and the actions appropriate to it.

Extended family was and is "the primary economic, religious, educational, and social network" in Mediterranean society.[43] Within the social network, family was also the locus of honor, carried exclusively by males, particularly the patriarch who headed the family and, for all intents and purposes, owned the females in it, whether they were daughters or wives. For a male to "lie with" another male, that is to act passively and allow himself to be penetrated like a female, seriously compromised male honor, not only that of the male being penetrated but also that of every male in the family or clan. The passivity of a male, who was expected to be active in all things, including the sexual, was always abhorred and dishonorable. In such a sociohistorical context, of course, male homosexual acts would be an abomination, not, however, qua homosexual acts but qua passive and dishonorable acts that threatened the patriarchal and hierarchical sexual arrangement that pervaded the Old Testament.[44] Xavier Lacroix writes that "'abomination' is the translation of the Hebrew *to-ebah*, which can evoke the *tohu-bohu* of the beginning of Genesis, that is, the chaos that preceded the creative action of God, that consisted in separating, introducing difference: between day and night, waters above and waters below, land and sea, male and female." This hermeneutic enables him to conclude that "homosexuality, therefore, is considered as a return to *tohu-bohu* [chaos]."[45] This conclusion displays creative imagination but is so removed from accurate etymology as to be itself an hermeneutical abomination. There is no etymological connection whatsoever between *tohu-bohu* and *to-ebah*.

But what of an utterly different social context: a context in which not every human being is assumed to be by "nature" heterosexual and some are known to be by "nature" homosexual; a context in which honor is not a dominant concern; a context in which male and female are understood to contribute equally to the procreation of new life? In such a context, male homogenital behavior need not be judged as dishonorable and ipso facto immoral; just and loving homosexual behavior, flowing from an innate homosexual orientation, cannot be regarded as a perversion of a universal heterosexual condition and, therefore, cannot be judged as ipso facto immoral; and the spilling of male semen or seed would no longer be regarded as the spilling of life, murder, and an abomination. In short, when the interpreter considers what the Bible says about male homosexual behavior and the sociohistorical context in which it says it, it is difficult to consider the Bible as saying anything more instructive in the present sociohistorical context than what it says about *kosher* laws.[46] As understood today, male homosexual behavior may or may not be immoral, but current judgment of its morality cannot be based on what the Old Testament says about it in the context of its own time and place.

Because many Christians consider the Old Testament fulfilled, or even superseded, by the New, they automatically give more credence to what the New Testament says about homosexual acts. We must, therefore, consider what the New Testament says and, in particular, we must consider what many consider the centerpiece of what it says about homogenitality, namely, chapter 1 of Paul's letter to the Romans. It is important, again, to note the context, which is a Pauline attack not on homosexual acts in particular but on degenerate, especially idolatrous, Gentile society in general.

After introductory greetings Paul launches into standard Jewish accusations about Gentile idolatry: "What can be known about God is plain to them [Gentiles] because God has shown it to them."[47] But however plain the existence of the true God of Israel might be and however much Gentiles ought to have known that God from the things God made, they did not acknowledge God, they "did not honor God as God or give thanks to God." Rather, "they exchanged the glory of the immortal God for images resembling a mortal human being or birds or four-footed animals or reptiles."[48] What is radically wrong with Gentiles, Paul believes, is that they do not worship the true God of Israel; they are idolaters, and he immediately moves on to describe the behavior of such idolaters. *Because* they are idolaters, in some divine punishment, "God *gave them up* in the lusts of their heart to impurity, to the dishonoring of their bodies. . . . God *gave them up* to dishonorable passions. . . . God *gave them up* to a base mind and to improper conduct."[49] The dishonorable passions and the male and female homosexual acts performed by perverted heterosexuals are God's punishment on Gentiles for their idolatry. It is Gentile *idolatry* that is directly at stake in the Pauline text, and the perverted homosexual acts of heterosexuals to which it is presumed to lead, not the homosexual acts of those who by "nature" share the homosexual condition and the just and loving homosexual acts in which it might issue.[50]

Language expresses meanings from and within a social system, and Paul's language clearly reveals the social system from which he writes. Women *exchanged* natural for unnatural relations, and men *gave up* relations with women for relations with men. Exchanged what, we might ask, gave up what? Exchanged or gave up the heterosexual actions to which their presumed heterosexuality obligated and entitled them. All men and women are heterosexual, Paul believes, with the Judaism of his time, and to engage in homosexual acts they have to *pervert* their true "nature." That perversion is, of course, immoral. First-century Paul has no insight into the contemporary psychosexual condition of homosexuality in which some people, homosexual by "nature," would have to pervert their true "nature" to engage in heterosexual acts. The language also reveals that Paul is speaking of relationships "heavy with lust,"[51] very possibly of pederasty, the only publicly discussed male same-sex activity in his time.[52] He is not talking of, because he has no concept of, relationships between homosexual couples who might justly love one another and might be committed to one another as faithfully as any heterosexual couple. The condemnation of the perverted homogenital actions of heterosexuals does not easily translate into the ipso facto condemnation of the just and loving actions of those whose condition is by "nature" the inversion, not the perversion, of heterosexuality. A further point of note, as Countryman points out, is that Paul nowhere in this text uses the language of *sin*; Gentiles have been given up only to *uncleanness*.[53]

The two remaining texts cited by the CDF as a solid foundation for the Church's teaching on the immorality of homosexual acts, 1 Corinthians 6:9–10 and 1 Timothy 1:10, present a serious difficulty of translation. We need only consider the former text in detail, for the difficulty is the same in both texts. Paul presents to the Corinthians a list of those who will not inherit the kingdom of God. "Do you not know that the unjust will not inherit the kingdom of God? Do not be deceived: neither fornicators, nor idolaters, nor adulterers, nor *malakoi*, nor *arsenokoitai*, nor thieves, the greedy, nor drunkards, nor slanderers, nor robbers will inherit the kingdom of God." The translation difficulty lies with both *malakoi* and *arsenokoitai*, and we shall have to consider each in some detail.

Malakos, the easier word to translate, literally means *soft*, and its cognate *malakia* means softness. It can be applied to people in a metaphorical sense, as it is, for instance, in Matthew 11:8 when Jesus asks about John the Baptizer: "Why then did you go out? To see a man clothed in soft raiment [*en malakois*]?" How does Paul use the word? There is some evidence that both *malakos* and *malakia* were used metaphorically of feminine sexual behavior without, however, being restricted to that meaning.[54] The Vulgate translated it as *molles* (the effeminate); the King James translated it along the same lines as *effeminacy*; the 1973 Revised Standard Version translated it as *adulterers*; the new Revised Standard Version translates it as *male prostitutes*; and the New English Bible translates it as *adultery*. There is no unanimity of translation. *Malakos* is clearly difficult to translate but, bearing in mind the Hebrew context we discussed in connection with Leviticus 18:22, there is a legitimate and clear contextual translation. Honor was a primary value in Hebrew culture, especially male honor that was earned and preserved by a man behaving like a man; masculinity was honored and femininity was correspondingly disparaged. Softness or effeminacy in men, therefore, qua effeminacy without any suggestion of homogenital behavior, was held in horror as an "abomination." D'Angelo articulates this

reading when she writes that "the biblical texts that have been read as condemnations of homo exuality originated in part as guardians of the kinds of sexual hierarchy that . . . is violated when *a male is 'reduced' to the status of a woman.*"[55] Philo
confirms this cultural value and the disparagement of its opposite.

The man–woman, *androgynos,* Philo judges, is "rightly judged worthy of death
by those who obey the law," and the man who loves him is worthy of the same
penalty. "He pursues an unnatural pleasure [and] he sees no harm in becoming a
tutor and instructor in the grievous vices of unmanliness [*anandrias*] and effeminacy
[*malakias*] by prolonging the bloom of the young and emasculating the flower of
their prime, which should rightly be trained to *strength and robustness.*"[56] For Philo,
a leading commentator on Jewish culture contemporary with Paul, a male is to be
masculine; he is to have "strength and robustness" and avoid *malakias* and every
soft, feminine way of behaving.

One feminine way of behaving is, undoubtedly, to act passively like a woman
rather than actively like a man in the act of sexual intercourse (we are speaking of
Paul's first-century culture, not our twenty-first-century culture with its more
advanced understanding of male and female sexuality), but that does not yet mean
that the passive act of intercourse is what is condemned. It is very likely that what
is condemned is masculine effeminacy in any of its forms. That reading is confirmed
by the other difficult word *arsenokoitai,* a most uncommon word, maybe even a
word coined by Paul himself. The common opinion is that it is inspired by the
Septuagint version of Leviticus 18:22. If that is true, then Paul uses it in the context
of the sexual acts between men prohibited in Leviticus, but again that does not
mean that it is precisely those acts qua homogenital that are an abomination. The
abomination may be again the more general disvalue of a man behaving like a
woman. Paul condemns both the *malakoi* and the *arsenokoitai* (which is also the
word at stake in 1 Tim 1:10), not for perverted homogenital acts as the Revised
Standard Version insinuates, but for the feminization of men whom the creator God
calls to be masculine.

The Bible and Contemporary Discourse on Homosexuality

This leads us to our third question and its answer: Can the Bible speak to the
confusion that characterizes contemporary Christians with respect to homosexuality?
It should first be noted that homosexual action is not a prominent biblical concern.
There is no mention of it in Israel's earliest moral codes, there is nothing about it
in the Decalogue, the gospels record no saying of Jesus about it, and there is not even
a word for it in either Hebrew or Greek. Malina's conclusion about the Romans text
is difficult to gainsay: "If we return to the twenty-first century after this excursion
into the first century we can see that Paul's perspectives, if taken consistently, simply
do not make sense."[57] Paul does not live in our context in which homosexuality is
scientifically recognized as a *natural* condition; we do not live in Paul's context of

bad biology, ritual purity, or cultural value; and the ancient context does not translate diachronically into the modern context on any issue, including homosexuality. The same conclusion applies to the even more distant texts of the Old Testament. They are articulated in the same context as Paul's texts. Everyone is presumed to be heterosexual and, therefore, any male homogenital act is a freely chosen perversion; the male is the sole source of life and, therefore, any spilling of the *homunculus* in a place where it cannot develop is murder and an abomination; the male is also the source of honor in the society and for a male to behave as a female, sexually or otherwise, shames not only him but every other male in the family or corporate clan: "The Old Testament narratives about the men of Sodom in Genesis 19 and the Levite's concubine in Judges 19 are more concerned with egregious failures in hospitality and gang rape than with homosexuality per se."[58]

Because of the difficulty of translating meanings diachronically across time, the Christian traditions are moving away from a *biblical rules* approach to moral judgments and are exploring a more profound, and perhaps even more morally ambiguous, interrelationship between rules, norms, values, and virtues. There are both historical and contemporary movements away from the simplistic judgment that what the Bible says is definitive for all time and is, therefore, the universal moral norm. Historically, Rodgers notes that this movement can be found in Thomas Aquinas's *Commentary on Romans*, which, when read closely, demonstrates a keen awareness of the interrelationship between scripture, anthropology, experience, natural law, and virtue; which has implications for interpreting scripture on homosexuality; and which "*requires* theologians to keep the matter open."[59] Contemporarily, Cahill puts the matter succinctly: "Realizing the impossibility of transposing rules from biblical times to our own, interpreters look for larger themes, values or ideals which can inform moral reflection without determining specific practices in advance."[60] Furnish articulates well the larger theme that we can abstract from both the Old Testament and New Testament texts on homosexual behavior: "Paul, in common with the tradition by which he was influenced and in accord with the wisdom of his day, saw the wickedness of homosexual practice to adhere in its lust and its perversion of the natural order."[61] The same wickedness, suggested as homosexual rape, and the same judgment of perversion of the presumed natural order are found in the Sodom account. Those judgments against uncontrolled and violent lust and a perversion of the natural order cannot automatically be applied to just and loving homosexual acts in persons whose natural sexual orientation is to persons of the same sex. Those acts may or may not be immoral, but any judgment of immorality will have to be substantiated on bases other than the simple fact that the Bible condemns the homosexual acts of heterosexual males. Sparks's judgment is also ours: "On scriptural evidence alone we are left short of a clear and clean condemnation of what might be called committed or covenantal homosexual acts."[62]

We agree with the majority of Catholic moral theologians that a universal and absolute moral norm exists and that such a norm dispels all possible confusion. We agree also with the Catholic moral theologian Dietmar Mieth, however, that the only absolute moral norm is the abstract norm that "good is to be done and evil left undone," and that every other moral judgment requires concrete, empirical discernment.[63] Joseph Fuchs agrees. "There is no discrepancy of theories and opinions within Catholic moral theology about the one ethical *absolutum*," he writes; "the translation of the ethical *absolutum* into the [concrete] *material plurality* of human reality is, however, a different matter."[64] The hermeneutic for that translation is controlled, as it is always controlled in the Catholic moral tradition, by the free human person seeking to be attentive, intelligent, rational, and responsible in the actual sociohistorical situation.[65] It cannot be otherwise for free persons who live in a physical and human world subject to historicity.

Bernard Lonergan was convinced that something new was happening in history in the twentieth century and that, because a living theology ought to be part of what was taking place in history, Christians were living in a new theological age that required a new theological approach. That new approach, he prophesied correctly, would be necessarily historical and empirical. Lonergan's distinction between a classicist and an empirical notion of culture has become widely accepted:[66] "The classicist notion of culture was normative: at least *de iure* there was but one culture that was both universal and permanent." The empirical notion of culture was "the set of meanings and values that informs a way of life. It may remain unchanged for ages. It may be in the process of slow development or rapid resolution."[67] Classicist culture is static, but empirical culture is dynamic. Theology, which is inescapably part of culture, mirrors this distinction.

In classicist mode theology is a static, permanent achievement that anyone can learn; in empirical mode it is a dynamic, ongoing process requiring a free person who is trained and committed. This distinction is as valid for moral theologians as for the practitioners of any other discipline. The classicist understanding, Fuchs writes, conceives of the human person as "a series of created, static, and thus definitively ordered temporal facts." The empirical understanding conceives of the person as a subject in process of "self-realization in accordance with a project that develops in God-given autonomy, that is, along a path of human reason and insight, carried out in the present with a view to the future."[68]

Classicist theology, like that of New Natural Law Theory, sees moral norms coming from the Magisterium as once and for all definitive; sexual norms enunciated in the fifth century continue to apply absolutely in the twenty-first century. Empirical theology sees past moral norms not as facts for uncritical and passive acceptance but as insights that are partial bases for active and critical understanding, pondering, and evaluating leading to a reasoned judgment and decision in the present sociohistorical situation. What the writers of Genesis and Leviticus, Paul, Augustine, and their medieval successors knew about sexuality cannot be the *exclusive* basis for a contemporary moral judgment about sexuality. At this point in our consideration of homosexuality, the theological news for contemporary Christians in classicist consciousness is twofold: first, that the Bible is undeniably subject to historicity and that, therefore, second, there are no definitive absolute norms about sexuality or homosexuality uncritically translatable from the sociohistorical contexts of the Bible to those of contemporary times. Christians will, therefore, have to discern moral judgments about natural homosexuals and homosexual behavior on bases other than what the Bible says. These bases include magisterial teaching and the reflection of the empirical sciences on human experience. To these we now turn.

Magisterial Teaching on Homosexual Acts and Relationships

Our analysis of the biblical texts, which can be extended to the equally historically and socially constructed theological texts of the Magisterium, points to the direction of moral discernment we propose as a way to arrive at a conscientious judgment about the morality or immorality of homosexual acts and homosexual relationships. Tradition teaches that homosexual acts are intrinsically disordered for the following reasons: They "are contrary to the natural law," the principles of which are reflected in human nature itself; "they close the sexual act to the gift of life"; and "they do not proceed from a genuine affective and sexual complementarity."[69] We will consider each of these teachings in turn.

Natural Law Argument

First, there is in every human being by "nature"—and remember that "nature" is always an interpreted category, and therefore there may be dialectical judgments about what is and what is not "nature"—a sexual orientation. The meaning of the phrase "sexual orientation" is complex and not universally agreed upon, but the Magisterium offers a description. It distinguishes between "a homosexual 'tendency,' which proves to be 'transitory,' and 'homosexuals who are definitively such because of some kind of innate instinct.'" It goes on to declare that "it seems appropriate to understand sexual orientation as a *deep-seated* dimension of one's personality and to recognize its *relative stability* in a person."[70] Sexual orientation is predominantly heterosexual, homosexual, or bisexual. This "natural" and historically, socially, and experientially revealed reality may be obscured by the obvious statistical preponderance of persons of heterosexual orientation, but it is in no way negated by that statistical preponderance. We are in complete agreement with the CDF when it teaches that "there can be no true promotion of man's [and woman's] dignity unless the essential order of his nature is respected."[71] We disagree with the CDF, however, on its exclusively heterosexual interpretation of that "essential order of nature."

"Nature" and natural law have always had a prominent place in Catholic moral theology and, in official Church teaching, not only homosexuality but also premarital, extramarital, contraceptive, and nonreproductive type marital sexual activity are condemned as contrary to the natural law. Any sexual activity that deviates from God's "wisely ordered laws of nature"[72] and is not open to the transmission of life, the Magisterium teaches, is morally wrong. The fundamental principles that dictate this moral judgment are contained "in the divine law—eternal, objective, and universal—whereby God orders, directs, and governs the entire universe and all the ways of the human community. . . . This divine law is *accessible to our minds*."[73] It is precisely this "accessible to our minds," however, as we explained in our prologue, that raises serious hermeneutical questions. Already in the thirteenth century, Aquinas taught that natural law is "nothing other than the light of understanding placed in us by God."[74] He also argues, however, that, although the precepts of natural law are universal and immutable, their application varies according to the circumstances of people's existence. We argued the same in chapter 2, and here we need only briefly summarize our argument.

Historical, reasonable men and women have no access to pure, unembellished "nature." "Nature" reveals to our attention, understanding, judgment, and decision only its naked facticity. Everything beyond that facticity is the result of interpretation by attentive, intelligent, rational, and responsible persons; that is, we experience "nature" only as interpreted and socially constructed. The uninterpreted experience of "nature," as indeed of every other reality, is restricted to its mere facticity and is void of meaning, a quality that does not inhere in nature but is assigned to it by rational beings in interpretive acts. "The potter, and not the pot, is responsible for the shape of the pot."[75] It is inevitable that different groups of equally reasonable and historically grounded women and men—traditionalist and revisionist theologians, for example—may derive different interpretations of "nature" and the moral obligations deriving from "nature," and that any given interpretation may be wrong. Because every interpretation of "nature" is a socially constructed reality dependent on human, perspectival interpretations, the reality of "nature" is always to be subjected to scrutiny, even if the interpretation be advanced by the Magisterium of the Church.

Our sexual anthropology recognizes sexual orientation as an intrinsic dimension of human "nature." As such, what is "natural" in sexual activity, which is an expression of the sexual person, will vary depending on whether or not the person's sexual orientation is homosexual or heterosexual. Homosexual sexual acts are "natural" for people with a homosexual orientation, just as heterosexual sexual acts are "natural" for people with a heterosexual orientation. They are natural because they coincide with, and reflect, the fundamental human "nature" of a person created in the image and likeness of God. We are not arguing here that homosexual activity is moral because it is natural for those with a homosexual orientation; that would be to treat natural facts as moral justification and to commit the naturalistic fallacy. Any sexual act, whether homosexual or heterosexual, must be not only natural but also, as we explained in chapter 4, just, loving, and in accord with holistic complementarity.

Procreation Argument

Second, the magisterial claim that homosexual acts "close the sexual act to the gift of life" has been addressed in chapter 4, and we need not repeat it here. Suffice to say that, if one explores "openness to the transmission of life" in biological terms, then potentially reproductive and permanently or temporarily nonreproductive heterosexual acts are essentially different types of acts. As Koppleman points out against Finnis, "A sterile person's genitals are no more suitable for generation than a gun with a broken firing pin is suitable for shooting." It is a conceptual stretch, he goes on, "to insist that the sexual acts of the incurably infertile are of the same kind as the sexual acts of fertile organs that occasionally fail to deliver the goods."[76] Heterogenital complementarity, therefore, becomes, as for New Natural Law Theory, the essential difference that distinguishes nonreproductive heterosexual acts from homosexual acts. If one explores "openness to the transmission of life" in metaphorical terms, then both homosexual and heterosexual couples can exhibit Hanigan's "iconic significance" in their embodied interpersonal unions and sexual acts.[77]

Complementarity Argument

Third, though the Magisterium consistently condemns homosexual acts on the grounds that they violate heterogenital and reproductive complementarity, it does not explain why they also violate personal complementarity other than to assert that homosexual acts "do not proceed from a genuine affective and sexual complementarity."[78] This statement, however, begs the question whether or not such acts can ever be truly human on the level of sexual and personal complementarity. Though the Magisterium has not confronted this question, monogamous, loving, committed, homosexual couples have confronted it experientially and testify that they do experience affective and communion complementarity in and through their homosexual acts. Margaret Farley notes that the experiential testimony of these couples witnesses "to the role of such loves and relationships in sustaining human well-being and opening to human flourishing" and "extends to the contributions that individuals and partners make to families, the church, and society as a whole."[79] This coincides precisely with our foundational principle on the immediate and mediate relational impact of truly human sexual acts. "Expressed in a manner which is truly human, these actions signify and promote that mutual self-giving by which spouses [immediately] enrich each other [and mediately enrich their family and community] with a joyful and a thankful will."[80] Farley's claim is amply supported by anecdotal and scientific research on the nature of homosexual relationships.

Some twenty years ago, while acknowledging that the question of same-sex relations is a question of dispute, Farley noted anecdotal experiences of homosexual couples and commented that we "have some clear and profound testimonies to the life-enhancing possibilities of same-sex relations and the integrating possibilities of sexual activity within these relations. We have the witness that homosexuality can be a way of embodying responsible love and sustaining human friendship." She concludes, logically, that "this witness alone is enough to demand of the Christian [and political] community that it reflect anew on the norms [and laws] for homosexual love."[81] Her judgment accords with that of Bernard Ratigan, a gay English consulting psychotherapist, who notes that "the gap between the caricature of us [gays] in Church documents and our lived reality seems so huge." He asks legitimately "on what evidence does the Vatican base its assertions about us?" and goes on to point out that psychoanalysis "has moved on from being solely concerned with genital sex to thinking much more about human relationships and love."[82] So, too, has revisionist Catholic moral theology.

This call for evidence can also be posed to the U.S. Conference of Catholic Bishops' most recent statement on homosexuality. Speaking of a homosexual inclination, the bishops note that it "predisposes one toward what is truly not good for the human person." The predisposition is towards homosexual acts that are "not ordered toward the fulfillment of the natural ends of human sexuality" and therefore "acting in accord with such an inclination simply cannot contribute to the true good of the human person."[83] The statement that homosexual acts, by definition, cannot contribute to the good of the human person seems to contradict the relational experiences of committed, monogamous, homosexual couples. Though this statement does not cite scientific studies to verify its claim, there are a number of studies that explicitly contradict it.

Lawrence Kurdek has done extensive research on gay and lesbian couples and notes the following characteristics when comparing these relationships with married heterosexual couples. Gay and lesbian couples tend to have a more equitable distribution of household labor, demonstrate greater conflict resolution skills, have less support from members of one's own family but greater support from friends, and, most significantly, experience similar levels of relational satisfaction compared with heterosexual couples.[84]

Not only do empirical studies challenge magisterial claims that homosexual acts, by definition, are detrimental to the human person and human relationships, such studies also challenge the Magisterium's claims regarding the detrimental effects of homosexual parenting on children. The CDF argues against same-sex couples socially parenting children based on the claim that, "as experience has shown, the absence of sexual complementarity in these unions creates obstacles in the normal development of children who would be placed in the care of such persons. . . . Allowing children to be adopted by persons living in such unions would actually mean doing violence to these children."[85] Not only is such a statement rhetorically unjust and discriminating,[86] but it is also empirically unsubstantiated. The CDF provides no scientific evidence, here or elsewhere, to substantiate its claim that homosexual unions are an obstacle to the normal development of children. There is, however, abundant evidence to the contrary.

While acknowledging that research on gay and lesbian parents is still evolving, especially with respect to gay fathers, Patterson summarizes the evidence available from twenty years of studies: "There is no evidence to suggest that lesbians and gay men are unfit to be parents or that psychosocial [including sexual] development among children of gay men or lesbians is compromised in any respect relative to that among offspring of heterosexual parents. *Not a single study* has found children of gay or lesbian parents to be disadvantaged in any significant respect relative to children of heterosexual parents."[87] In her overview of the research, Laird goes further to suggest that the scientific data indicate that homosexual parents are somewhat more nurturing and tolerant than heterosexual parents, and their children are, in turn, more tolerant and empathetic.[88] This preponderance of evidence led the American Psychological Association to approve and disseminate an important resolution. Because "lesbian and gay parents are as likely as heterosexual parents to provide supportive and healthy environments for their children, . . . [and because] research has shown that the adjustment, development, and psychological well-being of children is unrelated to parental sexual orientation and that the children of lesbian and gay parents are as likely as those of heterosexual parents to flourish," the association opposes any discrimination based on sexual orientation.[89]

The important and thoroughly child-centered Child Welfare League of America is also convinced by the data that there are no significant differences between the parental attitudes and skills of heterosexual, gay, and lesbian parents.[90] In 1994, the league's policy statement recommends that "gay/lesbian adoptive applicants should be assessed the same as any other adoptive applicant. It should be recognized that sexual orientation and the capacity to nurture a child are separate issues." The league further recommends that factual information about gays and lesbians should be provided "to dispel common myths about gays and lesbians."[91] It is not the sexual orientation of gay and lesbian parents that produces negative outcomes in their children but the social discrimination toward them generated by myths propagated about their parents.

The Second Vatican Council praises the advances of the social sciences that bring the human community "improved self-knowledge" and "influence on the life of social groups."[92] Pope John Paul II teaches that "the Church values sociological and statistical research when it proves helpful in understanding the historical context in which pastoral action has to be developed and when it leads to a better understanding of the truth."[93] The present question, namely, the effect of homosexual parents on their children, is a classic case in which the social sciences have clearly led to a better understanding of the truth. There is abundant social scientific data to support the claim that communion and affective complementarity are evident in homosexual relationships and that, in the case of homosexual parents, these complementarities facilitate both parental complementarity and the positive nurture of children.[94]

These assessments on the relational and parental experiences of homosexual couples recall John Courtney Murray's principle that practical, as distinct from theoretical, intelligence is preserved from ideology by having "a close relation to concrete experience."[95] As we saw above regarding the scientific studies of persons in homosexual relationships and children being raised by gay and lesbian parents, magisterial positions on gays and lesbians tend to be theoretical hypotheses unsubstantiated by the practical experience of those gays and lesbians. The magisterial position regarding its claim that homosexual acts "do not proceed from a genuine affective and sexual complementarity" is open to the same accusation, theoretical hypotheses unsubstantiated by practical experience.

The Moral Sense of the Christian People and Homosexual Acts

Data from the social sciences also suggest that the third foundation on which the CDF grounds its judgment on the immorality of homosexual acts, "the moral sense of the Christian people," is now as open to critique as the reading of biblical texts and the natural law argument. In a 1997 study, James Davidson and his colleagues describe "how American Catholics approach faith and morals."[96] They found, with respect to homosexual activity, that 41 percent of parishioners agree with the Magisterium that homosexual acts are always wrong and that 49 percent believe that, at least in certain circumstances, the decision to engage in such acts is up to the individual.[97] A 2001 study replicated that figure of 49 percent, believing the decision to engage in homosexual acts belongs to the individual; only 20 percent believed it had anything to do with the Magisterium.[98] The authors comment that their data "depict a trend away from conformity and toward personal autonomy" with respect to sexual issues.[99] That trend was most marked in "Post–Vatican II Catholics," those aged thirty-eight and younger.[100] Dean Hoge and his colleagues also document this trend away from authority to personal conscience in matters of morality. In his study, he found that 73 percent of Latino Catholics and 71 percent of non-Latino Catholics judged that, in matters of morality, the final authority is the individual's informed conscience.[101] The same trend is well documented in other Western countries.[102] A reasonable theological question then arises: Do sociological data of this sort tell us anything about magisterial teaching and the faith of the Church?

An immediate and crucial answer is that sociological data are not an expression of the belief and teaching of the Catholic Church. Nor do they tell us what the Church ought to believe and teach, for 50 percent, and even 100 percent, of Catholics could be wrong. The empirical data reported above, however, do two important things. They tell us what the beliefs of Catholics actually are with respect to the morality of homosexual acts and they demonstrate that these beliefs are at serious variance with the beliefs proposed by the Magisterium. These data may not tell us anything about the truth of magisterial teaching with respect to the morality of homosexual acts, but they do tell us something about its relevance to the life of the contemporary Church. It ought neither to be accepted uncritically nor dismissed out of hand as if it had no relevance to the life of the Church. Pope John Paul II teaches that "the Church values sociological and statistical research" but immediately adds the proviso that "such research is not to be considered in itself an expression of the *sensus fidei*."[103] The pope is correct. Empirical research neither expresses nor creates the faith of the Church, but it does manifest what Catholics actually believe and do not believe, and that experiential reality is a basis for critical reflection on any claim about what "the Church believes." It is this critical reflection, always required of the Church's theologians,[104] that we undertake in this chapter and throughout this book.

The theologian and sociologist Robin Gill complains that Christian ethicists have been "reluctant to admit that sociology has any constructive role to play in their discipline. It is rare to find a Christian ethicist prepared to examine data about the moral effects of Church-going. Instead, Christian communities have become *far too idealized.*"[105] "Christian communities" may be a euphemism for Catholic Magisterium, which tends to talk of the belief of the Church as it has been rather than as it is. If, as the Second Vatican Council clearly taught, "the body of the faithful as a whole cannot err in matters of belief,"[106] then they must be infallible in the beliefs they *actually* believe. It is that actual belief that is uncovered by sociological research. Avery Dulles argues that, to determine *sensus fidei,* which has important relevance in this discussion, "we must look not so much at the statistics, as at the quality of the witnesses and the motivation for their assent."[107] We agree. *Sensus fidei,* the connatural capacity to discern the truth into which the Spirit of God is leading the Church, must be carefully discerned by all who are competent. John Paul II is correct: A simple head count does not necessarily express the faith of the Church. A head count, however, which would include virtually all the faithful, especially virtually all the competent theological faithful, would most certainly manifest the actual faith of the whole Church. All we claim here about the sociological data with respect to the belief of the Church about the morality of homosexual acts is that they may manifest a development that Church theologians and the Magisterium ought to examine carefully.

What is clear from the above investigation of biblical and magisterial teaching on homosexual acts and homosexual relationships is the importance of experience as a source of moral knowledge. In the dialectic between the sources of moral knowledge for morally assessing homosexual acts and relationships, experience is foundational and even primary. We concur with Farley, who notes that experience "is an important part of the content of each of the other sources, and it is always a factor in interpreting the others."[108] It provides a sociohistorical context for interpreting the other sources of moral knowledge, and it illuminates if, and to what extent, the sources taken individually and as a whole and the normative conclusions that they reach "make sense" and "ring true" in terms of "our deepest capacity for truth and goodness."[109] Furthermore, "given the arguable inconclusiveness of Scripture, tradition, and secular disciplines" on the morality of homosexual relationships, "concrete experience becomes a determining source on this issue."[110] Relying upon the historical critical method espoused by the Magisterium, we have demonstrated that traditional interpretations of scripture condemning homosexual acts lack legitimacy. There seems to be a disconnect between the evolving tradition and its use of scripture to condemn homosexual acts on the one hand, and its relatively recent espousal of the historical-critical method for interpreting scripture on the other hand. The historical-critical method does not support traditional normative conclusions deduced from the Bible on this issue. This same historical-critical method, when applied to recent magisterial teaching on homosexual acts, reveals another disconnect between what empirical studies convey regarding the experiences of homosexual couples and parents and unsubstantiated magisterial claims to the contrary. Given the entrenched, and sometimes discriminatory and hurtful, magisterial rhetoric addressing the issue of homosexuality,[111] openness to a revised hermeneutic of the sources of moral knowledge that might allow for a revision of magisterial teaching on homosexual acts will take some time.

The Morality of Homosexual Acts Reconsidered

We defend what we believe to be a more adequate foundational principle, which is doubly grounded in sound biblical exegesis and the best of magisterial teaching on human sexuality, and which also incorporates the reflection of the empirical sciences on human experience. Bearing in mind our revised foundational principle and everything we said about complementary, just, and loving sexual intercourse in chapter 4, we conclude this section by, again, approving of Farley's judgment: "Sex between two persons of the same sex (just as between two persons of the opposite sex) should not be used in a way that exploits, objectifies, or dominates; homosexual (like heterosexual) rape, violence, or any harmful use of power against unwilling victims (or those incapacitated by reason of age, etc.) is never justified; freedom, integrity, privacy are values to be affirmed in every homosexual (as heterosexual) relationship; all in all, individuals are not to be harmed, and the common good is to be promoted."[112]

Heterosexual orientation is an innate, deep-seated, and stable orientation to, predominantly, persons of the opposite sex; homosexual orientation is a similarly innate, deep-seated, and stable orientation to, predominantly, persons of the same sex. "Ethics can have for its object only acts that are free, acts that can be imputed to personal responsibility. Whatever is determined, *insofar as it is determined*, is neither moral nor immoral; it simply *is*."[113] Sexual orientation is neither chosen nor readily changeable; it simply is. It is, therefore, in itself neither moral nor immoral nor even premoral. The sexual acts that flow from it, however, may be moral or immoral. We apply the principle we have already enunciated to arrive at the judgment of the morality or immorality of all heterosexual or homosexual acts.

Sexual acts are moral when they are natural, reasonable, and expressed in a truly human, just, and loving manner. All terms of this articulation are important and must be carefully understood. Sexual acts are moral when they are *natural*, and they are natural when they coincide with the "*nature*" of the human person according to right reason and what facilitates human flourishing.[114] For men and women who are by "nature" heterosexual, heterosexual acts are natural, reasonable, and therefore moral when all other requirements for moral acts are safeguarded, and homosexual acts are unnatural, unreasonable, and therefore immoral, even if all other requirements for moral acts are safeguarded. For those who are by "nature" homosexual, it is the reverse. Homosexual acts are natural, reasonable, and moral, and heterosexual acts are unnatural, unreasonable, and immoral. Sexual acts are moral when they are *reasonable*, and they are reasonable when, as a result of careful attention to and understanding of all the relevant human circumstances, a person makes an informed judgment that a given sexual action is according to right reason and facilitates human flourishing. The circumstances to be attended to will include sexual orientation and holistic, that is, orientation, personal, and biological, complementarity. Sexual acts are moral when they are *truly human*, that is, when they fulfill all the requirements of holistic complementarity.[115]

Heterosexual acts are truly human, and therefore reasonable and moral, when they are in line with holistic complementarity, which embraces orientation, personal, and genital (though not necessarily reproductive) complementarity. Personal complementarity embraces everything we considered in chapter 4 under the headings of the physical, emotional, psychological, spiritual, and relational dimensions of truly human sexuality. Any sexual act that violates any of these dimensions will ipso facto be deemed immoral; any sexual act that is true to all these dimensions will ipso facto be deemed moral. Heterosexual rape, therefore, or any heterosexual intercourse that is not just and loving, will be deemed immoral, and so too will homosexual rape. Heterosexual intercourse without relational connection—casual sex, for instance, or sex with a prostitute—will be similarly deemed immoral because it violates personal complementarity, and so too will homosexual intercourse without relational connection. Heterosexual intercourse that is predetermined to be free of responsibility for its outcome—the birth of a child, for instance, or the communication of a sexually transmitted disease—will be deemed immoral because it violates personal complementarity as justice; and so too will homosexual intercourse. However, heterosexual intercourse that is mutually freely chosen, just, and loving will be deemed moral, whether it is actually reproductive or not, and so too will homosexual intercourse.

Conclusion

We argued earlier in this book that, given the essential historicity of every human teaching, what Augustine and Aquinas, Trent and Vatican II, Pius, Paul, and John Paul taught in the past about human sexuality cannot be the *exclusive* basis for conscientious moral judgment about sexuality today. All must be subjected to critical scrutiny. It is that scrutiny we have attempted throughout this book, and again in this chapter with respect to homosexuality, enlightened by Ratzinger's judgment that remains true today: "Not everything that exists in the Church must for that reason be also a legitimate tradition. . . . There is a distorting as well as a legitimate tradition, . . . [and] . . . consequently tradition must not be considered only affirmatively but also critically."[116] With respect to historicity, the CDF teaches that "the meaning of the pronouncements of faith depends partly upon the expressive power of the language used at a given time and in given circumstances." That being so, a truth that is first expressed incompletely may, "at a later date, when considered in a broader context of faith or human knowledge, [be] expressed more fully and perfectly."[117] In the light of contemporary human knowledge about homosexual orientation, we have examined in this chapter the threefold bases on which the Catholic Church rests its judgment that homosexual acts are intrinsically disordered and gravely immoral, namely, the teaching of scripture, the teaching of the Magisterium, and the moral sense of the Christian people. On all three bases, we argued, the Church's teaching needs serious reevaluation.

We believe we have comprehensively shown that, following the Magisterium's sanctioned way of reading the sacred scriptures—namely, historical-critically—the texts cited in support of the claim of the serious depravity of the homosexual activity of persons of genuine homosexual orientation, which was simply unknown when the Scriptures in question were written, do not support such a judgment. The same historical-critical approach that was used to demonstrate the meanings of the biblical texts in their sociohistorical contexts applies equally to the sociohistorically conditioned texts of the Magisterium. We believe we have shown that the Magisterium's argument for the immorality of all homosexual acts on the basis of a classicist and ahistorical interpretation of "nature" is also unsound and open to critique as is the absolute assertion that homosexual acts can never "proceed from a genuine affective and sexual complementarity." So, too, is its argument on the basis of the constant belief of the Christian people, when faced with the data of contemporary research on what Catholics actually believe. A lack of understanding, indeed misunderstanding, of the full scope of sexuality in a human life until very recent history; a lack of understanding, indeed misunderstanding, of the essential contribution of both male and female in human reproduction until the latter half of the nineteenth century; a lack of understanding, indeed misunderstanding, of the natural reality of heterosexual and homosexual orientation until the twentieth century—these are not good bases for making any normative judgment about sexuality in general or about heterosexuality and homosexuality in particular.

Nothing we have argued in this chapter proves that homosexual acts are ipso facto morally right. We have argued only that the arguments advanced by the Church's Magisterium to sustain the judgment that *all* homosexual acts are ipso facto morally wrong are unsound and need to be revisited. Our present judgment endorses Farley's judgment: "At this point, . . . it is difficult to see how on the basis of sheer rationality alone, and all of its disciplines [including theology], an absolute prohibition of same-sex relationships or activities can be maintained." She goes on to point out that "we are still pressed to the task of discerning what must characterize same-sex relationships if they are to conduce to human flourishing."[118] Again we agree, though we also believe we have developed criteria in previous chapters for the judgment that *some* homosexual acts may be morally right. We content ourselves here by repeating the criteria with which we concluded a previous chapter. *Some* homosexual and *some* heterosexual acts, those that meet the requirements of complementary, just, and loving sexual relations, are truly human and moral; and *some* homosexual and *some* heterosexual acts, those that do not meet the requirements of complementary, just, and loving sexual relations, are immoral. This judgment, we believe, stands in spite of the rhetorical assertions of the Catholic Magisterium, and it stands for the good of the whole Church. We embrace Moore's judgment: "This is not a matter of dissent or materialism; it is simply that the Church at the moment produces no good arguments to assent to. Regrettably, in this area, the Church teaches badly."[119]

Chapter Eight

Artificial Reproductive Technologies

IN THE 1950s THE MARKETING of effective oral contraceptives made it possible to have sexual intercourse without reproduction; in the 1980s the marketing of artificial reproductive technologies (ARTs) made it possible to reproduce without having sexual intercourse. The Catholic Magisterium argues against the morality of both oral contraceptives and ARTs on the basis of its principle of the inseparability of the unitive and procreative meanings of sexual intercourse. We have already dealt at length with the teaching on contraception. In this chapter, we deal with the teaching on ARTs. The Congregation for the Doctrine of the Faith's (CDF's) *Instruction*, or *Donum vitae*, enunciates the principle: "The Church's teaching on marriage and human procreation affirms the 'inseparable connection, willed by God and unable to be broken by man on his own initiative, between the two meanings of the conjugal act: the unitive meaning and the procreative meaning.'"[1] This insep-arability principle prohibits *some* types of "artificial procreation" or "artificial fertil-ization," understood as "the different technical procedures directed towards obtaining a human conception in a manner other than the sexual union of man and woman."[2]

From the beginning of this book we have insisted that traditional Catholic sexual morality is essentially marital morality; sexuality is confined within marriage and is moral when open to procreation. There is a trinity that is intrinsically and insepara-bly interconnected: marriage, sexuality, and procreation. For the Magisterium, ARTs, defined as "non-coital methods of conception that involve manipulation of both eggs and sperm,"[3] interfere with this intrinsic connection by separating the unitive and procreative meanings of sexual intercourse. Revisionist theologians tend to think that, although ARTs often do not rely on sexual intercourse for reproduc-tion, they may still fulfill on occasion both the unitive and procreative ends of *marriage* considered as an intimate interpersonal whole. When the marital relation-ship is seen, as it has been seen since Vatican II in contemporary Catholic theology, as an interpersonal, procreative whole, and not just as a genital act, it seems reason-able to argue that, at least, some ARTs utilize modern science and technology to facilitate both the unitive and procreative meanings of the relationship. *Gaudium et spes* notes that "children really are the supreme gift of marriage"[4] and, if they are and ARTs can help infertile couples realize this supreme gift, we may legitimately ask about the credibility of the Magisterium's inseparability principle in condemning *all* ARTs that separate the two meanings of the conjugal act. This, then, concretely, is the debate in this chapter. First, we define various types of ARTs; second, we explain and critique magisterial teaching on ARTs, focusing primarily on the CDF's *Instruction*; and third, we analyze and evaluate ARTs in light of our foundational principle for the morality of any sexual activity.

Defining Artificial Reproductive Technologies

ARTs are used when, at least, one spouse in a marriage is believed to be infertile. The American Society for Reproductive Medicine puts the level of infertility, "generally defined as the inability of a couple to conceive after 12 months of intercourse without contraception,"[5] at around 10 percent.[6] The causes of infertility are varied. They include hormonal imbalance, endometriosis, venereal infection (20 percent), contraceptive practices, abortions, incompatibility of gametes, cancer, and other causes,[7] but scientific developments in the last forty years have offered couples the ability to overcome infertility.[8] These developments include fertility drugs, which cause the woman to produce a number of ripe ova that can result in multiple pregnancies, and surgical operations, which can remove blockages in, for example, the fallopian tubes. The most popular of these modern developments is, however, the ART.[9]

One of the earliest ARTs to be used was artificial insemination. In this procedure male sperm is collected, from either masturbation or a condom used in sexual intercourse, and is inserted into the woman's cervical canal at or near the time of ovulation in order to fertilize the released ovum. The collected sperm may be used within a few hours of collection or frozen for later use. When fertilization takes place within the woman's body, the procedure is known as *in vivo* (in the body) artificial insemination. When the sperm is collected from the woman's husband, the entire procedure is known as *homologous insemination*; when it is collected from a donor not the woman's husband, it is *heterologous insemination*.

Another ART, one that differs from *in vivo* in terms of where fertilization takes place, is *in vitro fertilization with embryo transfer* (IVF-ET). In this procedure, used in over 70 percent of all ART procedures,[10] both sperm and ova are collected, and fertilization takes place outside the woman's body in a laboratory. There are various ways to collect the ova. Hormonal treatments with human menopausal gonadotropin cause ova to mature in the woman's body, and these ripe eggs or oocytes are harvested via laparoscopic surgery or transportation by ultrasound guidance to the vagina. Once sperm and ova are collected, the sperm is washed or *capacitated* to enhance penetration and fertilization of several oocytes, creating several zygotes in a laboratory container. Because fertilization in this case takes place outside the woman's body in a laboratory container, the procedure is known as *in vitro* (in glass) fertilization. After fertilization and about forty hours of development, during which time the zygote is scientifically in the *pre-embryo* stage,[11] one to six healthy embryos are selected and transferred through the woman's cervix to her uterus anticipating implantation and development. Excess healthy embryos can be frozen, a process known as *cryopreservation*, and used later if the embryo transfer is unsuccessful or if the couple desires another pregnancy. They may also be used for research. Unhealthy embryos are typically destroyed. The processes of destruction, use in research, and the cryopreservation of fertilized embryos raise their own moral problems, and we must first address them before proceeding.

The Catholic principle is firm: "The human being must be respected—as a person—from the very first instant of his existence."[12] Whether fertilization and the first instance of existence take place *in vivo* or *in vitro*, "from the time the ovum is fertilized, a new life is begun which is neither that of the father nor of the mother; it is rather the life of a new human being with its own growth. It would never be made human if it were not human already."[13] Zygotes, pre-embryos, embryos, and fetuses, or whatever name is given to the new being postfertilization, are therefore human beings with all the rights of human beings, and it is immoral to deliberately destroy them or to place them unnecessarily at the risk of death. The Church condemns induced abortion as immoral because it is the direct killing of an innocent human being, and it similarly forbids as immoral acts against the life of artificially reproduced embryos.[14] For the very same reason, "respect for the dignity of the human being," it forbids as immoral all experimental manipulation or exploitation of the human embryo[15] and the freezing or cryopreservation of embryos. This latter "constitutes an offence against the respect due to human beings by exposing them to grave risks of death or harm to their physical integrity and depriving them, at least temporarily, of maternal shelter and gestation."[16]

The Church's moral stance could not be clearer. The human embryo is a human being from the moment of conception, has all the rights due to a human being including the right to life, and may not be deliberately destroyed or placed in a situation that may lead to its destruction. We agree with protecting innocent human life. That said, however, the question of the morality of ARTs, assured the safety of any resultant embryo, still remains for discussion, and with that question we now continue.

Other types of ARTs include the following. *Low tubal ovum transfer* (LTOT) is used when the fallopian tubes are blocked and the ova cannot get below the block or the sperm cannot get above it. To bypass the block, ripe eggs are harvested by laparoscopy and relocated below the tubal block in the hope of fertilization *in vivo* from sexual intercourse. Because LTOT has not been very successful, perhaps because fertilization normally takes place in the upper fallopian tube,[17] it has been replaced by *tubal ovarian transfer with sperm* (TOTS). In TOTS, sperm and ova are collected as in IVF and are placed in the upper fallopian tube where fertilization normally occurs. Given the placement of sperm and egg, technically called gametes, in the upper fallopian tube, TOTS cannot be used by women whose tubes are blocked. Another ART is *gamete intrafallopian transfer* (GIFT), which closely follows TOTS, except that the ova are harvested and incubated to allow for additional maturation. In both TOTS and GIFT, once the gametes are collected, they are placed in a catheter and injected in the upper fallopian tube where fertilization takes place *in vivo*.[18]

Pronuclear stage tubal transfer (PROST) is a procedure where ova are harvested, combined with sperm in a catheter, and transferred to the fallopian tube before syngamy is complete. *Zygote intrafallopian tube transfer* (ZIFT) transfers a single zygote to avoid multiple pregnancies or the destruction of other zygotes. In the case of low sperm counts or where gametes do not interact well, *intracytoplasmic sperm injection* (ICSI) may be utilized. In this procedure, sperm is collected and treated and then a single sperm is injected into an oocyte by a microscopic glass needle. The fertilized ovum is then transferred into the fallopian tube, as in embryo transfer. *Natural cycle oocyte retrieval intravaginal fertilization* (NORIF) retrieves an ovum during the natural ovulation cycle and places the ovum with the sperm in a special vial, which is placed for forty-eight hours in the vagina, where fertilization occurs. The vial is then removed, and the embryo is transferred, as in ET, into the uterus. Though fertilization technically occurs *in vivo*, NORIF still relies upon embryo transfer from the vial to the uterus.[19]

According to the CDF's *Instruction*, all these procedures are to be morally assessed on one basis: Does the technology assist or replace marital sexual inter-course? "If the technical means facilitates the conjugal act or helps it to reach its natural objectives, it can be morally acceptable."[20] In light of this principle, AI, IVF-ET, PROST, ZIFT, ICSI, and NORIF, all of which replace intercourse to varying degrees, are morally prohibited. There is debate among moral theologians about whether or not GIFT and TOTS are morally acceptable, and the Magisterium has made no conclusive judgment on the morality of these two procedures. Theologians who argue for the moral acceptability of GIFT and TOTS do so on the basis that these technological interventions are licit means to facilitate reproduction when used "in conjunction with the conjugal act."

Cataldo judges that "the number of steps in between the conjugal act and fertil-ization is not morally decisive for the difference between assistance and replacement, but rather it is whether any one or more of those steps constitute the immediate conditions by which fertilization takes place."[21] We agree with this judgment, because this perspective seems to morally assess conjugal intercourse in its total context, rather than confining its moral evaluation to its merely physical dimensions. Whether a couple utilizes one, two, or all of these procedures to facilitate sexual intercourse in reaching its reproductive finality is not morally decisive. It is the intention of the couple, in conjunction with their sexual intercourse, to *maintain the unitive and procreative meanings of their overall marital, interpersonal relationship* that defines the moral meaning of the technique. It must be noted that Cataldo's reasoning seems to allow for the moral acceptability of other ARTs as well, as long as there is sexual intercourse involved at some point in the process of reproduction.

Though he may not accept the implications of his reasoning, it seems that his argument for GIFT and TOTS reflects a profound disagreement with the Magisterium's inseparability principle as a moral foundation against ARTs.

Moral theologians who argue against the morality of GIFT and TOTS do so on the basis that "fertilization is not directly the result of the marital act, since the semen used is not deposited by that act in the vagina, but by a technician's manipulation which substitutes for the marital act."[22] Because the integrity of marital intercourse and its direct relationship with reproduction are at the heart of the Magisterium's moral analysis of ARTs, we next explore this analysis as it is articulated in the CDF's *Instruction*.

The CDF's *Instruction* and Artificial Reproductive Technologies

The *Instruction* was issued by the CDF in 1987 in response to questions posed by episcopal conferences, individual bishops, theologians, doctors, and scientists about the scientific and biomedical ability to intervene in the process of procreation.[23] It draws some clear lines on the morality of fertility-related interventions. We note at the outset that the *Instruction*'s rejection of some ARTs is based neither on a rejection of science nor on a distinction between what is *natural* and what is *artificial*. The *Instruction* explicitly notes that "these interventions are not to be rejected on the grounds that they are artificial. As such, they bear witness to the possibilities of the art of medicine." Rather, these technologies "must be given a moral evaluation in reference to the dignity of the human person, who is called to realize his vocation from God to the gift of love and the gift of life."[24]

As its full title indicates, the *Instruction* addresses two main issues. The first is the fundamental respect due to human life and the long-standing Catholic principle that "human life must be absolutely respected and protected from the moment of conception."[25] This principle rules out by definition, as we have already explained, any destruction of, experimentation with, and cryopreservation of embryos. The second issue, "Interventions upon Human Procreation,"[26] specifically addresses artificial insemination and IVF-ET. Interventions are to be assessed morally on the basis of "the respect, defense and promotion of man, his dignity as a person who is endowed with a spiritual soul and with moral responsibility,"[27] but no definition is offered for the dignity of the human person in relation to either natural law or the meaning and nature of marriage, human sexuality, procreation, and parenthood. All these dimensions of the question will be considered next.

Natural Law: Biological and Personalist Interpretations

In general, the CDF's Instruction "argues its case in terms of the traditional natural-law teaching of the Catholic Church, amplified by revelation and mediated though papal and magisterial teaching."[28] Much of the same critique we have leveled against traditionalist interpretations of natural law throughout this book, therefore, applies to the foundational principles the *Instruction* derives from natural law to condemn certain ARTs. The American Fertility Society, which met in 1987 to reconsider its statement about the morality of ARTs in light of the CDF's *Instruction*, questioned the procedure used by the CDF to derive its conclusions from the stated premises: "While stating that 'the individual integrally and adequately considered' is to be the basis of the moral judgment, the fact is that most conclusions are based on and referred to past Catholic statements."[29] We question the teaching of the *Instruction* largely because of its biological and physicalist approach to natural law.

Like *Gaudium et spes* and *Humanae vitae*, however, the *Instruction* evinces a tension between a biological approach and a personalist approach to natural law. Shannon demonstrates where this tension is present in *Gaudium et spes*. In its proposed norm for judging human activity, *Gaudium et spes* reflects a personalist approach to natural law, stating the norm in the following terms: "That in accord with the divine plan and will, it should harmonize with the genuine good of the human race, and allow men as individuals and as members of society to pursue their total vocation and fulfill it."[30] The articulation of this norm is followed by the assertion that "by the very circumstance of their having been created, all things are endowed with their own stability, truth, goodness, proper laws, and order."[31]

There is a dialectic between the ordination of humanity to God and physical reality and its laws, for humans tend toward God precisely as embodied beings. This dialectic is reflected in *Gaudium et spes*'s statement on human reproduction: "Therefore when there is question of harmonizing conjugal love with the responsible transmission of life, the moral aspect of any procedure does not depend solely on sincere intentions or on an evaluation of motives. It must be determined by objective standards. These are based on the nature of the human person and his acts."[32] Shannon points out that the Second Vatican Council "vacillated between a less biological and more personalistic understanding of natural law, suggesting that, while physical reality is important, one also needs to look at the good of humanity and one's vocation in that context."[33] It is, therefore, not a question of either/or, either the biological or the personal in natural law but a question of both/and, both biological and personal. This raises the further question about whether priority is to be given to the biological or the personal and, in magisterial documents seeking to deduce moral norms, interpretations of natural law are distinguished by the prioritization of either biological or personal dimensions. The personalist account of natural law in *Gaudium et spes* has yet to be fully integrated into normative magisterial teachings on both human sexuality and reproduction.

Though it does offer intimately personalist reflections on the unitive meaning of marital sexual intercourse, *Humanae vitae*'s absolute prohibition of artificial means of regulating conception demonstrates a clear prioritization of the biological over the personalist approach to natural law. This prioritization allows for "therapeutic means necessary to cure bodily diseases, even if a foreseeable impediment to procreation should result there from,"[34] but it does not allow such means to facilitate the unitive meaning of the marital relationship. For example, if for "serious reasons" a couple chooses not to reproduce, or for the sake of responsible parenthood chooses not to have more children, and practicing natural family planning proves to be detrimental to the unitive meaning of the marital relationship, artificial contraceptives are not permitted. In this situation, treating a biological pathology justifies using artificial contraceptives, but addressing relational complications that may arise from practicing natural family planning does not.

The *Instruction* also demonstrates a clear prioritization of the biological over the personalist emphasis in natural law, but it vacillates between these two interpretations in assessing different types of reproductive technologies. This vacillation is clearly evident in its analysis and moral assessment of heterologous artificial fertilization or artificial fertilization by donor (AFD) and homologous artificial fertilization (AFH).[35] Though the *Instruction* draws on personalist interpretations in its reflections on marriage, marital union, and parenthood, it is unwilling to follow through with the logical and normative implications of that interpretation in the case of certain ARTs. After addressing the *Instruction*'s personalist natural law foundation, we will explore how it vacillates in its use of natural law when addressing AFD and AFH.

The Instruction's *Personalist Language*

The CDF's *Instruction* relies heavily on the personalist language of *Gaudium et spes* and *Humanae vitae* to explain its perception of human dignity in relation to human sexuality, marriage, and the conjugal act: "The moral criteria for medical intervention in procreation are deduced from the dignity of human persons, of their sexuality and of their origin. *Medicine which seeks to be ordered to the integral good of the person must respect the specifically human values of sexuality.*"[36] These foundational values are grounded in "the integral dignity of the human person"[37] reflected in the "conjugal union"[38] of the spouses, which "must be actualized in marriage" through the conjugal act "in accordance with the laws inscribed in their persons and in their union."[39]

These laws, it is believed, establish the inseparable or intrinsic union between the unitive and procreative meanings of every conjugal act. The scientific and/or technological separation of these meanings, as a form of either artificial contraception or artificial reproduction, violates the intrinsic dignity of the marital act and renders the separation a violation and immoral. The relationship between sexuality and medicine must respect this act fundamentally. The *Instruction* notes that "the humanization of medicine . . . requires respect for the integral dignity of the human person *first of all in the act and at the moment in which the spouses transmit life to a new person.*"[40] The physical and relational integrity of the conjugal act is the only way human sexuality respects human dignity and the marital relationship. When human sexuality, as it is expressed in a conjugal act, separates the unitive and procreative meanings of the act, the *Instruction* teaches, the act loses its human dignity.[41]

There is, then, in the *Instruction* a clear "No" to ARTs, heavily based on the natural law inseparability principle.

Heterologous Artificial Insemination and the Personalist Principle

Although the *Instruction* utilizes personalist language to explain marriage and human sexuality, the tension between the personalist and biological interpretations of natural law is evident in its treatment of heterologous (AFD) and homologous (AFH) artificial insemination. The *Instruction* begins its treatment of AFD by answering the question: "Why must human procreation take place in marriage?" Its answer and its reference to *Gaudium et spes* reflect a personalist interpretation of natural law. Procreation "must be the fruit and the sign of the mutual self-giving of the spouses, of their love and of their fidelity."[42] Notice that the emphasis is not on the biological act of intercourse but on the interpersonal marital *relationship*, its mutual self-giving, love, and fidelity. Fidelity pertains to the marital relationship where there is "reciprocal respect of their right to become a father and a mother only through each other."[43] The *Instruction* grounds its moral assessment of AFD in the personalist dimension of natural law. Procreation must take place in marriage because of the personal and relational implications for the spouses with one another, "mutual self-giving," and with the child, "the child is the living image of their love," the "permanent sign of their conjugal union."[44] The clear focus of the *Instruction*'s treatment of AFD is on the personal and relational dimensions of the spouses, their union, and their relationship with the child.

In light of these relational criteria the *Instruction* then asks the question: "Does Heterologous Artificial Fertilization (AFD) Conform to the Dignity of the Couple and to the Truth of Marriage?" Here, again, the focus is not on the marital act but on the marital relationship as a whole, what is called the "Truth of Marriage." The *Instruction* formulates its response to its question by setting forth several ways in which AFD violates numerous relationships.

First, AFD violates the marital relationship. "*Heterologous artificial fertilization is contrary to the unity of marriage, to the dignity of the spouses, to the vocation proper to parents, and to the child's right to be conceived and brought into the world in marriage and from marriage.*"[45] Again, "respect for the unity of marriage and for conjugal fidelity demands that the child be conceived in marriage; the bond existing between husband and wife accords the spouses, in an objective and inalienable manner, the exclusive right to become father and mother solely through each other."[46] Second, the introduction of a third party into reproduction through the use of donor gametes "constitutes a violation of the reciprocal commitment of the spouses and a grave lack in regard to that essential property of marriage which is its unity." Third, AFD "violates the rights of the child; it deprives him of his filial relationship with his parental origins and can hinder the maturing of his personal identity." Fourth, AFD threatens the vocation to parenthood because "it offends the common vocation of the spouses who are called to fatherhood and motherhood. . . . It brings about and manifests a rupture between genetic parenthood, gestational parenthood and responsibility for upbringing." Finally, AFD has a negative impact on broader social relationships: "Such damage to the personal relationships within the family has repercussions on civil society: what threatens the unity and stability of the family is a source of dissension, disorder and injustice in the whole of social life." The fundamental violation of all these relationships leads "to a negative moral judgment concerning heterologous artificial fertilization."[47]

This entire section of the *Instruction* focuses on the various relationships the spouses have and argues to the immorality of AFD on the basis that it fundamentally violates those relationships. If the *Instruction* were consistent in its ethical reasoning, it would continue with this personalist, relational principle in morally evaluating homologous artificial insemination (AFH). It does not. When it addresses AFH, the *Instruction* shifts emphasis to a different foundational principle.

Homologous Artificial Insemination and the Biological Principle

The CDF's treatment of AFH opens with the question: "What connection is required from the moral point of view between procreation and the conjugal act?"[48] The shift in the question from "Dignity of the Couple and the Truth of Marriage" to "Procreation and the Conjugal Act" reflects a methodological shift from the primacy of a relational, personalist emphasis to the primacy of an act-centered, biological emphasis. This shift is indicated when the *Instruction* notes that "a question of principle must be clarified"[49] in addressing AFH. Following *Humanae vitae*, the foundational principle for the *Instruction*'s moral analysis of AFH is the inseparability principle: "The Church's teaching on marriage and human procreation affirms the 'inseparable connection, willed by God and unable to be broken by man on his own initiative, between the two meanings of the conjugal act: the unitive meaning and the procreative meaning. Indeed, by its intimate structure, the conjugal act, while most closely uniting husband and wife, capacitates them for the generation of new lives, according to laws inscribed in the very being of man and of woman.'"[50] Three questions emerge regarding the *Instruction*'s introduction of this principle. First, why does the *Instruction* make this methodological shift from a focus on relationships when morally evaluating AFD to focus on the inseparability principle when morally evaluating AFH? Second, what are the weaknesses of this inseparability principle with regard to AFH? Third, what would be the moral implications for AFH if the *Instruction* were methodologically consistent?

A Methodological Shift

First, though the arguments against AFD seem reasonable given the relational complications of donor gametes and their potential impact on the marital relationship, the relationship of the parents with the child, the donor's relationship with both the parents and the child, and the social implications with regard to the nature of the family, the same relational complications do not apply in AFH. Where the gametes belong to the parents, and a surrogate is not used to carry the embryo, the relational complications do not exist. All that can be claimed with certainty in the case of AFH is that the act of sexual intercourse is not *immediately* responsible for procreation. This point, however, though it gives us insight into the *procedure* facilitating reproduction, gives us no insight into the *moral meaning* of that procedure. As was indicated above, moral meaning is discerned not through the *givenness* of reality, in this case the givenness of the use of technology and science to assist reproduction, but in the *meaning* of those facts for human relationships. If the same personalist principle were to be applied to AFH as is applied to AFD, one could come to a different conclusion about the morality of AFH.

AFH and the Inseparability Principle

Second, by introducing the inseparability principle in its discussion of AFH, the *Instruction* clearly recognizes that there is a shift in the foundational moral principle in analyzing and morally evaluating AFH and AFD. The *Instruction*'s condemnation of AFH is "strictly dependent on the principles just mentioned."[51] In fact, there is a single principle, the inseparability principle. McCormick notes that the *Instruction*'s claim of strict dependence is a "remarkable statement" because previous magisterial documents indicated that the prohibition of AFH is "not strictly dependent on the analyses given or available to support it."[52] It follows from the *Instruction*'s strict dependence on a particular principle to justify its moral argument against AFH that the argument is only as strong as the principle; if the principle is weak, so too is any moral conclusion drawn from the principle.

We believe the "inseparability principle" used to prohibit AFH (and contraception) is a weak principle on several counts. First, there is no intrinsic procreative meaning to each and every sexual act unless one interprets procreative in a metaphorical or *formal* sense, meaning relationally life giving, as opposed to a biological or *material* sense, meaning biologically capable of *actual* reproduction. As we have noted several times, sexual acts in an infertile or postmenopausal relationship, or sexual acts during periods in which the woman is known to be infertile, do not have an intrinsic material procreative meaning, though they do contain a formal procreative meaning. In these cases, however, as well as in cases where the couple avoids procreation for serious reasons, the formal procreative meaning has merely been elided into the unitive meaning, because there seems to be nothing unique about the procreative meaning in a formal sense that would not apply to the unitive meaning of the sexual act. The act is only procreative in a material sense when actual, biological reproduction is possible, and only then can the procreative meaning of the act be strictly distinguished from its unitive meaning. That is why many theologians choose to discuss the unitive and procreative meanings of not every sexual act but the overall marital relationship.[53] As Rhonheimer notes, marital acts extend beyond sexual acts to include abstinence, and these acts are *both* procreative and unitive.[54]

This formal interpretation of procreation allows for conjugal acts other than the act of sexual intercourse to count as marital acts with both procreative and unitive meanings. If *procreation* in a formal sense is extended to include all just and loving marital acts that always express and give life to the marital union and is not restricted solely to acts of just and loving sexual intercourse that only on occasion give life to a new being, it is not logically clear why *procreation* in a material sense should not also be extended to include marital acts that are not acts of coitus. The distinction between procreation formally understood and procreation materially understood seems to open up the moral possibility of ARTs that are not necessarily an immediate result of marital coitus as traditionally defined. It is ironic that, in an effort to solidify the traditional arguments against both artificial birth control and artificial reproductive technologies, the shift from the unitive-procreative ends of marriage as a whole to the unitive-procreative meanings of only marital coitus has undermined the intended objective.

Second, the inseparability principle contains a "germ of truth" in what McCormick calls an "aesthetic or ecological (bodily integrity) concern." By that he means that all artificial interventions into the sexual relationship, whether they are to prevent or procure reproduction, are a kind of "second best."[55] This is in line with the *Instruction*'s claim that conception realized through IVF is "deprived of its proper function." To deprive a procedure of its "proper function," however, does not make the procedure ipso facto morally wrong in every situation. It does not do so, McCormick legitimately insists, unless we "elevate an aesthetic-ecological concern into an absolute moral imperative."[56]

Third, the basis for the "aesthetic-ecological concern" is a product of the biologism and physicalism that has controlled the Catholic natural law tradition, grounded in both a flawed biology and a flawed theology of marriage. In the Catholic tradition up until the Second Vatican Council, the *primary end* of marriage was always said to be procreation. This teaching reflected a long history that recognized procreation as the only legitimate meaning and purpose for sexual intercourse.[57] Our modern understanding of biology and human sexuality, however, teaches us that procreation is not even possible in the vast majority of sexual acts. A couple can morally justify having sexual intercourse without the material procreative meaning, but they can never justify having sexual intercourse without the unitive meaning. It is logical, therefore, to argue that not only are the unitive and material procreative meanings of the sexual act separable, and on occasion in fact legitimately separated, but also that the unitive meaning is now primary and the material procreative meaning secondary.

Fourth, while the *Instruction* correctly notes that "the one conceived must be the fruit of the parent's love," it has not adequately explained how the one conceived in AFH is not the fruit of the parent's love. It is not enough simply to state that AFH separates the unitive and procreative meanings of the sexual act and to conclude, therefore, that the child conceived in AFH is not the fruit of the parents' love, for that conclusion is a non sequitur; it does not follow from the premise. Elsewhere, the *Instruction* gives further insight into why it believes that IVF is not the fruit of the parent's love: "The one conceived . . . cannot be desired or conceived as the product of an intervention of medical or biological techniques; that would be equivalent to reducing him to an object of scientific technology."[58] To substitute the marital act and procreation with a technological act accomplished through doctors and technicians is to objectify the human person and treat him or her as a product. Grisez affirms this position, noting that to choose IVF is "to will the baby's initial status as a product."[59]

One can reasonably ask, however, whether or not there is an intrinsic moral meaning in ARTs. It seems that the *Instruction* and Grisez would claim that ARTs do have an intrinsic meaning that defines the morality of choice, namely, willing "the baby's status as an initial product," regardless of the parent's intention in choosing an ART. Universal human experience demonstrates that a couple can will a "baby's initial status as a product," through both normal intercourse and through ARTs, and treat the baby as a *mere* means to an end. It also demonstrates, however, that a couple can will a "baby's initial status as a product," through both normal intercourse and through ARTs, and still acknowledge his or her fundamental human dignity, still nurture him or her into functioning adulthood, and still fulfill the procreative meaning of the marital relationship as a whole through an ART as much as through an act of intercourse.

We argue, however, that "product" language, when referring to conception in ARTs or normal intercourse, is a foreign moral language for most couples. The thirty-year experience with artificial insemination appears to show that the frustration and desperation of infertile couples (even though it may be only one individual who is infertile that individual is so inseparably bound to the marital other that they are, in reality, an infertile couple) and all the inconvenience they are willing to undergo—social, emotional, physical, economic—is frequently a very powerful sign of their mutual love and their desire to offer to one another "the supreme gift of marriage," a child.[60] Furthermore, there is no intrinsic moral meaning to ARTs and there is no intrinsic moral intention in couples that might be driven in desperation to choose to use ARTs. The meaning of ARTs and the intentions for choosing them are determined concretely case by case within the context of concrete human relationships; meaning and intention are determined by the will, motives, desires, hopes, dreams, and reasons of the concrete couple choosing ARTs. To posit an intrinsic meaning to ARTs and an intrinsic intention for those who choose to use them is tantamount to determinism. Determinism, however, ignores the infinite relational and experiential complexities of an infertile couple driven to use an ART as a last desperate resort to enable their marital relationship to give life to a new human being, their child.[61]

Fifth, the tension between the personalist principle used to morally evaluate AFD and the inseparability principle used to morally evaluate AFH is highlighted all the more when the *Instruction* claims that "homologous IVF and ET fertilization is not marked by all that ethical negativity found in extra-conjugal procreation; the family and marriage continue to constitute the setting for the birth and upbringing of the children."[62] The relational considerations of AFD make it more morally objectionable than the violation of the inseparability principle in AFH. By its own admission, then, the inseparability principle on the basis of which the *Instruction* condemns AFH does not carry the same moral weight as the relational principle condemning AFD. The *Instruction* focuses on the marital act to argue against AFH; it focuses on relational dimensions to argue to the "ethical negativity" of AFD. It is relational considerations that make AFH less morally reprehensible than AFD. Because there may be no conjugal act in AFH, however, why would the *Instruction* base its moral condemnation of AFH on the conjugal act and the inseparability principle? It must do so because the relational considerations do not warrant an absolute prohibition of AFH, though the inseparability principle may so warrant if one accepts the principle as morally compelling. We do not find it morally compelling.

The Morality of AFH

On the basis of the foregoing analysis, we draw what we believe is a logical conclusion about the morality of AFH. As we noted at the beginning of this section, if the premise, in this case the inseparability principle, is weak, then any conclusion drawn from that premise will also be weak. We believe the inseparability principle cannot bear the weight of the *Instruction*'s conclusions absolutely prohibiting AFH. Given the desperation of an infertile couple to have a child and their intention—grounded in justice, mutual love, respect, responsibility, and human dignity—to have their marital relationship "crowned" by their child,[63] we believe the use of AFH can be moral and facilitate both the unitive and procreative meanings of marriage.

We are in agreement here with Cahill. Many Catholics, she notes, "perceive a difference larger than the Vatican allows between therapies used in marriage, even if they do temporarily circumvent sexual intercourse, and methods which bring donors into the marital procreative venture." She believes, and we agree, that "donor methods are more morally objectionable because they do not appreciate the unity as *relationships* of sexual expression, committed partnership, and parenthood."[64] Though procreation in AFH would not be the result of one act of marital coitus, it would be the fruit of an overall *marital relational act* that expresses and facilitates the just love, commitment, care, concern, and dignity of the couple shared with a new human being, their child. Our argument defending the moral acceptability of AFH is grounded not in the inseparability of the unitive and procreative meanings of a *sexual act*, but in the meaning and nature of *marital relationship, marital sexuality*, and parenthood that is its crown. It is in the overall marital relationship, not in each and every sexual act, that the unitive and procreative meanings are legitimately inseparable.[65] With the *Instruction*, we affirm the intrinsic connection of marriage, sexual love, and parenthood. We judge, however, that its claim that genuine marital love is absolutely incompatible with the occasional use of artificial means to bring about conception without a sexual act, or to avoid conception with a sexual act, is unsupported and meaningless apart from consideration of the context of particular marital relationships.

The Meaning and Nature of Parenthood

Although the *Instruction* uses the inseparability principle to condemn AFH, it indicates a parallel consideration between this principle and the relational emphasis it uses to condemn AFD. This parallel consideration revolves, first, around the relationship between the conjugal act and parenthood and, second, around the meaning and nature of parenthood in itself. After positing the inseparability principle as the foundational principle prohibiting AFH, the *Instruction* quotes *Humanae vitae*: "By safeguarding both these essential aspects, the unitive and the procreative, the conjugal act preserves in its fullness the sense of true mutual love and its ordination towards man's exalted vocation to parenthood."[66] In addressing AFD, the *Instruction* notes that "it offends the common vocation of the spouses who are called to fatherhood and motherhood: it objectively deprives conjugal fruitfulness of its unity and integrity; it brings about and manifests a rupture between genetic parenthood, gestational parenthood, and responsibility for upbringing."[67] Two points need to be addressed when parenthood is offered as a parallel consideration in the condemnation of AFD and AFH. First, we must investigate the *Instruction*'s assertion that the conjugal act is ordained toward parenthood. Second, we must investigate parenthood in its genetic, gestational, and social dimensions.[68]

The Interrelationship between Parenthood and the Conjugal Act

Gaudium et spes teaches that "children are really the supreme gift of marriage."[69] In the abstract and in general, one can say there is an intrinsic relationship between the conjugal act and parenthood in its three dimensions: genetic, gestational, and social. Approximately one out of five couples in the United States, however, is infertile,[70] and for these infertile couples it is impossible that any conjugal act will lead to genetic, gestational, or social parenthood. The CDF's teaching on ARTs that replace the marital act prescribes that the only morally acceptable path to parenthood for these infertile couples is through adoption or fostering.

The Magisterium applauds the moral validity and nobility of postnatal adoption.[71] Adoption is a noble act, incarnating the fundamental Christian imperative to care "for the least of these."[72] In the case of adoption, however, the nature of the relationship between the conjugal act and parenthood is fundamentally transformed. Though the conjugal act of infertile couples does not result in genetic or gestational parenthood, it does express and promote the union of the spouses, thereby strengthening their ordination to social parenthood, that is, the nurturing of a child into functional adulthood. The sexual acts of infertile, adoptive parents are certainly procreative, but only in a formal, relational sense, not in a material, biological, sense. In and through just and loving sexual intercourse, a couple promotes shared life in their relationship, and that shared life permeates all their relationships, including a possible relationship with an adopted child or children in social parenthood. It also, of course, makes possible a sacramental relationship with God, a fact deeply important for Catholics. Though adoption may not preserve "in its fullness" the relationship between the conjugal act and genetic and gestational parenthood, it certainly preserves the unitive, relational dimension of the marriage, and the social dimension of parenthood. In light of the reality of adoption and its implications for the relationship between parenthood and the conjugal act, the phrase "in its fullness," we propose, refers to a marital, interpersonal communion that may, though not necessarily, result in genetic and gestational parenthood.

The lack of parental fullness in the case of adoption, in which the genetic and gestational dimensions of parenthood are missing, does not constitute a *moral* disvalue. In the case of adoption, the relationship between sexual intercourse and parenthood lacks an *aesthetic-ecological* fullness, but this has no bearing on the *moral meaning* of the relationship. Rather, it constitutes a unique incarnation of the relationship between parenthood and conjugal intercourse that is as morally valuable as the relationship between genetic and gestational parenthood and intercourse. Not only does adoption force us to reconsider both the relationship between parenthood and conjugal intercourse and the very nature of parenthood itself, but technological developments also force us to reconsider both these realities.

Technology has complicated the definition of parenthood. Couples who utilize IVF-ET or its technological equivalents generally produce excess embryos that are frozen. If a couple decides not to have more children, these embryos remain frozen to be eventually destroyed, used for stem cell research, or adopted. The *Instruction*, as we have seen, clearly condemns destroying embryos or any experimentation that will damage or destroy them. Embryonic destruction or experimentation has been at the heart of social, political, and legal controversies as well. Currently in the United States, estimates indicate that there are 400,000 frozen embryos.[73] Though the vast majority (88.2 percent) of these frozen embryos are designated for use in future pregnancies and "family building,"[74] many will never be implanted and will remain cryopreserved. The first successful birth of an adopted frozen embryo occurred in Australia in 1984. Even though the publication of the *Instruction* followed that first case of frozen embryo adoption by three years, it did not address embryo adoption. The question of adopting frozen embryos has been discussed by theologians,[75] but the Magisterium's silence on the question continues. The reality of the possible adoption of frozen embryos, however, challenges us to rearticulate the meaning and nature of parenthood.

The *Instruction* notes that AFD "brings about and manifests a rupture between genetic parenthood, gestational parenthood and responsibility for upbringing,"[76] but it does not explain the moral meaning of that rupture. Nor does it explain the interrelationship between the three dimensions of parenthood or suggest any hierarchy among them. We offer two comments. First, as is indicated in both prenatal and postnatal adoption, there is no intrinsic relationship between the various dimensions of parenthood. A couple can experience one, two, or all three dimensions. Second, in the case of AFD, the *Instruction* makes no moral distinction between the three dimensions of parenthood. It would seem that these dimensions are of equal value and constitute ontological dimensions of the vocation of parenthood. In both prenatal and postnatal adoption, no genetic parenthood is involved; in prenatal adoption, there is both gestational and social parenthood; in postnatal adoption, there is neither genetic nor gestational but only social parenthood. Social parenthood is common to all three scenarios and, in fact, is the most important dimension of parenthood. On this we agree with Lauritzen, who writes that the core of parenthood is "the commitment to, and the activities of, caring for a child in a way that promotes human flourishing,"[77] and with Grisez, who writes that "parenthood is far more a moral than a biological relationship: its essence is not so much in begetting and giving birth as in readiness to accept the gift of life, commitment to nurture it, and faithful fulfillment of that commitment through many years."[78]

The primacy of social parenthood has moral implications for the definition of the rupture between the three types of parenthood the *Instruction* notes and for the relationship between parenthood and the conjugal act. The rupture *may* have moral implications for AFD, but its deliberate rupture in the case of embryo adoption leads to an untenable position in the case of AFH. Berkman highlights this position: "Catholic teaching seems to allow [adoptive embryo transfer] which separates genetic parenthood from gestational and 'raising' parenthood, but prohibits [AFH embryo transfer] that would maintain the bond between genetic, gestational, and 'raising' parenthood."[79] Though AFH does not rely upon the conjugal act for its realization, it does realize parenthood "in its fullness." And though the rupture between the three types of parenthood may be *descriptively* relevant, it is not necessarily *morally* relevant in evaluating ARTs.

The Magisterium's apparent approval of embryo adoption, and undoubted approval of postnatal adoption, also recognizes the moral legitimacy of separating the conjugal act from genetic parenthood and gives further credence to our distinction between formal and material procreation. In the case of AFH, like prenatal and postnatal adoption, there is not a conjugal act of the parents immediately responsible for procreation. The conjugal act between the spouses, however, is formally procreative in that it sustains and nurtures both the marital relationship between the spouses and the parental relationship between the parents and the child. The moral implications for defining parenthood that result from the adoption of abandoned embryos or postnatal embryos requires a more thorough exploration and clearer articulation by the Magisterium. The adoption of cryopreserved embryos also requires the Magisterium to clarify its teaching on the nature of the relationship between the sexual act and parenthood.

Parental Complementarity, Relational Considerations, and Social Ethics

Because the Magisterium's principle of the inseparability of the procreative and unitive meanings of the marital act, used to prohibit AFH, is subject to fundamental critiques, a credible moral analysis of ARTs needs to focus more on the relational dimensions and implications of these procedures. We agree with the *Instruction*'s prioritization of the relational considerations of ARTs over the inseparability principle in its moral assessment of AFD and, for the sake of internal consistency and credibility, we use the relational principle to analyze and evaluate all ARTs. Because there is not an act of spousal sexual intercourse immediately responsible for reproduction in most ARTs, because the genetic link is severed from the act of intercourse and parenthood in prenatal adoption, and because the genetic and gestational link is severed from the conjugal act in postnatal adoption, our option for this principle, we believe, is compelling. Focus on personal relationships is at the heart of the foundational, sexual, moral principle we have articulated in this book. Because reproduction is fundamentally about parenthood, we focus on the meaning of parenthood in morally assessing ARTs. Parenthood includes the relationship between the spouses, the relationship between the parents and their child, and the broader social relationships in which the family exists, functions, finds support, and contributes to society.

Because the relationship between husband and wife, the "coupled-we" in marriage, is the foundational relationship in which children are procreated, nurtured, and educated, this relationship requires special focus and attention in the case of ARTs. We share with many theologians and the CDF concerns about the potential spousal relational complications associated with AFD. Though it is not necessarily the case that the use of donor gametes is destructive of the marital, parental, or child–parent relationship, there are legitimate relational concerns that warrant a prima facie norm against the use of donor gametes. At the root of these concerns is the notion that "conjugal exclusivity should include the genetic, gestational and rearing dimensions of parenthood. Separating these dimensions (except through rescue, as in adoption) too easily contains a subtle diminishment of some aspect of the human person"[80] and the spousal relationship. The diminishment of the human person could take many different forms: feelings of reproductive inadequacy, loss of the self-esteem so necessary for a healthy sexual life, and resentment toward the other spouse. These personal issues may affect the marital relationship and create disharmony between the spouses. Where donor gametes are the only means for a couple to reproduce, the couple must discern the impact of gamete donation on their own relationship and their mutual relationship with the child who might be born. This discernment process requires frank, open, and honest reflection, dialogue, and prayer. A realistic assessment of the issues and their potential impact on human relationships must be made and, in light of this process of discernment, a responsible decision can be reached.

The great challenge in speculating about the relational implications and consequences of reproductive choices is, of course, that we are finite human beings, and our vision, knowledge, and understanding are limited. This is especially true of any reality that lies in the future. We cannot fully understand or accurately assess all the complications or blessings that may arise from our decisions on reproductive, or any other, issues. Though certitude is not an absolute requirement for moral judgment, prudence always is. We believe an infertile couple could make, in good conscience, a prudential moral judgment to use AFD. The couple would, however, bear the burden of proof that the concerns voiced by the *Instruction* about the use of donor gametes would not endanger their various relationships.

If, after reflection, an infertile couple comes to the conclusion that AFD would entail a disproportional risk to their human relationships, there are alternatives for reproduction. Rather than using AFD and creating new embryos or practicing artificial insemination, a couple could adopt existing, cryopreserved embryos. Though, technically, the woman is carrying the embryo of another couple, there is a fundamental difference between embryo adoption and surrogacy. In the former, the gestational mother will give birth to and nurture a wanted child; in the latter, the gestational mother will "surrender the child once it is born to the party who commissioned or made the agreement for the pregnancy."[81] Surrogacy is a means to an end, in which the gestational mother's obligations to the child end shortly after the child's birth and the responsibility of nurturing the child is taken over by another person or persons. Embryo adoption, conversely, includes both the gestational and social dimensions of parenthood.

The distinction between surrogacy and embryo adoption is helpful for addressing the issue of ARTs and same-sex parenthood. Some argue that, if AFD is permitted as a moral option, then there is nothing to prevent lesbian or gay couples (through surrogacy) from reproducing children. The same relational concerns we highlighted in the case of heterosexual couples and their marital relationship, with the exception of reproductive inadequacy, apply to homosexual couples and their union. Though these concerns do not rule out, ipso facto, AFD for homosexual couples, there is a prima facie norm against such procedures. Embryo adoption, however, is another matter and would provide, for lesbian couples, an opportunity to participate in both the gestational and nurturing dimensions of parenthood. As we indicated in chapter 7, there is no credible social scientific evidence to support the claim that homosexual parenting has a negative impact on children.[82]

Our proposal to posit the gestational and social dimensions of parenthood as the justification for embryo adoption by homosexual couples while maintaining genetic parenthood as the foundational principle for a prima facie norm against AFD is open to critique. A legitimate question would be whether or not our genetic parenthood principle used to prohibit AFD is every bit as much biologically rooted as the CDF's inseparability principle used to prohibit AFH. In other words, is it simply the biological reality of human genes that prevents us from supporting AFD for either heterosexual or homosexual couples? We address this point by noting the following.

There is no doubt that genes are biological material, but a more profound relational and ontological consideration defines the moral meaning of the genetic, biological consideration. If biological, genetic material were the only morally determinative reason that AFD is morally acceptable or unacceptable, then spousal rape that results in pregnancy could be morally justified, because parenthood is respected genetically, gestationally, and socially. No one, we trust, however, would ever condone spousal rape, even if it does fulfill all three dimensions of parenthood. Spousal rape is absolutely wrong because of the unjust violence and relational implications of the act. Similarly, in the case of AFD where the biological genes are not from one or both of the partners, the moral assessment of the procedure rests not in the presence or absence of the requisite genes but in the relational implications of the genetic connection for the partners individually, for them as a coupled-we, and in relation to any possible child. The genetic dimension of parenthood is morally relevant only in light of these relational considerations. If it could be demonstrated that the genetic dimension does not have a negative influence on these relationships, then, in theory, AFD could be morally acceptable. Scientific studies of those who use AFD and of the impact of that use on their relationships would be a great help in clarifying the concerns we have expressed in these pages. Barring such studies, we hold a presumption against AFD. The burden of proof, as we have already argued, rests with the couple to demonstrate that there would not be negative relational complications due to AFD. Though these concerns would apply to AFD, they would not apply to embryo adoption.

ARTs and Health Complications among Children

Although the relational implications of AFH and adoptive surrogacy for the spouses as individuals, as a couple, and as parents do not establish an *absolute* moral prohibition against ARTs, either AFH or AFD, other considerations would seem to indicate a cautious moral approval of the use of such procedures. The first important consideration is the multiple pregnancies that result from the use of an ART and the medical complications for the mother and child that accompany those pregnancies. In the United States in 2002, 35.4 percent of all fresh embryo, nondonor cycles utilizing ARTs were multiple births, and 3.8 percent involved triplets or more.[83] This statistic contrasts with 3 percent of multiple birth rates in natural reproduction. For the mother, the medical complications include anemia, increased risks of hypertensive disorders, *placenta previa* and placental abruption, premature labor and delivery, the possibility of cesarean section with the accompanying risks, and death. For infants the major risks include low birth weight, prematurity, congenital anomalies, and death.[84]

The second important consideration, which expands on medical risks to the child, is scientific studies that seem to indicate a direct correlation between ARTs and the heightened risk of birth defects among children. A systematic meta-review of the literature investigating the prevalence of birth defects in infants conceived through the use of IVF and/or ICSI suggests "that infants born following ART treatment are at increased risk [30–40 percent] of birth defects, compared to spontaneously conceived infants."[85] Though the increase in the likelihood of birth defects would not influence the moral assessment of embryo adoption for either heterosexual or homosexual couples, it would certainly have moral implications for those who choose to use ARTs (including both AFD or AFH) for reproductive purposes. Using ARTs knowing that such procedures have a higher incidence of birth defects may demonstrate a lack of care and concern for a child's human dignity. One may argue that most couples do not, in fact, know that there is a higher incidence of birth defects among children produced artificially. Studies that demonstrate this correlation recommend that couples seeking ARTs should be informed of this possibility.[86] We would expand this recommendation to require reproductive clinics to inform potential parents about the increased likelihood of birth defects from using ARTs. Informed parental ethical choice demands knowledge that is accurate, complete, and readily understood. This provides a strong argument for more legislation and moral guidelines in an industry that remains largely unlegislated.[87]

Although the higher incidence of birth defects among ART children *could* render the procedure morally objectionable, we should be prudentially hesitant to draw such a conclusion. For instance, a person who has a parent or fully genetically related sibling with Huntington's Disease (HD), a terminal neurological disease, has a 25 percent chance of passing that gene on to his or her child. If the person tests positive for HD, there is a 50 percent chance of passing on the HD gene to his or her child.[88] Even if the person knows that she may have, or even does have, the HD gene, she is not morally prohibited from reproducing. Just as responsible parenthood requires that a couple take into consideration genetic information when making reproductive choices, so, too, is a couple required to take into consideration the possibility of birth defects with ARTs. The possibility of genetically inherited mutations, however, could be an argument supporting AFD. Where one or both spouses have a serious genetic mutation, responsible parenthood may dictate that they use genetically screened donor gametes. Gamete screening for genetic mutations is certainly morally preferable to preimplantation genetic screening of embryos and the subsequent, immoral destruction of genetically flawed embryos. The mere increased statistical probability of giving birth to a child with a birth defect from the use of ART is not, ipso facto, morally decisive, though it is certainly a serious moral consideration for a couple trying to discern whether or not to use an ART. In the use of an ART that increases the chance of having a child with birth defects, and in natural procreation when the parents carry known genetic mutations, such information should be weighed carefully. With the mapping of the human genome and the availability of parental, embryonic, and gamete genetic screening, the ethical issues surrounding reproduction are going to become more, not less, morally complex.

In addition to consideration of a couple's emotional, psychological, and relational capabilities to care for a child with a birth defect, whether that child is the result of ART or natural procreation, there is also an economic consideration. The ethical challenge of factoring the financial consideration into the discernment process is that those who can "afford" to use ARTs can have access to the technology and those who cannot afford to do so are usually denied access. In addition, those who can afford to use ARTs may or may not be able to afford to pay for the short- and long-term health complications that may result from those technologies. The social justice issues become more prevalent the more we explore the issues surrounding ARTs.

Family and Society: ARTs and the Common Good

Another consideration related to the moral acceptability of ARTs is the relationship between the procedures and the Catholic tradition of the common good. A recent estimate puts the cost of *in vitro* fertilization with a woman's own eggs at $12, 500 to $25,000 and the cost with donor eggs up to $35,000,[89] and "less than 25% of cycles involving fresh, non-donor eggs result in a live birth."[90] Some insurance companies cover part of the initial costs. By far the greatest costs of ARTs, however, are associated with multiple births and postnatal care for those infants. In 2000, multiple births from ARTs accounted for more than $640 million in additional hospital costs,[91] an amount that does not include the cost of caring for a child with a lifelong disability that often results from the use of an ART.

This is where an important Catholic ethical question arises. The biblical prophets consistently proclaim that to know and love God requires action against the injustice perpetrated against God's people.[92] The reciprocation between God and the poor "underside"[93] reaches its high point in Jesus of Nazareth who, in Guttierez' pregnant words, is "precisely God become poor."[94] In the Catholic ethical tradition, this reciprocation is framed in the language of distributive justice, the common good, a preferential option for the poor, and solidarity.[95] Given the equal dignity of every human being before God, distributive justice demands that each and every person be accorded equal right to have their minimum human needs satisfied. Ambrose of Milan articulates the root principle: "Not from your own do you bestow upon the poor man, but you make return from what is his. What has been given as common for the use of all you appropriate to yourself alone. The earth belongs to all, not to the rich."[96] His disciple, Augustine of Hippo, agreed: "God commands sharing, not as being from the property of those he commands but as being from his own property, so that those who offer something to the poor should not think they are doing so from what is their own."[97] This is strange language in the contemporary highly individualistic world, but it is thoroughly consonant with the biblical action and teaching of Jesus.

Two items of statistical information frame the present question. First, besides the financial costs of ARTs and postnatal care to families, insurance companies, and hospitals, there are also major costs in medical resources, professional talent, and research and development. According to the Centers for Disease Control and Prevention, there were 428 fertility clinics in the United States in 2002, an exponential increase from the 30 or so in 1995. Second, there are approximately 46 million people in the United States without health insurance, many of them among the poorest in the nation. A serious question is whether or not fertility treatment for well-off individuals, almost exclusively in the developed world, is the wisest and most efficient use of limited medical resources and personnel. Are ARTs a luxury that should be offered only after we have provided necessary minimum health care for everyone, in the developing as well as in the developed world?

If we grant that ARTs are a luxury, second to basic health care for all on a medical hierarchy, does this national hierarchy have international implications as well? What about basic health care resources in developing countries? Should financial and medical aid to developing countries come before infertility treatments in our medical hierarchy? Though these considerations may seem to be blowing the moral question surrounding ART out of proportion, we believe that, just as the sexual relationship between a couple has both personal and social implications, so too the reproductive choices a couple makes have both personal and social implications. A holistic moral evaluation of ARTs requires that we take the common-good implications of their use into consideration when rendering a moral judgment on a couple's reproductive decisions: "The procreative interests of infertile persons have to be evaluated in light of the obligation of society to provide universal access to a decent minimum level of care. From our reading of Catholic social teaching, . . . guaranteeing basic primary and emergency care takes precedence over curative therapies that benefit a small number of individuals."[98]

The approach we recommend to this hierarchical question and to the questions surrounding the Catholic debate about ARTs is to shift the focus from sexual ethics and a biological understanding of natural law to social ethics, and a personalist, relational understanding of natural law. When the focus shifts, the questions and the answers found acceptable also shift. We submit that discussions about the moral acceptability of ARTs should not revolve exclusively around individual sexual acts. Reproduction is never simply a private, individual matter; the birth of a child, whether by natural intercourse or ART, is always a social reality. It establishes inescapable social relations, between the parent and the child, between the child and society, and between individuals and the social or common good. Maura Ryan frames the question: "How should we understand the relationship between individual wants, needs, and desires, and the social or 'common' good? How do we weigh the importance of 'saving' lives versus 'creating' lives?"[99] We agree with Cahill. "Low success rates, disproportionate expense, the priority of other medical needs, and the availability of other solutions should be part of public deliberation about the ethics and practice of assisted reproduction."[100] Shannon suggests a range of things that Catholic arguments should focus on: "the relative importance of biological child-bearing, funding for research into artificial reproduction, access to reproductive clinics, the place of artificial reproduction in relation to other health care services, and the status and role of children within society."[101] We suggest that the approach to questions about ARTs from a social theological ethics perspective, that is from a perspective in which distributive justice, preferential option for the poor, and agapaic love of neighbor hold priority, allied to the participatory theological ethics perspective proposed by Cahill,[102] is a more fruitful approach than the approach from the meaning of individual sexual acts and would help to restore much-needed credibility in the public forum to the Catholic voice on reproductive issues.

Conclusion

In this chapter we have explained artificial reproductive technologies, considered and critiqued the CDF's judgment on their morality, and examined their morality in light of our foundational principle guiding human sexual morality. We considered also the relational considerations between parents and between parents and their children that might have an impact on judgments about the morality of ARTs. Although we judge the use of the Magisterium's inseparability principle to condemn AFH lacks credibility, we also judge that the personalist and relational considerations of the CDF's *Instruction* are in line with our foundational principle guiding human sexuality.

According to this principle we argued that AFH is morally acceptable *in se*, though warning that the issues of multiple embryos and their human right to life, birth defects, and social justice must be factored into a couple's discernment process. These latter considerations, however, do not ipso facto prohibit the moral use of AFH. We further argued that, though there is a prima facie norm against AFD because of the potential relational complications between the spouses, the spouses and child, and the family and society, these considerations also do not lead to an absolute norm prohibiting the use of AFD. A couple is required to discern the relational implications of their reproductive choices on these various relationships and to make a socially just, prudent, faithful, and responsible moral decision. These considerations apply to both heterosexual and homosexual couples, though we warn that there are further complications with a gay couple and surrogacy. Embryonic adoption may be morally acceptable for all couples, though again, the surrogacy issue would arise for gay couples. We believe that, again, the strength of our argument rests in the consistency of a holistic, interpersonal approach to human sexuality and reproductive decisions, rather than in an act-centered, biological understanding of human sexuality grounded in exclusive heterogenital or organic complementarity.

Epilogue

THROUGHOUT THIS BOOK we have argued that Catholic sexual morality is institutionalized within the confines of marriage and procreation, and we have examined the foundations of two principles that articulate the essence of that Catholic morality. The first principle states that "any human genital act whatsoever may be placed only within the confines of marriage";[1] the second states that "each and every marriage act must remain open to the transmission of life."[2] In contemporary Catholic moral theology, two approaches to understanding these principles demarcate two schools of Catholic moral theology. First, the classicist approach holds the principles as universal, permanent, and unchangeable; this approach defines what we have called the traditionalist school. Second, the empirical or historically conscious approach holds that the principles *may* be unchangeable and unchanged or *may* be in the process of development or resolution in the contemporary sociohistorical context; this approach defines what we have called the revisionist school. Throughout the book, we have intentionally opted for a historically conscious and revisionist approach.

It is misleading, as we pointed out, to speak about reason *and* nature, as if they were two completely separate categories. They are not. Thinkers in the past, including sainted theologians, did not know the full reality of the human person as it has unfolded over the centuries, nor did they know the full reality of human biology and sexuality physiologically and psychologically. This restricted knowledge relates directly to the subject matter of this book—human anthropology in general and human sexuality specifically—and makes Josef Fuchs's claim difficult to gainsay: "One cannot take what Augustine or the philosophers of the Middle Ages knew about sexuality as the exclusive basis of a moral reflection."[3] Nor can one take the presumed facticity of nature as the exclusive basis for moral reflection, for "we never simply 'have' nature or that which is given in nature." We know nature, rather, "always as something that has already been interpreted in some way."[4] Put more directly, "nature" is a socially constructed category. To indicate and emphasize this socially constructed reality, throughout we have always placed the word "nature" in quotation marks.

Intrachurch Dialogue

Because theologians are essentially persons inculturated into a variety of human perspectives, only one of which is theology, this book has inevitably engaged in a twofold dialogue. The first dialogue is internal to theology and to the Catholic Church. It asks what a two-thousand-year ecclesial tradition has said theologically about human anthropology and sexuality and how that ancient tradition is to be mediated to, appropriated by, and transmitted onward in and by the contemporary Church. The young Joseph Ratzinger underscores why that internal dialogue must be pursued: "Not everything that exists in the Church must for that reason be also a legitimate tradition; in other words, not every tradition that arises in the Church is a true celebration of the mystery of Christ. There is a distorting, as well as a legitimate tradition . . . [and] . . . consequently tradition must not be considered only affirmatively but also critically."[5]

Three matters are crucial to both the critical consideration Ratzinger demands and the internal dialogue: the "nature" of Christian theology, the origin of sacred scripture, and the "nature" of the Church that claims its origin in the scriptures and seeks to mediate its meanings to each new Christian generation. For what has transpired in this book, the "nature" of the Church is, perhaps, the most pressing of these three, because how one conceives of the Church will determine how one conceives of another theological reality that is central to the internal dialogue, and to this book: *sensus fidei*, "the instinctive capacity of the whole Church to recognize the infallibility of the Spirit's truth."[6]

Before we consider *sensus fidei*, however, we need to add another word about theology and theologians. Traditional Catholic theology before the Second Vatican Council was enclosed within a classicist-traditionalist framework; it was universal, permanent, objective, and only to be learned. It was above all ahistorical, which led to its categorization as "non-historical orthodoxy."[7] That explains its evident lack of creativity. One of the achievements of Bernard Lonergan was to point the way beyond this classicist-traditionalist theology to an empirical, historically conscious, critical, and revisionist theology. Some continue to lament that "some recent Roman Catholic theology seems determined to live in a world that no longer exists,"[8] but we have eschewed that lamentation and have chosen the way forward that Lonergan has mapped in detail.

Horizon and Conversion

Horizon is an important category in Lonergan's philosophy and theology. In its everyday use, it denotes the line at which the Earth and the sky appear to meet, the outer limit of physical vision. Horizon is not immovably fixed. My horizon moves as I move, either receding in front of me or encroaching behind me. It is determined by my standpoint and, in turn, determines what I can and cannot see. "Beyond the horizon lie the objects that, at least for the moment, cannot be seen. Within the horizon lie the objects that can now be seen."[9] Physical horizon provides an easy analogy for the personal horizon of knowledge. The perspective that lies within my personal horizon is, to a greater or lesser degree, an object of interest and of knowledge: I can be attentive to it, understand it, make a judgment about its truth, and make a decision about it. What lies outside my perspective and horizon lies outside the range of my interest and knowledge. There is a difference, however, between the physical horizon and my personal horizon. My personal horizon is the product of both past socialization and individual achievement, and it constitutes both the condition and the limitation of any further development. In sociological language, my personal horizon is a socially constructed human product, and different products, different horizons, and different perspectives may be opposed dialectically. An understanding, a judgment, and a decision that are intelligible and true in one horizon may be unintelligible and false in another horizon. Because I have the freedom to move and adjust within a horizon, I also have the freedom to move from one horizon to another. The move from one horizon to another is what Lonergan means by conversion.

Conversion, the movement from one horizon to another, may be either intellectual, moral, or religious. Intellectual conversion is "the elimination of an exceedingly stubborn and misleading myth concerning reality, objectivity, and knowledge. The myth is that knowing is like looking, that objectivity is seeing what is out there to be seen and not seeing what is not there, and that the real is what is out there to be looked at."[10] This myth confuses the physical world of sensation—the sum of what is experientially seen, heard, touched, tasted, smelled—with the world mediated by meaning, which is a world known not by the act of sensation alone but also through the cognitive process of sensation, understanding, and judgment. Knowing is not simply seeing, hearing, touching, tasting, and smelling; it is also sensing, understanding, and judging. Until knowers reach the judgment that their understanding is true or false, there is no true knowledge. The myth that is to be clarified and eliminated has many possible consequences. It can lead to naive realism, thinking that the world of meaning can be known simply by looking at it, thinking that I achieve true knowledge simply by looking at and learning what Paul or John, Augustine or Aquinas, Pius IX or John Paul II said and wrote. Once intellectually converted from this prevalent myth, I come to understand that what Augustine or John Paul or Karl Marx said is only a first step in the process of my coming to know, to be followed by my own understanding and judgment not only of what was said but also, especially, of what is true. This converted horizon is what Lonergan means by critical realism.

Along with intellectual conversion there are also moral conversion and religious conversion. Following judgment and the attainment of truth comes the decision about what to do about the truth. Moral conversion "changes the criterion of one's decisions and choices from satisfactions to values."[11] Moral conversion involves progressively understanding the present situation, exposing and eradicating both individual and societal bias, constantly evaluating my scale of preferred values, paying attention to criticism and protest, and listening to others. Neither one instance of moral conversion nor one moral decision leads to moral perfection, for after one conversion there remains the possibility of either another conversion or relapse, and after moral decision there is still required moral action. Conversion is not to be conceived as a singular moment but as an ongoing process.

Religious conversion "is being grasped by ultimate concern. It is otherworldly falling in love. It is total and permanent self-surrender without conditions, qualifications, reservations."[12] In Christian terms, religious conversion is falling in love with God. Robert Doran, Lonergan's most authentic and creative interpreter, has beautifully described the love that is religious conversion: "Love alone releases one to be creatively self-transcendent. It is love that reveals values we would not otherwise see, commands commitments, dissolves bias, breaks the bonds of psychological and social determinisms, and so conditions the very emergence of the creative capacities for insight, judgment, and decision. The self-transcendence of intelligent, reasonable, responsible persons becomes a way of life . . . only to the extent that we are in love."[13]

When we are in love, especially in love with God, a new principle takes over, life begins anew, and love becomes the all-controlling horizon. Intellectually, morally, religiously converted theologians, both traditionalist and revisionist, have been much in evidence throughout this book.

Horizon and conversion have much to do with *sensus fidei* and its cognates, *sensus fidelium*, *sensus ecclesiae*, and *sensus catholicus*. *Sensus fidei* is a spiritual charism of discernment, possessed by the whole Church, which recognizes and receives a teaching as apostolic truth and, therefore, to be believed.[14] It has biblical roots in Paul's exhortation to the Philippians to "have this [common] mind (*phroneite*) among yourselves, which is yours in Christ Jesus" (2:5). It has modern validation in the Second Vatican Council, which taught that the doctrine of the Catholic Church is preserved in *all* the faithful, laity and hierarchy together: "The body of the faithful *as a whole*, anointed as they are by the Holy One (1 Jn 2:20, 27), cannot err in matters of belief [i.e., they are infallible]. Thanks to a supernatural sense of the faith [*sensus fidei*], which characterizes the people *as a whole*, it manifests this unerring quality when, 'from the bishops to the last of the faithful,'[15] it manifests its universal agreement in matters of faith and morals."[16]

Catholic doctrine enshrines this belief in the teaching that the Spirit is gifted to the whole Church. That teaching makes sense only in a Church that is believed to be and is lived as a *koinonia*-communion instituted by Christ, constituted by the Spirit of Christ, and "composed of all those who receive him in faith and in love,"[17] a historical communion "of life, love, and truth."[18] It is from and for such a Church that this book is written to invite conversion.

Extrachurch Dialogue

The second dialogue is external to theology and to the Church. It takes place between theology and the sociohistorical contexts in which theological doctrines develop and take root. Theology is not sociology or any other social science, but that does not mean that the two disciplines are completely unrelated. Sociology is eminently equipped, for instance, to elucidate empirically and scientifically what theologically *is*, forcing theologians to reflect on and evaluate what *is* and the sociohistorical context in which it *is*. It forces, for instance, the question we raised in the section on contraception: How can anyone claim that the Church believes that artificial contraception is morally wrong when some 89 percent of the communion-Church does not believe that claim?[19] Yves Congar highlights two approaches to an answer to this question. Obedience to authentic ecclesial authority is called for "if the Church is conceived as a society subject to monarchical authority," and dialogue and consensus are called for "when the universal Church is seen as a communion."[20] The theological fact that, after the Second Vatican Council, the Church is seen predominantly as a communion[21] demands critical dialogue and consensus about the *sensus fidei* of the Church rather than uncritical obedience. The ecclesiology in which this book is rooted is a communion ecclesiology.

The simple social fact that 89 percent of Catholics in the communion-Church believe that they can practice methods of contraception prohibited by the Church and still be good Catholics proves nothing theologically. It does, however, raise questions that theologians cannot ignore without fulfilling contemporary prophecies that theologians and their theologies have nothing to do with the real questions of the real world in which real women and men live, among other things, as members of the communion-Church. Another moral question we have considered in this book presses the Church in our day, perhaps more than contraception, namely, cohabitation prior to marriage. If the first union for some 75 to 80 percent of Western women is cohabitation and not marriage, again a social fact raises questions for theologians about what the communion-Church believes. The sociohistorical and theological fact of the nonreception and nuanced re-reception of long-held Catholic doctrines about usury, slavery, religious freedom, and membership in the Body of Christ[22] points to, and ecclesially legitimates, the direction in which the doctrines prohibiting contraception and premarital cohabitation (and also divorce and remarriage without annulment) *might* develop.

A word here about responsible behavior in the Church. The *Catechism* teaches that "the Church's social teaching proposes *principles for reflection*; it provides *criteria for judgment*; it gives *guidelines for action*.[23] This trinity—principles for reflection, criteria for judgment, and guidelines for action—came into Catholic social teaching via Pope Paul VI's *Octogesima adveniens* in 1971.[24] It was repeated in the Congregation for the Doctrine of the Faith's (CDF's) *Instruction on Freedom and Liberation* in 1986,[25] and it was underscored again a year later in John Paul II's *Sollicitudo rei socialis*.[26] This approach to social morality, an authentically established part of the Catholic moral tradition in modern times, introduces a model of converted personal responsibility that underscores the responsibility of each person in the communion-Church. John Paul II accentuates this Catholic perspective with the precept that, in its social teachings, the Church seeks "to *guide* people to *respond*, with the support of rational reflection and of the human sciences, to their vocation as *responsible builders of earthly society*."[27] The relationship between Church teaching and the individual believer's learning that this approach advances merits close attention in a Church that is communion. Church teaching *guides*; as responsible believers learn—drawing on Church guidance and their own attentiveness, intelligence, rationality, decisiveness, experience, and the findings of the human sciences—they *respond*.

The notion of responsibility introduces an important dimension of individual and communion-wide freedom to the unnuanced notion of uncritical obedience. In social reality, the Magisterium does not pretend to pronounce on every last detail or to impose final decisions; it understands itself as informing and guiding believers while leaving judgment, decision, and application to their faithful and responsible consciences.[28] Sociomoral principles are humanly constructed guidelines for attention, intelligence, judgment, decision, and action, not moral imperatives drawn from divine, natural, or ecclesiastical law, and demanding uncritical obedience to God, nature, or Church. John Paul adds what the Catholic tradition has always taken for granted. On the one hand, the Church's social teaching is "constant." On the other hand, "it is ever new, because it is subject to the necessary and opportune adaptations suggested by the changes in historical conditions and by the unceasing flow of the events which are the setting of the life of people and society."[29] Principles remain constant. Judgments and actions, as history amply demonstrates, can change after responsible reflection on changed sociohistorical contexts and the ongoing flow of human events illuminated by the social sciences. Because this approach is authoritatively advanced in social morality, and because social and sexual morality pertain to the same human person, it would seem that the same approach would apply to sexual morality. Indeed, because the whole person is more intimately involved in the sexual domain than in the social, should the sexual domain not "be *more than any other* the place where all is referred to the informed conscience?"[30] Part of the proposal of this book has been, under the guidance of ecclesial principles and the illumination of the contemporary sciences, to refer questions about sexual morality to the morally converted and informed conscience.

Christians in general and Christian theologians specifically do not live in a comfortable theological cocoon but in the world along with other human beings who appear to have decided that Christians have nothing to tell them about that world, about themselves in the world, or about the forces at work for good and evil in the world. Many of these others have perspectives on the world and answers for the world's questions that are different from Christian theological perspectives and answers. This raises the inevitable question of which perspective is right and true, a question that, in its turn, raises another question about a necessary external dialogue between theology and other socially constructed human perspectives. Individuals and the human world they inhabit are not two independent realities; they are realities that work in an ongoing dialectical and symbiotic interdependence. Human society, culture, perspective, and province of meaning are human products and nothing but human products, and yet these products act back upon their producers to conform and control them. The temptation of intellectually unconverted individuals, whether they are theologians or not, is always to assume that *our* way is the *right* way and *our* truth is the *real* truth. But the sociology of knowledge scotches this unconverted approach.

Human truth, we have argued elsewhere,[31] is relative to a given perspective or province of meaning and is supported by a plausibility structure that derives from that perspective. Each perspective has its own accent of reality, its own cognitive style, and its own consistency and compatibility, and outside a given perspective there is no possibility of grasping the truth held within that perspective. This raises the specter of relativism, which is so disconcerting to many. Relativism acknowledges that all human truth is inseparably bound to the sociohistorical perspective of the thinker and concludes that, therefore, all human truth is *relative* and unreliable. We do not accept that judgment. All human truth is indeed inseparably bound to the sociohistorical perspective of the thinker and is, therefore *relational*, but that does not suggest it is unreliable. It suggests only that truth-within-perspective is partial truth in need of dialectical complementation by truths held in other perspectives. This suggestion is even truer, the Christian traditions universally teach, when it comes to human truth about the God whom "no one has ever seen" (Jn 1:18; cf. Ex 33:20–24).

Augustine expresses the basic Christian, apophatic perspective when he argues "*Si comprehendis, non est Deus*" (If you have understood, then what you have understood is not God).[32] Thomas Aquinas expresses it in his mature doctrine of analogy: "Now we cannot know what God is but only what God is not; we must, therefore, consider the ways in which God does not exist rather than the ways in which God does exist."[33] Karl Rahner expresses the same perspective in modern theological language when he writes that "revelation does not mean that the mystery is overcome by gnosis bestowed by God. . . . On the contrary, it is the history of the deepening perception of God *as* the mystery."[34] The God whom the communion-Church believes in is always wholly other, *deus absconditus*, a hidden God, a transcendent Mystery, "blessedly present but conceptually inapprehensible, and so God."[35] Recognizing this Christian theme, the Magisterium of the Church teaches that "the fullness of truth received in Jesus Christ does not give individual Christians the guarantee that they have grasped that truth fully. . . . Christians must be prepared to learn and to receive from and through others the positive values of their traditions. Through dialogue they may be moved to give up ingrained prejudices [psychic conversion], to revise preconceived ideas [intellectual conversion], and even sometimes to allow the understanding of their faith to be purified."[36] Pope John Paul II approves. Dialogue, he teaches, as we pointed out in our prologue, "is rooted in the nature and dignity of the human person. . . . [It] is an indispensable step along the path towards *human self-realization*, the self-realization of *each individual* and of *every human community*. . . . It involves the human subject in his or her entirety."[37] We agree. We are wide open to dialogue in this book, and we look forward to the ongoing dialogue for the building up of the holy communion that is the Church.

Notes

Abbreviations for Sources

Works frequently cited in the notes are identified by the following abbreviations:

AAS   *Acta Apostolicae Sedis: Commentarium Officiale* (Rome; Typis Polyglottis Vaticanis)

CCC   *Catechism of the Catholic Church*

CMP   Germain Grisez, *The Way of the Lord Jesus, Vol. 1: Christian Moral Principles* (Chicago: Franciscan Herald Press, 1983)

CRP   Congregation for the Doctrine of the Faith, *Considerations Regarding Proposals to Give Legal Recognition to Unions between Homosexual Persons, AAS* (2003): 41–57

DS   *Enchiridion Symbolorum Definitionum et Declarationum de Rebus Fidei et Morum,* ed. H. Denziger and A. Schoenmetzer (Fribourg: Herder, 1965)

DV   *Dei verbum,* Vatican Council II, *Dogmatic Constitution on Divine Revelation*

EV   *Evangelium vitae,* John Paul II, *The Gospel of Life, AAS* 87 (1995): 401–522

FC   *Familiaris consortio,* John Paul II, *Exhortation on the Role of the Christian Family,* AAS 74 (1982), 81–191

GS   *Gaudium et spes,* Vatican Council II, *Pastoral Constitution on the Church in the Modern World*

HV   *Humanae vitae,* Paul VI, *On Human Life, AAS* 60 (1968): 481–522

LCL   Germain Grisez, *The Way of the Lord Jesus, Vol. 2: Living a Christian Life* (Quincy, IL: Franciscan Herald Press, 1993)

LG   *Lumen gentium,* Vatican Council II, *Dogmatic Constitution on the Church*

MD   *Mulieris dignitatem,* John Paul II, *On the Dignity of Woman, AAS* 80 (1988): 1653–1729

OT   *Optatum Totius,* Vatican Council II, *Decree on Priestly Formation*

PG   *Patrologiae cursus completus: Series Graeca,* ed. J. P. Migne

PH   *Persona humana,* Congregation for the Doctrine of the Faith, *Declaration on Certain Questions Concerning Sexual Ethics, AAS* 68 (1976): 77–96

PL   *Patrologiae cursus completus: Series Latina,* ed. J. P. Migne

SRS   *Sollicitudo rei socialis,* John Paul II, *The Social Concern of the Church, AAS* 80 (1988): 513–86

ST   *Summa theologiae Sancti Thomae de Aquino*

TS   *Theological Studies* (Marquette University)

VS   *Veritatis splendor,* John Paul II, *The Splendor of Truth, AAS* 85 (1993): 1133–1228

All translations from languages other than English are the authors'.

Notes to the Prologue

1. *PH*, 7.
2. *HV*, 11.
3. Thomas Aquinas, *ST*, II–IIae, 154, 11 corp.
4. *AAS* 43 (1951), 835–54.
5. Bernard J. F. Lonergan, *Insight: A Study of Human Understanding* (London: Longmans, 1958), esp. 431–87; Bernard J. F. Lonergan, *Method in Theology* (New York: Herder and Herder, 1972), 237–44, 270–71.
6. Robert M. Doran, *Theology and the Dialectics of History* (Toronto: University of Toronto Press, 1990), 35.
7. Ibid., 36.
8. Ibid.
9. Ibid.
10. Lonergan, *Method in Theology*, 270; emphasis added.
11. See Michael G. Lawler, *What Is and What Ought to Be: The Dialectic of Experience, Theology and Church* (New York: Continuum, 2005), 18–20.
12. *DV*, 12; and Pius XII, *Divino afflante spiritu*, *AAS* 35 (1943), 297–325.
13. *CCC*, 2357, n. 140.
14. *GS*, 62.
15. *GS*, 51.
16. John Paul II, "Ut unum sint," *Acta Apostolicae Sedis* 87 (1995): 28; emphasis added.
17. See Jean-Pierre Torell, *St. Thomas Aquinas*, vol. 1 (Washington, DC: Catholic University of America Press, 1996), 54–74.
18. Peter Cantor, *Verbum abbreviatum*, 1, in *PL* 205, 25; emphasis added.
19. International Theological Commission, *Theses on the Relationship between the Ecclesiastical Magisterium and Theology* (Washington, DC: United States Catholic Conference, 1977), 6.
20. Johann Sebastian Drey, *Brief Introduction to the Study of Theology with Reference to the Scientific Standpoint of the Catholic System*, trans. with an Introduction by Michael J. Himes (Notre Dame, IN: University of Notre Dame Press, 1944), xxv.
21. Ibid., xxvi.
22. For a recent exemplar of this approach, see Julie Hanlon Rubio, "Beyond the Liberal/Conservative Divide on Contraception," *Horizons* 32 (2005): 270–94.
23. See *LG*, 48.

Notes to Chapter One

1. Karl Rahner and Herbert Vorgrimler, *Concise Theological Dictionary* (London: Burns and Oates, 1965), 205.
2. Bernard J. F. Lonergan, *Method in Theology* (New York: Herder and Herder, 1972), 325.
3. Ibid., 263.
4. Joseph Fuchs, *Moral Demands and Personal Obligations* (Washington, DC: Georgetown University Press, 1993), 36.

5. Ibid.

6. Ibid., xi.

7. Ibid., 39.

8. *CCC*, 2423; emphasis added.

9. Paul VI, *Octogesima adveniens*, 4, *AAS* 63 (1971): 401–41.

10. CDF, *Instruction on Christian Freedom and Liberation*, 72, *AAS* 79 (1987): 586.

11. John Paul II, *SRS*, *AAS* 80 (1988): 571.

12. Ibid., 1; emphasis added.

13. Ibid., 41.

14. In her *Just Love: A Framework for Christian Sexual Ethics* (New York: Continuum, 2006), 211–15, Margaret Farley argues that "*autonomy* and *relationality*" are two basic features of human personhood that must be factored into every contemporary discussion of morality.

15. This notion of individual responsibility is brilliantly analyzed by Jean-Yves Calvez, "Morale sociale et morale sexuelle," *Etudes* 378 (1993): 642–44.

16. *SRS*, 3.

17. Calvez, "Morale sociale et morale sexuelle," 648; emphasis added.

18. Pierre-Olivier Bressoud, *Eglise et couple à petits pas: Vers un réevaluation théologique des formes de cohabitation contemporaines* (Fribourg: Editions Universitaires Fribourg Suisse, 1998), 134.

19. See, e.g., David Cohen, *Law, Sexuality, and Society: The Enforcement of Morality in Ancient Athens* (New York: Cambridge University Press, 1991); Kenneth J. Dover, *Greek Popular Morality in the Time of Plato and Aristotle* (Berkeley: University of California Press, 1974); Michel Foucault, *The History of Sexuality*, 3 vols., esp. vols. 2 and 3 (New York: Pantheon Books, 1978–); Otto Kiefer, *Sexual Life in Ancient Rome* (New York: AMS Press, 1975); Ross S. Kraemer and Mary Rose D'Angelo, *Women and Christian Origins* (New York: Oxford University Press, 1999); Martha C. Nussbaum and Juha Sihvola, eds., *The Sleep of Reason: Erotic Experience and Sexual Ethics in Ancient Greece and Rome* (Chicago: University of Chicago Press, 2002); Sarah Pomeroy, *Goddesses, Whores, Wives, and Slaves: Women in Classical Antiquity* (New York: Schocken Books, 1975); Aline Rousselle, *On Desire and the Body in Antiquity* (Oxford Blackwell, 1988); Marilyn B. Skinner, *Sexuality in Greek and Roman Culture* (Oxford: Blackwell, 2005); and various entries in *Sex from Plato to Paglia: A Philosophical Encyclopedia*, ed. Alan Soble (Westport, CT: Greenwood Press, 2006). That not all these sources agree about everything is eloquent testimony to the difficulty inherent in historical interpretation.

20. Judith P. Hallett, "Women's Lives in the Ancient Mediterranean," in *Women and Christian Origins*, ed. Kraemer and D'Angelo, 13–34.

21. Demosthenes, *Against Neaera*, 122, in *Demosthenis orationes*, ed. William Rennie (Oxford: Clarendon, 1931), 1385.

22. See John Boswell, *Christianity, Social Tolerance, and Homosexuality: Gay People in Western Europe from the Beginning of the Christian Era to the Fourteenth Century* (Chicago: University of Chicago Press, 1980); Kenneth Dover, *Greek Homosexuality* (Cambridge, MA: Harvard University Press, 1978); Pomeroy, *Goddesses, Whores, Wives, and Slaves;* Martti Nissenen, *Homoeroticism in the Biblical World: A Historical Perspective*, trans. Kirsi Stjerna (Minneapolis: Fortress Press, 1998); and Bernadette Brooten, *Love between Women: Early Christian Responses to Female Homoeroticism* (Chicago: University of Chicago Press, 1996).

23. See Demosthenes, *The Erotic Essays*, trans. N. W. Dewitt and N. J. Dewitt (Cambridge, MA: Harvard University Press, 1949). In the *Symposium*, 201d–212c, and in the *Laws*, VIII, Plato seems to prefer the elimination of all sex between men and boys for the sake of transcendence above sexual desire, but in the *Symposium*, 215b–222c, and the *Phaedrus* he proposes an alternate view. This is another example of the danger of generalizations about ancient Greece and Rome.

24. See Boswell, *Christianity, Social Tolerance, and Homosexuality*, 74–82; and Foucault, *History of Sexuality*, 2:193–97.

25. Plato, *Republic*, IX, the *Symposium, and the Laws*. Aristotle, *Nichomachean Ethics*, III.

26. Foucault, *History of Sexuality*, 1:3.

27. *PH*, 7.

28. *HV*, 11.

29. For a brief conspectus of the history of sexuality in Catholicism, see James F. Keenan, "Catholicism, History of," in *Sex from Plato to Paglia*, ed. Soble, 143–52, and Christine E. Gudorf, "Catholicism, Twentieth- and Twenty-First Century," in ibid., 153–63.

30. George Lindbeck, "Barth and Textuality," *Theology Today* 43 (1986): 361.

31. *Dei verbum* is the official title of the Second Vatican Council's Dogmatic Constitution on Divine Revelation.

32. *DV*, 8.

33. Ibid., 10.

34. This distinction is enunciated by Trent in its *Decretum de libris sanctis et traditionibus recipiendis*, *DS* 1501: "This truth and discipline [promulgated by our Lord Jesus Christ, the Son of God] are contained in written books *and* in unwritten traditions." This formulation created an ongoing debate among Catholic theologians about the precise relationship of scripture and tradition, specifically about whether the whole truth that God wants humans to know was contained in scripture alone, as the Reformers argued, in tradition alone, or in a combination of both. While not wishing to settle that debate, the Second Vatican Council still opted for the interpretation that scripture and ongoing tradition are related as written and unwritten tradition.

35. See Pontifical Biblical Commission, "The Interpretation of the Bible in the Church," *Origins* 23 (January 6, 1994): 497–524.

36. *Dei verbum* is the official title of the Second Vatican Council's *Constitution on Divine Revelation*.

37. *Divino afflante spiritu*, *AAS* 35 (1943): 310.

38. Ibid., 314–15.

39. *DV*, 12; emphasis added.

40. Pontifical Biblical Commission, "The Interpretation of the Bible in the Church," *Origins* 23 (January 6, 1994): 521.

41. Ibid., 500.

42. Ibid., 506.

43. Ibid., 524; emphasis added.

44. Ibid., 519.

45. *AAS*, 57 (1965): 758.

46. Ibid., 65 (1973): 402.

47. We mean by "construal" "to interpret," "to place a certain meaning on." We use it here to insinuate two connected meanings: first, the character of the theologian as construction worker within the Church; second, the character of theology as social construction, both

the theology that preceded the writings that came to be called scripture as well as the theology that succeeded them.

48. We reiterate the meaning of "construe," to interpret, to place a certain meaning on. We use it again here to insinuate two connected meanings: first, the character of the theologian as construction worker within the Church; second, the character of theology as social construction, both the theology that preceded the writings that came to be called scripture as well as the theology that succeeded them.

49. David H. Kelsey, *The Uses of Scripture in Recent Theology* (Philadelphia: Fortress Press, 1975).

50. See *DV*, 19.

51. Ibid.

52. *DV*, 12; emphasis added.

53. Shere Hite, *The Hite Report: Women and Love* (London: Penguin, 1988), 532.

54. Bryan S. Turner, *The Body and Society* (Oxford: Blackwell, 1984), 119.

55. Anne E. Carr, *Transforming Grace: Tradition and Women's Experience* (New York: Harper & Row, 1988), 207.

56. Mary Hayter, *The New Eve in Christ* (London: SPCK, 1987), 146.

57. The distinction between a sexual theology and a theology of sexuality derives from the classic work by James B. Nelson, *Embodiment: An Approach to Sexuality and Christian Theology* (Minneapolis: Augsburg Press, 1978), 115–16.

58. There are many good treatments of Jewish approaches to sexuality and sexual ethics, though, as with the Greco-Roman histories we saw, they do not all necessarily agree on everything. We recommend David Biale, *Eros and the Jews: From Biblical Israel to Contemporary America* (New York: Basic Books, 1992); Louis M. Epstein, *Sex, Laws, and Customs in Judaism* (New York: Block, 1948); Michael Kaufman, *Love, Marriage, and Family in Jewish Law and Tradition* (Northvale, NJ: Aronson, 1992); David Novak, *Jewish Social Ethics* (New York: Oxford University Press, 1992); and Judith Plaskow, *Standing Again at Sinai: Judaism from a Feminist Perspective* (San Francisco: Harper & Row, 1990).

59. For a different interpretation of the creation texts, see Ronald A. Simkins, "Marriage and Gender in the Old Testament," in *Marriage in the Catholic Tradition: Scripture, Tradition, and Experience*, ed. Todd A. Salzman, Thomas A. Kelly, and John J. O'Keefe (New York: Crossroad, 2004), 21–29.

60. Edward Schillebeeckx, *Marriage: Secular Reality and Saving Mystery* (New York: Sheed and Ward, 1965), 15.

61. F. R. Barry, *A Philosophy from Prison* (London: SCM Press, 1926), 151.

62. *Acta et documenta Concilio Vaticano II apparando: Series II (Praeparatoria)* (Rome: Typis Polyglottis Vaticanis, 1968), vol. II, pars III, 961.

63. Raymond F. Collins, *Christian Morality: Biblical Foundations* (Notre Dame, IN: University of Notre Dame Press, 1986), 176.

64. *Reliquiae* XIV, ed. O. Hense, in *C. Musonius Rufus reliquiae* (Leipzig: Teubner, 1990), 71.

65. Ibid., XIIIA, 67–68.

66. Ibid., XIV, 74–75. Aristotle argued that the community between parents and their children, in whom they could recognize part of themselves, was the highest. *Nichomachean Ethics*, VIII, 12.

67. William Moran, "The Ancient Near Eastern Background of the Love of God in Deuteronomy," *Catholic Biblical Quarterly* 25 (1963): 82.

68. Schillebeeckx, *Marriage*, 29.

69. The Revised Standard Version's translation modestly translates *sorerek* as "navel." But its location in the poem between thighs and belly suggests "vulva," as also the Arabic cognate of *sorerek* suggests. Marcia Falk translates it as "hips" in her *Love Lyrics from the Bible: A Translation and Literary Study of the Song of Songs* (Sheffield, U.K.: Almond Press, 1982), 41; see her explanation, 127–28.

70. Karl Barth, *Church Dogmatics* (Edinburgh: T. and T. Clark, 1958–61), 3, 1, 312.

71. Ibid., 3, 2, 294.

72. Marvin Pope, *Song of Songs: A New Translation with Introduction and Commentary* (New York: Doubleday, 1977); Helmut Gollwitzer, *Song of Love: A Biblical Understanding of Sex* (Philadelphia: Fortress Press, 1979); Falk, *Love Lyrics from the Bible*; Roland E. Murphy, *The Song of Songs: A Commentary on the Book of Canticles or Song of Songs* (Minneapolis: Fortress Press, 1990); Diane Bergant, *Song of Songs: The Love Poetry of Scripture* (Hyde Park, NY: New City Press, 1998).

73. Murphy, *Song of Songs*, 97.

74. Phyllis Trible, "Depatriarchalizing in Biblical Interpretation," *Journal of the American Society of Religion* 41 (1973): 45; her argument on 42–45 leads her to this conclusion.

75. Lisa Sowle Cahill, *Women and Sexuality* (New York: Paulist Press, 1992), 33. See also Raymond F. Collins, *Sexual Ethics and the New Testament: Behavior and Belief* (New York: Crossroad, 2000).

76. *DV*, 19.

77. Theodore Mackin, *What Is Marriage?* (New York: Paulist, 1982), 56.

78. See its definition of marriage as an "intimate partnership of life and love," *GS*, 48.

79. Whether that writer of Ephesians was the Apostle Paul or not, and the common opinion among Catholic scholars is that it was not, is of no relevance to the present discussion.

80. Markus Barth, *Ephesians: Translation and Commentary on Chapters Four to Six, The Anchor Bible* (New York: Doubleday, 1974), 618.

81. See Michael G. Lawler, *Symbol and Sacrament: A Contemporary Sacramental Theology* (Omaha: Creighton University Press, 1995), 29–62.

82. *GS*, 48.

83. Clement, *Stromatum* 3, 5, in *PG* 8, 1143–47.

84. Ibid. 3, 13, in *PG* 8, 1191.

85. For Greek society, see Paige duBois, *Sowing the Body: Psychoanalysis and Ancient Representations of Women* (Chicago: University of Chicago Press, 1988), 39–85. For Jewish Society, see Sirach 26:19; *Mishna*, Ketuboth, 1, 6. For Muslim society, see Carol Delaney, *The Seed and the Soil: Gender and Cosmology in Turkish Village Society* (Berkeley: University of California Press, 1991).

86. Clement, *Stromatum* 3, 12, in *PG* 8, 1186.

87. *Adv. haer.* 1, 28, 1, in *PG* 7, 690.

88. Ibid., 2, 23, in *PG* 8, 1086, 1090. See also *Paed.* 2, 10, in *PG* 8, 498.

89. Ibid., 3, 12, in *PG* 8, 1184, and 2, 23, in *PG* 8, 1090–91.

90. Ibid., 4, 19, in *PG* 8, 1333.

91. Lactantius, *Divinarum institutionum* 6, 23, in *PL* 6, 718.

92. Justin, *Apologia prima* 1, 29, in *PG* 6, 374.

93. Clement, *Stromatum* 3, 7, in *PG* 8, 1162. In his *Paed.* II, 10, Clement utilizes the argument of the Stoic, Musonius Rufus, to establish procreation as the major purpose of marriage.

94. Origen, *In gen. hom.* 3, 6, in *PG* 12, 180.

95. Ibid., 5, 4 in *PG* 12, 192.

96. See Eusebius, *Ecclesiastical History*, trans. J. E. L. Oulton (Cambridge, MA: Harvard University Press, 1980), book VI, no. viii, p. 29.

97. Tertullian, *Ad uxorem*, I, in *PL* 1, 1278.

98. Ibid., 1287.

99. See Jean-Claude Guy and Francois Refoulé, *Chrétiennes des premiers temps* (Paris: Cerf, 1965).

100. Tertullian, *Ad uxorem*, in *PL* 1, 1278–79.

101. Athanasius, *Epistola ad Amunem Monachum*, in *PG* 26, 1174.

102. John Chrysostom, *De virginitate* 9, in *PG* 48, 539.

103. Ibid., 10, 540.

104. Basil, *Liber de virginitate*, 38, in *PG* 30, 746. See also Gregory of Nyssa, *De virginitate* 7, in *PG* 46, 354.

105. *FC*, 14.

106. Tertullian, *Ad uxorem*, I, 2–3, in *PL* 1, 1277–79; emphasis added.

107. Ibid., II, 9, in *PL* 1, 1302–3.

108. Tertullian, *De pudicitia*, 16, in *PL* 2, 2, 1012.

109. *GS*, 48.

110. See Augustine, *De bono coniugali*, 6–7. See also Thomas Aquinas, *ST*, III (Suppl.), 41, 4.

111. Augustine, *De nupt. et concup.* 2, 32, 54, in *PL* 44, 468–69. See also Augustine, *De bono coniugali*, passim, in *PL* 40, 374–96.

112. *De gen. ad litt.* 9, 7, 12, in *PL* 34, 397; also Augustine, *De bono coniugali*, 24, 32, in *PL* 40, 394.

113. Augustine, *De bono coniugali*, 9, 9, in *PL* 40, 380.

114. *PL* 40, 375.

115. "The good of marriage, which even the Lord in the gospel confirmed, . . . seems to me to be not only about the procreation of children but also about the natural companionship/friendship [*societas*] between the sexes. Otherwise we would not be able to speak of marriage among the old"; Augustine, *De bono coniugali*, in *PL* 40, 380. Aquinas also had an incipient insight into the relationship of friendship between men and women and into the fact that sexual intercourse in marriage intensified that friendship. "From the point of view of the union between the spouses, a wife is to be loved more [than parents], because the wife is joined to the husband in one flesh, according to Matt 19:6. . . . To the extent of their marital and sexual unions, a man clings to his wife rather than to his parents." Aquinas, *ST*, II–II, 26, 11.

116. Mackin, *What Is Marriage?* 141.

117. *Contra Julianum*, 3, 23, 53, in *PL* 44, 729–30.

118. Augustine, *De bono coniugali*, 6, 6, in *PL* 40, 377–78; 10, 11, in *PL* 40, 381.

119. Ibid., 16, 18, in *PL* 40, 386.

120. Ibid., 6, 5, in *PL* 40, 377.

121. Gregory the Great, *Epistolarum liber IX epist.*, 64, in *PL* 77, 1196.

122. Augustine, *De bono coniugali*, 6, 6, in *PL* 40, 377–78.

123. James A. Brundage, *Law, Sex, and Christian Society in Medieval Europe* (Chicago: University of Chicago Press, 1987), 9.

124. Pierre J. Payer, *The Bridling of Desire: Views of Sex in the Later Middle Ages* (Toronto: University of Toronto Press, 1993), 14.

125. John T. McNeill and Helena M. Gamer, *Medieval Handbooks of Penance: A Translation of the Principal Libri Poenitentiales* (New York: Columbia University Press, 1990), vii.

126. Ibid., 95. Compare the same canon in the "Penitential of Cummean," in ibid., 105.

127. Pierre J. Payer, *Sex and the Penitentials: The Development of a Sexual Code 550–1150* (Toronto: University of Toronto Press, 1984), 165.

128. Ibid., 29.

129. Another reason for the sinfulness of every male pollution derived from an ignorance of sexual biology. The ancient Hebrew, Greek, and Roman understanding was that the male seed contained all that was necessary for a new human life; the woman merely provided a suitable "ground" or "field" for the male *seed*, a true *homunculus* or little man, to develop into a fully fledged human being. To spill the seed anywhere it could not develop properly, on the ground, in a mouth, or in an anal orifice, for instance, was regarded as murder, and murder was always judged to be a serious evil. For detail, see note 55 above.

130. McNeill and Gamer, *Medieval Handbooks*, 253.

131. Ibid., 185. Columban imposes a more severe penance: "If one commits fornication as the Sodomites did, he shall do penance for ten years, the first three on bread and water; but in the other seven years he shall abstain from wine and meat, and [he shall] not be housed with another person forever" (ibid., 252).

132. Payer, *Sex and the Penitentials*, 20.

133. McNeill and Gamer, *Medieval Handbooks*, 94. For adultery, Theodore prescribes a penance of "fast for three years, two days a week, and in the three forty-day periods" and no intercourse with one's own wife (see ibid., 196). Payer explains that the three forty-day periods are the forty days before Christmas, before Easter, and after Pentecost (*Sex and the Penitentials*, 24).

134. Ibid., 173; emphasis added.

135. Ibid., 104; emphasis added.

136. Ibid. See also the canons in the "Penitential of Theodore": "Those who are married shall abstain from intercourse for three nights before they communicate," and "A man shall abstain from his wife for forty days before Easter until the week of Easter" (ibid., 208).

137. See the figure on the sexual decision-making process according to the "Penitentials" in James A. Brundage, *Law, Sex, and Christian Society in Medieval Europe* (Chicago: University of Chicago Press, 1987), 162.

138. McNeil and Gamer, *Medieval Handbooks*, 197. See similar restrictions in Theodore, in ibid., 208.

139. Richard M. Gula, *Reason Informed by Faith: Foundations of Catholic Morality* (New York: Paulist, 1989), 26.

140. See, e.g., the negative and act-avoiding definition of chastity offered by Henry Davis in his influential *Moral and Pastoral Theology* (London: Sheed and Ward, 1936), vol. 2, 172; H. Noldin, *Theologiae Moralis* (Vienna: N.p., 1922), especially the treatment of "De Sexto Praecepto et de Usu Matrimonii"; Arturus Vermeersch, *Theologiae Moralis* (Rome: Pontificia Universitas Gregoriana, 1933), vol. 4, "De Castitate et Vitiis Oppositis"; and Gerald Kelly, *Modern Youth and Chastity* (Saint Louis: Queen's Work, 1941).

141. Aquinas, *ST*, III (Suppl.), 65, 1, c.

142. Aquinas, *ST*, III (Suppl.), 41, 3 ad 6.

143. Ibid., corp.; cp. *Contra gentiles* 3, 126.

144. Ibid., ad 1.

145. Aquinas, *ST*, III (Suppl.), 41, 4; 49, 5.

146. Aquinas, *ST*, II–II, 142, 1.

147. E. C. Messenger, *Two in One Flesh, Part 2: The Mystery of Sex in Marriage* (London: Sands, 1948), 178–79.

148. Peter Lombard, *Sententiae* 4, d. 1, c. 4.

149. Ibid., 4, d. 2, c. 1.

150. Ibid., d. 26, c. 6.

151. Albert the Great, *Comment in libros sententiarum*, 4, d. 26, a. 14, q. 2 ad 1.

152. Aquinas, *Comment in quartum librum sent.*, d. 26, q. 2, a. 3; repeated in Suppl. 42, 3c.

153. Aquinas, *Contra Gentiles*, 4, 78.

154. Aquinas, *ST*, II–II, 26, 11; also Aquinas, *Summa contra gentiles*, 3, II, 123, 6.

155. Aquinas, *Summa contra Gentiles*, III, 24, Bonaventure, *In quart. sent.*, 33, 1, 1.

156. For a discussion of this point, see Michael G. Lawler, "Faith, Contract, and Sacrament in Christian Marriage: A Theological Approach," in *TS* 52 (1991), 712–31.

157. David E. Fellhauer, "The *Consortium Omnis Vitae* as a Juridical Element of Marriage," *Studia Canonica* 13 (1979): 82.

158. Urban Navarrette, "Structura Juridica Matrimonii Secundum Concilium Vaticanum II," *Periodica* 56 (1967): 366.

159. Mackin, *What Is Marriage?* 214.

160. Gerald C. Treacy, ed., *Five Great Encyclicals* (New York: Paulist Press, 1939), 83–84.

161. Ibid.

162. Dietrich Von Hildebrand, *Marriage* (London: Longman,1939), v.

163. Ibid., 4 and vi.

164. Ibid., 6.

165. Ibid., 25; emphasis in original.

166. Heribert Doms, *The Meaning of Marriage*, trans. George Sayer (London: Sheed and Ward, 1939), 94–95.

167. See, e.g., Sara S. McLanahan and Gary Sandefur, *Growing Up with a Single Parent: What Hurts, What Helps* (Cambridge, MA: Harvard University Press, 1994); Paul R. Amato and Alan Booth, *A Generation at Risk: Growing Up in an Era of Family Upheaval* (Cambridge, MA: Harvard University Press, 1997); and Judith Wallerstein, Julia Lewis, and Sandra Blakeslee, *The Unexpected Legacy of Divorce* (New York: Hyperion, 2000).

168. *AAS* 36 (1944): 103.

169. *AAS* 43 (1951): 848–49.

170. Germain Grisez, *LCL*, 564.

171. *Acta et documenta Concilio Vaticano II Apparando: Series II (Praeparatoria)*, vol. 2, pars III, 937.

172. Ibid., 910 n. 16, 917 n. 50.

173. Ibid., 961.

174. Ibid.

175. Ibid., 952.

176. Remember, the so-called traditional language had been canonically traditional only since Gasparri and the 1917 *Code*.

177. See the votes recorded in the commission "according to the comments of Dopfner, Alfrink, and Suenens." *Acta et documenta Concilio Vaticano II apparando: Series II (Praeparatoria)*, 971–85.

178. *GS*, 47.

179. Ibid., 48.

180. Ibid.

181. *Acta Synodalia Sacrosancti Concilii Vaticani II*, vol. IV, *Periodus Quarta* (Rome: Typis Polyglottis Vaticanis, 1968), pars I, 536.

182. John Breck, *The Sacred Gift of Life: Orthodox Christianity and Bioethics* (New York: St. Vladimir's Seminary Press, 2000), 63.

183. Ibid., 62. While preferring *mysterion* or *sacrament* and eschewing *covenant*, John Meyendorff, *Marriage: An Orthodox Perspective* (New York: St. Vladimir's Seminary Press, 1984), still articulates the meanings Breck associates with covenant; see 18–20, 33–42.

184. *GS*, 48.

185. Ibid.; emphasis added.

186. *HV*, 11.

187. See Bernard Haring, *Commentary on the Documents of Vatican II* (New York: Herder, 1969), 5:234.

188. *GS*, 50.

189. Grisez, *LCL*, 565, n. 35.

190. See Michael G. Lawler, *Marriage in the Catholic Church: Disputed Questions* (Collegeville, MN: Liturgical Press, 2002), 27–42.

191. Those who are interested in that debate and its arguments can profitably begin in Charles E. Curran and Robert E. Hunt, *Dissent in and for the Church: Theologians and Humanae Vitae* (New York: Sheed and Ward, 1969) and Germain Grisez, John C. Ford, Joseph Boyle, John Finnis, and William E. May, *The Teaching of Humanae Vitae: A Defense* (San Francisco: Ignatius Press, 1988).

192. Norbert J. Rigali, "On the *Humanae Vitae* Process: Ethics of Teaching Morality," *Louvain Studies* 23 (1998): 3–21.

193. Clifford Longley, *The Worlock Archive* (London: Chapman, 2000), 232.

194. Robert McClory, *Turning Point: The Inside Story of the Papal Birth Control Commission, and How Humanae Vitae Changed the Life of Patty Crowley and the Future of the Church* (New York: Crossroad, 1995), 127.

195. Ibid., 99.

196. For detail on this, see Janet E. Smith, *Humanae Vitae: A Generation Later* (Washington, DC: Catholic University of America Press, 1991), 11–33.

197. *HV*, 11.

198. Cited by Robert Blair Kaiser, *The Politics of Sex and Religion* (Kansas City: Leaven Press, 1985), 260–61; emphasis added. See also Longley, *Worlock Archive*, 233.

199. Richard McCormick, *Notes on Moral Theology 1965–1980* (Lanham, MD: University of America Press, 1981), 164.

200. Margaret A. Farley, *Just Love: A Framework for Christian Sexual Ethics* (New York: Continuum, 2006), 278.

201. *GS*, 50.

202. Ibid.

203. *HV*, 11.

204. Farley, *Just Love*, 278.
205. *PH*, 64.
206. *HV*, 11.
207. *AAS* 35 (1943): 307.
208. Ibid., 310.
209. "The Interpretation of the Bible in the Church," *Origins* 23 (January 6, 1994): 511.
210. See Gen 38:9.

Notes to Chapter Two

1. See David Hume, *A Treatise of Human Nature*, ed. L. Selby-Bigges (Oxford: Clarendon, 1928), 469.

2. G. E. Moore, *Principia Ethica* (Cambridge: Cambridge University Press, 1903), 64; W. K. Frankena, *Ethics* (Englewood Cliffs, NJ: Prentice Hall, 1963), 101.

3. See Jean Porter, *Nature as Reason: A Thomistic Theory of Natural Law* (Grand Rapids: Eerdmans, 2005), 123–125

4. Ibid., 117.

5. See John T. Noonan Jr., *A Church That Can and Cannot Change: The Development of Catholic Moral Teaching* (Notre Dame, IN: University of Notre Dame Press, 2005); Michael G. Lawler, *What Is and What Ought to Be* (New York: Continuum, 2005), 127–29.

6. Alfred Schutz, *Collected Papers* (The Hague: Martinus Nijhoff, 1964–67), I, 230.

7. Alfred North Whitehead, *Symbolism: Its Meaning and Effect* (New York: Putnam's, 1959), 8.

8. See, e.g., Thomas Luckmann, *The Invisible Religion: The Transformation of Symbols in Industrial Society* (New York: Macmillan, 1967); Peter L. Berger and Thomas Luckmann, *The Social Construction of Reality: A Treatise in the Sociology of Knowledge* (New York: Doubleday, 1966).

9. See Bernard J. F. Lonergan, *Method in Theology* (New York: Herder and Herder, 1972).

10. Ibid., 263.

11. Ibid., 262.

12. Ibid., 263. For a fuller exposition, see Bernard J. F. Lonergan, *Insight: A Study of Human Understanding* (London: Longmans, 1958), 375–83.

13. See, e.g., Norwood Russell Hanson, *Patterns of Discovery: An Inquiry into the Conceptual Foundations of Science* (Cambridge: Cambridge University Press, 1958); and Norwood Russell Hanson, *Observation and Explanation: A Guide to Philosophy of Science* (New York: Harper & Row, 1971).

14. Joseph Ratzinger, "100 Years: The Magisterium and Exegesis," *Theology Digest* 51 (2004): 7.

15. Peter L. Berger, *The Sacred Canopy: Elements of a Sociological Theory of Religion* (Garden City, NY: Doubleday, 1967); Berger and Luckmann, *Social Construction of Reality*.

16. Berger and Luckmann, *Social Construction of Reality*, 60.

17. The use of "culture" in this broad sense to refer to the totality of human products is adopted from the discipline of American cultural anthropology. Sociologists tend to use it in

a sense restricted to symbolic spheres. The broader sense is more appropriate to the argument of this section.

18. Schutz, *Collected Papers*, I: 230; Lonergan, *Method in Theology*, 217.

19. David Martin, *Reflections on Sociology and Theology* (Oxford: Clarendon, 1997), 48.

20. Eric Voegelin, *The New Science of Politics* (Chicago: University of Chicago Press, 1952), 27.

21. See Berger and Luckmann, *Social Construction of Reality*, 129–73.

22. Berger, *Sacred Canopy*, 187.

23. Lonergan, *Method in Theology*, 217.

24. On limit language, see David Tracy, *Blessed Rage for Order: The New Pluralism in Theology* (New York: Seabury Press, 1975); David Tracy, *The Analogical Imagination: The Culture of Pluralism* (New York: Crossroad, 1987); and David Tracy, *Plurality and Ambiguity: Hermeneutics, Religion, and Hope* (San Francisco: Jossey-Bass, 1987).

25. Lonergan, *Insight*, 344; emphasis added. See also Lonergan, *Method in Theology*, 217–19.

26. *Sermo* 52, 16, PL 38, 360. For a detailed analysis, see Victor White, *God the Unknown* (New York: Harper, 1956) and William Hill, *Knowing the Unknown God* (New York: Philosophical Library, 1971).

27. Thomas Aquinas, *ST*, I, 3, preface.

28. Theodore Roszak, *The Making of a Counter Culture* (New York: Doubleday, 1969), 215.

29. *GS*, 51.

30. Joseph Fuchs, *Moral Demands and Personal Obligations* (Washington, DC: Georgetown University Press, 1993), 103.

31. Ibid., 104.

32. Dietmar Mieth, *Moral und Erfahrung: Beitrage zur theologisch-ethischen Hermeneutik* (Freiburg: 1977), 34.

33. Fuchs, *Moral Demands and Personal Obligations*, 27; emphasis in original.

34. Lonergan, *Method in Theology*, 20.

35. *GS*, 43.

36. Ibid., 51.

37. Ibid., 44; emphasis added.

38. See the section in chapter 1 titled "Historicity."

39. *OT*, 16; emphasis added.

40. See Pope John Paul II, *VS*, 1, 34, 84, 101, 106, 112.

41. See Todd A. Salzman, *What Are They Saying about Catholic Ethical Method?* (New York: Paulist Press, 2003).

42. *HV*, 11.

43. Cited in Clifford Longley, *The Worlock Archive* (London: Chapman, 2000), 233; emphasis added.

44. Aquinas, *ST*, I, 44, 4; see also I–II, 1, 6.

45. Brian V. Johnstone, "From Physicalism to Personalism," *Studia Moralia* 30 (1992): 71.

46. See, e.g., Ronald Lawler, Joseph Boyle, and William E. May, *Catholic Sexual Ethics: A Summary, Explanation, & Defense*, 2nd ed. (Huntington, IN: Our Sunday Visitor Publishing Division, 1998), 88.

47. The sources for the new natural law are extensive. Among them are Germain Grisez, *CMP*; Germain Grisez, *LCL*; Grisez and Russell Shaw, *Fulfillment in Christ* (Notre Dame, IN: University of Notre Dame Press, 1991); John Finnis, *Natural Law and Natural Rights*: *Fundamentals of Ethics* (Washington, DC: Georgetown University Press, 1983); *Moral Absolutes: Tradition, Revision, and Truth* (Washington, DC: Catholic University Press of America, 1991); Germain Grisez, Joseph M. Boyle, and John Finnis, *Nuclear Deterrence, Morality and Realism* (Oxford: Clarendon Press, 1987); and, Germain Grisez, Joseph M. Boyle, and John Finnis, "Practical Principles, Moral Truth and Ultimate Ends," *American Journal of Jurisprudence* 32 (1987): 99–151. For a synthesis of NNLT, see Jean Porter, "Basic Goods and the Human Good in Recent Catholic Moral Theology," *Thomist* 57 (1993): 28–42; and Jean Porter, "The Natural Law and the Specificity of Christian Morality: A Survey of Recent Work and an Agenda for Future Research," in *Method and Catholic Moral Theology*, ed. Todd A. Salzman (Omaha: Creighton University Press, 1999), 209–29.

48. Grisez, *CMP*, 180; emphasis deleted.

49. Grisez and Shaw, *Fulfillment in Christ*, 54.

50. Finnis, *Natural Law and Natural Rights*, 34.

51. Grisez, *CMP*, 124. See also Grisez, Boyle, and Finnis, "Practical Principles," 107–8.

52. *GS*, 48.

53. Grisez, *LCL*, 568; emphasis in original.

54. Ibid., 568 n. 43.

55. Ibid., 651.

56. Ibid., 652.

57. Ibid., 568. See also Robert P. George and Gerard V. Bradley, "Marriage and the Liberal Imagination," *Georgetown Law Journal* 84, no. 261 (1995): 301.

58. John Finnis, "Law, Morality, and 'Sexual Orientation,'" *Notre Dame Law Review* 69, no. 5 (1994): 1066; emphasis in original.

59. Finnis, "Law, Morality," 1066.

60. Ibid., 1067.

61. Ibid., 1069; Grisez, *CMP*, 216.

62. Grisez, *CMP*, 182, 202 n. 21.

63. Robert P. George, "Natural Law and Human Nature," in *Natural Law Theory: Contemporary Essays*, ed. Robert P. George (Oxford: Clarendon Press, 1992), 39.

64. Grisez, *CMP*, 902.

65. E.g., Grisez and Ford claim that the Magisterium's teaching against artificial contraception is infallible. See Grisez and John C. Ford, SJ, "Contraception and the Infallibility of the Ordinary Magisterium," *TS* 39 (1978): 258–312; Germain Grisez, "Infallibility and Specific Moral Norms: A Review Discussion," *Thomist* 49 (1985): 248–87; and, Germain Grisez, "*Quaestio Disputata*: The Ordinary Magisterium's Infallibility: A Reply to Some New Arguments," *TS* 55 (1994): 720–32, 737–38.

66. Johnstone, "From Physicalism to Personalism," 95.

67. Grisez, *CMP*, 216.

68. Grisez, *LCL*, 634–35.

69. See Todd A. Salzman and Michael G. Lawler, "New Natural Law Theory and Foundational Sexual Ethical Principles: A Critique and a Proposal," *Heythrop Journal* 47 (2006): 182–205; "Catholic Sexual Ethics: Complementarity and the Truly Human," *TS* 67, no. 3 (2006): 625–52. As our argument has developed, we have reformulated *genital* complementarity as *heterogenital* complementarity to designate magisterial teaching. This reformulation applies to our critique of NNLT as well.

70. Grisez, *LCL*, 570.

71. Finnis, "Law, Morality," 1067; emphasis added.

72. See Finnis, "Law, Morality," 1066–67.

73. Aquinas, *ST*, I–II, 91, 2.

74. Ibid., I–II, 90, 2.

75. Ibid., I–II, 94, 2.

76. Ibid., I–II, 94, 2.

77. Finnis, "Law, Morality," 1067; emphasis added.

78. United States Conference of Catholic Bishops (USSCB), *Always Our Children* (Washington, DC: USSCB, 1997), 4–5; *PH*, 8.

79. Finnis, "Is Natural Law Theory Compatible with Limited Government," in *Natural Law, Liberalism, and Morality: Contemporary Essays*, ed. Robert P. George (Oxford: Clarendon Press, 1996), 16.

80. Finnis, "Law, Morality," 1067; emphasis added.

81. Grisez, *CMP*, 124.

82. Finnis, "Law, Morality," 1053.

83. Germain Grisez, *The Way of the Lord Jesus, Volume Three: Difficult Moral Questions* (Quincy, IL: Franciscan Press, 1997) (hereafter, *DMQ*), 105. It is interesting to note that in his article, "Law, Morality, and 'Sexual Orientation,'" Finnis focuses almost entirely on homosexual activity. There is no evidence that he has consulted, or is familiar with, the contemporary scientific literature on psychosexual development or the meaning and nature of homosexual orientation. In his presentation of the "standard modern position," he demonstrates both unfamiliarity with, and insensitivity to, studies on orientation in this disparaging remark: "Nor have such states renounced the judgment that a life involving homosexual conduct is bad even for anyone *unfortunate enough* to have innate or quasi-innate homosexual inclinations" (emphasis added, 1052).

84. USSCB, *Always Our Children*, 4–5; emphasis added. See also *PH*, 8.

85. Robert Nugent, "Sexual Orientation in Vatican Thinking," in *The Vatican and Homosexuality: Reactions to the "Letter to the Bishops of the Catholic Church on the Pastoral Care of Homosexual Persons,"* ed. Jeannine Gramick and Pat Furey (New York: Crossroad, 1988), 55.

86. There are scholars who reject a biological or genetic determination of homosexual orientation. See Christopher Wolfe, ed., *Homosexuality and American Public Life* (Dallas: Spence Publishing Co., 1999), esp. chaps. 1–4. Grisez recognizes several potential factors contributing to one's orientation: genetic or biological, psychodynamic, and social experiences that affect individual development. See Grisez, *DMQ*, 105.

87. This terminology has been borrowed from John E. Perito, *Contemporary Catholic Sexuality: What Is Taught and What Is Practiced* (New York: Crossroad, 2003). He explains: "Genetic loading is given by nature. . . . The best we can do is to name the quality properly. . . . Heavy psychological loading has to do with the cultural and family influences that have contributed to the sexual orientation" (p. 96). We embrace the term as articulating our position that sexual orientation is neither exclusively genetic nor exclusively social in origin.

88. See William Paul, J. Weinreich, J. Gonsioerek, and M. E. Motvedt, eds., *Homosexuality: Social, Psychological, and Biological Issues* (Beverly Hills, CA: Sage, 1982); Pim Pronk, *Against Nature? Types of Moral Argumentation Regarding Homosexuality* (Grand Rapids: Eerdmans, 1993); Richard C. Pillard and J. Michael Bailey, "A Biological Perspective on Sexual

Orientation," *Clinical Sexuality* 18 (1995): 1–14; Lee Ellis and Linda Ebertz, *Sexual Orientation: Toward Biological Understanding* (Westport, CT: Praeger, 1997); and Richard C. Friedman and Jennifer I. Downey, *Sexual Orientation and Psychoanalysis: Sexual Science and Clinical Practice* (New York: Columbia University Press, 2002).

89. See the section above titled "Sexual Anthropology, Marriage, and Absolute Norms." Also, Grisez notes: "Though human sexuality's meaning and value transcend the biological, sexual behavior fundamentally pertains to a person's reproductive capacity. This basic meaning and value of sex grounds every other aspect of its personal and interpersonal significance, so that humans can fulfill themselves through sexual behavior only in marriage—the stable communion of a man and a woman that is appropriate for having children and raising them" (*DMQ*, 107).

90. See chapter 4.

91. Finnis, "Law, Morality," 1066. Grisez notes that, at best, homosexual acts can only achieve "an unsatisfying illusion of intimacy" (*DMQ*, 108).

92. Grisez, *DMQ*, 108 n. 86, favorably cites studies indicating the high levels of promiscuity and the inability among homosexuals to maintain stable relationships, and the "psychological causes *within* such people that account for those phenomena," but he does not address the reality of monogamous, loving, committed homosexual relationships.

93. Margaret A. Farley, "An Ethic for Same-Sex Relations," in *A Challenge to Love: Gay and Lesbian Catholics in the Church*, ed. Robert Nugent (New York: Crossroad, 1983), 99–100.

94. John Courtney Murray, *We Hold These Truths: Catholic Reflections on the American Experience* (New York: Sheed and Ward, 1960), 106.

95. Stephen J. Pope, "Scientific and Natural Law Analyses of Homosexuality: A Methodological Study," *Journal of Religious Ethics* 25 (1997): 111.

96. Grisez, *LCL*, 509.

97. Ibid., 267.

98. Ibid., 483–84; Finnis, *Moral Absolutes*, 56–57, 78–79.

99. Germain Grisez, Joseph M. Boyle, John Finnis, and William E. May, "NFP: Not Contralife," in *Dialogue about Catholic Sexual Teaching, Readings in Moral Theology No. 8*, ed. Charles E. Curran and Richard A. McCormick (New York: Paulist Press, 1993), 126–34.

100. Grisez, *LCL*, 511; emphasis added.

101. Grisez et al., "NFP," 130.

102. Grisez, *LCL*, 511; emphasis added.

103. Grisez, *CMP*, 58–59.

104. Grisez, *LCL*, 469 n. 19. See also John Finnis, "Object and Intention in Moral Judgments According to Aquinas," *Thomist* 55 (1991): 1–27.

105. Grisez et al., "NFP," 131.

106. CCE, *Educational Guidance in Human Love: Outlines for Sex Education* (Rome: Typis Polyglottis Vaticanis, 1983) (hereafter *EGHL*), 35.

107. See G. Simon Harak, *Virtuous Passions: The Formation of Christian Character* (New York: Paulist, 1993).

108. See Jean Porter, *Nature as Reason: A Thomistic Theory of the Natural Law* (Grand Rapids: Eerdmans, 2005), 274–84.

109. John Finnis, "Is Natural Law Theory Compatible with Limited Government," in *Natural Law, Liberalism, and Morality*, ed. Robert P. George, 16.

110. Finnis, "Law, Morality," 1067; emphasis added.

111. Though it seems clear that NNLT theorists commit the naturalistic fallacy, their commitment to a strict logical distinction between metaphysics and basic goods, fact and value, is and ought, raises anthropological questions as well. Though NNLT is correct to hold that one cannot logically deduce conclusions that do not contain terms of reference in their premises, in this case an "illicit inference from facts to norms" (Finnis, *Natural Law and Natural Rights*, 33), it seems that a shift in natural law from human "nature" biologically understood to the relational human person obfuscates the naturalistic fallacies clarity. E.g., whereas human "nature" includes the teleology of the reproductive organs to reproduce, the human person entails a fundamentally human and relational dimension in that teleology. Thus, we would concur with Henry Veatch that "the very 'is' of human nature has . . . an 'ought' built into it"; Henry Veatch, "Natural Law and the 'Is'-'Ought' Question," *Catholic Lawyer* 26 (1981): 258. The disagreement on whether or not the naturalistic fallacy is legitimate to critique naturalistic ethical theories is dependent, at least in part, on how one defines the human person.

112. See *PH*, 1.

113. Grisez, *CMP*, 902.

114. See Jeffrey D. Sachs, *The End of Poverty: Economic Possibilities for Our Time* (New York: Penguin Press, 2005), 64–66, 323–26.

115. Ibid., 1.

116. See Grisez, *CMP*, chap. 6.

117. Grisez, Boyle, and Finnis, *Nuclear Deterrence*, 284.

118. Grisez, *CMP*, 205–16.

119. Grisez, *LCL*, 38–55.

120. Ibid., 685; emphasis added.

121. See Christine E. Gudorf, "Western Religion and the Patriarchal Family," in *Feminist Ethics and the Catholic Moral Tradition: Readings in Moral Theology No. 9*, ed. Charles E. Curran, Margaret E. Farley, and Richard A. McCormick (New York: Paulist Press, 1996), 251–77.

122. Porter, *Nature as Reason*, 128. See also Charles E. Curran, *The Catholic Moral Tradition Today: A Synthesis* (Washington, DC: Georgetown University Press, 1999), 158–60.

123. See Grisez, *CMP*, 901–2.

124. Porter, *Nature as Reason*, 131.

125. Grisez claims that the basic goods do not have an independent existence, "as if they were Platonic Ideas"; Germain Grisez and Russell Shaw, *Beyond the New Morality* (Notre Dame, IN: University of Notre Dame Press, 1974), 71. However, Bernard Hoose challenges this claim. Bernard Hoose, "Proportionalists, Deontologists and the Human Good," *Heythrop Journal* 33 (1992): 180; and Bernard Hoose, "Basic Goods: Continuing the Debate," *Heythrop Journal* 35 (1994): 58–63.

126. Porter, *Nature as Reason*, 130.

127. Though NNLT does have recourse to the virtues in its theory (e.g., see Grisez, *LCL*, 633–80), the clear emphasis is on the basic goods.

128. Martin Rhonheimer, *Natural Law and Practical Reason: A Thomist View of Moral Autonomy*, trans. G. Malsbary (New York: Fordham University Press, 2000), 44 n. 7, 556; Martin Rhonheimer, "The Cognitive Structure of the Natural Law and the Truth of Subjectivity," *Thomist* 67 (2003): 22 n. 50.

129. Rhonheimer, "Cognitive Structure," 38.

130. Rhonheimer, *Natural Law*, 117. For another traditionalist attempt to ground sexual ethics in virtue, see John Grabowski, *Sex and Virtue: An Introduction to Sexual Ethics* (Washington, DC: Catholic University of America Press, 2003). Though this is an admirable attempt to formulate a sexual anthropology grounded in scripture, personalism, and virtue, Grabowski's theory is subject to some of the same classicist critiques of human "nature," intentionality, and a univocal correlation between acts and virtues that we address below.

131. Jean Porter, *Nature as Reason*, 188.

132. Rhonheimer, Natural Law, 557; Rhonheimer, "Cognitive Structure," 1–4.

133. Rhonheimer, Natural Law, 182–83; Rhonheimer, "Cognitive Structure," 7 n. 12.

134. Porter, *Nature as Reason*, 188.

135. Rhonheimer, "Cognitive Structure," 4.

136. From this perspective, natural law's "objective" realm constitutes the "natural order" and its subjective realm constitutes reason or moral knowledge. The subjective "ought" of natural law is deduced from the objective "is" of the natural order, thus committing the naturalistic fallacy. Ibid., 1–4.

137. Ibid., 5.

138. Ibid., 15.

139. Rhonheimer, *Natural Law*, 570–74.

140. Ibid., 581.

141. Rhonheimer, "Cognitive Structure," 38.

142. Rhonheimer, *Natural Law*, 569.

143. Ibid., 569–70.

144. Rhonheimer, "Contraception," 29.

145. Ibid., 32–38.

146. Ibid., 39.

147. Ibid.

148. Ibid.

149. Ibid., 40.

150. Ibid., 23.

151. Ibid., 41.

152. Ibid.

153. Ibid., 42.

154. Ibid.

155. Ibid., 44; emphasis in original.

156. Aquinas, *ST*, I–II, 94, 3.

157. Grisez, *CMP*, 192.

158. Rhonheimer, "Contraception," 56 n. 34.

159. See Lawler, Boyle, and May, *Catholic Sexual Ethics*, 304 n. 72. They admit it is possible for couples to use NFP for selfish reasons, in which case NFP would be wrong, but they argue that "it is not wrong because it is contraceptive." We argue that the selfishness involved in using NFP is a "contraceptive mentality," and the intentionality for abstaining at this time is to engage in sexual intercourse at a later time when procreation is not possible. At the heart of the difference between the two positions is action-theory, and the definition of the human act. For a similar critique, see Lisa Sowle Cahill, "Catholic Sexual Ethics and the Dignity of the Person: A Double Message," *TS* 50 (1989): 136–37.

160. Rhonheimer, "Contraception," 44.

161. Ibid., 56 n. 34.

162. Ibid., 42–43.

163. Ibid., 44.

164. Ibid., 41.

165. A similar point is made by Gareth Moore, *The Body in Context: Sex and Catholicism*, *Contemporary Christian Insights* (New York: Continuum, 2001), 163–65.

166. Rhonheimer, "Contraception," 44.

167. See Todd A. Salzman, "The Human Act and Its Moral Evaluation in the *Catechism of the Catholic Church*: A Critical Analysis," in *Ethics and the Catechism of the Catholic Church*, ed. Michael E. Allsopp (Scranton: University of Scranton Press, 1999), 68–71.

168. Rhonheimer, "Contraception," 41–42.

169. Ibid.

170. *HV*, 12.

171. Rhonheimer, "Contraception," 41; emphasis added.

172. See *GS*, 48–50; *Code of Canon Law*, can. 1055; Michael G. Lawler, *Marriage in the Catholic Church: Disputed Questions* (Collegeville, MN: Liturgical Press, 2002), 27–42.

173. Rhonheimer, "Contraception," 43; emphasis in original.

174. Grisez, *LCL*, 508.

175. Ibid., 508–9.

176. Edward Vacek, "Contraception Again—A Conclusion in Search of Convincing Arguments: One Proportionalist's [Mis?]understanding of a Text," in *Natural Law and Moral Inquiry: Ethics, Metaphysics, and Politics in the Work of Germain Grisez*, ed. Robert P. George (Washington, DC: Georgetown University Press, 1998), 57.

177. Rhonheimer, "Contraception," 41–42.

178. Porter, *Nature as Reason*, 185–86. See also Rosalind Hursthouse, *On Virtue Ethics* (New York: Oxford University Press, 1999), 25–42.

179. We are indebted for this insight to James F. Keenan, "Virtue Ethics and Sexual Ethics," *Louvain Studies* 30 (2005): 188.

180. Paul Ricoeur, "Love and Justice," in *Radical Pluralism and Truth: David Tracy and the Hermeneutics of Religion*, ed. Werner G. Jeanrond and Jennifer L. Rike (New York: Crossroad, 1991), 196.

181. Keenan, "Virtue Ethics and Sexual Ethics," 189.

182. Eberhard Schockenhoff, *Natural Law and Human Dignity: Universal Ethics in an Historical World*, trans. B. McNeil (Washington, DC: Catholic University of America Press, 2003), 165.

183. See, e.g., Karol Wojtyla, *Love and Responsibility*, trans. H. T. Willetts (New York: Farrar, Straus & Giroux, 1982, reprinted), 51–54; *VS*, 13, 48, 50, 67, 79.

184. Wojtyla, *Love and Responsibility*, 52.

185. Ibid., 41.

186. Lawler, Boyle, and May, *Catholic Sexual Ethics*, 279 n. 60.

187. Pope John Paul II developed this position in a series of general audience talks he gave from 1979 to 1981. These talks are published in a single volume, *The Theology of the Body: Human Love in the Divine Plan*, with a foreword by John S. Grabowski (Boston: Pauline Books and Media, 1997).

188. John Paul II, *Theology of the Body*, 48.

189. Ibid.

190. Ibid., 49.

191. See ibid., 48–49, 58, 69–70, 276–78, 298–99, 368–70.

192. John Paul II, *Redemptoris mater*, *AAS* 79 (1987): 20, 23.

193. John Paul II, *Mulieris dignitatem*, 26, 27, *Origins* 18 (1988): 278–80.

194. *FC*, 11; and John Paul II, *Mulieris dignitatem*, 17, 21.

195. It is important to note that the distinction between biological sex (male/female) and socially conditioned gender (masculine/feminine) is frequently absent in magisterial discussions of complementarity; see Susan A. Ross, "The Bridegroom and the Bride: The Theological Anthropology of John Paul II and Its Relation to the Bible and Homosexuality," in *Sexual Diversity and Catholicism: Toward the Development of Moral Theology*, ed. Patricia Beattie Jung with Joseph Andrew Coray (Collegeville, MN: Liturgical Press, 2001), 56 n. 5.

196. Charles E. Curran, *The Moral Theology of Pope John Paul II* (Washington, DC: Georgetown University, 2005), 190–91.

197. Ibid., 168.

198. Ibid., 191.

199. Ross, "Bridegroom and the Bride"; and David Matzko McCarthy, "The Relationship of Bodies: A Nuptial Hermeneutics of Same-sex Unions," in *Theology and Sexuality: Classic and Contemporary Readings*, ed. Eugene F. Rogers Jr. (Oxford: Blackwell, 2002), 206–10.

200. John Paul II, "Authentic Concept of Conjugal Love," *Origins* 28 (1999): 655.

201. John Paul II, "Letter to Women No. 7," *Origins* 25 (1995): 141.

202. *FC*, 19.

203. *HV*, 10; see also Pope Pius XII, "The Apostolate of the Midwife," in *The Major Addresses of Pope Pius XII, Vol. I: Selected Addresses*, ed. Vincent A. Yzermans (Saint Paul: North Central Publishing, 1961), 169.

204. John Paul II, "Letter to Women," 7.

205. See *CRP*, 4; *CCC*, 2357.

206. Pope John Paul II, "World Day of Peace" (January 1, 1995), in *The Genius of Women* (Washington: United States Catholic Conference, 1999), 3.

207. Edward Collins Vacek, "Feminism and the Vatican," *TS* 66 (2005): 173–74, referring to John Paul II, "Authentic Concept of Conjugal Love," *Origins* 28 (March 4, 1999): 655.

208. John Paul II, "Letter to Women," 7.

209. Ibid; emphasis in original. *FC*, 19. For a response to "ontological complementarity," see Kevin Kelly, *New Directions in Sexual Ethics* (London: Cassell, 1999), 51–52.

210. John Paul II, "Letter to Women," 8; John Paul II, *Mulieris dignitatem*, 6.

211. John Paul II, "Authentic Concept of Conjugal Love," 5.

212. *FC*, 32.

213. *EV*, 14.

214. *FC*, 32. Though the falsification of conjugal love specifically addresses contraception in this paragraph, according to magisterial teaching, it applies to reproductive technologies as well. See CDF, *Instruction on Respect for Human Life in Its Origin and on the Dignity of Procreation: Replies to Certain Questions of the Day* (*Donum Vitae*) (Washington, DC: United States Catholic Conference, 1987).

215. "Introduction to the Present Edition," in *Love and Responsibility*, by Wojtyla, 12.

216. John Paul II, *Theology of the Body*, 387.

217. See Ronald Modras, "Pope John Paul II's Theology of the Body," in *John Paul II and Moral Theology: Readings in Moral Theology No. 10*, ed. Charles E. Curran and Richard A. McCormick (New York: Paulist Press, 1998), 149–56.

218. See Cahill, "Catholic Sexual Ethics," 145–46; and Luke Timothy Johnson, "A Disembodied 'Theology of the Body': John Paul II on Love, Sex, and Pleasure," *Commonweal* 128, no. 2 (January 26, 2001): 11–17. Farley resurrects the so-called Methodist Quadrilateral—scripture, tradition, secular disciplines, contemporary experience—in her discussion of the sources of Christian ethics. She points out correctly that "today there is general recognition among Christian ethicists that adequate moral discernment requires attention to all four of the sources." See Margaret A Farley, *Just Love: A Framework for Christian Sexual Ethics* (New York: Continuum, 2006), 182.

219. Wojtyla, *Love and Responsibility*, 229–30.

220. Ibid., 53.

221. See also Pontifical Council for the Family, "Family, Marriage and 'De Facto' Unions," *Origins* 30, no. 30 (January 11, 2001): 8: "According to this ideology [of gender], being a man or a woman is not determined fundamentally by sex but by culture. Therefore *the very bases of the family and interpersonal relationships are attacked*" (emphasis added). Biological sex is the foundation for interpersonal relationships, according to this statement.

222. *CCC*, 2357.

223. See the subsection above titled "NNLT's Sexual Anthropology: A Critique."

224. USCCB, *Always Our Children* (Washington, DC: USCCB, 1997), 4–5; emphasis added.

225. CDF, "Vatican List of Catechism Changes," *Origins* (September 25, 1997): 257.

226. *CCC*, 2357; *CRP*, 4.

227. *CRP*, 4.

228. Lawrence A. Kurdek, "Differences between Partners from Heterosexual, Gay, and Lesbian Cohabiting Couples," *Journal of Marriage and Family* 68 (May 2006): 509–28; Lawrence A. Kurdek, "What Do We Know about Gay and Lesbian Couples?" *Current Directions in Psychological Science* 14, no. 5 (2005): 251–54; Lawrence A. Kurdek, "Lesbian and Gay Couples," in *Lesbian, Gay and Bisexual Identities over the Lifespan*, ed. Anthony R. D'Augelli and Charlotte J. Patterson (New York: Oxford University Press, 1995), 243–61; Lawrence A. Kurdek, "Are Gay and Lesbian Cohabiting Couples *Really* Different from Heterosexual Married Couples?" *Journal of Marriage and Family* 66 (2004): 880–900; Ritch C. Savin-Williams and Kristin G. Esterberg, "Lesbian, Gay, and Bisexual Families," in *Handbook of Family Diversity*, ed. David H. Demo, Katherine R. Allen, and Mark A. Fine (New York: Oxford University Press, 2000), 207–12; and P. Blumstein and P. Schwartz, *American Couples: Money, Work, Sex* (New York: Morrow, 1983).

229. Margaret A. Farley, "An Ethic for Same-Sex Relations," in *Challenge to Love*, ed. Nugent, 99–100.

230. See *GS*, 48–50; *Code of Canon Law*, can. 1055, 1; Lawler, *Marriage in the Catholic Church*, 27–42.

231. Franz Böckle, "Nature as the Basis of Morality," in *Personalist Morals: Essays in Honor of Professor Louis Janssens*, ed. Joseph A. Selling (Leuven: Leuven University Press), 58.

232. See Grisez, *LCL*, 564.

233. Joseph A. Selling, "The Development of Catholic Tradition and Sexual Morality," in *Embracing Sexuality: Authority and Experience in the Catholic Church*, ed. Joseph A. Selling (Aldershot, U.K.: Ashgate, 2001), 152.

Notes to Chapter Three

1. Germain Grisez, *LCL*, 506–19.

2. Joseph A. Selling, "The Development of Catholic Tradition and Sexual Morality," in *Embracing Sexuality: Authority and Experience in the Catholic Church*, ed. Joseph A. Selling (Aldershot, U.K.: Ashgate, 2001), 152.

3. Ibid., 153.

4. Karl Rahner, *Foundations of Christian Faith* (New York: Seabury Press, 1978), 94; emphasis in original.

5. See Karl Rahner, "Reflections on the Unity of the Love of Neighbour and the Love of God," in *Theological Investigations*, vol. 6, trans. Karl-H. Kruger and Boniface Kruger (London: Darton, Longman & Todd, 1974), 231–49.

6. Ronald Modras, "The Implications of Rahner's Anthropology for Fundamental Moral Theology," *Horizons* 12 (1985): 74.

7. See Josef Fuchs, *Human Values and Christian Morality* (Dublin: Gill and Macmillan, 1970), 92–111; and Josef Fuchs, *Christian Morality: The Word Becomes Flesh* (Washington, DC: Georgetown University Press, 1987), 3–133.

8. *PH*, 10.

9. John Paul II, *VS*, 71.

10. Charles E. Curran, *The Catholic Moral Tradition: A Synthesis* (Washington, DC: Georgetown University Press, 1999), 97.

11. Karl Rahner, "Some Thoughts on 'A Good Intention,'" in *Theological Investigations*, vol. 3, trans. Karl-H. Kruger and Boniface Kruger (London: Darton, Longman & Todd, 1967), 113. See Modras, "Implications," 86; and Richard A. McCormick, *Critical Calling: Reflections on Moral Dilemmas since Vatican II* (Washington, DC: Georgetown University Press, 1999), 173.

12. Rahner, *Foundations of Christian Faith*, 95. For an analysis of transcendental freedom, see 93–97.

13. Ibid., 37; emphases in original.

14. See Modras, "Implications," 82.

15. Rahner, "Basic Observations on the Subject of Changeable and Unchangeable Factors in the Church," in *Theological Investigations*, vol. 14 (New York: Seabury Press, 1976), 14.

16. Rahner, *Foundations of Christian Faith*, 39–41.

17. See Titus F. Guenther, *Rahner and Metz: Transcendental Theology as Political Theology* (Lanham, MD: University Press of America, 1994).

18. Curran, *Catholic Moral Tradition*, 97.

19. Richard McCormick, *How Brave a New World? Dilemmas in Bioethics* (Garden City, NY: Doubleday, 1981), 5; Richard McCormick, "Theology and Biomedical Ethics," *Logos* 3 (1982): 27; Richard McCormick, "A Commentary on the Commentaries," in *Doing Evil to Achieve Good: Moral Choice in Conflict Situations*, ed. Richard McCormick and Paul Ramsey (Chicago: Loyola University Press, 1978), 251–52.

20. See, e.g., Bernard Hoose, "Basic Goods: Continuing the Debate," *Heythrop Journal* 35 (1994): 58. Hoose refers to the basic goods as they are used in NNLT as "Platonic Ideas."

21. McCormick, *Critical Calling*, 230.

22. Norbert Rigali, SJ, "Christian Morality and Universal Morality: The One and the Many," *Louvain Studies* 19 (1994): 29.

23. Ibid., 32.

24. McCormick, "Ambiguity in Moral Choice," in *Doing Evil to Achieve Good*, ed. McCormick and Ramsey, 42–44.

25. See Michael G. Lawler, *What Is and What Ought to Be: The Dialectic of Experience, Theology and Church* (New York: Continuum, 2005), 10–14.

26. This dialectic is worked out extensively by Peter L. Berger and Thomas Luckman, *The Social Construction of Reality* (New York: Anchor Books, 1967). See also Lawler, *What Is and What Ought to Be*, 8–16.

27. E.g., in *Tertio millennio adveniente*, Pope John Paul II proposes "reducing substantially, if not canceling outright, the international debt which seriously threatens the future of many nations"; *Origins* 24, no. 24 (November 24, 1994): 51, 414.

28. See Lawler, *What Is and What Ought to Be*.

29. On the biological, genetic, and environmental sources of sexual orientation, see Magnus Hirschfeld, *The Homosexuality of Men and Women*, trans. Michael A. Lombardi-Nash (New York: Prometheus Books, 2000). This book was originally published in 1914. It is listed here because it is "the most comprehensive study of homosexuality in the first half of the twentieth century" and because "many a scholar has cribbed from [Hirschfeld] without giving him credit or even without realizing that the data came from him"; Vern L. Bullough, in the Introduction, 17. See also Simon LeVay, "A Difference in Hypothalamic Structure between Heterosexual and Homosexual Men," *Science* 253 (1991): 1034–37; J. Michael Bailey and Richard C. Pillard, "A Genetic Study of Male Sex Orientation," *Archives of General Psychiatry* 48 (1991): 1089–96; Simon LeVay, *The Sexual Brain* (Cambridge: MA: MIT Press), 1993; Dean H. Hamer, S. Hu, V. L. Magnuson, and S. Pattatucci, "A Linkage between DNA Markers on the X-Chromosome and Male Sexual Orientation," *Science* 261 (1993): 321–27; J. Michael Bailey, Richard C. Pillard, M. C. Neale, and Y. Agyei, "Heritable Factors Influence Sexual Orientation in Women," *Archives of General Psychiatry* 50 (1993): 217–23; Dean Hamer and Peter Copeland, *The Science of Desire: The Search for the Gay Gene and the Biology of Behavior* (New York: Simon & Schuster, 1994); B. A. Gladue, "The Biopsychology of Sexual Orientation," *Current Directions in Psychological Science* 3 (1994): 150–54; John Corvino, ed., *Same Sex: Debating the Ethics, Science, and Culture of Homosexuality* (Lanham, MD: Rowman & Littlefield, 1997); Timothy F. Murphy, *Gay Science: The Ethics of Sexual Orientation Research* (New York: Columbia University Press, 1997); Charlotte J. Patterson and Anthony R. D'Augelli, eds., *Lesbian, Gay, and Bisexual Identities in Families: Psychological Perspectives* (New York: Oxford University Press, 1998); W. Byrne, S. Tobet, L. A. Mattiace, M. S. Lasco, and E. Kemether, "The Interstitial Nuclei of the Human Anterior Hypothalamus: An Investigation of Variation with Sex, Sexual Orientation, and HIV Status," *Hormones and Behavior* 40 (2001): 86–92 (this is a replication of LeVay's 1991 study above; it found the same difference between heterosexual and homosexual men but in smaller degree); and S. LeVay and S. M. Valente, *Human Sexuality, Second Edition* (Sunderland, MA: Sinauer, 2006), esp. 151–86, 217–52.

30. Pope John Paul II, "The Fabric of Relations among People," *Origins* 25, no. 18 (October 19, 1995): 10, 297.

31. *GS*, 48.

32. Ibid., 51.

33. Louis Janssens, "Artificial Insemination: Ethical Considerations," *Louvain Studies* 8 (1980): 4.

34. Ibid., 5–13.

35. Lisa Sowle Cahill, *Sex, Gender, and Christian Ethics* (Cambridge: Cambridge University Press, 1996), 233; "Catholic Sexual Ethics and the Dignity of the Person: A Double Message," *TS* 50 (1989): 147.

36. McCormick, *How Brave a New World?*, 5; McCormick, "Commentary on the Commentaries," 251–52.

37. McCormick, *Critical Calling*, 306.

38. Cristina L. H. Traina, *Feminist Ethics and Natural Law: The End of the Anathemas* (Washington, DC: Georgetown University Press, 1999), 218–19. See McCormick, "Human Significance," in *Norms and Context in Christian Ethics*, ed. Gene H. Outka and Paul Ramsey (New York: Charles Scribner's Sons, 1968), 249.

39. McCormick, *Critical Calling*, 341.

40. Ibid., 341–42.

41. Ibid., 343.

42. Ibid.

43. Ibid, 341.

44. Janssens, "Artificial Insemination," 25–29.

45. McCormick, *Critical Calling*, 341.

46. Richard McCormick, *Notes on Moral Theology, 1981 through 1984* (Lanham, MD: University Press of America, 1984), 11, citing Lisa Sowle Cahill, "Moral Methodology: A Case Study," in *A Challenge to Love*, ed. Robert Nugent (New York: Crossroad, 1983), 91; emphasis added.

47. McCormick, *Critical Calling*, 312.

48. CDF, "Vatican List of Catechism Changes," *Origins*, September 25, 1997, 257.

49. *PH*, 1.

50. McCormick, *Critical Calling*, 310.

51. Ibid., 311.

52. *PH*, 8.

53. McCormick, *Critical Calling*, 309.

54. *PH*, 8; United States Conference of Catholic Bishops, *Always Our Children* (Washington, DC: United States Conference of Catholic Bishops, 1997), 6.

55. See McCormick, "Human Significance," 247–61; McCormick, *Notes on Moral Theology*, 181–82.

56. *PH*, 1.

57. Traina, *Feminist Ethics and Natural Law*, 217. This critique applies to Cahill's treatment of homosexuality as well ("Moral Methodology: A Case Study," 87–88). See also James F. Keenan, "The Open Debate: Moral Theology and the Lives of Gay and Lesbian Persons," *TS* 64 (2003): 134–37.

58. Margaret A. Farley, "Feminism and Universal Morality," in *Prospects for a Common Morality*, ed. Gene Outka and John P. Reeder Jr. (Princeton, NJ: Princeton University Press, 1993), 171.

59. See Gustavo Gutierrez, *A Theology of Liberation*, 2nd ed. (Maryknoll, NY: Orbis Books, 1988); Michael E. Allsopp, *Renewing Christian Ethics: The Catholic Tradition* (Scranton: University of Scranton Press, 2005), 73–106; and various essays in *Feminist Ethics and the Catholic Moral Tradition: Readings in Moral Theology No. 9*, ed. Charles E. Curran, Margaret E. Farley, and Richard A. McCormick (New York: Paulist Press, 1996).

60. See Traina, *Feminist Ethics and Natural Law*, 102–6; 317; Albert R. Jonsen and Stephen Toulmin, *The Abuse of Casuistry: A History of Moral Reasoning* (Berkeley: University of California Press, 1988); and James F. Keenan and Thomas A. Shannon, eds., *The Context of Casuistry* (Washington, DC: Georgetown University Press, 1995).

61. Traina, *Feminist Ethics and Natural Law*, 315–16.

62. Ibid., 315–19.

63. Cahill, *Sex, Gender, and Christian Ethics*, 1.

64. Ibid., 13.

65. Ibid., 54.

66. Ibid., 51.

67. Ibid., 55.

68. Martha Nussbaum, "Introduction," in *The Quality of Life*, ed. Martha Nussbaum and Amartya Sen (Oxford: Clarendon Press, 1993), 4. See Lisa Sowle Cahill, "Feminist Ethics, Differences, and Common Ground: A Catholic Perspective," in *Feminist Ethics and the Catholic Moral Tradition*, ed. Curran, Farley, and McCormick, 195; and Cahill, *Sex, Gender, and Christian Ethics*, 55–61.

69. Cahill, "Feminist Ethics, Differences, and Common Ground," 196–97; and Cahill, *Sex, Gender, and Christian Ethics*, 59.

70. Cahill, *Sex, Gender, and Christian Ethics*, 59.

71. See Farley, "Feminism and Universal Morality," 181–85.

72. Cahill, *Sex, Gender, and Christian Ethics*, 10.

73. See Susan Parsons, *Feminism and Christian Ethics* (Cambridge: Cambridge University Press, 1996); and Lisa Sowle Cahill, "Gender and Christian Ethics," in *The Cambridge Companion to Christian Ethics*, ed. Robin Gill (Cambridge: University Press, 2001), 121–22.

74. *MD*, 6; emphases in original.

75. *FC*, 22; *MD*, 16; John Paul II, "Letter to Women No. 7," *Origins* 25 (1995): 4. See Charles Curran's explanation and critique of John Paul II's position on the dignity and equality of women in *The Moral Theology of Pope John Paul II* (Washington, DC: Georgetown University Press, 2005), 187–95.

76. *FC*, 23.

77. John Paul II, *Ordinatio sacerdotalis*, 1; *MD*, 26. These arguments based on maleness were first articulated by the CDF in "*Inter Insigniores*" (Declaration on the Question of the Admission of Women to the Ministerial Priesthood), *AAS* (1977): 99–116.

78. Michael Novak, "Women, Ordination and Angels," *First Things* 32 (April 1993): 32; cited by James F. Keenan, "Current Theology Note: Christian Perspectives on the Human Body," *TS* 55 (1994): 345.

79. *MD*, 10.

80. Curran, *Moral Theology of Pope John Paul II*, 193.

81. Cahill, *Sex, Gender, and Christian Ethics*, 89.

82. Ibid., 97–102, 156–60.

83. Cahill, "Moral Methodology," 88. Even though Cahill claims the homosexual orientation is nonnormative, and though she does not posit "a negative moral judgment on homosexual persons, on their potential for praiseworthy relationships, nor necessarily on homosexual acts" (p. 90), labeling such acts premorally evil (p. 91) seems to carry a pejorative connotation for homosexual orientation.

84. Anthony Kosnik, W. Carroll, A. Cunningham, R. Modras, and J. Schulte, *Human Sexuality: New Directions in American Catholic Thought* (New York: Paulist Press, 1977), 2;

Peter Brown, *The Body and Society: Men, Women and Sexual Renunciation in Early Christianity* (New York: Columbia University Press, 1988; Susan Parsons, "Feminist Ethics," in *Christian Ethics: An Introduction*, ed. Bernard Hoose (Collegeville, MN: Liturgical Press, 1998), 140.

85. See James F. Keenan, "Christian Perspectives on the Human Body," *TS* 55 (1994): 330–46.

86. A. Kinsey, W. Pomeroy, C. Martin, and P. Gebhard, *Sexual Behavior in the Human Female* (Philadelphia: Saunders, 1953), 163–64, 391; cited by Christine E. Gudorf, *Body, Sex, and Pleasure: Reconstructing Christian Sexual Ethics* (Cleveland: Pilgrim Press, 1994), 31.

87. Gudorf, *Body, Sex, and Pleasure*.

88. Parsons, "Feminist Ethics," 139.

89. Brett Wilbur, "Health and Fitness: We Are Not Barbie," www.montereycounty weekly.com/issues/Issue.01–20–2005/cover/Article.cover_feature_1.

90. See Don Olcott Jr. and Darcy W. Hardy, eds., *Dancing on the Glass Ceiling: Women, Leadership, and Technology* (Madison, WI: Atwood, 2006); Ann M. Morrison, *Breaking the Glass Ceiling: Can Women Reach the Top of America's Largest Corporations?* (Reading, MA: Addison-Wesley, 1994); and Federal Glass Ceiling Commission, "The Glass Ceiling: The Findings and Recommendations of the Federal Glass Ceiling Commission," www.inmotion magazine.com/glass.html.

91. James F. Keenan, "Virtue Ethics and Sexual Ethics," *Louvain Studies* 30 (2005): 186.

92. Alasdair MacIntyre, *After Virtue: A Study in Moral Theory* (Notre Dame, IN: University of Notre Dame Press, 1988). For a historical overview of virtue ethics, see Jean Porter, "Virtue Ethics," in *Cambridge Companion to Christian Ethics*, ed. Gill, 96–111.

93. Keenan, "Virtue Ethics and Sexual Ethics," 187.

94. In this section, we are indebted to James F. Keenan's work on virtue ethics. See James F. Keenan, "Proposing Cardinal Virtues," *TS* 56 (1995): 709–29; James F. Keenan, *Virtues for Ordinary Christians* (Kansas City: Sheed and Ward, 1996); and Keenan, "Virtue Ethics and Sexual Ethics," 180–97.

95. Anne E. Patrick, *Liberating Conscience: Feminist Explorations in Catholic Moral Theology* (New York: Continuum, 1996), 76–80.

96. Ibid., 77.

97. Martin Rhonheimer, *Natural Law and Practical Reason: A Thomist View of Moral Autonomy*, trans. G. Malsbary (New York: Fordham University Press, 2000); John S. Grabowski, *Sex and Virtue: An Introduction to Sexual Ethics* (Washington, DC: Catholic University Press of America, 2003).

98. *CCC*, 2337.

99. See *PH*, 10.

100. See *CCC*, 2351–57.

101. Patrick, *Liberating Conscience*, 79.

102. Rhonheimer and Grabowski have attempted this on the traditionalist side. However, Grabowski's comment regarding Cahill's work on a virtue-based approach to human sexuality sums up well a primary ecclesiological consideration guiding traditionalist virtue approaches: "An overall difficulty with [Cahill's] works is that [her] revisionist commitments place her at odds with the Church's tradition and teaching on issues such as the morality of contraception, homogenital sex, and reproductive technologies" (Grabowski, *Sex and Virtue*, xiii n. 14). This tells us much about Grabowski's ecclesiology, but it leaves open the question concerning moral methodology and virtue ethics.

103. Keenan, "Virtue Ethics and Sexual Ethics," 192.

Notes to Chapter Four

1. United States Conference of Catholic Bishops (USCCB), *Always Our Children* (Washington, DC: USCCB, 1997), 3.

2. *GS*, 49.

3. USCCB, *Human Sexuality: A Catholic Perspective for Education and Lifelong Learning* (Washington, DC: USCCB, 1991), 9.

4. Simon LeVay and Sharon M. Valente, *Human Sexuality* (Sunderland, MA: Sinauer Associates, 2006); LeVay and Curt Freed, *Healing the Brain* (New York: Times Books, 2002); Simon LeVay, *The Sexual Brain* (Cambridge, MA: MIT Press, 1995). See also *PH*, 1.

5. See Charles A. Gallagher, G. A. Maloney, M. F. Rousseau, and Paul F. Wirczak, *Embodied in Love: Sacramental Spirituality and Sexual Intimacy* (New York: Crossroad, 1985), 21–37.

6. Tom W. Smith, *American Sexual Behavior: Trends, Socio-Demographic Differences, and Risk Behavior* (Chicago: University of Chicago), 74; www.norc.uchicago.edu/issues/American_Sexual_Behavior_2003.

7. 1 Cor 7:3–5; *GS*, 51.

8. Aristotle, *Generation of Animals*, I, 21, 729b. For greater detail, see also Paige duBois, *Sowing the Body: Psychoanalysis and Ancient Representations of Women* (Chicago: University of Chicago Press, 1988), 39–85; Sirach 26:19; *Mishna*, Ketuboth, 1, 6; Carol Delaney, *The Seed and the Soil: Gender and Cosmology in Turkish Village Society* (Berkeley: University of California Press, 1991).

9. Diogenes Laertius, *Lives of Eminent Philosophers*, VIII, 1, 9.

10. Aristotle, *Problems*, IV, 9, 877b.

11. Michel Foucault, *The History of Sexuality*, vol. 1, trans. Robert Hurley (New York: Vintage Books, 1990), 105.

12. These thoughts on Genesis 2:24 are developed from the section "Peneter-Etre Penetrer," in Xavier Lacroix, *Le Corps de chair: Les dimensions éthiques, esthétiques, et spirituelles de l'amour* (Paris: Cerf, 1992), 111–14.

13. F. R. Barry, *A Philosophy from Prison* (London: SCM, 1926), 151.

14. Gen 1–3.

15. Michel Foucault, *L'Usage des plaisirs* (Paris: Gallimard, 1984), 142.

16. W. H. Masters and Virginia E. Johnson, *Human Sexual Response* (Boston: Little, Brown, 1966), 3–8.

17. June M. Reinisch and Ruth Beasley, *The Kinsey Institute New Report on Sex: What You Must Know to Be Sexually Literate* (New York: St. Martin's Press, 1990), 84.

18. Michel Foucault, *The Care of the Self. History of Sexuality*, vol. 3, trans. Robert Hurley (New York: Vintage Books, 1988), 182–83.

19. Thomas Aquinas, *ST*, III (Suppl.), 41, 3 ad 6.

20. Ibid., corp.; cp. Thomas Aquinas, *Contra Gentiles*, 3, 126.

21. Aquinas, *ST*, III (Suppl.), 41, 3 ad 1.

22. Ibid., 41, 4; 49, 5.

23. Aquinas, *ST*, II–II, 142, 1.

24. E.C. Messenger, *Two in One Flesh: The Mystery of Sex in Marriage* (London: Sands, 1948), 178–179.

25. Augustine, *De bono coniugali*, *PL* 40, 16, 18.

26. For an investigation of pleasure as an essential component of human sexuality, see Christine E. Gudorf, *Body, Sex, and Pleasure: Reconstructing Christian Social Ethics* (Cleveland: Pilgrim Press, 1995).

27. In this section, we are indebted to the excellent essay by Jack Dominian, "Sexuality and Interpersonal Relationships," in *Embracing Sexuality: Authority and Experience in the Catholic Church*, ed. Joseph A. Selling (Burlington, VT: Ashgate, 2001), 12–15.

28. See Michael G. Lawler, *Marriage and Sacrament: A Theology of Christian Marriage* (Collegeville, MN: Liturgical Press, 1993); and *Marriage in the Catholic Church: Disputed Questions (*Collegeville, MN: Liturgical Press, 2002), 1–26.

29. Ernst Cassirer, *An Essay on Man: An Introduction to Philosophy* (New Haven: Yale University Press, 1944), 36.

30. Paul Ricoeur, *The Symbolism of Evil*, trans. Emerson Buchanan (New York: Harper & Row, 1967), 15.

31. Dominian, "Sexuality and Interpersonal Relationships," 20.

32. Ibid., 13.

33. See Lawler, *Marriage and Sacrament*, 52–56.

34. The connection of marriage and Eucharist is beautifully developed in Germain Martinez, *Worship: Wedding to Marriage* (Washington, DC: Pastoral Press, 1993).

35. Luke 22:19.

36. Adrian Thatcher, *Liberating Sex: A Christian Sexual Theology* (London: SPCK, 1993), 89.

37. For the Catholic preference of celibacy/virginity over marriage, see the encyclical letter of Pius XII, *Sacra Viginitas*, *AAS* 46 (1954): 174f.; also the Apostolic Exhortation of John Paul II, *Familiaris Consortio*, *AAS* 74 (1982): 98–99.

38. *LG*, 39–42.

39. Gen 1:26–27.

40. Cited by Robert Williams, "Toward a Theology for Gay and Lesbian Marriage," in *Christian Perspectives on Sexuality and Gender*, ed. Adrian Thatcher and Elizabeth Stuart (Grand Rapids: Eerdmans, 1996), 297.

41. USCCB, *Human Sexuality*, 10.

42. Gallagher, *Embodied in Love*, 108; emphasis in original.

43. USCCB, *Human Sexuality*, 9.

44. J. Paul Sampley, *And the Two Shall Become One Flesh: A Study of Traditions in Ephesians 5:21–33* (Cambridge: Cambridge University Press, 1971), 30.

45. See *CCC*, Can. 1055, 1.

46. *CCC*, 2207.

47. *FC*, 21.

48. Matt 5:43–48.

49. See Maura Ryan, *Ethics and Economics of Assisted Reproduction: The Cost of Longing* (Washington, DC: Georgetown University Press, 2001), 134.

50. Mark D. Jordan, *The Silence of Sodom: Homosexuality in Modern Catholicism* (Chicago: University of Chicago Press, 2000), 74.

51. *CCC*, 2538.

52. James F. Keenan, SJ, "The Open Debate: Moral Theology and the Lives of Gay and Lesbian Persons," *TS* 1, no. 64 (2003): 146.

53. *CCC*, 2337.

54. *CCC*, 2358; USCCB, *Always Our Children*, 5.

55. *CCC*, 2359.

56. See *LG*, 12, 34. See also Leo J. O'Donovan, *A World of Grace: An Introduction to the Themes and Foundations of Karl Rahner's Theology* (New York: Seabury, 1980) and Thomas F. O'Meara, *Loose in the World* (New York: Paulist Press, 1974).

57. Joseph A. Selling, "Gaudium et Spes, A Manifesto for Contemporary Moral Theology," in *Vatican II and Its Legacy*, ed. M. Lamberigts and L. Kenis (Leuven: Leuven University Press, 2002), 145–62.

58. *GS*, 49; emphasis added.

59. Commissio Pontificia Codici Iuris Canonici Recognoscendo, "De Matrimonio," *Communicationes* 5 (1973): 79.

60. *Code of Canon Law*, Can. 1061, 1.

61. John P. Beal, James A. Coriden, and Thomas J. Green, eds., *New Commentary on the Code of Canon Law* (New York: Paulist Press, 2000), 1258; James A. Coriden, Thomas J. Green, and Donald E. Heintschel, eds., *The Code of Canon Law: A Text and Commentary* (New York: Paulist Press, 1985), 745.

62. Beal, Coriden, and Green, *New Commentary on the Code*, 1364.

63. *CRP*, 7.

64. *FC*, 19. In this passage, Pope John Paul II speaks of a "natural complementarity."

65. *CRP*, 3.

66. *Code of Canon Law*, Can. 1084, 1.

67. *CRP*, 3.

68. *HV*, 10; see also Pope Pius XII, "The Apostolate of the Midwife," in *The Major Addresses of Pope Pius XII*, ed. Vincent A. Yzermans, vol. 1, *Selected Addresses* (Saint Paul: North Central Publishing, 1961), 169.

69. *HV*, 11.

70. Thomas Aquinas, *Summa contra Gentiles* 3, 122.

71. Gareth Moore, *The Body in Context: Sex and Catholicism*, Contemporary Christian Insights (New York: Continuum, 2001), 162.

72. Andrew Koppleman, "Natural Law (New)," in *Sex from Plato to Paglia: A Philosophical Encyclopedia*, ed. Alan Soble (Westport, CT: Greenwood Press, 2006), II:708.

73. James P. Hanigan, "Unitive and Procreative Meaning: The Inseparable Link," in *Sexual Diversity and Catholicism: Toward the Development of Moral Theology*, ed. Patricia Beattie Jung with Joseph Andrew Coray (Collegeville, MN: Liturgical Press, 2001), 33. For a critique of Hanigan's earlier work, *Homosexuality: The Test Case for Christian Sexual Ethics* (New York: Paulist Press, 1988), see Robert Nugent and Jeannine Gramick, *Building Bridges: Gay & Lesbian Reality and the Catholic Church* (Mystic, CT: Twenty-Third Publications, 1992), 172–83.

74. Hanigan, "Unitive and Procreative Meaning," 35.

75. Ibid., 30; emphasis added.

76. Moore, *Body in Context*, 200–1.

77. David Matzko McCarthy, "The Relationship of Bodies: A Nuptial Hermeneutics of Same-Sex Unions," in *Theology and Sexuality: Classic and Contemporary Readings*, ed. Eugene F. Rogers Jr. (Oxford: Blackwell, 2002), 201.

78. Ibid., 210.

79. Ibid., 212.

80. USCCB, *Always Our Children*, 4–5; *PH*, 8.

81. CDF, "Letter to the Bishops of the Catholic Church on the Pastoral Care of Homosexual Persons," 5, AAS 79 (1987): 3; CDF, "Vatican List of Catechism Changes," *Origins* 27 (1997): 257.

82. CCE, *Educational Guidance in Human Love: Outlines for Sex Education* (hereafter, *EGHL*) (Rome: Typis Polyglottis Vaticanis, 1983), 35.

83. McCarthy, "Relationship of Bodies," 212–13; emphasis added.

84. Ibid., 213.

85. We will address "orientation complementarity" in more detail below.

86. *CRP*, 3.

87. Ibid., 4; *CCC*, 2357.

88. *FC*, 19.

89. John Paul II, "Letter to Women No. 7," *Origins* 25 (1995): 7.

90. *EGHL*, 35.

91. John Paul II, *Women: Teachers of Peace*, 3, Message of His Holiness Pope John Paul II for the XXVIII World Day of Peace (January 1, 1995), www.vatican.va/holy_father/ john_paul_ii/messages/peace/documents/hf ejp-ii_mes_08121994_xxviii-world-day-for-peace_en.html.

92. Christine E. Gudorf, "Encountering the Other: The Modern Papacy on Women," in *Feminist Ethics and the Catholic Moral Tradition, Readings in Moral Theology No. 9*, ed. Charles E. Curran, Margaret A. Farley, and Richard A. McCormick (New York: Paulist Press, 1996), 75; Charles E. Curran, *The Moral Theology of Pope John Paul II* (Washington, DC: Georgetown University Press, 2005), 192–93.

93. Edward Collins Vacek, "Feminism and the Vatican," *TS* 66 (2005): 173–74, referring to John Paul II, "Authentic Concept of Conjugal Love," *Origins* 28 (1999): 655.

94. John Paul II, "Letter to Women," 7.

95. Ibid.; emphasis in original. *FC*, 19.

96. Kevin Kelly, *New Directions in Sexual Ethics* (London: Cassell, 1999), 51. He goes on (p. 52) to critique ontological complementarity as ultimately "oppressive and deterministic."

97. John Paul II, "Letter to Women," 8; *MD*, 6.

98. John Paul II, "Authentic Concept of Conjugal Love," 5.

99. *FC*, 19.

100. John Paul II, "Authentic Concept of Conjugal Love," 5.

101. John Paul II, "Letter to Women," 7–8.

102. Moore, *Body in Context*, 121–27.

103. See *FC*, 23; John Paul II, "Letter to Women," 9; *MD*, 18; and *Women: Teachers of Peace*.

104. Cristina L. H. Traina, "Papal Ideals, Marital Realities: One View from the Ground," in *Sexual Diversity and Catholicism*, 280–82.

105. See Elaine L. Graham, *Making the Difference: Gender, Personhood, and Theology* (Minneapolis: Fortress Press, 1996); Margaret A. Farley, *Just Love: A Framework for Christian Sexual Ethics* (New York: Continuum, 2006), 156–57.

106. See Traina, "Papal Ideals," 281.

107. Ibid., 282.

108. *CRP*, 7.

109. For a review of these data, see Osnat Erel and Bonnie Burman, "Interrelatedness of Marital Relations and Parent-Child Relations: A Meta-Analytic Review," *Psychological Bulletin* 118 (1995): 108–32; Paul R. Amato and Alan Booth, *A Generation at Risk: Growing Up*

in an Era of Family Upheaval (Cambridge, MA: Harvard University Press, 1997), 67–83; Stacy J. Rogers and Lynn K. White, "Satisfaction with Parenting: The Role of Marital Happiness, Family Structure, and Parents' Gender," *Journal of Marriage and Family* 60 (1998): 293–316; and David H. Demo and Martha J. Cox, "Families with Young Children: A Review of the Research in the 1990s," *Journal of Marriage and Family* 62 (2000): 876–900.

110. *CCC*, 2357.

111. *EGHL*, 4.

112. *PH*, 1; emphasis added.

113. See the subsection in chapter 2 titled "NNLT's Sexual Anthropology: A Critique."

114. Robert Nugent, "Sexual Orientation in Vatican Thinking," in *The Vatican and Homosexuality: Reactions to the "Letter to the Bishops of the Catholic Church on the Pastoral Care of Homosexual Persons,"* ed. Jeannine Gramick and Pat Furey (New York: Crossroad, 1988), 55.

115. See William Paul, J. Weinreich, J. Gonsioerek, and M. E. Motvedt, eds., *Homosexuality: Social, Psychological, and Biological Issues* (Beverly Hills, CA: Sage, 1982); Pim Pronk, *Against Nature? Types of Moral Argumentation Regarding Homosexuality* (Grand Rapids: Eerdmans, 1993); Richard C. Pillard and J. Michael Bailey, "A Biological Perspective on Sexual Orientation," *Clinical Sexuality* 18 (1995): 1–14; Lee Ellis and Linda Ebertz, *Sexual Orientation: Toward Biological Understanding* (Westport, CT: Praeger, 1997); and Richard C. Friedman and Jennifer I. Downey, *Sexual Orientation and Psychoanalysis: Sexual Science and Clinical Practice* (New York: Columbia University Press, 2002). Robert L. Spitzer, "Can Some Gay Men and Lesbians Change Their Sexual Orientation? 200 Participants Reporting a Change from Homosexual to Heterosexual Orientation," *Archives of Sexual Behavior* 32 (2003): 403–17, presents a contrary and minority perspective.

116. CDF, "Vatican List of Catechism Changes," *Origins* 27 (1997): 257.

117. *CCC*, 2357; *CRP*, 4.

118. See *GS*, 48–50; *CCC*, Can. 1055, 1; Michael G. Lawler, *Marriage in the Catholic Church: Disputed Questions* (Collegeville, MN: Liturgical Press, 2002), 27–42.

119. Though it is beyond the scope of this chapter, as in the Magisterium's model, *how* these elements complement one another in a "truly human sexual act," heterosexual or homosexual, needs to be more fully developed.

120. Though we recognize the reality of bisexual persons, focus and space do not allow us to address this orientation in detail.

121. *PH*, 9.

122. Thomas Aquinas, *De malo* 15.1c.

123. Moore, *Body in Context*, 81.

124. See Aristotle, *Generation of Animals*, I, 21, 729b. For greater detail, see also Paige duBois, *Sowing the Body: Psychoanalysis and Ancient Representations of Women* (Chicago: University of Chicago Press, 1988), 39–85; Sirach 26:19; *Mishna*, Ketuboth, 1, 6; Carol Delaney, *The Seed and the Soil: Gender and Cosmology in Turkish Village Society* (Berkeley: University of California Press, 1991).

125. Joseph Ratzinger, "The Transmission of Divine Revelation," in *Commentary on the Documents of Vatican II*, vol. 3, ed. Herbert Vorgrimler (New York: Herder and Herder, 1969), 185.

126. Moore, *Body in Context*, 64–91. We are indebted to Moore's overall treatment of the purpose of sexual organs in this section.

127. *FC*, 11.

128. Stephen J. Pope, "Scientific and Natural Law Analyses of Homosexuality: A Methodological Study," *Journal of Religious Ethics* 25 (1997): 111.

129. Margaret Farley, "An Ethic for Same-Sex Relations," in *A Challenge to Love: Gay and Lesbian Catholics in the Church*, ed. Robert Nugent (New York: Crossroad, 1983), 100.

130. See Aquinas, *ST*, I–II, 28, 1c.

131. Ibid., II–II, 58, 1.

132. Ibid., I, 4, 1, 1344a.

133. We advise the reader that the original draft for this chapter was completed before Farley's beautiful book *Just Love* became available to us. We are affirmed that both the importance we assign to just love and our analysis of it are matched in general and independently by Farley. See Farley, *Just Love*, esp. 200–6.

134. See Gen 5:1.

135. *Nicomachean Ethics*, 8, 2; see Aquinas, *ST*, II–II, q. 23, a. 1c.

136. For a fuller development of this point, see Michael G. Lawler, *Family: American and Christian* (Chicago: Loyola University Press, 1998), 166–74.

137. See the subsection above titled "Chastity."

138. The formal criteria listed for what constitutes a morally right or wrong truly human sexual act, though not the specific acts themselves, are common in magisterial and moral theological discourse.

139. See Alasdair MacIntyre, *After Virtue: A Study in Moral Theory* (Notre Dame, IN: University of Notre Dame Press, 1981); Martha Nussbaum, *The Fragility of Goodness: Luck and Ethics in Greek Tragedy and Philosophy* (New York: Cambridge University, 1988); Martha Nussbaum, "Non-Relative Virtues: An Aristotelian Approach," in *Ethical Theory: Character and Virtue*, ed. Peter A. French, Theodore E. Uehling, Jr., and Howard K. Wettstein (Notre Dame, IN: University of Notre Dame Press, 1988), 32–53; James F. Keenan, "Proposing Cardinal Virtues," *TS* 56 (1995): 709–29; James F. Keenan, *Virtues for Ordinary Christians* (Kansas City: Sheed & Ward, 1996); and James F. Keenan, "Virtue Ethics and Sexual Ethics," *Louvain Studies* 30 (2005): 180–97.

140. See Matt 5:43–48.

141. Farley, "Ethic for Same-Sex Relations," 105.

Notes to Chapter Five

1. This teaching is a conclusion from the universal Catholic teaching that continence or virginity is better than marriage. Pius followed Augustine, who had taught that virginity is better than marriage (*De bono coniugali*, III, 3, in *PL* 40, 375) and that, even in marriage, "in these days no one perfect in piety seeks to have children other than spiritually" (ibid., XVII, 19, in *PL* 40, 387). The Council of Trent taught the same thing. See *Catechism of the Council of Trent for Parish Priests,* trans. John A. McHugh and Charles J. Callan (New York: Wagner, 1945), 338, 343.

2. *AAS* 43 (1951), 835–54. John Paul II taught the same thing in *FC*, 32.

3. Germain Grisez, *LCL*, 636; see Robert P. George and Gerard V. Bradley, "Marriage and the Liberal Imagination," *Georgetown Law Journal* 84/261 (1995), 301–2, 302 n. 5, 305–6.

4. John Finnis, "Law, Morality, and 'Sexual Orientation,'" *Notre Dame Law Review* 69, no. 5 (1994): 1067; see also George and Bradley, "Marriage," 303–13.

5. Finnis, "Law," 1066.

6. Ibid.

7. George and Bradley, "Marriage," 301–2; emphasis added.

8. Ibid., 302.

9. F. R. Barry, *A Philosophy from Prison* (London: SCM Press, 1926), 151.

10. Finnis, "Law," 1066; emphasis added.

11. Gratian, *Decretum Gratiani*, pars ii, causa XXVII, q. 2, cap. 34, in *PL* 187, 1406.

12. *Code of Canon Law* (1983), Can. 1061, 1.

13. Ibid., Can. 1141.

14. *GS*, 48.

15. See Theodore Mackin, *What Is Marriage?* (New York: Paulist Press, 1982), 29–33, 158–64; Michael G. Lawler, *Marriage in the Catholic Church: Disputed Questions* (Collegeville, MN: Liturgical Press, 2002), 77–85.

16. See Lawler, *Marriage in the Catholic Church*, 1–26.

17. Finnis, "Law," 1062–63, 1066–67.

18. This book, we judge, is not the place to enter into the contemporary discussion of same-sex marriage. What we say about the conditions under which homosexual activity may be moral is not in any way to be interpreted as an approbation of same-sex marriage. The possible implications of our foundational principle for same-sex marriage remain to be worked out.

19. Finnis, "Law," 1066–67; emphasis added.

20. George and Bradley, "Marriage," 302.

21. CDF, *Persona humana*, *AAS* 68 (1976): 1.

22. Robert Nugent, "Sexual Orientation in Vatican Thinking," in *The Vatican and Homosexuality: Reactions to the "Letter to the Bishops of the Catholic Church on the Pastoral Care of Homosexual Persons*," ed. Jeannine Gramick and Pat Furey (New York: Crossroad, 1988), 55.

23. This terminology has been borrowed from John E. Perito, *Contemporary Catholic Sexuality: What Is Taught and What Is Practiced* (New York: Crossroad, 2003), 96. It articulates our belief that homosexual orientation is caused exclusively neither by genetics nor by social conditioning.

24. Grisez, *LCL*, 654 n. 194.

25. Karl Rahner, "Concerning the Relationship between Nature and Grace," in *Theological Investigations* I (London: Darton, Longman & Todd, 1965), 302. See also Louis Malevez, "La Gratuité du surnaturel," *Nouvelle Revue Théologique* 75 (1953): 561–86, 673–89.

26. George and Bradley, "Marriage," 305; emphasis added. See also ibid., 304; and Finnis, "Law," 1064–65.

27. Grisez, *LCL*, 555–68.

28. Finnis, "Law," 1066.

29. *Divinarum institutionum* 6, 23, in *PL* 6, 718; emphasis added.

30. Grisez, *LCL*, 558.

31. In ibid., 557 n. 8, Grisez cites John T. Noonan Jr., *Contraception: A History of Its Treatment by Catholic Theologians and Canonists* (Cambridge, MA: Harvard University Press, 1965), 131, where Noonan argues, reasonably, that Augustine did not invent the notion of

the procreative good but took it from the Stoics. Grisez also admits, unnecessarily reluctantly given the historical evidence, that Noonan provides "enough evidence to make clear that, without stating it, several other Fathers of the Church shared the view that marriage is only an instrumental good."

32. *Etymologiae*, 9, 7, 27, in *PL* 82, 367.

33. Thomas Aquinas, *ST*, III (Suppl.), 65, 1c.

34. Grisez, *LCL*, 561.

35. Charlton T. Lewis and Charles Short, *A Latin Dictionary* (Oxford: Clarendon, 2002), 303.

36. See Joseph Gredt, *Elementa philosophiae Aristotelico-Thomisticae* (Barcelona: Herder, 1946), II:147–48.

37. This is not the first time we have had to point out error in Grisez's (and Finnis's) translation. See Michael G. Lawler, "Indissolubility, Divorce, and Holy Communion: An Open Response to Germain Grisez, John Finnis, and William E. May," *New Blackfriars* 76 (1995): 229–36.

38. *Catechismus Concilii Tridentini*, 2, 8, 12.

39. *AAS* 22 (1930): 548–49.

40. Those desiring the detail of the convoluted debate can consult Giovanni Turbanti, *Un concilio per il mondo moderno: La redazione della costituzione pastorale "Gaudium et spes" del Vaticano II* (Bologna: Editrice Il Mulino, 2000); Charles Moeller, "History of the Constitution," in *Commentary on the Documents of Vatican II*, ed. Herbert Vorgrimler (New York: Herder, 1969), vol. 5, 1–76; and Mackin, *What Is Marriage?* 249–74.

41. *GS*, 47.

42. Ibid., 48.

43. Ibid.

44. See Bernard Häring, *Commentary on the Documents of Vatican II* (New York: Herder and Herder, 1969), vol. 5, 234. Häring, of course, played an active role on the subcommission that established the definitive text of *Gaudium et spes*. See Turbanti, *Un concilio per il mondo moderno*.

45. Grisez, *LCL*, 565 n. 35.

46. Ibid., 565.

47. Ibid., 561. See also Finnis, "Law," 1065; and George and Bradley, "Marriage," 302, 304, 315.

48. *GS*, 48; Can. 1057.

49. George and Bradley, "Marriage," 301–2.

50. Leslie Woodcock Tentler, *Catholics and Contraception: An American History* (Ithaca, NY: Cornell University Press, 2004); Julio Hanlon Rubio, "Beyond the Liberal/Conservative Divide on Contraception," *Horizons* 32 (2005): 270–94.

51. Rubio, "Beyond the Liberal/Conservative Divide," 271.

52. Margaret A. Farley, *Just Love: A Framework for Christian Sexual Ethics* (New York: Continuum, 2006), 278.

53. International Theological Commission, *Theses on the Relationship between the Ecclesiastical Magisterium and Theology* (Washington, DC: United States Conference of Catholic Bishops, 1977), 6.

54. The official title of the famous Majority Report of the Papal Birth Control Commission was *Schema documenti de responsabili paternitate*, Outline of a Document on Responsible

Parenthood. See Robert McClory, *Turning Point: The Inside Story of the Papal Birth Control Commission and How Humanae Vitae Changed the Life of Patty Crowley and the Future of the Church* (New York: Crossroad, 1995), 171.

55. See *History of Vatican II*, 3 vols., ed. Giuseppe Alberigo and English version ed. Joseph A. Komonchak (Maryknoll: Orbis, 2000).

56. See *Origins* 18 (March 2, 1989): 632.

57. Ibid., 632.

58. Bernard Häring, "Does God Condemn Contraception? A Question for the Whole Church," *Commonweal* 116 (February 10, 1989): 71.

59. Noonan, *Contraception*, 6.

60. Ibid.

61. For a detailed account of the Papal Commission, see McClory, *Turning Point*, passim.

62. Paul Evdokimov, "Le sacerdoce conjugal," in *Le Mariage*, ed. Georges Crespy, Paul Evdokimov, and Christian Duquoc (Paris: Maison Mame, 1966), 94–95.

63. Augustine, *De bono coniugio*, 3, 3, in *PL* 40, 375; emphasis added.

64. Aquinas, *ST*, 3 (Suppl.), 65, 1, c.

65. See Urban Navarette, "Structura Juridica Matrimonii Secundum Concilium Vaticanum II," *Periodica* 56 (1967): 366.

66. William V. D'Antonio, J. D. Davidson, D. R. Hoge, and R. A. Wallace, *Laity American and Catholic: Transforming the Church* (Kansas City: Sheed and Ward, 1996), 79. Corroborating evidence is supplied by James D. Davidson, A. S. Williams, R. A. Lamanna, J. Stenftenagel, K. Maas Weigert, W. J. Whalen, and P. Wittenberg, *The Search for Common Ground: What Unites and Divides Catholic Americans* (Huntington, IN: Our Sunday Visitor, 1997), 47.

67. See Andrew M. Greeley, William C. McCready, and Kathleen McCourt, *Catholic Schools in a Declining Church* (Kansas City: Sheed and Ward, 1976), 35; D'Antonio et al., *Laity American and Catholic*, 140; Davidson et al., *Search for Common Ground*, 131.

68. Michael Hornsby-Smith, *Roman Catholicism in England: Customary Catholicism and Transformation of Religious Authority* (Cambridge: Cambridge University Press, 1991), 177.

69. John J. Lynch, "Current Theology: Notes on Moral Theology," *TS* 23 (1962): 239.

70. Richard A. McCormick, *Notes on Moral Theology 1965–1980* (Lanham, MD: University Press of America, 1981), 38.

71. Ibid., 41–42; emphasis in original.

72. Ibid., 164.

73. *HV*, 11. The encyclical was written in Italian (see Lucio Brunelli, "The Pill That Divided the Church," *Thirty Days* 4, July–August, 1988, 66), probably because its main editor was the Franciscan Padre Ermenegildo Lio, of the Pontifical Athenaeum Antonianum, who made such *sustained* efforts to reintroduce Ottaviani's rejected schema, *De castitate, virginitate, matrimonio, familia*, into Schema XIII that became *Gaudium et spes* (See Turbanti, *Un concilio per il mundo moderno*). Janet Smith references several English translations and offers her own translation "based on the Latin, though on a few occasions, when the Latin seemed irrecoverably obscure, recourse was made to the Italian"; Janet Smith, *Humanae Vitae: A Generation Later* (Washington, DC: Catholic University of America Press, 1991), 269. She does not tell us why or where the Latin is "irrecoverably obscure" or how the Italian is any less obscure but, when compared with the official Latin text and official English translation, the translation she offers is rather free.

74. Clifford Longley, *The Worlock Archive* (London: Chapman, 2000), 232.

75. See McClory, *Turning Point*, 127.

76. Ibid., 99.

77. Some of the majority theologians and the four of the minority are named in *The Catholic Case for Contraception*, ed. Daniel Callahan (London: Macmillan, 1969), 149, 174. Tentler writes that the Minority Report was "largely written by Germain Grisez, then a Georgetown University theologian, and the Jesuit John Ford"; *Catholics and Contraception*, 227.

78. For the details of this, see Smith, *Humanae vitae*, 11–33.

79. *HV*, 11.

80. Cited in Longley, *Worlock Archive*, 233; emphasis added.

81. McCormick, *Notes on Moral Theology*, 164.

82. Rubio, "Beyond the Liberal/Conservative Divide," 271.

83. Bernard Häring, "The Encyclical Crisis," *Commonweal* 88 (1968): 588.

84. Longley, *Worlock Archive*, 232.

85. International Theological Commission, *Theses on the Relationship between the Ecclesiastical Magisterium and Theology* (Washington, DC: United States Conference of Catholic Bishops, 1977), 6.

86. See Robert Blair Kaiser, *The Politics of Sex and Religion* (Kansas City: Leaven Press, 1985), 260–61; emphasis added. Also see Longley, *Worlock Archive*, 233. Both Kaiser and Longley translate the French word *finalité* as *finality*; we prefer the more traditional theological word *end*, which is, in fact, what the French *finalité* intends.

87. The quoted words are from Stephen Sloesser, *Jazz Age Catholicism: Mystic Modernism in Postwar Paris* (Toronto: University of Toronto Press, 2005), an insightful look into this period.

88. *AAS* 22 (1930): 548–49; emphasis added.

89. Ibid., 25; emphasis in original.

90. Heribert Doms, *The Meaning of Marriage*, trans. George Sayer (London: Sheed and Ward, 1939), 94–95.

91. See Michael Lamb and Abraham Sagi, *Fatherhood and Family Policy* (Hillsdale, NJ: Erlbaum, 1983); Ronald J. Angel and Jacqueline L. Angel, *Painful Inheritance: Health and the New Generation of Fatherless Families* (Madison: University of Wisconsin Press, 1993); Jean Bethke Elshtain, "Family Matters: The Plight of America's Children," *Christian Century* 110, no. 21 (1993): 710–12; Sara McLanahan and Gary Sandefur, *Growing Up with a Single Parent* (Cambridge, MA: Harvard University Press, 1994); David Blankenhorn, *Fatherlessness in America: Confronting Our Most Urgent Social Problem* (New York: Basic Books, 1995); David Popenoe, *Life without Father* (New York: Free Press, 1996); Arlene R. Skolnick and Jerome H. Skolnick, *Family in Transition* (New York: Longman, 1999); Linda J. Waite and Maggie Gallagher, *The Case for Marriage: Why Married People Are Happier, Healthier, and Better Off Financially* (New York: Doubleday, 2000); and Judith Wallerstein and Julia Lewis, *The Unexpected Legacy of Divorce: A 25 Year Landmark Study* (New York: Hyperion, 2000).

92. *AAS* 36 (1944): 103.

93. *AAS* 43 (1951): 848–49.

94. Ibid., 846.

95. Joseph A. Selling, "Marriage and Sexuality in the Catholic Church," in *Embracing Sexuality: Authority and Experience in the Catholic Church*, ed. Joseph A. Selling (Burlington, VT: Ashgate, 2001), 185.

96. *GS*, 47–48.

97. *Acta Synodalia Sacrosancti Concilii Vaticani II*, vol. IV, Periodus Quarta, pars I, 536.

98. *GS*, 48.

99. Ibid., emphasis added.

100. For an extended analysis of covenant, see Michael G. Lawler, "Marriage as Covenant in the Catholic Tradition," in *Covenant Marriage in Comparative Perspective*, ed. John Witte Jr. and Eliza Ellison (Grand Rapids: Eerdmans, 2005), 70–91.

101. See Marcia Falk, *Love Lyrics from the Bible: A Translation and Literary Study of the Song of Songs* (Sheffield, U.K.: Almond Press, 1982); and Helmut Gollwitzer, *Song of Love: A Biblical Understanding of Sex* (Philadelphia: Fortress, 1979).

102. *GS*, 49.

103. Ibid., 48.

104. Ibid., 50; emphasis added.

105. Grisez, *LCL*, 565 n. 35.

106. See, e.g., George Gallup Jr. and Jim Castelli, *The American Catholic People: Their Beliefs, Practices, and Values* (New York: Doubleday, 1987); Andrew M. Greeley, William C. McCready, and Kathleen McCourt, *Catholic Schools in a Declining Church* (Kansas City: Sheed and Ward, 1976).

107. See Fergus Kerr, *Twentieth-Century Catholic Theologians* (Oxford: Blackwell, 2007), 219.

108. See John T. Noonan Jr., *A Church That Can and Cannot Change* (Notre Dame, IN: University of Notre Dame Press, 2005); and Michael G. Lawler, *What Is and What Ought to Be: The Dialectic of Experience, Theology, and Church* (New York: Continuum, 2005), 119–42.

109. *LG*, 37.

110. Augustine, *De praed. sanct.*, 14, 27, in *PL* 44, 980. See also *LG*, 12.

111. *GS*, 48.

112. See Lawler, *Marriage in the Catholic Church*, 1–26.

113. Ibid., 66–91.

114. *GS*, 50; emphasis added.

115. Can. 1055; emphasis added.

116. See Audrey Richards, *Chisungu* (London: Faber, 1956), 120–21; and Michael G. Lawler, *Symbol and Sacrament: A Contemporary Sacramental Theology* (Omaha: Creighton University Press, 1995), 5–15.

117. Margaret Farley, *Personal Commitments: Beginning, Keeping, Changing* (San Francisco: Harper & Row, 1986), 34.

118. *FC*, 11; emphasis added. John Paul repeats this argument, though in slightly different terms, in *FC*, 32. Paul M. Quay, "Contraception and Conjugal Love," *TS* 22 (1961): 18–40, had argued in the same way twenty years prior to *FC*. Smith, in *Humanae vitae*, 108–12, does not so much argue the position as cite with favor both Quay and John Paul II, allowing her to conclude that "the evil of contraception, then, is that it belies the truth that the 'language of our bodies' should be expressing: the truth that we are seeking complete union with the beloved" (p. 112).

119. Lisa Sowle Cahill, "Human Sexuality," in *Moral Theology: Challenges for the Future*, ed. Charles E. Curran (New York: Paulist Press, 1990), 198.

120. Ibid., 199.

121. *HV*, 12.
122. *FC*, 32.
123. *HV*, 12.
124. Ibid., 11.
125. Vincent J. Genovesi, *In Pursuit of Love: Catholic Morality and Human Sexuality* (Collegeville, MN: Liturgical Press, 1966), 194; emphasis in original.
126. *FC*, 32; emphasis added.
127. See, e.g., John R. Cavanagh, MD, "The Rhythm of Sexual Desire in the Human Female," *Bulletin of the Guild of Catholic Psychiatrists* 14 (1967): 87–100. Cavanagh was a member of the Papal Commission who originally was a strong advocate of periodic abstinence but, instructed by the commission's debates, changed his opposition to artificial contraception. For more on Cavanagh, see Charles E. Curran, *Critical Concerns in Moral Theology* (Notre Dame, IN: University of Notre Dame Press, 1984), 216–24. See also June M. Reinisch and Ruth Beasley, *The Kinsey Institute New Report on Sex* (New York: St. Martin's Press, 1990), 119; and Tentler, *Catholics and Contraception*, 225.
128. *HV*, 10.
129. Ibid., 16.
130. Ibid.
131. Ibid.

Notes to Chapter Six

1. Emmanuel Ntakarutimana, "Being a Child in Central Africa Today," *Concilium* 2 (1996): 15.
2. Kevin T. Kelly, "Cohabitation: Living in Sin or Occasion of Grace," *The Furrow* 56 (2005): 652.
3. Louis Roussel, *La cohabitation sans mariage: Des faits aux interpretations*, *Dialogue* 92 (1986): 47; emphasis added. See also Louis Roussel, *La famille incertaine* (Paris: Odile Jacob, 1989); and Jean-Claude Kaufmann, *Sociologie du Couple* (Paris: Presses Universitaires de France, 1993); emphasis added.
4. Barbara Dafoe Whitehead, "The Changing Pathway to Marriage: Trends in Dating, First Unions, and Marriage among Young Adults," in *Family Transformed: Religion, Values, and Society in American Life*, ed. Steven Tipton and John Witte Jr. (Washington, DC: Georgetown University Press, 2005), 172–73.
5. Larry L. Bumpass, "What's Happening to the Family? Interactions between Demographic and Institutional Change," *Demography* 27 (1990): 486; Larry L. Bumpass, *The Declining Significance of Marriage: Changing Family Life in the United States* (Madison: Center for Demography and Ecology, University of Wisconsin–Madison, 1995), 8; Larry L. Bumpass and Hsien-Hen Lu, *Trends in Cohabitation and Implications for Children's Family Contexts* (Madison: Center for Demography and Ecology, University of Wisconsin–Madison, 1998), 7; Larry L. Bumpass and James A. Sweet, "National Estimates of Cohabitation," *Demography* 26 (1989): 619; Larry L. Bumpass, James A. Sweet, and Andrew Cherlin, "The Role of Cohabitation in Declining Rates of Marriage," *Journal of Marriage and the Family* 53 (1991): 914; Center for Marriage and Family, *Time, Sex, and Money: The First Five Years of Marriage* (Omaha: Center for Marriage and Family, Creighton University, 2000); David Popenoe and

Barbara Dafoe Whitehead, *Should We Live Together? What Young Adults Need to Know about Cohabitation before Marriage* (New Brunswick: National Marriage Project, Rutgers, the State University of New Jersey, 1999), 6; Linda J. Waite, ed., *The Ties That Bind* (New York: De Gruyter, 2000).

6. John Haskey, "Patterns of Marriage, Divorce, and Cohabitation in the Different Countries of Europe," *Population Trends* 69 (1992): 27–36; F. Hopflinger, "The Future of Household and Family Structures in Europe," paper presented at seminar on present demographic trends and lifestyles in Europe, Council of Europe, Strasbourg, 1991; L. Roussel, *La famille incertaine* (Paris: Éditions Odile Jacob, 1989); H. J. Hoffmann-Howotny, "The Future of the Family" in *European Population Conference 1987* (Helsinki: Central Statistical Office of Finland, 1987).

7. John Haskey, "Pre-Marital Cohabitation and the Probability of Subsequent Divorce: Analyses Using the New Data from the General Household Survey," *Population Trends* 68 (1992): 10–19.

8. Oystein Kravdal, "Does Marriage Require a Stronger Economic Underpinning than Informal Cohabitation?" *Population Studies* 53 (1999): 63–80.

9. Neil G. Bennett, Ann Klimas Blanc, and David E. Bloom, "Commitment and the Modern Union: Assessing the Link between Premarital Cohabitation and Subsequent Marital Stability," *American Sociological Review* 53 (1988): 127–38; Ann-Zofie E. Duvander, "The Transition from Cohabitation to Marriage: A Longitudinal Study of the Propensity to Marry in Sweden in the Early 1990s," *Journal of Family Issues* 20 (1999): 698–717.

10. Aart C. Liefbroer, "The Choice between a Married or Unmarried First Union by Young Adults," *European Journal of Population* 7 (1991): 273–98; Aart C. Liefbroer and Jenny De Jong Gierveld, "The Impact of Rational Considerations and Perceived Opinions on Young Adults' Union Formation Intentions," *Journal of Family Issues* 14 (1993): 213–35.

11. Henri Leridon, "Cohabitation, Marriage, Separation: An Analysis of Life Histories of French Cohorts from 1968 to 1985," *Population Studies* 44 (1990): 127–44.

12. R. Lesthaeghe, G. Moors, and L. Halman, "Living Arrangements and Values among Young Adults in the Netherlands, Belgium, France and Germany, 1990," paper presented at annual meetings of Population Association of America, Cincinnati, April 1–3, 1993.

13. Charles Hobart and Frank Grigel, "Cohabitation among Canadian Students at the End of the Eighties," *Journal of Comparative Family Studies* 23 (1992): 311–37; T. R. Balakrishnan, K. V. Rao, Evelyne Lapierre-Adamcyk, and Karol J. Krotki, "A Hazard Model Analysis of the Covariates of Marriage Dissolution in Canada," *Demography* 24 (1987): 395–406.

14. Michael Bracher, Gigi Santow, S. Philip Morgan, and James Trussell, "Marriage Dissolution in Australia: Models and Explanations," *Population Studies* 47 (1993): 403–25.

15. Haskey, "Patterns of Marriage, Divorce, and Cohabitation," 30; and Duncan Dormor, *Just Cohabiting: The Church, Sex and Getting Married* (London: Darton, Longman & Todd, 2004), 3.

16. Larry L. Bumpass and James A. Sweet, "National Estimates of Cohabitation," *Demography* 26 (1989): 615–25; Bumpass and Lu, "Trends in Cohabitation."

17. Bumpass, *Declining Significance of Marriage*; Larry L. Bumpass, R. Kelly Raley, and James A. Sweet, "The Changing Character of Stepfamilies: Implications of Cohabitation and Nonmarital Childbearing," *Demography* 32 (1995): 425–36; Bumpass and Sweet, "National Estimates of Cohabitation," 615–30; Bumpass, Sweet, and Cherlin, "Role of Cohabitation," 913–27; Arland Thornton, "Cohabitation and Marriage in the 1980s," *Demography* 25

(1988): 497–508; William G. Axinn and Arland Thornton, "The Relationship between Cohabitation and Divorce: Selectivity or Causal Influence," *Demography* 29 (1992): 357–74; Robert Schoen, "First Unions and the Stability of First Marriages," *Journal of Marriage and Family* 54 (1992), 281–84; Elizabeth Thomson and Ugo Colella, "Cohabitation and Marital Stability," *Journal of Marriage and Family* 54 (1992): 259–67; Neil G. Bennett, Ann Klimas Blanc, and David E. Bloom, "Commitment and the Modern Union: Assessing the Link between Premarital Cohabitation and Subsequent Marital Instability," *American Sociological Review* 53 (1988): 127–38; David R. Hall and John Z. Zhao, "Cohabitation and Divorce in Canada: Testing the Selectivity Hypothesis," *Journal of Marriage and Family* 57 (1997): 421–27.

18. See, as an example replicated in diocesan policies across the United States, Committee on Marriage and Family, National Conference of Bishops, *Marriage Preparation and Cohabiting Couples* (Washington, DC: United States Catholic Conference, 1999), 10. See also Pontifical Council for the Family, *Marriage, Family, and De Facto Unions* (Rome: Typis Polyglottis Vaticanis, 2000), 4.

19. Schoen, "First Unions and the Stability of First Marriages," 283.

20. Susan McRae, "Cohabitation: A Trial Run for Marriage?" *Sexual and Marital Therapy* 12 (1997): 259.

21. Lakeesha N. Woods and Robert E. Emery, "The Cohabitation Effect on Divorce: Causation or Selection," *Journal of Divorce and Remarriage* 37 (2002): 101–21.

22. David de Vaus, Lixia Qu, and Ruth Weston, "Does Pre-marital Cohabitation Affect the Chances of Marriage Lasting?" paper presented at Eighth Australian Institute of Family Studies Conference, Melbourne, February 2003; available at www.aifs.org.au.

23. Jay Teachman, "Premarital Sex, Premarital Cohabitation, and the Risk of Subsequent Marital Dissolution among Women," *Journal of Marriage and the Family* 65 (2002): 63.

24. Scott M. Stanley, Communication to the Smart Marriages Website, April 21, 2003, www.smartmarriages.com.

25. Linda J. Waite, "Cohabitation: A Communitarian Perspective," in *Marriage in America: A Communitarian Perspective*, ed. Martin King Whyte (Lanham, MD: Rowman & Littlefield, 2000), 26.

26. Ibid., 18. See also Steven L. Nock, "A Comparison of Marriages and Cohabiting Relationships," *Journal of Family Issues* 16 (1995): 53; Susan L. Brown and Alan Booth, "Cohabitation versus Marriage: A Comparison of Relationship Quality," *Journal of Marriage and the Family* 58 (1996): 668–78; Susan L. Brown, "Relationship Quality Dynamics," *Journal of Family Issues* 24 (2003): 583–601; David Popenoe and Barbara Defoe Whitehead, "Ten Important Research Findings on Marriage and Choosing a Marriage Partner," Research Note 6, November 2004, available at http://marriage.rutgers.edu.

27. Waite, "Cohabitation," 26; emphasis added.

28. Whitehead, "Changing Pathway to Marriage," 172.

29. See National Marriage Project, *The State of Our Unions 2001* (New Brunswick: Rutgers, the State University of New Jersey, 2001), for the variety of reasons that people cohabit.

30. *FC*, 13.

31. Kelly, "Cohabitation," 652.

32. Scott M. Stanley, *The Power of Commitment: A Guide to Active, Lifelong Love* (San Francisco: Jossey-Bass, 2005), 23; emphasis added.

33. Ibid., 24.

34. See Blaine Fowers, *Beyond the Myth of Marital Happiness* (San Francisco: Jossey-Bass, 2000).

35. Stanley, *Power of Commitment*, 24.

36. Ibid., 62–63.

37. Ibid., 93–95. See also W. Bradford Wilcox, *Soft Patriarchs, New Men: How Christianity Shapes Fathers and Husbands* (Chicago: University of Chicago Press, 2004); Wilcox and Steven L. Nock, "What's Love Got to Do with It? Equality, Equity, Commitment, and Women's Marital Happiness," *Social Forces* (forthcoming).

38. Stanley, *Power of Commitment*, 126.

39. Ibid., 176–79.

40. See *GS*, 44, 58, 59, and esp. 62. John Paul II frequently teaches that the cultural situation is a major source for theological reflection. He explains that "since God's plan for marriage and family touches men and women in the concreteness of their daily existence in specific social and cultural situations, the Church ought to apply herself to understanding the situations within which marriage and family are lived today, in order to fulfill her task of serving"(*FC*, 4). Elsewhere, he states that "a faith which does not become culture is a faith not fully accepted, not entirely thought out, not faithfully lived" (*L'Osservatore Romano*, March 8, 1982).

41. See Michael G. Lawler, "Toward a Theology of Christian Family," in *Marriage in the Catholic Church: Disputed Questions*, by Michael G. Lawler (Collegeville, MN: Liturgical Press, 2002), 193–219.

42. It is of note that in 1996, under the pressure of the movement to legalize same-sex marriages, the U.S. Congress passed the Defense of Marriage Act, which repeated the assertions of these Roman definitions that marriage was a union between a *man* and a *woman*.

43. The addition to the 1983 *Code of Canon Law* that the consummation of a marriage is achieved only by sexual intercourse *humano modo* (Can. 1061), and the lack of definition for intercourse *humano modo*, has made it impossible to say clearly when a marriage is consummated in the law of the Catholic Church. That inability introduces major problems to the entire Catholic theology of marriage, but those problems do not touch the subject under analysis in this chapter.

44. Jean Remy, "The Family: Contemporary Models and Historical Perspective," in *The Family in Crisis or Transition*, ed. Andrew Greeley, *Concilium* 121 (1979): 9.

45. See Ntakarutimana, "Being a Child in Central Africa Today," *Concilium* 2 (1996): 15; M. Legrain, *Mariage chretien, modele unique: Questions venus d'Afrique* (Paris: Chalet, 1978).

46. Lawrence Stone, *The Family, Sex, and Marriage in England: 1500–1800* (London: Weidenfeld and Nicolson, 1979), 626.

47. Alan Macfarlane, *Marriage and Love in England: Modes of Reproduction 1300–1840* (Oxford: Blackwell, 1987), 291.

48. Ibid., 309.

49. G. R. Quaife, *Wanton Wives and Wayward Wenches: Peasants and Illicit Sex in Early Seventeenth Century England* (London: Croom Helm, 1979), 59.

50. Ibid., 61.

51. Stephen Parker, *Informal Marriage, Cohabitation, and the Law, 1750–1989* (New York: St. Martin's Press, 1990), 19.

52. *DS*, 1813–16.

53. John R. Gillis, *For Better, for Worse: British Marriages 1600 to the Present* (Oxford: University Press, 1985), 135.

54. This chapter focuses on heterosexual cohabitation. The conclusions reached here, however, apply mutatis mutandi, to homosexual cohabitation.

55. Adrian Thatcher, *Marriage after Modernity: Christian Marriage in Postmodern Times* (Sheffield, U.K.: Academic Press, 1999), 119; emphasis in original.

56. Andre Guindon, "Case for a 'Consummated' Sexual Bond before a 'Ratified' Marriage," *Eglise et Theologie* 8 (1977): 137–82; M. Legrain, *Mariage chrétien, modele unique? Questions venues d'Afrique* (Paris: Chalet, 1978).

57. Legrain, *Mariage chretien*, 62.

58. Ibid., 77.

59. Jean-Claude Kaufmann coined a perfect phrase to describe this stage theory, "*couple à petits pas*," couple by small steps. See Jean-Claude Kaufmann, *Sociologie du couple* (Paris: Presses Universitaires de France, 1993), 44. The phrase was picked up by Pierre-Olivier Bressoud in *Eglise et couple à petits pas* (Fribourg: Editions Universitaires Fribourg Suisse, 1998).

60. See Michael G. Lawler, *Marriage and Sacrament: A Theology of Christian Marriage* (Collegeville, MN: Liturgical Press, 1993), 67.

61. Thatcher, *Marriage after Modernity*, 128; emphasis in original. See also Adrian Thatcher, *Living Together and Christian Ethics*, New Studies in Christian Ethics (Cambridge: Cambridge University Press, 2002).

62. Thatcher, *Marriage after Modernity*, 129; emphasis in original.

63. Ibid., emphasis in original.

64. Ibid.

65. See Lawler, *Marriage in the Catholic Church*, 27–42.

66. *PH*, 7.

67. See Christine E. Gudorf, *Body, Sex, and Pleasure: Reconstructing Christian Sexual Ethics* (Cleveland: Pilgrim Press, 1994), 29–50.

68. See, e.g., Clement of Alexandria, *Stromatum*, 3, 23, in *PG* 8, 1086, 1090; Origen, *In gen hom*, 3, 6, in *PG* 12, 180; Augustine, *De gen ad litt*, 9, 7, 12, in *PL* 34, 397; Augustine, *De bono coniug*, 24, 32, in *PL* 40, 394; and ibid., 9, 9, in *PL* 40, 380.

69. See Joan Roughgarden, *Evolution's Rainbow: Diversity, Nature, and Sexuality in Nature and in People* (Berkeley: University of California Press, 2004).

70. Karl Barth, *Church Dogmatics* (Edinburgh: T. and T. Clark, 1961), vol. 3, part 4, 186.

71. See Judith S. Wallerstein and Sandra Blakeslee, *Second Chances: Men, Women, and Children a Decade after Divorce* (New York: Ticknor and Fields, 1989); Judith S. Wallerstein, "Children of Divorce: Preliminary Report of a Ten-Year Follow-Up of Older Children and Adolescents," *Journal of the American Academy of Child Psychiatry* 24 (1985): 545–53; Judith S. Wallerstein, Julia M. Lewis, and Sandra Blakeslee, *The Unexpected Legacy of Divorce: A 25 Year Landmark Study* (New York: Hyperion, 2000); and Sara McLanahan and Gary Sandefur, *Growing Up with a Single Parent* (Cambridge, MA: Harvard University Press, 1994), 65–68.

72. See, e.g., Carl Rogers, *Becoming Partners: Marriage and Its Alternatives* (New York: Delacorte Press, 1972); and McLanahan and Sandefur, *Growing Up with a Single Parent*.

73. Pierre-Olivier Bressoud, *Eglise et couples a petits pas*; and Pierre-Olivier Bressoud, "Eglise catholique et couples non maries: Suggestions en vue d'une reevaluation theologique,"

INTAMS Review 6 (2000): 105–9. The latter piece is a contribution to a debate on cohabitation that includes essays from Lisa Sowle Cahill ("Living Together, Christian Morality, and Pastoral Care") and Hubert Windisch ("Ehe-Wege").

74. See Michael G. Lawler, "A Marital Catechumenate: A Proposal," *INTAMS Review* 13, no. 2 (2007): 161–77.

75. See Kelly, "Cohabitation," 652–58.

76. Gudorf, *Body, Sex, and Pleasure*, 14–18; Charles E. Curran, "Sexuality and Sin: A Current Appraisal," in *Moral Theology No. 8: Dialogue about Catholic Sexual Teaching*, by Charles E. Curran and Richard A. McCormick (New York; Paulist Press, 1993), 411–14; Vincent Genovesi, *In Pursuit of Love: Catholic Morality and Human Sexuality* (Wilmington, DE: Glazier, 1987), 154–55; Philip Keane, *Sexual Morality: A Catholic View* (New York: Paulist Press, 1977), 98; Xavier Lacroix, *Le Corps de Chair: Les dimensions éthique, esthétique, et spirituelle de l'amour* (Paris: Éditions du Cerf, 1992), 346–50.

77. Lisa Sowle Cahill, *Sex, Gender and Christian Ethics* (New York: Cambridge University Press, 1996), 112.

78. Ibid., 11.

79. Keane, *Sexual Morality*, 107.

80. John Paul II, *The Theology of the Body: Human Love in the Divine Plan*, foreword by John S. Grabowski (Boston: Pauline, 1997), 48.

81. Ibid., emphasis in original; *FC*, 19. It is important to note that the distinction between biological sex (male/female) and socially conditioned gender (masculine/feminine) is frequently absent in magisterial discussions of complementarity. See Susan A. Ross, "The Bridegroom and the Bride: The Theological Anthropology of John Paul II and Its Relation to the Bible and Homosexuality," in *Sexual Diversity and Catholicism: Toward the Development of Moral Theology*, ed. Patricia Beattie Jung with Joseph Andrew Coray (Collegeville, MN: Liturgical Press, 2001), 56 n. 5.

82. Kevin Kelly, *New Directions in Sexual Ethics* (London: Cassell, 1999), 51. Kelly goes on to critique ontological complementarity as ultimately "oppressive and deterministic" (p. 52).

83. John Paul II, "Authentic Concept of Conjugal Love," *Origins* 28, no. 37 (1999): 655–56.

84. John Paul II, *Theology of the Body*, 58; emphasis added.

85. *FC*, 66; Pontifical Council for the Family, *Preparation for the Sacrament of Marriage*, 1996, 46; www.cin.org/vatcong/prepmarr.html.

86. John Paul II, "Authentic Concept of Conjugal Love," 655–56.

87. Pontifical Council for the Family, *Preparation for the Sacrament of Marriage*, 7; emphasis added.

88. Guindon, "Case for a 'Consummated' Sexual Bond," 157.

89. Thatcher, *Living Together and Christian Ethics*, 217.

90. Can. 1057, 1.

91. Can. 1057, Can. 1061.

92. John Paul II, "Authentic Concept of Conjugal Love," 3.

93. Pontifical Council for the Family, *Preparation for the Sacrament of Marriage*, 63.

94. Thatcher, *Living Together and Christian Ethics*, 249.

95. Ibid., 228.

96. Ibid., chap. 8.

97. Ibid., 242.

98. Ibid., 252.

99. Ibid.

100. Bressoud, "Eglise catholique et couples non maries," 108.

101. We refer here only to same-sex *relationship*, not to the contemporary concept of same-sex *marriage*. In this book, we repeat, we do not enter into the discussion of same-sex marriage. The possible implications of our foundational principle for same-sex marriage remain to be worked out.

102. See Center for Marriage and Family, *Marriage Preparation in the Catholic Church: Getting It Right* (Omaha: Creighton University Press, 1995); and Scott M. Stanley, "Making a Case for Premarital Education," *Family Relations* 50 (2001): 272–80.

Notes to Chapter Seven

1. Joseph Ratzinger, "The Transmission of Divine Revelation," in *Commentary on the Documents of Vatican II*, vol. 3, ed. Herbert Vorgrimler (New York: Herder and Herder, 1969), 185.

2. In Catholic theological discourse, Tradition refers not simply to the process and structure of handing down but also to the content of what is handed down, whereas traditions refer to particular determinations of the Tradition, which may be permanent in certain contexts but are not necessarily enduringly normative. See Yves Congar, *Tradition and Traditions*, trans. Michael Naseby and Thomas Rainborough (New York: Macmillan, 1967). Even within this discourse, however, there is fluidity in interpreting these two terms. E.g., while the International Theological Commission published a document titled "The Interpretation of Dogmas," and uses the terms Tradition and tradition throughout the text, it provides no explanation of the terms. See "De interpretatione dogmatum," *Gregorianum* 72 (1991): 5–37.

3. *PH*, 8; *CCC*, 2357.

4. *PH*, 8.

5. *Letter to the Bishops of the Catholic Church on the Pastoral Care of Homosexual Persons*, 5, *AAS* 79 (1987): 545.

6. Ibid., 546.

7. *CCC*, 2357.

8. Ronald Lawler, Joseph Boyle Jr., and William E. May, *Catholic Sexual Ethics: Summary, Explanation, and Defense* (Huntington, IN: Our Sunday Visitor, 1998), 197. When Lawler, Boyle, and May cite the "specific biblical passages," they omit Genesis 19:1–11.

9. *DV*, 12. See also Pius XII, *Divino afflante spiritu*, *AAS* 35 (1943): 297–325.

10. Gerald D. Coleman, "The Vatican Statement on Homosexuality," *TS* 48 (1987): 727–34. A similar point is made also by Richard B. Hays, "Relations Natural and Unnatural: A Response to John Boswell's Exegesis of Romans 1," *Journal of Religious Ethics* 14 (1986): 184–215.

11. Lawler, Boyle, and May, *Catholic Sexual Ethics*, 199.

12. See William J. Paul, J. Weinreich, J. Gonsiorek, and M. E. Motvedt, eds., *Homosexuality: Social, Psychological, and Biological Issues* (Beverly Hills, CA: Sage, 1982); Pim Pronk, *Against Nature? Types of Moral Argumentation Regarding Homosexuality* (Grand Rapids: Eerdmans, 1993); Richard C. Pillard and J. Michael Bailey, "A Biological Perspective on Sexual

Orientation," *Clinical Sexuality* 18 (1995): 1–14; Lee Ellis and Linda Ebertz, *Sexual Orientation: Toward Biological Understanding* (Westport, CT: Praeger, 1997); Richard C. Friedman and Jennifer I. Downey, *Sexual Orientation and Psychoanalysis: Sexual Science and Clinical Practice* (New York: Columbia University Press, 2002); CDF, *Letter to the Bishops of the Catholic Church on the Pastoral Care of Homosexual Persons*, AAS 79 (1987): 543–54; and United States Conference of Catholic Bishops, *Always Our Children* (Washington, DC: United States Conference of Catholic Bishops, 1997).

13. This terminology articulates our position that homosexual orientation is neither exclusively genetic nor exclusively social in origin. See John E. Perito, *Contemporary Catholic Sexuality: What Is Taught and What Is Practiced* (New York: Crossroad, 2003), 96.

14. Pillard and Bailey, "Biological Perspective on Sexual Orientation," 1.

15. D. Sherwin Bailey, *Homosexuality and the Western Christian Tradition* (New York: Longman, 1955), x; emphasis added.

16. Donald W. Cory, *The Homosexual in America* (New York: Julian Press, 1951), 8; emphasis in original.

17. See Maria Harris and Gabriel Moran, "Homosexuality: A Word Not Written," in *Homosexuality and Christian Faith: Questions of Conscience for the Churches*, ed. Walter Wink (Minneapolis: Fortress Press, 1999), 33.

18. See Joseph A. McCaffrey and Suzanne M. Hartung, eds., *The Homosexual Dialectic* (Englewood Cliffs, NJ: Prentice-Hall, 1972), 3–30.

19. See *HP*, 10; United States Conference of Catholic Bishops, *Always Our Children*, passim.

20. Our argument in what follows is in full agreement with Gareth Moore: "There are no good arguments, from either scripture or natural law, against what have come to be known as homosexual relationships. The arguments put forward to show that such relationships are immoral are bad. Either their premises are false or the argument by means of which the conclusion is drawn from them itself contains errors." See his Gareth Moore, *A Question of Truth: Christianity and Homosexuality* (London: Continuum, 2003), x. See also Robin Scroggs, *The New Testament and Homosexuality* (Philadelphia: Fortress Press, 1983).

21. See Edward Vacek, "A Christian Homosexuality," *Commonweal*, December 5, 1980, 681–84.

22. See Martti Nissinen, *Homoeroticism in the Biblical World: A Historical Perspective* (Minneapolis: Fortress Press, 1998), 93–95.

23. Gen 18:2, 3, 10, 13, 14, 17, 17, 22.

24. Lev 20:33–34.

25. Gen 18:4–5.

26. Gen 19:1.

27. Gen 19:5.

28. G. A. Barton, "Sodomy," in *Encyclopedia of Religion and Ethics*, ed. James Hastings (Whitefish, MT: Kessinger Publishing, 2003), 11, 672. Derrick Sherwin Bailey, *Homosexuality in the Western Christian Tradition* (London: Darton, Longman, Green, 1955), 1–6, advances the same argument; the men of Sodom simply wanted to know the identity of the strangers.

29. Gen 19:7.

30. Gen 19:8, emphasis added.

31. Moore, *Question of Truth*, 5; emphasis in original.

32. Ezek 16:49.

33. See Michael G. Lawler, "Being Christ-ian and the Service of Love and Justice," *Liturgical Ministry* 13 (2004): 10–22.

34. Is 1:17.

35. Wisdom 19:14.

36. Luke 10:10–12; cf. Matt 10:14–15.

37. Matt 25:34–46.

38. Lawler, Boyle, and May, *Catholic Sexual Ethics*, 305 n. 58.

39. Lev 18:22.

40. Lev 20:13.

41. For Greek society, see Paige duBois, *Sowing the Body: Psychoanalysis and Ancient Representations of Women* (Chicago: University of Chicago Press, 1988), 39–85. For Jewish Society, see Sirach 26:19; and *Mishna*, Ketuboth, 1, 6. For Muslim society, see Carol Delaney, *The Seed and the Soil: Gender and Cosmology in Turkish Village Society* (Berkeley: University of California Press, 1991).

42. Lev 24:17, 21; Num 35:30; Exod 20:13.

43. Bruce J. Malina and Richard L. Rohrbaugh, *Social Science Commentary on the Synoptic Gospels* (Minneapolis: Fortress Press, 1992), 202. See also Carolyn Osiek and David L. Balch, *Families in the New Testament World: Households and House Churches* (Louisville: Westminster / John Knox Press, 1997); and Halvor Moxnes, *Constructing Early Christian Families* (London: Routledge, 1997).

44. The same system of honor and shame existed among the Greeks. Though it was acceptable for a boy to behave passively sexually, it was not acceptable for an adult male. Taking the passive, female role in sexual activity brought him dishonor and negatively impacted his status and role in society. See Foucault, *The Use of Pleasure: The History of Sexuality, Vol. 2*, trans. Robert Hurley (New York: Pantheon, 1985), 187–225.

45. Xavier Lacroix, "Une parole éthique recevable par tous?" in *L'amour du semblable: Questions sur l'homosexualité*, ed. Xavier Lacroix (Paris: Cerf, 2001), 150.

46. Lev 11.

47. Rom 1:19.

48. Rom 1:21–23.

49. Rom 1:24–28; emphasis added.

50. See Dale B. Martin, "Heterosexism and the Interpretation of Romans 1:18–31," *Biblical Interpretation* 3 (1995): 332–55. For a contrary reading, see Hays, "Relations Natural and Unnatural," 184–215; and Richard B. Hays, *The Moral Vision of the New Testament: Community, Cross, New Creation: A Contemporary Introduction to the New Testament* (San Francisco: HarperSanFrancisco, 1996), esp. chap. 16.

51. Walter Wink, "Homosexuality and the Bible," in *Homosexuality and Christian Faith*, ed. Wink, 36.

52. See Scroggs, *New Testament and Homosexuality*, 44–65.

53. William Countryman, *Dirt, Greed, and Sex: Sexual Ethics in the New Testament and Their Implications for Today* (London: SCM Press, 1989), 100–17.

54. See Scroggs, *New Testament and Homosexuality*, 62–65.

55. Mary Rose D'Angelo, "Perfect Fear Casteth Out Love: Reading, Citing, and Rape," in *Sexual Diversity and Catholicism: Toward the Development of Moral Theology*, ed. Patricia Beattie Jung with Joseph A. Corey (Collegeville, MN: Liturgical Press, 2001), 181; emphasis added.

56. Philo, *Special Laws*, III, trans. Francis H. Colson, *Loeb Classical Library. Philo, Vol. VII* (London: Heinemann, 1937), 37–39; emphasis added.

57. Bruce J. Malina, "The New Testament and Homosexuality," in *Sexual Diversity and Catholicism*, ed. Jung, 168.

58. Daniel Harrington and James Keenan, *Jesus and Virtue Ethics: Building Bridges between New Testament Studies and Moral Theology* (Lanham, MD: Sheed and Ward, 2002), 166.

59. Eugene F. Rogers Jr., "Aquinas on Natural Law and the Virtues in Biblical Context," *Journal of Religious Ethics* 27 (1999): 52.

60. Lisa Sowle Cahill, "Is Catholic Ethics Biblical?" Warren Lecture Series in Catholic Studies, No. 20, University of Tulsa, Tulsa, 1992, 5–6.

61. Victor Paul Furnish, *The Moral Teaching of Paul: Selected Issues* (Louisville: Abingdon, 1985), 78.

62. Richard Sparks, *Contemporary Christian Morality* (New York: Crossroad, 1996), 81.

63. Dietmar Mieth, *Moral und Erfahrung: Beitrage zur theologisch-ethischen Hermeneutik* (Freiburg: 1977), 34.

64. Joseph Fuchs, *Moral Demands and Personal Obligations* (Washington, DC: Georgetown University Press, 1993), 27; emphasis in original.

65. Bernard J. F. Lonergan, *Method in Theology* (New York: Herder and Herder, 1972), 20.

66. For elaboration of this point, see Michael G. Lawler, *What Is and What Ought to Be* (New York: Continuum Press, 2005).

67. Ibid., xi.

68. Fuchs, *Moral Demands*, 39.

69. *CCC*, 2357; *CRP*, 4.

70. United States Conference of Catholic Bishops, *Always Our Children*, 4–5; emphasis added. See also *PH*, 8.

71. *PH*, 3.

72. *HV*, 11.

73. Ibid., 3; emphasis added.

74. *CCC*, 426.

75. Alfred North Whitehead, *Symbolism: Its Meaning and Effect* (New York: Putnam's, 1959), 8.

76. Andrew Koppleman, "Natural Law (New)," in *Sex from Plato to Paglia: A Philosophical Encyclopedia*, ed. Alan Soble (Westport, CT: Greenwood Press, 2006), II:708.

77. Todd A. Salzman and Michael G. Lawler, "*Quaestio Disputata*: Catholic Sexual Ethics: Complementarity and the Truly Human," *TS* 67, no. 3 (September 2006): 631–35; David Matzko McCarthy, "The Relationship of Bodies: A Nuptial Hermeneutics of Same-Sex Unions," in *Theology and Sexuality: Classic and Contemporary Readings*, ed. Eugene F. Rogers Jr. (Oxford: Blackwell, 2002), 200–16.

78. *CCC*, 2357.

79. Margaret A. Farley, *Just Love: A Framework for Christian Sexual Ethics* (New York: Continuum, 2006), 287. Frans Vosman affirms this claim as well, noting, e.g., that homosexuals contribute to the "social good" in terms of "mutual support, care, and justice." Frans Vosman, "Can the Church Recognize Homosexual Couples in the Public Sphere?" *INTAMS Review* 1, no. 12 (2006): 37.

80. *GS*, 49.

81. Margaret A. Farley, "An Ethic for Same-Sex Relations," in *A Challenge to Love: Gay and Lesbian Catholics in the Church*, ed. Robert Nugent (New York: Crossroad, 1983), 99–100. In her most recent book, Farley returns to the question of gay and lesbian experience and judges that "we do have strong witnesses to the role of such [gay and lesbian] relationships in sustaining human well-being and opening to human flourishing. This same witness extends to the contributions that individuals and partners make to families, the church, and society as a whole"; Farley, *Just Love*, 287. The recent Vatican document on homosexuality and the priesthood is also guilty of ignoring the experience of many gay men. After having stated that gay men "must be accepted with respect and sensitivity; every sign of unjust discrimination in their regard should be avoided," the document proceeds to assert unjustly that such men "find themselves in a situation that seriously obstructs them from properly relating to men and women"; Congregation for Catholic Education, *Instruction Concerning the Criteria for the Discernment of Vocations with Regard to Persons with Homosexual Tendencies*, 2; available at www.vatican.va/roman_curia/congregations/. No evidence is advanced for such a sweeping statement; contrary evidence, known to anyone who accepts gays and lesbians with "respect and sensitivity," is ignored.

82. Bernard Ratigan, "When Faith and Feelings Conflict," *The Tablet*, December 10, 2005, 13.

83. United States Conference of Catholic Biships, "Ministry to Persons with a Homosexual Inclination: Guidelines for Pastoral Care," *Origins* 24, no. 36 (November 23, 2006): 381.

84. Lawrence A. Kurdek, "What Do We Know about Gay and Lesbian Couples?" *Current Directions in Psychological Science* 14 (2005): 251; Lawrence A. Kurdek, "Differences between Partners from Heterosexual, Gay, and Lesbian Cohabiting Couples," *Journal of Marriage and Family* 68 (May 2006): 509–28; Lawrence A. Kurdek, "Lesbian and Gay Couples," in *Lesbian, Gay and Bisexual Identities over the Lifespan*, ed. Anthony R. D'Augelli and Charlotte J. Patterson (New York: Oxford University, 1995), 243–61; and Lawrence A. Kurdek, "Are Gay and Lesbian Cohabiting Couples *Really* Different from Heterosexual Married Couples?" *Journal of Marriage and Family* 66 (2004), 880–900. See also, Ritch C. Savin-Williams and Kristin G. Esterberg, "Lesbian, Gay, and Bisexual Families," in *Handbook of Family Diversity*, ed. David H. Demo, Katherine R. Allen, and Mark A. Fine (New York: Oxford University Press, 2000), 207–12; and Philip Blumstein and Pepper Schwartz, *American Couples: Money, Work, Sex* (New York: Morrow, 1983).

85. *CRP*, 7.

86. See Stephen J. Pope, "The Magisterium's Arguments against 'Same-Sex Marriage': An Ethical Analysis and Critique," *TS* 65 (2004): 530–65.

87. Charlotte J. Patterson, "Lesbian and Gay Parenting" (Washington, DC: APA Press, 1995), www.apa.org/pi/parent.html; emphasis added. See also Marybeth J. Mattingly and Robert N. Bozick, "Children Raised by Same-Sex Couples: Much Ado about Nothing," paper given at Conference of the Southern Sociological Society, Atlanta, 2001.

88. Joan Laird, "Lesbian and Gay Families," in *Normal Family Processes*, ed. Froma Walsh (New York: Guilford, 1993), 316–17.

89. APA, "Resolution on Sexual Orientation and Marriage," 2004, http://www.apa.org/releases/gaymarriage_reso.pdf.

90. Ann Sullivan, ed., *Issues in Gay and Lesbian Adoption: Proceedings of the Fourth Annual Peirce-Warwick Adoption Symposium* (Washington, DC: Child Welfare League of America, 1995), 24–28.

91. Ibid., 41.

92. *GS*, 5.

93. *FC*, 5.

94. For a review of these data, see Osnat Erel and Bonnie Burman, "Interrelatedness of Marital Relations and Parent-Child Relations: A Meta-Analytic Review," *Psychological Bulletin* 118 (1995): 108–32; Paul R. Amato and Alan Booth, *A Generation at Risk: Growing Up in an Era of Family Upheaval* (Cambridge, MA: Harvard University Press, 1997), 67–83; Stacy J. Rogers and Lynn K. White, "Satisfaction with Parenting: The Role of Marital Happiness, Family Structure, and Parents' Gender," *Journal of Marriage and Family* 60 (1998): 293–316; and David H. Demo and Martha J. Cox, "Families with Young Children: A Review of the Research in the 1990s," *Journal of Marriage and Family* 62 (2000): 876–900.

95. John Courtney Murray, *We Hold These Truths: Catholic Reflections on the American Experience* (New York: Sheed & Ward, 1960), 106.

96. James D. Davidson, A. S. Williams, R. A. Lamanna, J. Stenftenagel, K. Maas Weigert, W. J. Whalen, and P. Wittenberg, *The Search for Common Ground: What Unites and Divides Catholic Americans* (Huntington, IN: Our Sunday Visitor, 1997), 11.

97. Ibid., 47.

98. William V. D'Antonio, J. D. Davidson, and D. R. Hoge, *American Catholics: Gender, Generation, and Commitment* (Lanham, MD: Altamira Press, 2001), 76.

99. Ibid., 85.

100. Ibid., 84.

101. Dean R. Hoge, W. D. Dinges, M. Johnson, and J. L. Gonzales Jr., *Young Adult Catholics: Religion in the Culture of Choice* (Notre Dame: University of Notre Dame Press, 2001), 59–60.

102. See Michael Hornsby-Smith, *Roman Catholicism in England: Customary Catholicism and Transformation of Religious Authority* (Cambridge: Cambridge University Press, 1991); Timothy J. Buckley, *What Binds Marriage? Roman Catholic Theology in Practice* (London: Chapman, 1997); and John Fulton, ed., *Young Catholics at the New Millennium: The Religion and Morality of Young Adults in Western Countries* (Dublin: University College Press, 2000).

103. *FC*, 5.

104. See International Theological Commission, *Theses on the Relationship between the Ecclesiastical Magisterium and Theology* (Washington, DC: United States Conference of Catholic Bishops, 1977), thesis 8, 6.

105. Robin Gill, *Churchgoing and Christian Ethics* (Cambridge: Cambridge University Press, 1999), 1; emphasis added.

106. *LG*, 12.

107. Avery Dulles, "*Sensus Fidelium*," *America*, November 1, 1986, 242.

108. Farley, *Just Love*, 190.

109. Ibid., 195–96.

110. Ibid., 287.

111. Mark D. Jordan, *The Silence of Sodom: Homosexuality in Modern Catholicism* (Chicago: University of Chicago Press, 2000), 46.

112. Farley, "Ethic for Same-Sex Relations," 105.

113. Lacroix, "Une parole ethique recevable par tous," 148; emphasis in original.

114. See Stephen J. Pope, "Scientific and Natural Law Analyses of Homosexuality: A Methodological Study," *Journal of Religious Ethics* 25, no. 1 (Spring 1997): 110–11.

115. See Todd A. Salzman and Michael G. Lawler, "New Natural Law Theory and Foundational Sexual Ethical Principles: A Critique and a Proposal," *Heythrop Journal* 47, no. 2 (April 2006): 182–205; Salzman and Lawler, "*Quaestio Disputata*," 625–52; and James F. Keenan, "Can We Talk? Theological Ethics and Sexuality," *TS* 1, no. 68 (2007) (forthcoming).

116. Ratzinger, "Transmission of Divine Revelation," 185.

117. CDF, *Mysterium Ecclesiae*, AAS 65 (1973): 402–3.

118. Farley, *Just Love*, 286.

119. Moore, *Question of Truth*, 282.

Notes to Chapter Eight

1. CDF, *Instruction on Respect for Human Life in Its Origin and on the Dignity of Procreation: Replies to Certain Questions of the Day* (Washington, DC: Office of Publishing and Promotion Services, United States Catholic Conference, 1987) (hereafter, *Instruction*), II, B, 4, a.

2. Ibid., II.

3. Linda J. Beckman and S. Marie Harvey, "Current Reproductive Technologies: Increased Access and Choice?" *Journal of Social Issues* 61 (2005): 2.

4. *GS*, 50.

5. Office of Technology Assessment, *Infertility, Medical and Social Choices* (Washington, DC: Office of Technology Assessment, U.S. Congress, 1988), 3; Mary B. Mahowald, "Ethical Considerations in Infertility," in *Infertility: A Comprehensive Text, Second Edition*, ed. Machelle M. Seibel (Stamford, CT: Appleton and Lange, 1997), 823.

6. American Society for Reproductive Medicine, "Frequently Asked Questions about Infertility," www.asrm.org/Patients/faqs.html. See also Seibel, *Infertility*, 4.

7. Benedict Ashley and Kevin O'Rourke, *Health Care Ethics: A Theological Analysis,* 4th ed. (Washington, DC: Georgetown University Press, 1997), 241.

8. For a historical overview of ARTs, see Don P. Wolf and Martin M. Quigley, "Historical Background and Essentials for a Program in *In Vitro* Fertilization and Embryo Transfer," in *Human in Vitro Fertilization and Embryo Transfer*, ed. Don P. Wolf and Martin M. Quigley (New York: Plenum Press, 1984), 1–11; and Annette Burfoot, ed., *Encyclopedia of Reproductive Technologies* (Boulder, CO: Westview Press, 1999).

9. For more detailed descriptions of ARTs, see Burfoot, *Encyclopedia of Reproductive Technologies*; Ashley and O'Rourke, *Health Care Ethics*, 240–48; and Peter J. Cataldo, "Reproductive Technologies," *Ethics & Medics* 21, no. 1 (January 1996): 1–3.

10. Resolve of Minnesota, "Assisted Reproductive Technologies," www.resolvemn.org/index.php?option = com_content&task = view&id = 17&Itemi d; eq2.

11. The pre-embryo stage lasts from the completion of fertilization to the development of the primitive streak, which occurs "on about the fourteenth day of development." Howard W. Jones and Susan L. Crockin, "On Assisted Reproduction, Religion and Civil Law," *Fertility and Sterility* 73 (2000): 450.

12. *Instruction*, I, 1.

13. Ibid.

14. Ibid., I, 5.

15. Ibid., I, 4.

16. Ibid., I, 6.

17. Richard T. Hull, "Gamete Intrafallopian Transfer (GIFT)," in *Encyclopedia of Reproductive Technologies*, ed. Burfoot, 252.

18. See ibid., 251–54.

19. More recent reproductive procedures have utilized ovary transplants from one woman to another. In this procedure, ovarian tissue is transferred to an infertile woman, and the tissue is able to produce fertilizable eggs. The conjugal act then results in procreation. Also, women's ova have been frozen, thawed, injected with sperm (ICSI), transferred to the fallopian tubes, and have resulted in birth.

20. *Instruction*, II, B, 7.

21. Cataldo, "Reproductive Technologies," 2–3. See also Stephen Bozza, "Counseling the Infertility Couple," *Ethics & Medics* 26, no. 11 (November 2001): 1–3; Donald G. McCarthy, "TOTS Is for Kids," *Ethics & Medics* 13, no. 12 (December 1988): 1–2; Donald G. McCarthy, "Response," in *Reproductive Technologies, Marriage and the Church*, ed. Donald G. McCarthy (Braintree, MA: Pope John Center, 1988), 140–45; and Donald G. McCarthy, "GIFT? Yes!" *Ethics & Medics* 18, no. 9 (September 1993): 3–4.

22. Ashley and O'Rourke, *Health Care Ethics*, 247. See also Germain Grisez, *Difficult Moral Questions: The Way of the Lord Jesus, Volume Three* (Quincy, IL: Franciscan Press, 1997) (hereafter, *DMQ*), 244–49; Donald T. DeMarco, "Catholic Moral Teaching and TOT/GIFT," in *Reproductive Technologies*, ed. McCarthy, 122–39; and John M. Haas, "GIFT? No!" *Ethics & Medics* 18, no. 9 (September 1993): 1–2.

23. *Instruction*, "Foreword."

24. Ibid., "Introduction," 3.

25. Ibid., I, 1.

26. Ibid., II.

27. Ibid., "Introduction," 1.

28. Thomas A. Shannon and Lisa Sowle Cahill, *Religion and Artificial Reproduction: An Inquiry into the Vatican "Instruction on Respect for Human Life in its Origin and on the Dignity of Human Reproduction"* (New York: Crossroad, 1988), 55.

29. Cited by Jones and Crockin, "On Assisted Reproduction," 449.

30. *GS*, 35.

31. Ibid., 36.

32. Ibid., 51.

33. Thomas A. Shannon, "Reproductive Technologies: Ethical and Religious Issues," in *Reproductive Technologies: A Reader*, ed. Thomas A. Shannon (New York: Sheed and Ward, 2004), 47.

34. *HV*, 15.

35. The *Instruction* distinguishes between heterologous artificial fertilization or procreation and homologous artificial fertilization or procreation. Within each classification, it addresses two types of reproductive technology: artificial insemination (AI) and in vitro fertilization and embryo transfer (IVF-ET). In this chapter, we use AFD to designate both types of heterologous artificial fertilization, and AFH to designate both types of homologous artificial fertilization. We will specifically distinguish between AI or IVF-ET when it is necessary for a point of clarification.

36. *Instruction*, II, B, 7; emphasis in original.

37. Ibid.

38. Ibid., II, B, 5.

39. Ibid., "Introduction," 5.

40. Ibid., II, B, 7; emphasis added.

41. Ibid., II, B, 5.

42. Ibid., II, A, 1.

43. Ibid.

44. Ibid.

45. Ibid., II, A, 2; emphasis in original.

46. Ibid.

47. Ibid.

48. Ibid., II, B, 4.

49. Ibid., II, B.

50. Ibid., II, B, 4, a.

51. Ibid., II, B, 5.

52. Richard A. McCormick, *The Critical Calling: Reflections on Moral Dilemmas since Vatican II* (Washington, DC: Georgetown University Press, 1989), 347. We are indebted to McCormick's critique of the "inseparability principle" (pp. 347–49).

53. See, e.g., ibid., 346–47; Joseph A. Selling, "The Development of Catholic Tradition and Sexual Morality," in *Embracing Sexuality: Authority and Experience in the Catholic Church*, ed. Joseph A. Selling (Burlington, VT: Ashgate, 2001), 149–162; Joseph A. Selling, "Magisterial Teaching on Marriage 1880–1986: Historical Constancy or Radical Development," in *Dialogue about Catholic Sexual Teaching: Readings in Moral Theology No. 8*, ed. Charles Curran and Richard McCormick (New York: Paulist Press, 1993), 93–97; Bernard Häring, "The Inseparability of the Unitive-Procreative Functions of the Marital Act," in ibid., 163–64; and Lisa Sowle Cahill, "Sexuality: Personal, Communal, Responsible," in *Embracing Sexuality*, ed. Selling, 165–72.

54. Martin Rhonheimer, "Contraception, Sexual Behavior, and Natural Law: Philosophical Foundation of the Norm of '*Humanae Vitae*,'" *Linacre Quarterly* 56, no. 2 (1989): 41–42.

55. McCormick, *Critical Calling*, 348.

56. Ibid.

57. See Michael G. Lawler, *Marriage in the Catholic Church: Disputed Questions* (Collegeville, MN: Liturgical Press, 2002), 27–42.

58. *Instruction*, II, B, 4, c.

59. Germain Grisez, *LCL*, 267; Grisez, *DMQ*, 240–41.

60. *GS*, 50.

61. "Since 1981, approximately 177,000 babies have been born via ART; and, in one year alone (2000), some 100,000 cycles of ART were attempted, resulting in 60,253 live births"; www.medicalnewstoday.com, January 19, 2005, 1. It is ludicrous to suggest that desperate spouses went to so much time, psychological stress, and expense merely to have a technological product.

62. *Instruction*, II, B, 5.

63. See *GS*, 48.

64. Lisa Sowle Cahill, *Women and Sexuality* (New York: Paulist Press, 1992), 75; emphasis in original. See also Shannon and Cahill, *Religion and Artificial Reproduction*, 103–32.

65. The Ethics Committee of the American Fertility Society accuses the CDF of "barnyard physiology." "This means that the concept that intercourse is intended entirely for reproduction derives from observation of those animals who exhibit 'heat' and give an external sign of ovulation during which period the female will accept the male and at no other time." Cited by Jones and Crockin, "On Assisted Reproduction," 449.

66. *Instruction*, II, B, 4, a.

67. Ibid., II, A, 2.

68. The classic legal case that demonstrates the *Instruction*'s legitimate concern for the relational complications of surrogacy is the case of "Baby M" and the contractual and custodial dispute between Elizabeth and William Stern, who contracted with Mrs. Whitehead to both donate her egg and her womb to bear a child for the Sterns. The bond that Mrs. Whitehead developed over the nine-month gestational period as well as through the genetic link with "Baby M" led her to deny her contractual obligations to the Sterns. In turn, this denial led to a complex legal custody battle that illustrates well the relational complications of AFD, with which the *Instruction* is legitimately concerned. In the end, the New Jersey Supreme Court nullified the surrogacy contract, arguing that commercial surrogacy was tantamount to selling babies and unethical. The basis for deciding the case was on the parental considerations of genetic, gestational, and social parenthood. While Mrs. Whitehead fulfilled the first two criteria of parenthood, social parenthood seems to be morally decisive. We agree with Glannon: "the social mother (or father) is arguably more important than genetic or gestational mothers, because the social mother is responsible for the welfare of the child from birth onward" (*Biomedical Ethics* [New York: Oxford University Press, 2005], 84). In the end, the Supreme Court granted full custody to Mr. Stern and Mrs. Whitehead was granted visitation rights. For our purposes, the important points in this case are twofold: first, the importance of the distinction the New Jersey Supreme Court made between different types of parenthood, genetic, gestational, and social, a distinction that the *Instruction* highlights as well; and second, the primacy of social parenthood over genetic and gestational parenthood.

69. *GS*, 50.

70. Cataldo, "Reproductive Technologies," 1.

71. *FC*, 14.

72. Matt 25:40.

73. Law & Health Research Brief, www.rand.org/publications/RB/RB9038/.

74. Ibid.

75. See John Berkman, "The Morality of Adopting Frozen Embryos," *Studia Moralia* 40, no. 1 (2002): 115–41; Grisez, *DMQ*, 239–44; Mary Geach, "Are There Any Circumstances in Which It Would Be Morally Admirable for a Woman to Seek to Have an Orphan Embryo Implanted in Her Womb?—1," in *Issues for a Catholic Bioethic*, ed. Luke Gormally (London: Linacre Centre, 1999), 341–46; William B. Smith, "Rescue the Frozen?" *Homiletic and Pastoral Review* 96 (October 1995): 72–74; William B. Smith, "Response," *Homiletic and Pastoral Review* 96 (August–September 1995): 16–17; and Geoffrey Surtees, "Adoption of a Frozen Embryo," *Homiletic and Pastoral Review* 96 (August–September 1995): 7–16.

76. *Instruction*, II, A, 2.

77. Paul Lauritzen, *Pursuing Parenthood: Ethical Issues in Assisted Reproduction* (Bloomington: Indiana University Press, 1993), 76–84.

78. Grisez, *LCL*, 689.

79. Berkman, "Morality of Adopting," 132.

80. McCormick, *Critical Calling*, 341.

81. *Instruction*, II, A, 3.

82. See Charlotte J. Patterson, *Lesbian and Gay Parenting* (Washington, DC: APA Press, 1995), 9; Joan Laird, "Lesbian and Gay Families," in *Normal Family Processes*, ed. Froma Walsh (New York: Guilford Press, 1993), 316–17; APA, "Resolution on Sexual Orientation and Marriage," 2004, 7; Ann Sullivan, ed., *Issues in Gay and Lesbian Adoption: Proceedings of the Fourth Annual Peirce-Warwick Adoption Symposium* (Washington, DC: Child Welfare League of America, 1995), 24–28. See also E. D. Gibbs, "Psychosocial Development of Children Raised by Lesbian Mothers: A Review of Research," *Women and Therapy* 8 (1988): 65–68; P. J. Falk, "Lesbian Mothers: Psychosocial Assumptions in Family Law," 44 (1989): 941–47; Fiona Tasker and Susan Golombok, "Children Raised by Lesbian Mothers: The Empirical Evidence," *Family Law* (1991): 184–87; Fiona Tasker and Susan Golombok, *Growing Up in a Lesbian Family: Effects on Child Development* (New York: Guilford Press, 1997); Susan Golombok and Fiona Tasker, "Children in Lesbian and Gay Families: Theories and Evidence," *Annual Review of Sex Research* 5 (1994): 73–100; Jeffrey Weeks, Brian Heaphy, and Catherine Donovan, *Same-Sex Intimacies: Families of Choice and Other Life Experiments* (London: Routledge, 2001); Stephen Hicks, "The Christian Right and Homophobic Discourse: A Response to 'Evidence' That Lesbian and Gay Parenting Damages Children," *Sociological Research Online* 8, no. 4 (2003), www.socresonline.org.uk/8/4/kicks.html; and Lawrence A. Kurdek, "Are Gay and Lesbian Cohabiting Couples Really Different from Heterosexual Married Couples?" *Journal of Marriage and Family* 66 (2004): 880–900.

83. Centers for Disease Control and Prevention, American Society for Reproductive Medicine, and Society for Reproductive Technology, "2002 Assisted Reproductive Technology Success Rates: National Summary and Fertility Clinic Reports," www.cdc.gov/reproductivehealth/ART02/sect5_fig40–46.htm.

84. Robert W. Rebar and Alan H. De Cherney, "Assisted Reproductive Technology in the United States," *New England Journal of Medicine* 350, no. 16 (April 15, 2004): 1603.

85. Michèle Hansen, C. Bower, E. Micne, N. de Klerk, and J. Kurrinczuk, "Assisted Reproductive Technologies and the Risk of Birth Defects—A Systematic Review," *Human Reproduction* 20 (2005): 335; Z. Kozinsky, "Obstetric and Neonatal Risk of Pregnancies after Assisted Reproductive Technology: A Matched Control Study," *Acta Obstet Gynecol Scand.* 82, no. 9 (September 2003): 850–56. These studies contradict earlier studies that indicate there is minimal, if any, risk to IVF-ET embryos. See Shannon and Cahill, *Religion and Artificial Reproduction*, 7–9, and their references, including John D. Biggers, "Risks of In Vitro Fertilization and Embryo Transfer in Humans," in *In Vitro Fertilization and Embryo Transfer* , ed. R. F. Harrison, J. Bonnar, and W. Thompson (London: Academic Press, 1983), 393–409; and Ian L. Pike, "Biological Risks of In Vitro Fertilization and Embryo Transfer," in *Clinical In Vitro Fertilization*, ed. Carl Wood and Alan Trounson (Berlin: Springer-Verlag, 1984), 137–46.

86. Hansen et al., "Assisted Reproductive Technologies."

87. Rebar and De Cherney, "Assisted Reproductive Technology," 1603–4, note that while assisted reproduction in the United States "is not legislated, . . . it is highly regulated" (p. 1604). One source of this regulation passed by Congress in 1992 to curb misleading advertising on success rates by fertility clinics as well as ethical, financial, and scientific scandals is the Fertility Clinic Success Rate and Certification Act (also known as the "Wyden Law," which is a misnomer because reporting is voluntary). This act "promotes uniformity

in data reporting and requires the listing of clinics that do not report their data" (p. 1604), but it does not require clinics to participate. See also W. Y. Chang and A. H. DeCherney, "History of Regulation of Assisted Reproductive Technology (ART) in the USA: A Work in Progress," *Human Fertility* 6 (2003): 64–70; and Andrea D. Gurmankin, Arthur L. Caplan, and Andrea M. Braverman, "Screening Practices and Beliefs of Assisted Reproductive Technology Programs," *Fertility and Sterility* 83 (2005): 61–67.

88. See John C. Avise, *The Genetic Gods: Evolution and Belief in Human Affairs* (Cambridge, MA: Harvard University Press, 1998), 56–62.

89. Gina Kolata, "The Heart's Desire," *New York Times*, May 11, 2004; see also Maura A. Ryan, *Ethics and Economics of Assisted Reproduction: The Cost of Longing* (Washington, DC: Georgetown University Press, 2001), 2.

90. Linda J. Beckman and S. Marie Harvey, "Current Reproductive Technologies: Increased Access and Choice?" *Journal of Social Issues* 61 (2005): 2.

91. Carol J. Rowland Hogue, "Successful Assisted Reproductive Technology: The Beauty of One," *Obstetrics and Gynecology* 100, no. 5 (November 2002): 1017. See also John A. Collins, "Reproductive Technology: The Price of Progress," *New England Journal of Medicine* 331, no. 4 (July 28, 1994): 270–71.

92. See Deut 24:18–22; Jer 7:2–7; Is 61:1–8; Matt 25: 31–46.

93. We borrow this metaphor from Jorg Rieder, *Remember the Poor: The Challenge to Theology in the Twenty-First Century* (Harrisburg: Trinity Press International, 1998), 1–5.

94. Gustavo Guttierez, *The Power of the Poor in History* (New York: Orbis, 1983), 13.

95. See John Paul II, *Sollicitudo Rei Socialis, AAS* (1987): 39–42; Christina Traina, *Feminist Ethics and Natural Law* (Washington, DC: Georgetown University Press, 1999); David Hollenbach, *The Common Good and Christian Ethics* (Cambridge: Cambridge University Press, 2002); and Michael G. Lawler, "Being Christian and the Service of Love and Justice," *Liturgical Ministry* 13 (Winter 2004): 10–22.

96. Ambrose, *De Nabuthe Jezraelita*, 1, in *PL*, 14, 747.

97. Augustine, *Sermo L*, 1, in *PL* 38, 326.

98. Ryan, *Ethics and Economics of Assisted Reproduction*, 134.

99. Ibid., 8.

100. Lisa Sowle Cahill, *Theological Bioethics: Participation, Justice, Change* (Washington, DC: Georgetown University Press, 2005), 210.

101. Shannon, "Reproductive Technologies," 53.

102. Cahill, *Theological Bioethics*, esp. 43–69. See also Ryan, *Ethics and Economics of Assisted Reproduction*.

Notes to the Epilogue

1. *PH*, 7.

2. *HV*, 11.

3. Joseph Fuchs, *Moral Demands and Personal Obligations* (Washington, DC: Georgetown University Press, 1993), 36.

4. Ibid.

5. Joseph Ratzinger, "The Transmission of Divine Revelation," in *Commentary on the Documents of Vatican II*, ed. Herbert Vorgrimler (New York: Herder and Herder, 1969), 185.

6. John E. Thiel, *Senses of Tradition: Continuity and Development in the Catholic Faith* (New York: Oxford University Press, 2000), 47.

7. See Michael Novak, "The 'Open Church' 40 Years Later: A Reckoning," in *Unfinished Journey: The Church 40 Years after Vatican II*, ed. Austin Ivereigh (New York: Continuum, 2003), 48. Novak comments that the practitioners of this nonhistorical orthodoxy "did not worry overmuch about that system's historical justification, or about making it relevant to the historical present" (p. 48).

8. Robert M. Doran, *Theology and the Dialectics of History* (Toronto: University of Toronto Press), 4.

9. Ibid., 236.

10. Ibid., 238.

11. Ibid., 240.

12. Ibid.

13. Ibid., 41.

14. For a fuller analysis of *sensus fidei* and reception, see Michael G. Lawler, *What Is and What Ought to Be: The Dialectic of Experience, Theology, and Church* (New York: Continuum, 2005), 119–34.

15. Augustine, *De praed sanct.*, 14, 27, in *PL* 44, 980.

16. *LG*, 12; emphasis added.

17. *GS*, 32.

18. *LG*, 9; cf. *AG*, 19.

19. See George H. Gallup Jr., *Religion in America 1996* (Princeton, NJ: Princeton Religion Research Center, 1996), 44. See also James D. Davidson, A. S. Williams, R. A. Lamanna, J. Stenftenagel, K. Maas Weigert, W. J. Whalen, and P. Wittenberg, *The Search for Common Ground: What Unites and Divides Catholic Americans* (Huntingdon, IN: Our Sunday Visitor, 1997); William V. D'Antonio, J. D. Davidson, and D. R. Hoge, *American Catholics: Gender, Generation, and Commitment* (Lanham, MD: Rowman & Littlefield, 2001); Dean R. Hoge, W. D. Dinges, M. Johnson, and J. L. Gonzales Jr., *Young Adult Catholics: Religion in the Culture of Choice* (Notre Dame, IN: University of Notre Dame Press, 2001).

20. Yves M. J. Congar, "Reception as an Ecclesiological Reality," *Concilium* 77 (1965): 62.

21. See Yves Congar, *Divided Christendom: A Catholic Study of the Problem of Reunion*, trans. M. Bousfield (London: Bles, 1939); Henri de Lubac, *Catholicism: A Study of Dogma in Relation to the Corporate Destiny of Mankind*, trans. Lancelot Sheppard (New York: Longmans Green, 1950); Marie Joseph Gouillou, *Mission et unite: Les exigencies de la communion* (Paris: Desclee, 1960); Jerome Hamer, *The Church Is a Communion* (New York: Sheed and Ward, 1965); Gustave Martelet, *Les idees maitresses de Vatican II* (Paris: Desclee, 1966); and Michael G. Lawler and Thomas J. Shanahan, *Church: A Spirited Communion* (Collegeville: Liturgical Press, 1995).

22. See John T. Noonan, *A Church That Can and Cannot Change* (Notre Dame, IN: University of Notre Dame Press, 2005); Lawler, *What Is and What Ought to Be,* 127–29.

23. *CCC*, 2423; emphasis added.

24. Paul VI, *Octogesima adveniens* 4, *AAS* 63 (197): 403 ff.

25. CDF, *Instruction on Christian Freedom and Liberation* 72, *AAS* 79 (1987): 586.

26. *SRS*, 571.

27. Ibid., 1; emphasis added.

28. This notion of individual responsibility is brilliantly analyzed by Jean-Yves Calvez in his essay, "Morale sociale et morale sexuelle," *Etudes* 378 (1993): 642–44.

29. *SRS*, 3.

30. Calvez, "Morale sociale et morale sexuelle," 648; emphasis added.

31. See Lawler, *What Is and What Ought to Be*, 44–67.

32. Augustine, *Sermo 52*, in *PL* 38, 360.

33. Thomas Aquinas, *ST*, 1, 3, preface.

34. Karl Rahner, "The Hiddenness of God," in *Theological Investigations*, vol. 16 (London: Darton, Longman & Todd, 1979), 238.

35. Elizabeth A. Johnson, *She Who Is: The Mystery of God in Feminist Theological Discourse* (New York: Crossroad, 1992), 105.

36. Pontifical Council for Interreligious Dialogue, *Dialogue and Proclamation* (Rome: Typis Polyglottis Vaticanis, 1991), 49.

37. John Paul II, "Ut unum sint," *Acta Apostolicae Sedis* 87 (1995): 28.

Index